CRITICAL SURVEY

OF

LONG FICTION

Novelists with Gay and Lesbian Themes

Editor

Carl Rollyson

Baruch College, City University of New York

SALEM PRESS

Ipswich, Massachusetts • Hackensack, New Jersey

Cover photo:
Anthony Burgess (© Sophie Bassouls/Sygma/Corbis)

978-1-4298-3677-7

CONTENTS

CONTRIBUTORS

Randy L. Abbott
University of Evansville

Gerald S. Argetsinger
*Rochester Institute of
Technology*

David Barratt
Farnsfield, England

Kate Begnal
Original Contributor

Jacquelyn Benton
*Metropolitan State College of
Denver*

Cynthia A. Bily
Adrian, Michigan

Margaret Boe Birns
New York University

B. Diane Blackwood
*International Press Club of
Chicago*

Harold Branam
Savannah, Georgia

Mitzi M. Brunsdale
Original Contributor

Edgar L. Chapman
Original Contributor

Samuel Coale
Original Contributor

Richard N. Coe
Original Contributor

Richard Hauer Costa
Texas A&M University

June M. Frazer
Original Contributor

Miriam Fuchs
*University of Hawaii at
Manoa*

Keith Garebian
Mississauga, Ontario

Lucy Golsan
Stockton, California

Arthur D. Hlavaty
Yonkers, New York

Gregory D. Horn
*Southwest Virginia
Community College*

Rebecca Kuzins
Pasadena, California

Penelope A. LeFew
Original Contributor

Naomi Lindstrom
Original Contributor

S. Thomas Mack
*University of South Carolina
Aiken*

Mary E. Mahony
*Wayne County Community
College*

Charles E. May
*California State University,
Long Beach*

Laurence W. Mazzeno
Alvernia College

Robert A. Morace
Daemen College

Earl Paulus Murphy
Original Contributor

Donald Palumbo
Original Contributor

David B. Parsell
Furman University

William E. Pemberton
*University of Wisconsin-La
Crosse*

J. Thomas Rimer
University of Pittsburgh

R. Baird Shuman
*University of Illinois at
Urbana-Champaign*

Jaquelyn W. Walsh
McNeese State University

Shawncey Webb
Taylor University

Craig Werner
Original Contributor

Roger E. Wiehe
Original Contributor

Scott D. Yarbrough
*Charleston Southern
University*

GAY AND LESBIAN LONG FICTION

Homosexuality, traditionally regarded as a disease or perversion by church, state, and society, was rigorously denounced and condemned by those same institutions. In the case of the arts and literature, works featuring homoeroticism or gays and lesbians as characters were often censored, if they were recognized at all. English-language writers, for example, wrote "gay novels" under pseudonyms and published them either privately or in foreign countries.

Gay characters and sensibilities were introduced into literature only by arch subterfuge, with writers following society's unwritten decree that homoerotic fiction must end with the death, destruction, or extraordinary "conversion" of the questionable characters. In Bayard Taylor's *Joseph and His Friend* (1870), a disastrous marriage causes Joseph to drift toward Philip, a young, golden-haired man; the novel ends, however, with Joseph's sudden, almost inexplicable interest in Philip's look-alike sister. This plot shift presumably was made to "save" Joseph from a fate worse than death. Henry James's *Roderick Hudson* (1876) sketches wealthy Rowland Mallet's infatuation with a young sculptor, but after a rift between them, the eponymous character sinks into a decadent languor from which he is rescued only by Christina Light, a beautiful, bored girl. Like other novels of the time, homoerotic love is forced to yield to the heterosexual imperative.

Europe saw many clandestine homoerotic novels—such as the lurid *Gamiani* (1833; *Gamiani: Or, Two Nights of Excess*, 1923), attributed to Alfred de Musset and featuring lesbian sexuality—but none of these was a major work. Honoré de Balzac masked homosexuality by artifice. In his vast sequence of interrelated novels about French society, *La Comédie humaine* (1829-1848; *The Comedy of Human Life*, 1885-1893, 1896; also as *The Human Comedy*, 1895-1896, 1911), the exuberantly masculine Vautrin is imprisoned after taking the blame for a crime committed by Lucien, the gentle, handsome young man he loves. Vautrin dreams of owning a plantation in the American South, where he can have absolute power over his slaves, especially their bodies. Only by living outside hypocritical French society can Vautrin have insight into its excesses and his own nature.

Irish writer and poet Oscar Wilde defied Victorian hypocrisy, but he paid a mortal price. *The Picture of Dorian Gray* (serial 1890; expanded 1891) represents a Faustian pact between young Dorian and the forces of evil. Wilde defiantly embraces and gilds what his society deems evil. Society enjoyed the ultimate revenge by destroying Wilde's reputation and life: He was jailed for homosexual "offences" and went bankrupt while in prison.

If gay fiction wished to vividly portray homosexuality, it had to balance sensuality with social determinism—as in the case of Adolpho Caminha's Brazilian novel *Bom crioulo* (1895; *Bom-Crioula: The Black Man and the Cabin Boy*, 1982), the first explicitly gay work in Latin American fiction. The violent Amaro, often described with animal imagery, escapes from slavery and sexual strictures, but his "animal" nature drives him to kill his male lover in a jealous fit. Caminha uses laws of heredity to justify slavery and exploitation, and his novel is flawed by contradictions: Homosexuality is unnatural, yet heroic; it is against nature, yet it is natural for Bom Crioulu. Nevertheless, his novel is an example of the manner in which homosexuality haunts the "normal" world.

EARLY TWENTIETH CENTURY OBLIQUENESS

Lesbian sexuality was a major theme in Colette's novels about teenagers who were infatuated with older women. Male love figured in Robert Musil's *Die Verwirrungen des Zöglings Törless* (1906; *Young Törless*, 1955), set in a military school, and Thomas Mann's *Der Tod in Venedig* (1912; *Death in Venice*, 1925), the story of Gustav von Aschenbach's fatal infatuation with Tadzio, a fourteen-year-old Polish boy of Apollonian beauty and stillness.

Gay novelists in England and the United States resorted to setting love stories in faraway lands or using other techniques of evasion. Charles Warren Stoddard's *For the Pleasure of His Company: An Affair of the Misty City, Thrice Told* (1903), the story of Paul Clitheroe's love affair with two darkly handsome men, runs sour until Paul ends up in the company of three South Sea islanders. Edward Prime-Stevenson's *Imre: A Memorandum* (1906), privately published abroad in a small run of 125 copies, ends with a young Englishman, Oswald, in the arms of Imre, a twenty-five-year-old Hungarian army officer; but this "openness" is undercut by the novelist's pretense to be no more than the editor of a manuscript sent to him by a British friend. The guardedness of gay novelists continued for decades, even when the theme was a "coming out" of sorts. Henry Blake Fuller's *Bertram Cope's Year* (1919), set near Chicago, is about the ruined love affair between Randolph and Bertram Cope, but Fuller pretends that the rupture is based on age rather than on rival love.

The 1920's, an age of reckless, fast living, did not end gay fiction's camouflage. Sophisticates knew of Sigmund Freud's radical sex theories and D. H. Lawrence's carnal characters, but there was no progress in attitudes about homosexuality. Camouflage through euphuism became the mode, as in Ronald Firbank's high-camp affectation in his novellas or Carl Van Vechten's frothy tone in *The Blind Bow-Boy* (1923), where the notorious Duke of Middlebottom dresses as a sailor and has stationery printed with the motto "A thing of beauty is a boy forever." The spirit of the times did not welcome serious novels of social protest or self-disclosure, as Radclyffe Hall discovered when she published her semiautobiographical lesbian novel, *The Well of Loneliness* (1928). Virginia Woolf masked her love affair with Vita Sackville-West with the fantastical, androgynous world of *Orlando: A Biography* (1928).

Through the 1930's and 1940's, the "tough guy" novels of Ernest Hemingway and Raymond Chandler, as well as the war novels of Norman Mailer and James Jones, depicted gay characters with contempt, as if they were weak "pansies" and the antitheses of masculine heroes. In contrast, novels featuring African Americans and Jews, for example, often were proletarian novels of social protest. Consequently, gay fiction was left to hacks, with a few outstanding exceptions, including Parker Tyler and Frederick Rolfe. Tyler's *The Young and Evil* (1933; with Charles Henri Ford) is a slice-of-life story about life in Greenwich Village, New York, and Rolfe's *The Desire and Pursuit of the Whole* (1934) features a male protagonist who can entertain desire only when his beloved adopts male attire and behavior.

Other novelists, such as Frederic Prokosch, used numerous filters to conceal gayness in his works. His novels, including *The Asiatics* (1935) and *The Seven Who Fled* (1937), were lyrical tales of handsome bachelors in extreme circumstances and exotic places (such as Aden, Turkey, Iraq, or Tibet). Prokosch allowed his heroes, ostensibly heterosexual males, to be placed in sexually charged situations, but his filtrations and dilutions of homosexuality were concessionary. Djuna Barnes's *Nightwood* (1936) expressed the intensity of lesbian love, but its Parisian world was broodingly gothic. Researcher Alfred Kinsey's studies *Sexual Behavior in the Human Male* (1948) and *Sexual Behavior in the Human Female* (1953) rebuked assumptions about sexuality, including homosexuality, while the horrors of World War II prompted Americans to question traditionally accepted morals and values. Nevertheless, although the "open" homosexual in long fiction became increasingly frequent, literary camouflage and subterfuge remained necessary.

Novelist Carson McCullers, who was lesbian, did not concern herself principally with the subject of sexuality. Although each of her novels includes a man with a crush on another man, these works actually concern abnormality and yearning. In her *The Heart Is a Lonely Hunter* (1940), homosexuality is one of the few things not attributed to protagonist Singer by other characters, despite the fact that Singer's homoerotic love is his only joy and his only reason for living. Truman Capote writes of a young man's love for a handsome prizefighter in *Other Voices, Other Rooms* (1948), but Capote, too, skirted the issue of homosexuality by simply affirming that any love could be beautiful as long as it belonged to a person's intrinsic nature.

William Maxwell Jr.'s *The Folded Leaf* (1945) camouflages Lymie Peters's homosexual interest as an aesthetic one; worse, the athletic Spud Latham is never allowed to realize his friend's sexual desire for him. Novelist John Horne Burns, who thought it necessary to be gay to be a good writer, created a gay bar and a vivid set of rapacious, spontaneous, erotic characters in *The Gallery* (1947). However, his story is not about sex or love per se, but rather human nature. In *Lucifer with a Book* (1949), Burns acts almost apologetic about his erotic male characters by designing for them last-minute conversions to heterosexuality.

BREAKING THE PATTERN

The protagonist in Fritz Peters's *The World Next Door* (1949) admits that he loves a man while denying that he is gay. Helped by new trends in Europe, Patricia Highsmith and Gore Vidal dared to break the pattern of gay and lesbian invisibility and shame. Highsmith's *The Price of Salt* (1952, as Claire Morgan; also published as *Carol*) has a clear lesbian theme, while Vidal's *The City and the Pillar* (1948; revised 1965) depicts men undressing and kissing. Vidal's Jim Willard is presented as a reproach to society's censors: After Willard is vilely denounced by the man with whom he tries to rekindle their boyhood homoeroticism, he strangles the object of his affection

Vidal's all-male Eden was shocking to American literary critics. Vidal, however, was not in the league of Jean Genet, whose dark, decadent fiction—*Notre-Dame des Fleurs* (1944, 1951; *Our Lady of the Flowers*, 1949), *Miracle de la rose* (1946, 1951; *Miracle of the Rose* 1966), *Querelle de Brest* (1947, 1953; *Querelle of Brest*, 1966), and the semiautobiographical *Journal du voleur* (1948, 1949; *The Thief's Journal*, 1954)—never flinches from portraying the emotional and psychological depths of gay relations. Sex and violence are mixed with lurid and salacious density, and Genet often creates an extremely perverse but original perspective on theft, rape, and even murder.

Genet's deliberate idealization of outlawed desire is reflected in Yukio Mishima's Japanese fiction. A martial artist and sexual outlaw, Mishima resorts to metaphor for deception. The narrator of *Kamen no kokuhaku* (1949; *Confessions of a Mask*, 1958) enters into anonymous relationships with women, for whom he harbors secret distaste, simply to "fit" into conventional society.

THE 1950'S AND EARLY 1960'S

The 1950's was a time of anticommunist—and antigay—hysteria in the United States. Fearing the critics, gay male writers often became grotesque, parasitic, clownish, or campy characters in their own lives. Capote embraced Manhattan whimsy and capriciousness; Burns wrote a weak, straight novel shortly before he died; and Vidal put his energy into nonfiction and politics. Many versions of the "apprenticeship" gay novel appeared as well, with themes of a problematic childhood.

Gay fiction divided itself into two main categories: traditional realism (James Baldwin and J. R. Ackerley) and counterculture writing (William S. Burroughs), though there were fascinating exceptions to the rule—as in James Purdy's *Malcolm* (1959), an allegorical story about a teenager befriended by a possible pedophile; Peters's *Finistère* (1951) is set in a France more apt to accept the adolescent protagonist's burgeoning gayness than are his parents; James Barr's *Quatrefoil* (1950), a male love story told in a lofty, intellectual manner; and William Talsman's playfully witty and stylish *The Gaudy Image* (1958). Most of these novels, however, ended in wistfulness or death for the protagonist. Young Matt in *Finistère* drowns himself; Baldwin's *Giovanni's Room* (1956) ends on a bridge, where David tries to discard his lover's letter, only to have the wind blow the fragments back to him; and in *Quatrefoil*, Phillip, after his lover is killed in an aircrash, contemplates suicide, only to decide that love has made him strong.

Lesbian pulp novels, intended for a heterosexual readership, were sold at places such as drugstores and newsstands in the 1950's and most often featured a male-fantasy version of lesbian sex. The novels also cast women who have sex with women as shamed and isolated. Many of the later pulps, however, began to depict these young women as fully embracing their sexuality. The novels of Ann Bannon, for example, sent a crucial message to readers: that a condemning society, and not homosexuality, is morally wrong. For lesbians growing up around this time, the new pulp novels were, in many ways, lifesavers. Bannon's novels include her first, *Odd Girl Out* (1957), featuring college students Beth and Laura, and *Beebo Brinker* (1962), which introduces Bannon's favorite protagonist, the soft butch Beebo Brinker, to the lesbian world of Greenwich Village.

Gay writers in the early 1960's became increasingly open about homosexuality, having been inspired by the creative courage of the Belgian-born Marguerite Yourcenar, whose books defy classification because they mix modes as they tackle different kinds of love. She wrote of homosexuality, however, through her gay characters, and avoided, for the most part, the topic of lesbian sexuality. Her novels include the early work *Alexis: Ou, Le Traité du vain combat* (1929; *Alexis*, 1984) and the influential *Mémoires d'Hadrien* (1951; *Memoirs of Hadrian*, 1954; also known as *Hadrian's Memoirs*).

The newly open writers include Baldwin, who, in *Another Country* (1962), depicts a sleazy New York hell where individuals are caught up in the general malaise of American society. However, Baldwin's gay characters have a greater awareness of their misery than does society at large, which remains ignorant. Christopher Isherwood's *A Single Man* (1964) affirms the value of an aging gay man who, in a departure from custom, is not a doomed homosexual with neurotic self-loathing or sexual guilt but a bachelor who entertains a fantasy of killing or torturing bigots unless they agree to end homophobic practices.

Isherwood's quiet prose contrasts with the louder brutality of Charles Wright's *The Messenger* (1963), where New York is a hell filled with junkies (and gays), or Hubert Selby's *Last Exit to Brooklyn* (1964), replete with pimps, whores, and thugs (and queers). The most controversial novels were John Rechy's *City of Night* (1963) and *Numbers* (1967). In *City of Night*, Rechy takes a hard look at the joyless and dangerous side of male prostitution, based on his own experiences, but his writing is not primarily confessional. It has a gritty realism that exposes its central character's refusal to express emotion for fear of revealing his sexual identity. *Numbers* is also a horror story with dark imagery, as its protagonist sets off on a journey of self-discovery, literally counting sexual experiences as if numbers could themselves ward off age and death.

NEW TAXONOMY

Homoeroticism became iconic after the Stonewall Inn bar uprising in New York City in 1969, a small revolt of bar patrons and others that ultimately strengthened an emerging modern gay and lesbian rights movement in the United States. Gay and lesbian writers began to produce works of full self-disclosure. By the end of the 1960's, gay and lesbian fiction expanded to include various subgenres: In other words, gay and lesbian literature was no longer simply about homosexuality as a "problem." In Europe, Pier Paolo Pasolini and

Genet reveled in picaresque novels. Marie-Claire Blais brought stories of French Canadian lesbians to readers outside Canada, and Ursula K. Le Guin wrote science fiction in which fantasy worlds included gender equality.

The 1970's was rich in gay inventiveness. Anne Rice and Marion Zimmer Bradley also wrote in the science fantasy genre, with Bradley becoming one of the first science-fiction writers to use independent female characters to explore gender roles. Guy Hocquenghem explored the connections between the body and technology. Mary Renault used classical history to show how bisexuality was once a cultural norm.

During the 1970's and 1980's, the new taxonomy of gay and lesbian writing was consolidated. The rise of small presses specializing in gay and lesbian (and lesbian feminist) writing ensured the publication of diverse writers and genres. The "coming-out" and semiautobiographical novels of Andrew Holleran, David Leavitt, Rita Mae Brown, and Jeanette Winterson explore a wide range of experiences, including parental disgust and rejection, dispossession of home, the death of innocence, and various discourses on love. Also remaining popular was the "colonialist" tradition of upper-class men seeking erotic adventure with foreigners or working-class people—already encountered in nineteenth century and early twentieth century novels. Alan Hollinghurst is most notable in this tradition.

The 1970's also included Ann Allen Shockley's *Loving Her* (1974), the first black lesbian novel published in the United States. In 1977, Barbara Smith, in "Toward a Black Feminist Criticism," decried the overt dismissal of literature by black women and black lesbians. Her essay led to a radical rethinking of the place of African American literature in the literary canon. Novels such as Alice Walker's *The Color Purple* (1982), which feature lesbian sexuality as central themes, soon followed. Also in the 1970's, black gay men, working to promote literature by men of color, especially through small presses, were influenced by black lesbians and feminists of all races and ethnicities.

The confluence of the gay and lesbian rights movement and the rise of third-wave feminism ensured that lesbian writers could tell their stories from a lesbian-feminist perspective. June Arnold envisions women taking control of their own destinies and Dutch writer Anna Blaman uses language to upend social stereotypes. Feminist literary theorists helped to shape lesbian writing as well, even outside the academy. Canadian theorist and novelist Nicole Brossard associates the lesbian body with an "intelligent body," thereby envisioning utopia. In France, theorist and writer Monique Wittig suggests that women can liberate themselves only by using language in radical ways. Novelist-critic Hélène Cixous developed a theory and style called "writing from the body." Her bold celebration of lesbian sexuality as a lever to dismantle oppressive social structures helped clear a path for writers such as Dorothy Allison and Blanche McCrary Boyd.

While Allison won acclaim with *Bastard Out of Carolina* (1992) and *Cavedweller* (1998), which explores domestic, personal, and psychic violence from the perspective of a working-class lesbian, Boyd has ensured that each of her own novels is female centered.

Each features a young woman who comes out as lesbian and learns to overcome obstacles to existential and sexual autonomy, as in the case of Ellen Larraine Burns, the protagonist of the Lambda Award-winning *The Revolution of Little Girls* (1991) and *Terminal Velocity* (1997).

The new consciousness enhanced gay and lesbian writers' gambits into social and political themes, even to the point of criticizing their own subculture—as with Larry Kramer's *Faggots* (1978), whose antipromiscuity theme aroused a backlash. Lisa Alther incorporates cultural satire into such works as *Kinflicks* (1975), *Original Sins* (1981), and *Five Minutes in Heaven* (1995). The preeminent writer of the era, however, is Sarah Schulman, who examines inherent tensions between the nature of art and the reality of politics in her novels, plays, and journalistic essays. Beginning with *The Sophie Horowitz Story* (1984), which reads like a detective story but is really a meditation on lesbian politics and sexuality, and continuing with *Girls, Visions and Everything* (1986), *People in Trouble* (1990), *Empathy* (1992), *Rat Bohemia* (1995), *Shimmer* (1998) and *The Child* (2007), Schulman examines, among other topics, individual responsibility and with the horrors of the AIDS crisis. *Rat Bohemia* is a favorite and ranks as one of the best novels of lesbian and gay fiction. Schulman's involvement with various gay activist groups deeply influences her writing. She was a cofounder of the New York Lesbian and Gay Experimental Film Festival and of the direct-action activist group Lesbian Avengers.

Gay and lesbian literature, however, does not limit itself to political themes. British novelist Sarah Waters's first novel, *Tipping the Velvet* (1998), is a lighthearted picaresque story of lesbian love featuring protagonist Kitty Butler, a stage performer and male impersonator in Victorian England. The novel was an immediate success, and it has been translated into more than twenty languages. Waters also set her next two novels, *Affinity* (1999) and *Fingersmith* (2002), in the Victorian period, but moved to the 1940's for *The Night Watch* (2006) and *The Little Stranger* (2009). Her first three novels were adapted for film and television. Katherine V. Forrest, a Canadian-born American writer, established the American lesbian detective novel with the first book in her Kate Delafield series, *Amateur City* (1984). Three of the eight novels in the series won the Lambda Literary Award, including *Hancock Park* (2004). Mark Richard Zubro is the author of two best-selling detective series, the Tom and Scott mysteries and the Paul Turner mysteries. *A Simple Suburban Murder* (1990), the first in the series about Chicago high school teacher Tom Mason and his pro-baseball-player husband Scott Carpenter, won a Lambda Literary Award as well. In the twelfth book in the series, *Schooled in Murder* (2008), a meeting at Tom's high school ends with a murder.

Schulman's playful experimentation with the detective genre, especially in *After Delores* (1988), a hard-boiled detective story in the style of James M. Cain and Dashiell Hammett, displays the modern gay and lesbian writer's literary freedom. English-language writers are no longer forced to envy foreign-language gay writers—such as Manuel Puig (*El beso de la mujer araña*, 1976; *Kiss of the Spider Woman*, 1979), Mutsuo

Takahashi (*Zen no henreki*, 1974; partial translation, 1999 and 2000; Zen's pilgrimage of virtue), or Michel Tournier (*Gilles et Jeanne*, 1983; *Gilles and Jeanne*, 1987)—for their ability to take risks. Notable, too, are the achievements of Paul Monette, Armistead Maupin, and Kitty Tsui, as are the more experimental and ambitious works of Dale Peck, Edmund White, and Samuel M. Steward.

Reacting to the subtle and pervasive censorship inherent even in political correctness, Peck, White, and Steward began experimenting with mixed styles and modes. Steward's detective and modernist parodies examine the position of the artist in modern society, while promoting erotica as pure entertainment. Peck's *Martin and John* (1993) is an absorbing patchwork of conflicting stories, all with characters named Martin and John, but death is its driving force. His *Body Surfing* (2009) is a wild and funny story about the Mogran, a race of demons known primarily for their sexual appetites. However, neither writer matches White's mainstream success, especially with the semiautobiographical trilogy *A Boy's Own Story* (1982), *The Beautiful Room Is Empty* (1988), and *The Farewell Symphony* (1997), a mature example of the elegant sensitivity of modern gay fiction.

Keith Garebian
Updated by Cynthia A. Bily

BIBLIOGRAPHY

Austen, Roger. *Playing the Game: The Homosexual Novel in America*. Indianapolis, Ind.: Bobbs-Merrill, 1977. Dated but literate and still relevant history of the "gay novel" from its beginnings into the 1960's. Covers two hundred novels and includes a bibliography and an index.

Cart, Michael, and Christine Jenkins. *The Heart Has Its Reasons: Young Adult Literature with Gay/Lesbian/Queer Content, 1969-2004*. Lanham, Md.: Scarecrow Press, 2006. Examines the historical development of gay and lesbian young adult fiction. Comprehensive resource on an undervalued genre. Appendixes include "Young Adult Novels with GLBTQ Content, 1969-2004: Author/Title Bibliography with GLBTQ Portrayal, Inclusion, and Narrative Role," and "Young Adult Fiction with GLBTQ Content, 1969-2004: A Chronological Bibliography."

Castle, Terry, ed. *The Literature of Lesbianism: A Historical Anthology from Ariosto to Stonewall*. New York: Columbia University Press, 2003. Collection of hundreds of literary works about lesbian sexuality. Authors include William Shakespeare, John Donne, Aphra Behn, Alexander Pope, the Marquis de Sade, Samuel Taylor Coleridge, Emily Dickinson, Guy de Maupassant, Willa Cather, Virginia Woolf, Ernest Hemingway, Nella Larsen, and Graham Greene.

Lilly, Mark. *Gay Men's Literature in the Twentieth Century*. New York: New York University Press, 1993. Reintroduction to famous texts and an entry into less known work from the standpoint of gay men's experiences, sensibilities, and sexual desires.

Malinowski, Sharon, ed. *Gay and Lesbian Literature*. 2 vols. Detroit, Mich.: St. James

Press, 1994, 1998. Extensive compilation of more than two hundred writers of the twentieth century. Inclusion in this work is based on thematic content, not sexual identity, forcing readers to rethink what makes a work "gay" or "lesbian." Each volume has a separate introduction to lesbian literature and gay literature, respectively.

Markowitz, Judith A. *The Gay Detective Novel: Lesbian and Gay Main Characters and Themes in Mystery Fiction.* Jefferson, N.C.: McFarland, 2004. Survey of series and stand-alone detective and mystery novels published since 1964, analyzing main characters, themes, and plot elements. Includes an extensive bibliography.

Pollack, Sandra, and Denise D. Knight, eds. *Contemporary Lesbian Writers of the United States: A Bio-bibliographical Critical Sourcebook.* Westport, Conn.: Greenwood Press, 1993. Biographical essays that include writers' personal history, an analysis of major works and themes, an overview of critical reception, and bibliographies. Introduction to this collection places lesbian literature in its historical and political contexts. Contains one hundred articles, a general bibliography, and appendixes of selected periodicals and journals.

Schwarz, A. B. Christa. *Gay Voices of the Harlem Renaissance.* Bloomington: Indiana University Press, 2003. Examines the work of four leading gay writers of the Harlem Renaissance—Countée Cullen, Langston Hughes, Claude McKay, and Richard Bruce Nugent—and their sexually nonconformist writings.

Slide, Anthony. *Lost Gay Novels: A Reference Guide to Fifty Works from the First Half of the Twentieth Century.* New York: Harrington Park Press, 2003. Detailed plot summary, character analysis, discussion of critical reception, and author biography for each of fifty "forgotten" works of lesbian and gay literature.

Summers, Claude J., ed. *The Gay and Lesbian Literary Heritage: A Reader's Companion to the Writers and Their Works, from Antiquity to the Present.* Rev. ed. New York: Routledge, 2002. This expanded edition features more than four hundred biographical essays on writers of all sexualities. Essays include overviews of ethnic literatures and literary themes, such as aesthetics, and cover genres such as modernism, science fiction, and young adult literature.

JAMES BALDWIN

Born: New York, New York; August 2, 1924
Died: St. Paul de Vence, France; December 1, 1987
Also known as: James Arthur Baldwin

PRINCIPAL LONG FICTION

Go Tell It on the Mountain, 1953
Giovanni's Room, 1956
Another Country, 1962
Tell Me How Long the Train's Been Gone, 1968
If Beale Street Could Talk, 1974
Just Above My Head, 1979

OTHER LITERARY FORMS

Before he published his first novel, James Baldwin had established a reputation as a talented essayist and reviewer. Many of his early pieces, later collected in *Notes of a Native Son* (1955) and *Nobody Knows My Name: More Notes of a Native Son* (1961), have become classics; his essays on Richard Wright, especially "Everybody's Protest Novel" (1949) and "Many Thousands Gone" (1951), occupy a central position in the development of "universalist" African American thought during the 1950's. Culminating in *The Fire Next Time* (1963), an extended meditation on the relationship of race, religion, and the individual experience in America, Baldwin's early prose demands a reexamination and redefinition of received social and cultural premises. His collections of essays *No Name in the Street* (1971) and *The Devil Finds Work* (1976) reflected a more militant stance and were received less favorably than Baldwin's universalist statements. *The Evidence of Things Not Seen* (1985) is a book-length essay on the case known as the Atlanta child murders, and *The Price of the Ticket* (1985) includes all of Baldwin's essay collections as well as a number of previously uncollected pieces. Less formal and intricate, though in some cases more explicit, reflections of Baldwin's beliefs can be found in *A Rap on Race* (1971), an extended discussion between Baldwin and anthropologist Margaret Mead, and *A Dialogue* (1975), a conversation with poet Nikki Giovanni.

Baldwin also wrote children's fiction (*Little Man, Little Man*, 1975), the text for a photographic essay (*Nothing Personal*, 1964, with Richard Avedon), an unfilmed scenario (*One Day, When I Was Lost: A Scenario Based on "The Autobiography of Malcolm X,"* 1972), dramas, and short stories. Most critics prefer Baldwin's first play, *The Amen Corner* (pr. 1954), to his *Blues for Mister Charlie* (pr. 1964) despite the latter's four-month Broadway run. Although he published little short fiction after the collection *Going to Meet the Man* (1965), Baldwin was an acknowledged master of the novella form. "Sonny's Blues" (1957), the story of the relationship of a jazz musician to his "respect-

James Baldwin
(Library of Congress)

able" narrator-brother, anticipates many of the themes of Baldwin's later novels and is widely recognized as one of the great American novellas.

Achievements

James Baldwin's role as a major spokesman on race guarantees his place in American cultural history. Although not undeserved, this reputation more frequently obscures than clarifies the nature of his literary achievement, which involves his relationship to African American culture, existential philosophy, and the moral tradition of the world novel. To be sure, Baldwin's progression from an individualistic, universalist stance through active involvement with the integrationist Civil Rights movement to an increasing sympathy with militant pan-Africanist thought parallels the general development of African American thought between the early 1950's and the mid-1970's. Indeed, Baldwin's novels frequently mirror both the author's personal philosophy and its social context. Some, most notably *Another Country*, attained a high degree of public visibility when published, leading to a widely accepted vision of Baldwin as a topical writer. Consideration of Baldwin primarily as a racial spokesman, however, imposes a stereotype that distorts many of his most penetrating insights and underestimates his status as a literary craftsman.

More accurate, although ultimately as limited, is the view of Baldwin primarily as an exemplar of the African American presence in the "mainstream" of the American tradition. Grouped with Ralph Ellison as a major "post-Wright" black novelist, Baldwin represents, in this view, the generation that rejected "protest literature" in favor of "universal" themes. Strangely at odds with the view of Baldwin as racial spokesman, this view emphasizes the craftsmanship of Baldwin's early novels and his treatment of "mainstream" themes such as religious hypocrisy, father-son tensions, and sexual identity. Ironically, many younger African American novelists accept this general view of Baldwin's accomplishment, viewing his mastery of Jamesian techniques and his involvement with continental literary culture as an indication of alienation from his racial identity. Recasting political activist Eldridge Cleaver's political attack on Baldwin in aesthetic terms, the African American writer Ishmael Reed dismisses Baldwin as a great "white" novelist. A grain of truth lies in Reed's assertion; Baldwin rarely created new forms. Rather, he infused a variety of Euro-American forms, derived from Wright and William Faulkner as well as from Henry James, with the rhythms and imagery of the African American oral tradition.

Like the folk preacher whose voice he frequently assumed in secular contexts, Baldwin combined moral insight with an uncompromising sense of the concrete realities of his community, whether defined in terms of family, lovers, race, or nation. This indicates the deepest level of Baldwin's literary achievement; whatever his immediate political focus or fictional form, he possessed an insight into moral psychology shared by only a handful of novelists. Inasmuch as the specific circumstances of this psychology involve American racial relations, this insight aligns Baldwin with Wright, Faulkner, Mark Twain, and Harriet Beecher Stowe. Inasmuch as Baldwin's insight involves the symbolic alienation of the individual, it places him with American romantics such as Nathaniel Hawthorne and European existentialists such as Albert Camus. Since his insight recognizes the complex pressure exerted by social mechanisms on individual consciousness, it reveals affinities with James Joyce, George Eliot, and Ellison. As a writer who combined elements of all of these traditions with the voice of the anonymous African American preacher, Baldwin cannot be reduced to accommodate the terms of any one of them. Refusing to lie about the reality of pain, he provided realistic images of the moral life possible in the inhospitable world that encompasses the streets of Harlem and the submerged recesses of the mind.

BIOGRAPHY

James Arthur Baldwin once dismissed his childhood as "the usual bleak fantasy." Nevertheless, the major concerns of his fiction consistently reflect the social context of his family life in Harlem during the Depression. The dominant figure of Baldwin's childhood was clearly that of his stepfather, David Baldwin, who worked as a manual laborer and preached in a storefront church. Clearly the model for Gabriel Grimes in *Go Tell It on the Mountain*, David Baldwin had moved from New Orleans to New York City, where he married Baldwin's mother, Emma Berdis. The oldest of what was to be a group of nine children in the household, James assumed a great deal of the responsibility for the care of his half brothers and half sisters. Insulated somewhat from the brutality of Harlem street life by his domestic duties, Baldwin, as he describes in *The Fire Next Time*, sought refuge in the church. Undergoing a conversion experience, similar to that of John in *Go Tell It on the Mountain*, at age fourteen in 1938, Baldwin preached as a youth minister for the next several years. At the same time, he began to read, immersing himself in works such as Harriet Beecher Stowe's *Uncle Tom's Cabin* (1852) and the novels of Charles Dickens. Both at his Harlem junior high school, where the African American poet Countée Cullen was one of his teachers, and at his predominantly white Bronx high school, Baldwin contributed to student literary publications. The combination of family tension, economic hardship, and religious vocation provides the focus of much of Baldwin's greatest writing, most notably *Go Tell It on the Mountain*, *The Fire Next Time*, and *Just Above My Head*.

If Baldwin's experience during the 1930's provided his material, his life from 1942 to 1948 shaped his characteristic approach to that material. After he graduated from high school in 1942, Baldwin worked for a year as a manual laborer in New Jersey, an experience that increased both his understanding of his stepfather and his insight into American economic and racial systems. Moving to Greenwich Village in 1943, Baldwin worked during the day and wrote at night for the next five years; his first national reviews and essays appeared in 1946. The major event of the Village years, however, was Baldwin's meeting with Richard Wright in the winter of 1944-1945. Wright's interest helped Baldwin secure first a Eugene F. Saxton Memorial Award and then a Rosenwald Fellowship, enabling him to move to Paris in 1948.

After his arrival in France, Baldwin experienced more of the poverty that had shaped his childhood. Simultaneously, he developed a larger perspective on the psychocultural context conditioning his experience, feeling at once a greater sense of freedom and a larger sense of the global structure of racism, particularly as reflected in the French treatment of North Africans. In addition, he formed many of the personal and literary friendships that contributed to his later public prominence. Baldwin's well-publicized literary feud with Wright, who viewed the younger writer's criticism of Wright's novel *Native Son* (1940) as a form of personal betrayal, helped establish Baldwin as a major presence in African American letters. Although Baldwin's first novel, *Go Tell It on the Mountain*, was well received critically, it was not so financially successful that he could devote all of his time to creative writing. As a result, Baldwin continued to travel widely, frequently on journalistic assignments, while writing *Giovanni's Room*, which is set in France and involves no black characters.

Returning to the United States as a journalist covering the Civil Rights movement, Baldwin made his first trip to the American South in 1957. The essays and reports describing that physical and psychological journey propelled Baldwin to the position of public prominence that he maintained for more than a decade. During the height of the movement, Baldwin lectured widely and was present at major events such as the March on Washington and the voter registration drive in Selma, Alabama. In addition, he met with most of the major African American activists of the period, including Martin Luther King, Jr., Elijah Muhammad, James Meredith, and Medgar Evers. Attorney General Robert F. Kennedy asked Baldwin to bring together the most influential voices in the black community; even though the resulting meeting accomplished little, the request testifies to Baldwin's image as a focal point of African American opinion.

In addition to this political activity, Baldwin formed personal and literary relationships—frequently tempestuous ones—with numerous white writers, including William Styron and Norman Mailer. A surge in literary popularity, reflected in the presence of *Another Country* and *The Fire Next Time* on best-seller lists throughout most of 1962 and 1963, accompanied Baldwin's political success and freed him from financial insecurity for the first time. He traveled extensively throughout the decade, and his visits to Puerto Rico and Africa were to have a major influence on his subsequent political thought.

Partly because of Baldwin's involvement with prominent whites and partly because of the sympathy for gays evinced in his writing, several black militants, most notably Eldridge Cleaver, attacked Baldwin's position as "black spokesman" beginning in the late 1960's. As a result, nationalist spokesmen such as Amiri Baraka and Bobby Seale gradually eclipsed Baldwin in the public literary and political spotlights. Nevertheless, Baldwin, himself sympathetic to many of the militant positions, continued his involvement with public issues, such as the fate of the group of North Carolina prisoners known as the Wilmington 10, which he addressed in an open letter to Jimmy Carter shortly after Carter's election to the U.S. presidency. In his later years, though he returned periodically to the South, Baldwin lived for much of the time in France and Turkey. He died in St. Paul de Vence, France, on November 30, 1987.

ANALYSIS

Uncompromising in his demand for personal and social integrity, James Baldwin from the beginning of his career charged the individual with full responsibility for his or her moral identity. Both in his early individualistic novels and in his later political fiction, he insisted on the inadequacy of received definitions as the basis for self-knowledge or social action. Echoing the existentialist principle "existence precedes essence," he intimated the underlying consistency of his vision in the introductory essay in *Notes of a Native Son*: "I think all theories are suspect, that the finest principles may have to be modified, or may even be pulverized by the demands of life, and that one must find, therefore, one's own moral center and move through the world hoping that this center will guide one aright."

This insistence on the moral center and movement in the world cautions against associating Baldwin with the atheistic or solipsistic currents of existential thought. Never denying the possibility of transcendent moral power—which he frequently imaged as the power of love—he simply insisted that human conceptions must remain flexible enough to allow for the honest perception of experience. Fully recognizing the reality of existential pain and despair, Baldwin invoked honesty and self-acceptance as the necessary supports for the love capable of generating individual communication and at least the groundwork for political action.

Baldwin's social vision, reflecting his experience in a racist culture, acknowledges the forces militating against self-knowledge and moral responsibility. Each of his novels portrays a series of evasive and simplifying definitions built into religious, economic, and educational institutions. These definitions, which emphasize the separation of self and other, control the immediate contexts of individual experience. As a result, they frequently seem to constitute "human nature," to embody the inevitable limits of experience. While sympathizing with the difficulty of separating the self from context without simultaneously denying experience, Baldwin insists that acquiescing to the definitions inevitably results in self-hatred and social immorality. The individual incapable of accepting his or her existential complexity flees to the illusion of certainty provided by the institutions that assume responsibility for directing moral decisions. This cycle of institutional pressure encouraging existential evasion ensuring further institutional corruption recurs in each of Baldwin's novels. On both personal and social levels, the drive to deny the reality of the other—racial, sexual, or economic—generates nothing save destruction. Derived from the streets of Harlem rather than from Scripture, Baldwin's response echoes Christ's admonition to "love thy neighbor as thyself." The derivation is vital; in Baldwin's novels, those who extract the message from the Bible rather than from their lives frequently aggravate the pain that makes evading reality seem attractive.

The immediate focus of Baldwin's attention gradually shifted from consciousness to context, creating the illusion of a change in his basic concerns. While he always worked in the realistic tradition of the novel, his choice of specific forms paralleled this shift in thematic focus, though again his later work indicates an underlying unity in his fiction. His first novel, *Go Tell It on the Mountain*, employs a tightly focused Jamesian form to explore the developing awareness of the adolescent protagonist John Grimes, who is not yet aware of the evasive definitions conditioning his experience. After a second Jamesian novel, *Giovanni's Room*, Baldwin adapted the relatively unstructured Dreiserian mode in *Another Country* and *Tell Me How Long the Train's Been Gone*. Characters such as Rufus Scott and Vivaldo Moore in *Another Country* continue to struggle for individual awareness, but Baldwin's new narrative stance emphasizes the impact of the limiting definitions on a wide range of particular social circumstances. Attempting to balance the presentation of consciousness and context, Baldwin's last two novels, *If Beale Street Could Talk* and *Just Above My Head*, synthesize the earlier technical approaches. Returning to the immediate focus on the individual consciousness in these first-person narratives, Baldwin creates protagonists capable of articulating their own social perceptions. Consciousness and context merge as Baldwin's narrators share their insights and, more important, their processes with their fellow sufferers.

These insights implicitly endorse William Blake's vision of morality as a movement from innocence through experience to a higher innocence. Beginning with an unaware innocence, individuals inevitably enter the deadening and murderous world of experience, the world of the limiting definitions. Those who attempt to deny the world and remain children perish alongside those who cynically submit to the cruelty of the context for imagined personal benefit. Only those who plunge into experience, recognize its cruelty, and resolve to forge an aware innocence can hope to survive morally. Specifically, Baldwin urges families to pass on a sense of the higher innocence to their children by refusing to simplify the truth of experience. This painful honesty makes possible the commitment to love despite the inevitability of pain and isolation. It provides the only hope, however desperate, for individual or social rejuvenation.

To a large extent, Baldwin's career developed in accord with the Blakean pattern. John Grimes begins his passage from innocence to experience in *Go Tell It on the Mountain*; Rufus Scott and Vivaldo Moore, among others, struggle to survive experience in *Another Country*, which intimates the need for the higher innocence. Baldwin's last two novels portray the entire process, focusing on the attempt first to find and then to pass on the higher innocence. *Just Above My Head*, with its middle-aged narrator and his teenage children, clearly represents a more highly developed and realistic stage of the vision than *If Beale Street Could Talk*, with its teenage-mother narrator and her newborn infant.

GO TELL IT ON THE MOUNTAIN

Go Tell It on the Mountain centers on the religious conversion and family relationships of John Grimes, whose experience parallels that of Baldwin during his youth. Although he believes himself to be the natural son of Gabriel Grimes, a preacher who, like Baldwin's stepfather, moved to New York after growing up in the South, John is actually the son of Gabriel's wife, Elizabeth, and her lover, Richard, who committed suicide prior to John's birth. Growing up under the influence of his hypocritical and tyrannical stepfather, John alternately attempts to please and transcend him. Gabriel expends most of his emotional energy on his openly rebellious son Roy, whose immersion in the violent life of the Harlem streets contrasts sharply with John's involvement with the "Temple of the Fire Baptized," the storefront church where his conversion takes place.

To the extent that Baldwin organizes *Go Tell It on the Mountain* around John's attempt to come to terms with these pressures, the novel appears to have a highly individualistic focus. The overall structure of the novel, however, dictates that John's experience be viewed in a larger context. Of the three major sections of *Go Tell It on the Mountain*, the first, "The Seventh Day," and the third, "The Threshing Floor," focus directly on John. The long middle section, "The Prayers of the Saints," a Faulknerian exploration of history, traces the origins of John's struggle to the experience of his elders, devoting individual chapters to Elizabeth, Gabriel, and Gabriel's sister Florence. Together the prayers portray the Great Migration of African Americans from South to North, from rural to urban settings. Far from bringing true freedom, the movement results in a new indirect type of oppression. As Elizabeth recognizes,

> There was not, after all, a great difference between the world of the North and that of the South which she had fled; there was only this difference: the North promised more. And this similarity: what it promised it did not give, and what it gave, at length and grudgingly with one hand, it took back with the other.

Even in his most individualistic phase, Baldwin is aware of the power of institutional pressures. The origins of John's particular struggle against the limiting definitions go back to their impact on both Elizabeth and Gabriel.

Elizabeth's relationship with John's true father, at least in its early stages, appears to offer hope for at least a limited freedom from external definition. Highly intelligent and self-aware, Richard struggles to transcend the limitations imposed on black aspiration through a rigorous program of self-education, which he shares with Elizabeth. Despite his intelligence and determination, however, Richard maintains a naïve innocence concerning the possibility of self-definition in a society based on racist assumptions. Only when arrested on suspicion of a robbery he had nothing to do with does he recognize that his context defines him as simply another "nigger." Unable to reconcile this imposed definition with his drive for social transcendence, he despairs and commits suicide. This act, in turn, destroys Elizabeth's chance for obtaining a greater degree of freedom. She is not, however, simply a victim. Fearing that Richard will be unable to cope with the responsibility of a family, she fails to tell him of her pregnancy. Far from protecting him, this evasion contributes to his destruction by allowing Richard to view his situation as purely personal. Elizabeth's own choice, conditioned by the social refusal to confront reality, combines with the racist legal system to circumscribe her possibilities. Forced to care for her infant son, she marries Gabriel, thus establishing the basic terms for John's subsequent struggle.

Seen in relation to John in "The Seventh Day," Gabriel appears to be one of the most despicable hypocrites in American literature. Seen in relation to his own history in "The Prayers of the Saints," however, he appears victimized by the institutional context of his youth. In turn, he victimizes his family by attempting to force them into narrowly defined roles. The roots of Gabriel's character lie in the "temple-street" dichotomy of his southern childhood. Encouraged by his religious mother to deny his sensuality, Gabriel undergoes a conversion experience and immerses himself in the role of preacher. As a result, he enters into a loveless, asexual marriage with his mother's friend Deborah, herself a victim of the racist psychology—enforced by blacks and whites—that condemns *her* after she has been brutally raped by a group of whites.

Eventually, Gabriel's repressed street self breaks out and he fathers a son by the sensual Esther. Again attempting to deny his sensuality, Gabriel refuses to acknowledge this son, Royal. Like John's half brother Roy, the first Royal immerses himself in the street life that Gabriel denies; he dies in a Chicago barroom brawl. Gabriel fears that Roy will share Royal's fate, but his attempt to crush his second son's street self merely strengthens the resulting rebellion. Faced with the guilt of Royal's death and the sense of impending doom concerning Roy, Gabriel retreats into a solipsism that makes a mockery of his Christian vocation. Far from providing a context for moral responsibility, the church—both in the South and in the North—simply replaces the original innocence of religious fervor with a cynical vision of religion as a source of the power needed to destroy the innocence of others.

Against this backdrop, John's conversion raises a basic question that will recur in slightly different circumstances in each of Baldwin's novels: Can an individual hope to break the cycle of evasion that has shaped his or her personal and social context? In John's case, the problem takes on added dimensions, since he remains ignorant of many of the events shaping his life, including those involving his own birth. By framing the prayers with John's conversion, Baldwin stresses the connection between past and present, but the connection can be perceived as either oppressive or liberating. The complex irony of "The Threshing Floor" section allows informed readings of John's conversion as either a surrender to evasion or a movement toward existential responsibility. Focusing primarily on John's internal experience as he lies transfixed on the church floor, "The Threshing Floor" revolves around a dialogue between an "ironic voice" that challenges John to return to the street and the part of John that seeks traditional salvation. Throughout John's vision, the narrative voice shifts point of view in accord with John's developing perception. As John accepts the perceptions implied by his vision, the ironic voice shifts its attention to yet deeper levels of ambiguity. To the extent that John resolves these ambiguities by embracing the Temple, his experience seems to increase the risk that he will follow Gabriel's destructive example.

Several image patterns, however, indicate that John may be moving nearer to a recognition of his actual complexity. Chief among these are those involving the curse of Ham, the rejection of the father, and the acceptance of apparent opposites. From the beginning of the vision, the ironic voice ridicules John for accepting the curse of Ham, which condemns him both as son and as "nigger." Manipulating John's sense of guilt for having indulged his street self by masturbating, the ironic voice insists that John's very existence "proves" Gabriel's own sexual weakness. If Gabriel condemns John, he condemns himself in the process. As a result, John comes to view himself as the "devil's son" and repudiates his subservience before his "father." Without this essentially negative, and ultimately socially derived, definition of himself, John finds himself in an existential void where "there was no speech or language, and there was no love."

Forced to reconstruct his identity, John progresses from this sense of isolation to a vision of the dispossessed with whom he shares his agony and his humanity. John's vision of the multitude whose collective voice merges with his own suggests suffering as the essential human experience, one obliterating both the safety and the isolation of imposed definitions. Significantly, this vision leads John to Jesus the Son rather than God the Father, marking an implicit rejection of Gabriel's Old Testament vengeance in favor of the New Testament commitment to an all-encompassing love. The son metamorphoses from symbol of limitation to symbol of liberation. Near the end of his vision, John explicitly rejects the separation of opposites—street and temple, white and black—encouraged by his social context: "The light and the darkness had kissed each other, and were married now, forever, in the life and the vision of John's soul." Returning to his immediate environment from the depths of his mind, John responds not to the call of Gabriel but to that of Elisha, a slightly older member of the congregation with whom he has previously engaged in a sexually suggestive wrestling match reminiscent of that in D. H. Lawrence's *Women in Love* (1920). John's salvation, then, may bring him closer to an acceptance of his own sensuality, to a definition of himself encompassing both temple and street. Baldwin ends the novel with the emergence of the newly "saved" John onto the streets of Harlem. His fate hinges on his ability to move ahead to the higher innocence suggested by his vision of the dispossessed rather than submit to the experiences that have destroyed and deformed the majority of the saints.

ANOTHER COUNTRY

Another Country, Baldwin's greatest popular success, analyzes the effects of deforming pressure and experience on a wide range of characters, black and white, male and female, homosexual and heterosexual. To accommodate these diverse consciousnesses, Baldwin employs the sprawling form usually associated with political rather than psychological fiction, emphasizing the diverse forms of innocence and experience in American society. The three major sections of *Another Country*—"Easy Rider," "Any Day Now," and "Toward Bethlehem"—progress generally from despair to renewed hope, but no single consciousness or plot line provides a frame similar to that of *Go Tell It on the Mountain*. Rather, the novel's structural coherence derives from the moral concerns present in each of the various plots.

Casting a Melvillean shadow over the novel is the black jazz musician Rufus Scott, who is destroyed by an agonizing affair with Leona, a white southerner recently arrived in New York at the time she meets him. Unable to forge the innocence necessary for love in a context that repudiates the relationship at every turn, Rufus destroys Leona psychologically. After a period of physical and psychological destitution, he kills himself by jumping off a bridge. His sister Ida, an aspiring singer, and his friend Vivaldo Moore, an aspiring white writer, meet during the last days of Rufus's life and fall in love as they console each other over his death. Struggling to overcome the racial and sexual definitions that destroyed Rufus, they seek a higher innocence capable of countering Ida's sense of the world as a "whorehouse." In contrast to Ida and Vivaldo's struggle, the relationship of white actor Eric Jones and his French lover Yves seems edenic. Although Baldwin portrays Eric's internal struggle for a firm sense of his sexual identity, Eric and Yves's shared innocence at times seems to exist almost entirely outside the context of the pressures that destroyed Rufus. The final major characters, Richard and Cass Silenski, represent the cost of the American Dream. After Richard "makes it" as a popular novelist, the couple's personal relationship decays, precipitating Cass's affair with Eric. Their tentative reunion after Richard discovers the affair makes it clear that material success provides no shortcut to moral responsibility.

Baldwin examines each character and relationship in the context of the institutional pressures discouraging individual responsibility. His portrait of Rufus, the major accomplishment of *Another Country*, testifies to a moral insight and a raw artistic power resembling that of Wright and Émile Zola. Forgoing the formal control and emotional restraint of his earlier novels, Baldwin opens *Another Country* with the image of Rufus as a man who "had fallen so low, that he scarcely had the energy to be angry." Both an exceptional case and a representative figure, Rufus embodies the seething anger and hopeless isolation that render Baldwin's United States a landscape of nightmare. Seeing his own situation as unbearable, Rufus meditates on the fate of a city tormented by an agony like his own: "He remembered to what excesses, into what traps and nightmares, his loneliness had driven him; and he wondered where such a violent emptiness might drive an entire city." Forcing readers to recognize the social implications of Rufus's situation, Baldwin emphasizes that his specific situation originates in his own moral failure with Leona. Where Gabriel Grimes remained insulated from his immorality by arrogance and pride, Rufus feels the full extent of his self-enforced damnation. Ironically and belatedly, his destitution clarifies his sense of the extent of his past acceptance of the social definitions that destroy him.

Wandering the streets of Manhattan, Rufus feels himself beyond human contact. Desperately in need of love, he believes his past actions render him unfit for even minimal compassion. His abuse of Leona, who as a white woman represents both the "other" and the source of the most obvious social definitions circumscribing his life as a black male, accounts for his original estrangement from family and friends, who find his viciousness uncharacteristic. All, including Rufus, fail to understand soon enough that his abuse of Leona represents both a rebellion against and an acceptance of the role dictated by racial and sexual definitions.

Separated from the psychological source of his art—jazz inevitably rejects the substructure of Euro-American definitions of reality—Rufus falls ever further into a paranoia that receives ample reinforcement from the racist context. Largely by his own choice, he withdraws almost entirely from his acquaintances, both black and white. Once on the street following Leona's breakdown, he begins to recognize not only his immediate but also his long-term acceptance of destructive definitions. Thinking back on a brief same-sex affair with Eric to which he submitted out of pity rather than love, Rufus regrets having treated his friend with contempt. Having rejected the "other" in Eric and Leona, Rufus realizes he has rejected a part of himself. He consigns himself to the ranks of the damned, casting himself beyond human love with his plunge off the bridge.

While not absolving Rufus of responsibility for his actions, Baldwin treats him with profound sympathy, in part because of his honesty and in part because of the enormous power of the social institutions that define him as the "other." Throughout *Another Country*, Baldwin emphasizes that white heterosexual males possess the power of definition, although their power destroys them as surely as it does their victims. Television producer Steve Ellis, a moral cripple embodying the basic values of the American economic system, nearly destroys Ida and Vivaldo's relationship by encouraging Ida to accept a cynical definition of herself as a sexual commodity. Vivaldo, too, participates in the cynicism when he visits the Harlem prostitutes, indirectly perpetuating the definitions that reduce black people to sexual objects and thus implicating himself in Rufus's death. In fact, every major character with the exception of Eric bears partial responsibility for Rufus's destruction, since each at times accepts the definitions generating the cycle of rejection and denial. The constituting irony, however, stems from the fact that only those most actively struggling for moral integrity recognize their culpability. Vivaldo, who attempts to reach out to Rufus earlier on the night of his suicide, feels more guilt than Richard, who simply dismisses Rufus as a common "nigger" after his mistreatment of Leona.

This unflinching portrayal of moral failure, especially on the part of well-meaning liberals, provides the thematic center of *Another Country*. Baldwin concludes the novel with the image of Yves's reunion with Eric, who is apparently on the verge of professional success with a starring role in a film of a Fyodor Dostoevski novel. This combination of personal and financial success seems more an assertion of naïve hope than a compelling part of the surrounding fictional world. The majority of the narrative lines imply the impossibility of simple dissociation from institutional pressure. Ultimately, the intensity of Rufus's pain and the intricacy of Ida and Vivaldo's struggle overshadow Eric and Yves's questionable innocence. As Ida tells Vivaldo, "Our being together doesn't change the world." The attempt to overcome the cynicism of this perception leads to a recognition that meaningful love demands total acceptance. Ida's later question "How can you say you loved Rufus when there was so much about him you didn't want to know?" could easily provide the epitaph for the entire society in *Another Country*.

JUST ABOVE MY HEAD

In *Just Above My Head*, Baldwin creates a narrator, Hall Montana, capable of articulating the psychological subtleties of *Go Tell It on the Mountain*, the social insights of *Another Country*, and the political anger of *Tell Me How Long the Train's Been Gone*. Like other observer-participants in American literature, such as Nick Carraway in F. Scott Fitzgerald's *The Great Gatsby* (1925) and Jack Burden in Robert Penn Warren's *All the King's*

Men (1946), Hall tells both his own story and that of a more publicly prominent figure, in this case his brother Arthur, a gospel singer who dies two years prior to the start of the novel.

Significantly, *Just Above My Head* also reconsiders Baldwin's own artistic history, echoing countless motifs from his earlier writings. Though not precisely a self-reflexive text, *Just Above My Head* takes on added richness when juxtaposed with Baldwin's treatment of religious concerns in *Go Tell It on the Mountain*, the homosexuality theme in *Giovanni's Room*, the relationship between brothers and the musical setting in "Sonny's Blues," racial politics in *Blues for Mister Charlie* and *Tell Me How Long the Train's Been Gone*, the Nation of Islam in *The Fire Next Time* and *No Name in the Street*, and, most important, the intermingled family love and world politics in *If Beale Street Could Talk*. Baldwin's reconsideration of his own history, which is at once private like Hall's and public like Arthur's, emphasizes the necessity of a continual reexamination of the nature of both self and context in order to reach the higher innocence.

Similarly, Hall's resolve to understand the social and existential meaning of Arthur's experience originates in his desire to answer honestly his children's questions concerning their uncle. Refusing to protect their original innocence—an attempt he knows would fail—Hall seeks both to free himself from the despair of experience and to discover a mature innocence he can pass on to the younger generation. Tracing the roots of Arthur's despair to pressures originating in numerous limiting definitions and failures of courage, Hall summarizes his, and Baldwin's, social insight:

> The attempt, more the necessity, to excavate a history, to find out the truth about oneself! is motivated by the need to have the power to force others to recognize your presence, your right to be here. The disputed passage will remain disputed so long as you do not have the authority of the right-of-way. . . . Power clears the passage, swiftly: but the paradox, here, is that power, rooted in history, is also, the mockery and the repudiation of history. The power to define the other seals one's definition of oneself.

Recognizing that the only hope for meaningful moral freedom lies in repudiating the power of definition, Hall concludes: "Our history is each other. That is our only guide. One thing is absolutely certain: one can repudiate, or despise, no one's history without repudiating and despising one's own."

Although Baldwin recognizes the extent to which the definitions and repudiations remain entrenched in institutional structures, his portrayal of Hall's courage and honesty offers at least some hope for moral integrity as a base for social action. If an individual such as Hall can counteract the pressures militating against personal responsibility, he or she may be able to exert a positive influence on relatively small social groups such as families and churches, which in turn may affect the larger social context. Nevertheless, Baldwin refuses to encourage simplistic optimism. Rather than focusing narrowly on Hall's individual process, he emphasizes the aspects of the context that render that success atypical.

Although Hall begins with his immediate context, his excavation involves the Korean War, the Civil Rights movement, the rise of Malcolm X, and the role of advertising in American culture. Hall's relationships with his family and close friends provide a Jamesian frame for the Dreiserian events of the novel, somewhat as John's conversion frames the historical "Prayers of the Saints" in *Go Tell It on the Mountain. Just Above My Head*, however, leaves no ambiguity concerning the individual's ability to free him- or herself from history. Only a conscious decision to accept the pain and guilt of the past promises any real hope for love, for the higher innocence. Similarly, Baldwin reiterates that, while the desire for safety is understandable, all safety is illusion. Pain inevitably returns, and, while the support of friends and lovers may help, only a self-image based on existential acceptance rather than repudiation makes survival possible.

Arthur's death, occupying a thematic and emotional position similar to the death of Rufus in *Another Country*, provides the point of departure for Hall's excavation. A gifted gospel singer as a teenager, Arthur rises to stardom as the "emperor of soul." Despite his success, however, he never frees himself from doubts concerning his own identity or feels secure with the experience of love. Even though his parents offer him a firm base of love and acceptance, Arthur feels a deep sense of emotional isolation even as a child, a sense reinforced by his observations of life in Harlem and, later, in the South. Though he accepts his own homosexuality with relatively little anxiety, his society refuses him the freedom necessary for the development of a truly satisfying emotional life. The edenic innocence of Eric and Yves in *Another Country* clearly fails to provide a sufficient response to the institutional context of *Just Above My Head*.

Arthur's childhood experiences provide clear warnings against the attempt to maintain innocence through simplistic self-definition. Julia Miller, like John in *Go Tell It on the Mountain*, undergoes a salvation experience and embarks on a career as a child evangelist. Encouraged by her parents, friends of the Montanas who rely on their daughter for economic support, she assumes a sanctimonious attitude, which she uses to manipulate her elders. Arthur's parents deplore the indulgence of Julia, unambiguously rejecting the idea that her religious vocation lifts her beyond the "naughty" street side of her personality. Ultimately, and in great pain, Julia confronts this truth. After her mother's death, she discovers that her father, Joel, views her primarily as an economic and sexual object. His desire to exploit her earning potential even when she says she has lost her vocation reflects his underlying contempt for the spirit. This contempt leads to an incestuous rape that destroys Julia's remaining innocence and drives her to a life as a prostitute in New Orleans. Eventually, Julia recovers from this brutalization, but her example provides a clear warning to Arthur against confusing his vocation as a gospel singer with a transcendence of human fallibility.

The experiences of the members of Arthur's first gospel group, the Trumpets of Zion, reveal how institutions infringe even on those not actively committed to simplifying definitions. At one extreme, the social definitions establish a context that accepts and encourages murder—symbolic and real—of the other. Peanut, a member of the Trumpets and later Arthur's companion on the road, vanishes into the Alabama night following a civil rights rally, presumably murdered by whites seeking to enforce the definition of blacks as "niggers." Equally devastating, although less direct, is the operation of the context on Red, another member of the Trumpets, who turns to drugs in an attempt to relieve the pain of the Harlem streets.

Even Hall finds himself an unwilling accomplice to the imposition of social definitions when he is drafted and sent to Korea. Powerless to alter the institutional structure, Hall recognizes, and tells Arthur, that the American military spreads not freedom but repudiation in the developing world. Hall's subsequent employment by an advertising agency involves him in another aspect of the same oppressive system. Viewed as an anomaly by his employers, as an atypical high-class "nigger," Hall nevertheless participates in the creation of images designed to simplify reality for economic gain, which will be used to strengthen the oppressive system. The juxtaposition of Julia's false innocence with the destructive experiences of Peanut, Red, and Hall protects Arthur against the urge to dismiss any aspect of his awareness. A large part of his power as a singer derives from his recognition of the reality of both street and temple, expressed in his ability to communicate sexual pain in gospel songs and spiritual aspiration in the blues.

Arthur, then, appears ideally prepared for the responsible exercise of existential freedom. His failure even to survive underscores the destructive power of the corrupt institutional context. The roots of Arthur's doom lie in his homosexual relationship with Crunch, the final member of the Trumpets. Highly desirable physically, Crunch feels locked into a definition of himself as a sexual object prior to his involvement with Arthur. In its early stages, Arthur and Crunch's love, like that of Yves and Eric in *Another Country*, seems an idyllic retreat, a spot of innocence in the chaos of experience. The retreat, however, proves temporary, in part because Crunch cannot free himself from the urge for self-simplification and in part because of the continuing presence of the outside world. Uneasy with his sexual identity, Crunch becomes involved with Julia when he discovers the extent of her father's abuse. Arthur recognizes that Crunch is not abandoning him by reacting to Julia's pain and accepts the relationship. Granted sufficient time for adjustment, Arthur and Crunch seem capable of confronting their experience and forging a higher innocence as the basis for a lasting love. The time does not exist, however. Crunch is drafted and sent to Korea. Separated from Arthur's reassurance and tormented by self-doubt, Crunch never fully accepts his sexuality. After his return to Harlem, he and Arthur gradually lose contact.

The repeated losses—of Peanut, Red, and Crunch—create a sense of isolation that Arthur never overcomes. The expectation of loss periodically overpowers his determination to communicate, the determination that makes him a great singer. Even during periods of real joy, with his French lover Guy in Paris or with Julia's brother Jimmy, who is both his pianist and his lover, Arthur suffers acute emotional pain. Attempting to survive by rededicating himself to communication, to his artistic excavation of history, Arthur drives himself past the limits of physical and psychological endurance. He dies in the basement bathroom of a London pub after a lovers' quarrel, clearly only temporary, with Jimmy. By concluding Arthur's life with an image of isolation, Baldwin emphasizes the power of limiting definitions to destroy even the most existentially courageous individual.

Arthur's death, however, marks not only a conclusion but also the beginning of Hall's quest for the higher innocence that he, along with his wife Ruth, Julia, and Jimmy, can pass on to the younger generation. This higher innocence involves both individual and social elements, ultimately demanding the mutual support of individuals willing to pursue excavation of their own histories. This support expresses itself in the call-and-response dynamic, a basic element of African American oral culture that Arthur employs in his interaction with audiences while singing. As Baldwin re-creates the traditional form, the interaction begins with the call of a leader who expresses his own emotional experience through the vehicle of a traditional song that provides a communal context for the emotion. If the members of the community recognize and share the experience evoked by the call, they respond with another traditional phrase that provides the sense of understanding and acceptance that enables the leader to go on. Implicitly, the process enables both individual and community to define themselves in opposition to dominant social forces. If the experience of isolation is shared, it is no longer the same type of isolation that brought Rufus to his death. In *Just Above My Head*, the call-and-response rests on a rigorous excavation requiring individual silence, courage, and honesty expressed through social presence, acceptance, and love. Expressed in the interactions between Arthur and his audiences, between Hall and his children, between Baldwin and his readers, this call-and-response provides a realistic image of the higher innocence possible in opposition to the murderous social definitions.

As in John's vision in *Go Tell It on the Mountain* and Rufus's self-examination in *Another Country*, the process begins in silence, which throughout Baldwin's novels offers the potential for either alienation or communication. The alienating silence coincides thematically with institutional noise—mechanical, social, political. The majority of Americans, Baldwin insists, prefer distracting and ultimately meaningless sounds to the silence that allows self-recognition. Only individuals sharing Arthur's willingness to remove himself from the noise can hope to hear their own voices and transform the silence into music. Every moment of true communication in *Just Above My Head* begins in a moment of silence that effectively rejects the clamor of imposed definitions. The courage needed for the acceptance of silence prepares the way for the honest excavation of history that must precede any meaningful social interaction. The excavation remains a burden, however, without that interaction. No purely individual effort can alter the overwhelming sense of isolation imposed by social definitions. The individual stage of the process merely heightens the need for acceptance, presence, and love. Arthur sounds the call amid the noise; he cannot provide the response. Perhaps, Baldwin indicates, no one, not even

Jimmy, can provide a response capable of soothing the feeling of isolation emanating from early experiences. Nevertheless, the attempt is vital. Julia recognizes both the necessity and the limitation of presence when she tells Hall of her relationship with Jimmy: "I don't know enough to change him, or to save him. But I know enough to be there. I *must* be there."

If presence—being there—is to provide even momentary relief, it must be accompanied by the honest acceptance underlying love. Refusing to limit his acceptance, Hall answers his son Tony's questions concerning Arthur's sexuality with complete honesty. Understanding fully that his acceptance of Arthur entails an acceptance of the similar complexity in himself and in Tony, Hall surrenders his voice to Jimmy's, imaginatively participating in a love that repudiates social definition, that rises up out of the silence beyond the noise. Implicitly, Hall offers both Tony and his daughter Odessa the assurance of presence, of acceptance, of love. They need not fear rejection if they have the courage to accept their full humanity. The assurance cannot guarantee freedom, or even survival. It can, and does, intimate the form of mature innocence in the world described by the composite voice of Baldwin, Jimmy, and Hall, a world that "doesn't have any morality. Look at the world. What the world calls morality is nothing but the dream of safety. That's how the world gets to be so fucking moral. The only way to know that you are safe is to see somebody else in danger—otherwise you can't be sure you're safe."

Against this vicious safety, a safety that necessitates limiting definitions imposed on others, Baldwin proposes a responsibility based on risk. Only by responding to the call sounding from Arthur, from Jimmy and Hall, from Baldwin, can people find freedom. The call, ultimately, emanates not only from the individual but also from the community to which he or she calls. It provides a focus for repudiation of the crushing definitions. Hall, using Jimmy's voice, describes the call: "The man who tells the story isn't *making up* a story. He's listening to us, and can only give back, to us, what he hears: from us." The responsibility lies with everyone.

Craig Werner

OTHER MAJOR WORKS

SHORT FICTION: *Going to Meet the Man*, 1965.

PLAYS: *The Amen Corner*, pr. 1954; *Blues for Mister Charlie*, pr., pb. 1964; *A Deed from the King of Spain*, pr. 1974.

POETRY: *Jimmy's Blues: Selected Poems*, 1983.

SCREENPLAY: *One Day, When I Was Lost: A Scenario Based on "The Autobiography of Malcolm X,"* 1972.

NONFICTION: *Notes of a Native Son*, 1955; *Nobody Knows My Name: More Notes of a Native Son*, 1961; *The Fire Next Time*, 1963; *Nothing Personal*, 1964 (with Richard Avedon); *No Name in the Street*, 1971; *A Rap on Race*, 1971 (with Margaret Mead); *A Dialogue*, 1975 (with Nikki Giovanni); *The Devil Finds Work*, 1976; *The Evidence of Things*

Not Seen, 1985; *The Price of the Ticket*, 1985; *Conversations with James Baldwin*, 1989; *Collected Essays*, 1998; *Native Sons: A Friendship That Created One of the Greatest Works of the Twentieth Century—"Notes of a Native Son*," 2004 (with Sol Stein).
CHILDREN'S LITERATURE: *Little Man, Little Man*, 1975.

BIBLIOGRAPHY

Balfour, Lawrie Lawrence, and Katherine Lawrence Balfour. *The Evidence of Things Not Said: James Baldwin and the Promise of American Democracy.* Ithaca, N.Y.: Cornell University Press, 2001. Explores the political dimension of Baldwin's essays, stressing the politics of race in American democracy.

Campbell, James. *Talking at the Gates: A Life of James Baldwin.* New York: Viking Press, 1991. Good narrative biography is organized into five sections, each focusing on a particular period of Baldwin's life. Places Baldwin's work within the context of his times. Includes detailed notes and bibliography.

Fabré, Michel. "James Baldwin in Paris: Love and Self-Discovery." In *From Harlem to Paris: Black American Writers in France, 1840-1980.* Chicago: University of Illinois Press, 1991. Discusses Baldwin's Paris experiences. Brings biographical details to the European experiences of the bicontinental playwright, who owed France "his own spiritual growth, through the existential discovery of love as a key to life." The notes offer interview sources of quotations for further study.

Harris, Trudier, ed. *New Essays on "Go Tell It on the Mountain."* New York: Cambridge University Press, 1996. Collection of essays examines the composition, themes, publication history, public reception, and contemporary interpretations of Baldwin's first novel. Some of the essays discuss Baldwin's treatment of God, the American South, and homosexuality in the novel.

Kinnamon, Keneth, ed. *James Baldwin: A Collection of Critical Essays.* Englewood Cliffs, N.J.: Prentice Hall, 1974. A good introduction to Baldwin's early work featuring a collection of diverse essays by such well-known figures as Irving Howe, Langston Hughes, Sherley Anne Williams, and Eldridge Cleaver. Includes a chronology of important dates, notes on the contributors, and a select bibliography.

Leeming, David. *James Baldwin: A Biography.* New York: Alfred A. Knopf, 1994. A biography of Baldwin written by one who knew him and worked with him for the last quarter century of his life. Provides extensive literary analysis of Baldwin's work and relates his work to his life.

McBride, Dwight A., ed. *James Baldwin Now.* New York: New York University Press, 1999. Collection of essays reevaluates Baldwin's work, stressing the usefulness of interdisciplinary approaches in understanding Baldwin's appeal, political thought and work, and legacy. The contributors maintain that Baldwin was not an exclusively gay, expatriate, black, or activist writer but instead was a complex combination of all of those things.

Miller, D. Quentin, ed. *Re-viewing James Baldwin: Things Not Seen*. Philadelphia: Temple University Press, 2000. Collection of essays explores the ways in which Baldwin's writing touched on issues that confront all people, including race, identity, sexuality, and religious ideology. Works analyzed include the novels *Giovanni's Room, Another Country,* and *Just Above My Head.*

Scott, Lynn Orilla. *James Baldwin's Later Fiction: Witness to the Journey*. East Lansing: Michigan State University Press, 2002. Analyzes the decline of Baldwin's reputation after the 1960's, the ways in which critics have often undervalued his work, and the interconnected themes in his body of work.

Sylvander, Carolyn Wedin. *James Baldwin*. New York: Frederick Ungar, 1980. Good overview of Baldwin's work provides an aesthetic perspective, a bibliographical summary, and an analysis of individual works, with greatest emphasis given to Baldwin's plays, novels, and short stories.

Troupe, Quincy, ed. *James Baldwin: The Legacy*. New York: Simon & Schuster, 1989. Contains eighteen essays by and about Baldwin, five of which were written for this collection, and homage and celebration from many who were profoundly influenced by him, including Pat Mikell's account of Baldwin's last days in St. Paul de Vence. With a foreword by Wole Soyinka.

Weatherby, W. J. *James Baldwin: Artist on Fire*. New York: Donald I. Fine, 1989. Lengthy personal reminiscence of Baldwin by a close friend who calls his biography a portrait. Based on conversations with more than one hundred people who knew Baldwin. Rich in intimate detail; reveals the man behind the words.

DJUNA BARNES

Born: Cornwall-on-Hudson, New York; June 12, 1892
Died: New York, New York; June 18, 1982
Also known as: Djuna Chappell Barnes

PRINCIPAL LONG FICTION
Ryder, 1928
Nightwood, 1936

OTHER LITERARY FORMS

Although primarily known for her singular novel *Nightwood*, Djuna Barnes wrote in many genres throughout her long life. She initially earned her living in New York City as a freelance reporter and theater critic, publishing articles in the *Brooklyn Daily Eagle*, *New York Morning Telegraph*, *Vanity Fair*, *The New Yorker*, *New York Press*, *The Dial*, and other periodicals. Her artistic skills showed in her drawings, some of which appeared as early as 1915 in *The Book of Repulsive Women*, her first published chapbook. Her artwork also appeared as illustrations for *Ladies Almanack*, a roman à clef about lesbian circles in Paris, a book she cleverly structured in the format of an almanac. Another collection of her drawings was published in 1995 as *Poe's Mother: Selected Drawings of Djuna Barnes*. Her first collection of short stories, *A Book* (1923), was reissued as *A Night Among the Horses* in 1928 with a number of additional stories.

Barnes also was a dramatist. Her one-act plays were performed at the Provincetown Playhouse in Greenwich Village, New York City. She wrote and rewrote the full-length verse drama, *The Antiphon*, over a twenty-year period before poet T. S. Eliot, in his position as a literary editor with publisher Faber and Faber, approved the manuscript for publication. The action of the play occurs in a fictional township in England during World War II, as family members from America reunite; family drama ensues. Their memories of love and aggression probably reflect Barnes's own upbringing and family dynamics.

Barnes's last book before she died was *Creatures in an Alphabet* (1982), a collection of short rhyming poems. Since her death in 1982, collections of her journalism, short fiction, poetry, short plays, previously published work, and manuscript selections have appeared, confirming her versatile talents in many literary and artistic forms.

ACHIEVEMENTS

Djuna Barnes was initially known as a literary modernist, someone who wrote formally and linguistically complex and allusive works. In the 1970's, critics began to examine her work in the context of feminist studies and feminist literary theory. They also began researching Barnes, long known for her role in the American expatriate literary scene in Paris in the 1920's. Like Gertrude Stein, Barnes is now appreciated as a formative figure in studies of modernism and of lesbian and gay cultural history. The concessions she made to adhere to U.S. censorship regulations are less widely known, but the published type-script of *Nightwood* shows what Eliot deleted while editing. *Ryder*, in this regard, also was problematic, and Barnes used asterisks in the text to indicate the changes that she was forced to make.

Because her protagonists often refer to individuals that Barnes knew from her years in Paris or from childhood, her books lend themselves to biographical, psychobiographical, and life-writing approaches. Barnes was knowledgeable about women's rights, and her fiction investigates the nature of sexuality, gender, sexual expression, equality, and choice. Barnes received recognition for her role in American literature when she was elected in 1961 to the National Institute of Arts and Letters.

BIOGRAPHY

As a child, Djuna Chappell Barnes received no formal education, but she was educated at home in Cornwall-on-Hudson. She was one of five children in a difficult and polyga-mist family structure. She left for New York City after a brief and inappropriate marriage and then studied art at the Pratt Institute (1912-1913) and the Art Students League (1915-1916). While living in Greenwich Village, she became a reporter and covered political is-sues such as women's suffrage (her grandmother had been a suffragist), and wrote popular feature stories and conducted interviews.

Barnes moved to Paris and by the early 1920's was well established in expatriate cir-cles on the Left Bank. She came to know James Joyce, Stein, Eliot, and many others. Memoirs from this period describe her as a dramatic, striking woman with an acerbic wit and strong will. Her *Ladies Almanack* both celebrates and satirizes the women she knew in Natalie Clifford Barney's lesbian salon on the rue Jacob, which met regularly to read writings by women. Barnes lived in Paris for about twenty years, primarily with her lover Thelma Wood. Other individuals close to her were Peggy Guggenheim, who helped sup-port her; Emily Holmes Coleman, a writer and exhaustive diarist; and Robert McAlmon, who was responsible for privately printed *Ladies Almanack*.

Barnes also spent time in the early 1930's at the Guggenheim manor house, Hayford Hall, in the English countryside, with Guggenheim, Coleman, writer Antonia White, and an array of male and female visitors. Hayford Hall was a supportive and lively community, and the living arrangements gave Coleman the opportunity to read and critique the manu-script of *Nightwood*. Coleman's diaries reveal something most readers of Barnes do not know: Coleman's resourceful determination and urging letters were instrumental in con-vincing Eliot to accept the manuscript for publication by Faber and Faber and to write his somewhat ambiguous introduction.

With the onset of World War II, Barnes returned to New York and moved to a small apartment on the historic Patchin Place in Greenwich Village. She lived there for decades, eventually in failing health and famously unreceptive to visitors, including scholars. She sold her correspondence and manuscripts to the McKeldin Library at the University of Maryland in College Park in 1972 but destroyed parts of her personal archive. According to various accounts, Barnes's neighbors at Patchin Place could smell smoke coming from her apartment, and they knew that she was methodically burning information she did not want to become part of her history and legacy.

ANALYSIS

The difficulties of negotiating identity in a culture whose moral values and cultural expectations are powerful and repressive run throughout Djuna Barnes's canon, from her satirical and witty works to the profoundly serious and dark *Nightwood*. Emotions, which run high through the generations of the families she depicts, are reflected in the struggles, violence, or loyalties of individuals. Characters across a broad Euro-American landscape try to locate and free themselves from old patterns of quest and fulfillment, seeking authentic channels of emotional and sexual intimacy. Barnes's work incorporates multiple levels of meaning and multiple layers of figurative allusiveness, which make it challenging for readers to distinguish truth from falsehood and sincerity from fabrication; the characters themselves may not articulate their positions and often may not know themselves.

From the vantage point of the early twenty-first century Barnes remains a modernist concerned with literary innovation, but she is indisputably a saboteur of traditional culture, a woman who extended her writing beyond traditional modernism and who lived according to her own standards. Like other women writers of the period, such as H. D., Jean Rhys, Anaïs Nin, and Gertrude Stein, she cared about women's freedom and was certainly a feminist. It could be said, however, that her greatest allegiance was to language, to creating it and controlling it either through elaborate expression or declared silence.

RYDER

Published in 1928 with the author's own illustrations, Barnes's first novel, *Ryder*, is an elaborately structured story about the Ryder family, extending through four generations up to the early twentieth century. There are many family members, some of whom appear briefly while others, like the patriarch and polygamist Wendell Ryder (based on Barnes's father), loom large. The book sold well for a time, but the complexities of its language (Chaucerian, Elizabethan, and Rabelaisian) and harsh portrayal of family relationships failed to sustain a readership.

Highly ambitious, *Ryder* works through literary pastiche and satire, relying also on quick changes of style, tone, and narrative points of view. On some levels it resembles a family chronicle, but it progresses episodically with part of its energy created by many embedded genres, including letters, poems, ghost stories, lullabies, parables, and epigrams. The book creates tension between patriarchy and matriarchy and gradually foregrounds women's struggles for autonomy and integrity through the mothers and daughters it portrays.

NIGHTWOOD

Nightwood is Barnes's major work of fiction and is undoubtedly the book on which her strong reputation will continue to be based. Its literary style is dazzling, and its language is highly structured. Although like other modernist masterpieces, it brilliantly undermines traditional elements of plot, character development, and linearity. The story is minimalist, taking place primarily in Europe between the two world wars and projecting a landscape of postwar disillusionment. The characters attempt to move beyond their individual despair to find new communities.

At the center is Robin Vote, whose silences make her unknowable and protean, regardless of where and with whom she goes. Felix Volkbein, a supposed Old World aristocrat, marries Robin in anticipation of producing strong progeny, but Robin leaves him and her young son and goes off with Nora Flood, the "Westerner" from the United States. Nora is devoted to Robin even after Robin abandons her. She follows Robin in her wanderings and witnesses Robin's horrific breakdown in the final chapter. Nora carries the weight of loyalty and has the equilibrium of balanced self-knowledge. In contrast, Robin is forever in flux, the "eternal momentary," and thus a source to be pursued and repeatedly lost.

The person who reigns over events is Dr. Matthew O'Connor, who functions as a modern-day Tiresias, imparting advice to the individuals who seek him out for predictions and wisdom from his private *quartier* in Paris. Matthew comes to occupy the center stage of *Nightwood* as chronology recedes and long monologues replace direct narrative action. Matthew's monologues respond to each character's questions and their own respective monologues. Increasingly, the doctor exposes his uncertain identity and own collection of self-performances.

In the chapter "Go Down, Matthew," Matthew explains the message that Robin's abandonments suggest: Life is not to be known or understood, despite the relentless attempts. Whatever one does, individually or coupled or communally, life will not reveal itself, and whatever stories the narrative seems to tell, the accounting is flawed, merely one of many possible and impossible fabrications. There are formulas for actions and prescriptions for truths, and they all fall into dissolution. These revelations have repercussion within the plot and beyond it, repercussions for *Nightwood* as a literary text: Structure rebounds on itself, and then order blurs into different orders or into disorder. In other words, *Nightwood* incorporates some of the familiar modernist conclusions, but it does so with Barnes's unique genius.

The last few pages of the novel, titled "The Possessed," depict the most pessimistic scene in the book. Robin, who has quested through marriage, childbirth, motherhood, and bisexuality, makes her way to Nora's country property in the United States. Reaching a decaying chapel on the property reminiscent of the one in Eliot's modernist poem *The Waste Land* (1922), Robin collapses and swings at Nora's dog, both of them barking before going entirely silent. The scene is open to different interpretations but is surely a reckoning of the woman, and women, whose socialized and rebellious sides fight one another in a psychic and mythic war of attrition. There are many ways to approach and understand *Nightwood*. What is unlikely to change is *Nightwood*'s central position in the evolving history of prose narrative.

Miriam Fuchs

OTHER MAJOR WORKS

SHORT FICTION: *A Night Among the Horses*, 1929; *Spillway*, 1962; *Smoke, and Other Early Stories*, 1982; *Collected Stories*, 1996.

PLAYS: *Three from the Earth*, pr., pb. 1919; *The Antiphon*, pb. 1958; *At the Roots of the Stars: The Short Plays*, 1995.

POETRY: *The Book of Repulsive Women*, 1915 (includes drawings); *Collected Poems: With Notes Toward the Memoirs*, 2005.

NONFICTION: *Interviews*, 1985 (journalism); *I Could Never Be Lonely Without a Husband*, 1987 (Alyce Barry, editor); *New York*, 1989 (journalism).

CHILDREN'S LITERATURE: *Creatures in an Alphabet*, 1982.

MISCELLANEOUS: *A Book*, 1923 (enlarged edition published as *A Night Among the Horses*, 1929; abridged as *Spillway*, 1962); *Ladies' Almanack*, 1928; *Selected Works*, 1962; *Poe's Mother: Selected Drawings of Djuna Barnes*, 1995 (Douglas Messerli, editor).

BIBLIOGRAPHY

Benstock, Shari. *Women of the Left Bank, 1900-1940*. Austin: University of Texas Press, 1986. Classic biocritical study of women artists, writers, and intellectuals. Chapter seven covers Barnes's life and writing while she lived on the Left Bank of Paris, a thriving center for American expatriates.

Broe, Mary Lynn, ed. *Silence and Power: A Reevaluation of Djuna Barnes*. Carbondale: Southern Illinois University Press, 1991. Pivotal collection of essays that emphasize the feminist and communal aspects of Barnes's life.

Chait, Sandra M., and Elizabeth M. Podnieks, eds. *Hayford Hall: Hangovers, Erotics, and Aesthetics*. Carbondale: Southern University Illinois Press, 2005. Critical essays examine the characters living and learning at Hayford Hall, the Devonshire estate in England where Barnes lived for a time.

Fuchs, Miriam. "Djuna Barnes and T. S. Eliot: Resistance and Acquiescence." *Tulsa Studies in Women's Literature* 12, no. 2 (Fall, 1993): 288-313. Uses unpublished correspondence to map the collaborative dynamics between Barnes and poet T. S. Eliot.

_____. "The Triadic Association of Emily Holmes Coleman, T. S. Eliot, and Djuna Barnes." *ANQ: A Journal of Short Articles, Notes, and Reviews* 12, no. 4 (Fall, 1999): 28-39. Examines Emily Holmes Coleman's unpublished diary entries to relate the drama behind T. S. Eliot's decision to publish Barnes's novel *Nightwood*.

Herring, Phillip F. *Djuna: The Life and Work of Djuna Barnes*. New York: Viking Press,

1995. A useful, comprehensive, and critical biography of Barnes that traces her inspirations and influences. Herring examined private papers and manuscripts and interviewed family and friends for this scholarly but accessible work.

Kannenstine, Louis F. *The Art of Djuna Barnes: Duality and Damnation.* New York: New York University Press, 1977. The first university press study of Barnes, which aligns Barnes with James Joyce. A groundbreaking work that nevertheless has been criticized by feminist and other scholars.

Review of Contemporary Fiction 13, no. 3 (Fall, 1993). Special issue on Barnes's fiction. Features papers presented at the Djuna Barnes Centennial Conference at the University of Maryland in 1992.

Warren, Diane. *Djuna Barnes' Consuming Fictions.* Cornwall, England: Ashgate, 2008. Study that positions itself in relation to ongoing dialogues and debates about Barnes's work. Emphasizes her ideas of identity, language, and culture.

ANTHONY BURGESS
John Anthony Burgess Wilson

Born: Manchester, Lancashire, England; February 25, 1917
Died: London, England; November 25, 1993
Also known as: John Anthony Burgess Wilson; John Wilson; Joseph Kell

PRINCIPAL LONG FICTION

Time for a Tiger, 1956
The Enemy in the Blanket, 1958
Beds in the East, 1959
The Doctor Is Sick, 1960
The Right to an Answer, 1960
Devil of a State, 1961
One Hand Clapping, 1961 (as Joseph Kell)
The Worm and the Ring, 1961
A Clockwork Orange, 1962 (reprinted with final chapter, 1986)
The Wanting Seed, 1962
Honey for the Bears, 1963
Inside Mr. Enderby, 1963 (as Kell)
The Eve of Saint Venus, 1964
Nothing Like the Sun: A Story of Shakespeare's Love-Life, 1964
The Long Day Wanes, 1965 (includes *Time for a Tiger, The Enemy in the Blanket*, and *Beds in the East*)
A Vision of Battlements, 1965
Tremor of Intent, 1966
Enderby, 1968 (includes *Inside Mr. Enderby* and *Enderby Outside*)
Enderby Outside, 1968
MF, 1971
The Clockwork Testament: Or, Enderby's End, 1974
Napoleon Symphony, 1974
Beard's Roman Woman, 1976
Moses: A Narrative, 1976
Abba, Abba, 1977
1985, 1978
Man of Nazareth, 1979
Earthly Powers, 1980
The End of the World News, 1983
Enderby's Dark Lady, 1984
The Kingdom of the Wicked, 1985

The Pianoplayers, 1986
Any Old Iron, 1989
A Dead Man in Deptford, 1993
Byrne, 1995

OTHER LITERARY FORMS

In addition to his novels, Anthony Burgess published eight works of literary criticism. He paid tribute to his self-confessed literary mentor, James Joyce, in such works as *Re Joyce* (1965) and *Joysprick: An Introduction to the Language of James Joyce* (1972). His book reviews and essays were collected in *The Novel Now* (1967), *Urgent Copy: Literary Studies* (1968), and *Homage to Qwert Yuiop* (1985; also known as *But Do Blondes Prefer Gentlemen? Homage to Qwert Yuiop, and Other Writings*, 1986). His fascination with language and with the lives of writers led to such works as *Language Made Plain* (1964), *Shakespeare* (1970), and *Flame into Being: The Life and Work of D. H. Lawrence* (1985). An autobiographical work, *Little Wilson and Big God*, was published in 1987 (part of which was republished in 1996 as *Childhood*), and a collection of short fiction, *The Devil's Mode*, in 1989. A posthumous volume of his uncollected writings, *One Man's Chorus* (1998), includes a variety of essays divided into sections on travel, contemporary life, literary criticism, and personality sketches.

ACHIEVEMENTS

In his novels, Anthony Burgess extended the boundaries of English fiction. His inventive use of language, his use of symphonic forms and motifs, his rewriting of myths and legends, his examination of cultural clashes between the developing world and the West, and his pursuit of various ways to tell a story established him as one of the chief exemplars of postmodernism. His novels are studied in contemporary fiction courses, and he also achieved popular success with such works as *A Clockwork Orange* and *Earthly Powers*, for which he received the Prix du Meilleur Livre Étranger in 1981. Stanley Kubrick's controversial film *A Clockwork Orange* (1971) further established Burgess's popular reputation.

BIOGRAPHY

John Anthony Burgess Wilson was born in Manchester, England, on February 25, 1917. His mother and sister died in the influenza epidemic of 1918. Of Irish background, his mother had performed in the music halls of the period and was known as the Beautiful Belle Burgess. His father performed as a silent-film pianist and, when he remarried, played piano in a pub called the Golden Eagle, owned by his new wife; Burgess himself began to compose music when he was fourteen. Burgess graduated from the Bishop Bilsborrow School and planned to study music at Manchester University. When he failed a required physics entrance exam there, he changed his focus to literature and graduated from Xaverian College in Manchester; in 1940, he wrote his senior honors thesis on Christopher Marlowe while Nazi bombs fell overhead.

In October, 1940, Burgess joined the army and was placed in the Army Medical Corps. He was later shifted to the Army Educational Corps—a prophetic move, given that he became a teacher for nearly twenty years afterward. In 1942, Burgess married Llewela Isherwood Jones, a Welsh fellow student. He spent three years, from 1943 to 1946, with the British Army on Gibraltar, during which time he wrote his first novel, *A Vision of Battlements* (which was not published until 1965).

Burgess left the army as a sergeant major and as a training college lecturer in speech and drama in 1946 to become a member of the Central Advisory Council for Adult Education in the British armed forces. He lectured at Birmingham University until 1948, when he served as a lecturer in phonetics for the Ministry of Education in Preston, Lancashire. From 1950 until 1954, he taught English literature, phonetics, Spanish, and music at the Banbury grammar school in Oxfordshire.

Throughout these years, Burgess was painfully aware of his Irish heritage and Catholic religion. Although he had renounced Catholicism early, the Irish Catholic stigma remained with him in rigorously Protestant England. His decision to apply for the job of education officer for the Colonial Service may have had something to do with his desire to leave England and his need to exile himself physically from a homeland that had already exiled him in spirit. From 1954 to 1957, he was the senior lecturer in English at the Malayan Teachers Training College in Kahta Baru, Malaya. There, he had more leisure time to write, and he published his first novel, *Time for a Tiger*, in 1956 under his middle names, Anthony Burgess. (Members of the Colonial Service were not allowed to publish fiction under their own names.)

Burgess continued working for the Colonial Service as an English-language specialist in Brunei, Borneo, from 1957 to 1959 and published two more novels, which, with his first, eventually constituted his Malayan trilogy, *The Long Day Wanes*. The clash between East and West in manners and morals became the major focus of his early novels.

Apparent tragedy struck in 1959, when Burgess collapsed in his Borneo classroom. After excruciating medical tests, he was diagnosed with an inoperable brain tumor. He was given a year to live and was sent back to England. Unable to teach and virtually penniless, Burgess set himself to writing as much as he could in order to provide for his wife. Not only had she already shown signs of the cirrhosis of the liver that was eventually to kill her, but she also had attempted suicide. In the next three years, Burgess wrote and published nine novels, including *A Clockwork Orange* and *Inside Mr. Enderby*.

On the first day of spring, March 20, 1968, Llewela Burgess finally died. That October, Burgess married Liliana Macellari, a member of the linguistics department at Cambridge, intensifying the scandal that had originally developed when their affair produced a son, Andreas, in 1964. The personal guilt involved with his first wife's death always haunted Burgess and provided one of the major underlying themes of his fiction. "Guilt's a good thing," Burgess once said, "because the morals are just ticking away very nicely." In fact, persistent guilt shadows all of his characters and consistently threatens to overwhelm them completely.

Burgess, Liliana, and Andrew left England in October, 1968; they moved to Malta, then to Bracciano in Italy, and eventually settled in Monaco. Burgess's life changed dramatically in 1971, when the film version of *A Clockwork Orange*, directed by Stanley Kubrick, was released, making Burgess a celebrity. Regardless of his continuous production of new works in several genres, Burgess lived in the shadow of his 1962 novel. In 1980, he published *Earthly Powers*, a long and ambitious novel on which he had been working for more than ten years. He continued to compose symphonies and write reviews and articles for major newspapers and periodicals. He also became a skilled dramatic writer, with credits that include a version of Edmond Rostand's *Cyrano de Bergerac* (pr. 1897), produced on Broadway in 1972; the screenplay for Franco Zeffirelli's 1977 extravaganza *Jesus of Nazareth*; and *A Clockwork Orange 2004*, produced at the Barbizon Theater, London, in 1990. Burgess's production never slackened. In the last decade of his life, he produced six more novels, his last, *A Dead Man in Deptford*, being published just before his death from lung cancer in 1993.

ANALYSIS

Anthony Burgess shares with many postmodernist writers an almost obsessive awareness of his great modernist predecessors—particularly James Joyce. The vision that Burgess inherited from modernism is informed by the anguish of a sensitive soul lost in a fragmented, shattered world. Each of Burgess's novels reveals one central character virtually "at sea" in a landscape of battered, broken figures and events. Burgess conveys this fragmented worldview by means of many of the literary devices of his modernist predecessors. Often he employs a stream-of-consciousness narration in which his main characters tell their own stories; he also uses what T. S. Eliot, reviewing Joyce's *Ulysses* (1922), called the "mythic method," in which contemporary chaos is compared with and contrasted to heroic myths, legends, religious ceremonies, and rituals of the past. As Eliot remarked, the mythic method "is simply a way of controlling, of ordering, of giving a shape and significance to the intense panorama of futility and anarchy which is contemporary history."

Like many postmodernists, convinced that most literary forms are serious games devised to stave off approaching chaos and collapse, Burgess delights in the play of language for its own sake. Here again, Joyce is a prime source of inspiration: surprising images, poetic revelations, linguistic twists and turns, and strange, evocative words nearly overwhelm the narrative shape of *Ulysses* and certainly overwhelm it in *Finnegans Wake* (1939). Burgess's best novels are those in which language for its own sake plays an important role, as in *Enderby, Nothing Like the Sun, A Clockwork Orange*, and *Napoleon Symphony*.

At the heart of his vision of the world lies Burgess's Manichaean sensibility, his belief that there is "a duality that is fixed almost from the beginning of the world and the outcome is in doubt." God and the Devil reign over a supremely divided universe; they are equal in power, and they will battle to the end of the world. In the Manichaean tradition—most notably, that of the Gnostics—Burgess sees the world as a materialistic trap and a prison of the spirit, a place devised by the Devil to incarcerate people until their deaths. Only art can break through the battle lines; only art can save him. The recasting of a religious commitment in aesthetic terms also belongs to the legacy of modernism. Burgess's Manichaean vision produces such clashes of opposites as that between East and West, between the self and the state, and between a single character and an alien social environment. These recurring polarities structure Burgess's fiction.

THE RIGHT TO AN ANSWER

This principle of polarity or opposition is evident in the early novel *The Right to an Answer*, in which J. W. Denham, businessman and exile, returns to his father's house in the suburban British Midlands and finds a provincial, self-satisfied community engaged in wife swapping, television viewing, and pub crawling. He remains a detached observer, longing for a kind of communion he cannot find, and in his telling of his own tale, he reveals himself as friendless, disillusioned, and homeless.

The wife-swapping quartet at the Black Swan pub is disturbed by the entrance of Mr. Raj, a Ceylonese gentleman who is interested in English sociology and in satisfying his lust for white women. He plays by no rules but his own and espouses a kind of deadly Eastern realism that threatens the suburban sport. Moving in with Denham's father, Raj unfortunately kills the old man by "currying" him to death with his hot dishes. The upshot of this clash of cultural and social values is that Raj kills Winterbottom, the most innocent member of the *ménage à quatre*, and then kills himself.

Throughout the novel, Burgess explores both Denham's point of view and Raj's within the seedy suburban landscape. Their viewpoints reflect the irreconcilable differences between East and West, between black and white, between sex and love, and between true religion and dead ritual. Denham's stream-of-consciousness narration eventually reveals his own spirit of exile, which he cannot overcome. He remains disconnected from both worlds, from England and the East, and epitomizes the state of lovelessness and isolation that has permeated modern culture. This early novel clearly explores Burgess's main themes and narrative forms.

TREMOR OF INTENT

In the guise of a thriller à la James Bond, *Tremor of Intent* explores a world of "God" and "Not-God," a profoundly Manichaean universe. Soviet spies battle English spies while the real villains of the novel, the "neutralists," play one camp off against the other purely for personal gain. Burgess derides the whole notion of the spy's realm, but he insists that taking sides is essential in such a world, whether ultimate good or evil is ever really confronted.

Denis Hillier, aging technician and spy, writes his confessional memoirs in the light of his possible redemption. His Catholic sense of Original Sin never falters for an instant, and he is constantly in need of some higher truth, some ultimate communion and revelation. In the course of the novel, he fights every Manichaean division, drinks "Old Mortality," sees himself as a "fallen Adam," and works his way toward some vision of hope. Finally, he abandons the spy game and becomes a priest, exiling himself to Ireland. From this new perspective, he believes, he can approach the real mysteries of good and evil, of free will and predestination, beyond the limiting and limited categories of the Cold War.

Hillier's opposite in the novel is Edwin Roper, a rationalist who has jettisoned religious belief and who hungers for an ultimately unified universe based on scientific truth and explanation. Such rationalism leads him to the Marxist logic of Soviet ideology, and he defects to the Russian side. Hillier has been sent to rescue him. One section of the novel consists of Roper's autobiographical explanation of his actions; its flat, logical prose reflects his methodical and disbelieving mind, in contrast to Hillier's more religious sensibility.

Within the complicated plot of the novel, self-serving scoundrels such as Mr. Theodorescu and Richard Wriste set out to destroy both Hillier and Roper and to gather information to sell to the highest bidder. They fail, owing largely to the actions of Alan and Clara Walters, two children on board the ship that is taking Hillier to meet Roper. The children become initiated into the world of double agents and sexual intrigue, and Theodorescu and Wriste are assassinated. Burgess displays his love of language for its own sake in exotic descriptions of sex, food, and life aboard a cruise ship. Such language intensifies the Manichaean divisions in the book, the constant battle between the things of this world and the imagined horrors of the next. The very language that Hillier and Roper use to tell their own stories reveals their own distinctly different personalities and visions.

Tremor of Intent insists on the mystery of human will. To choose is to be human; that is good. Thus, to choose evil is both a good and a bad thing, a Manichaean complication that Burgess leaves with the reader. In allegorical terms the novel presents the problems of free will and its consequences, which underlie all of Burgess's fiction.

NOTHING LIKE THE SUN

Nothing Like the Sun, Burgess's fanciful novel based on the life of William Shakespeare, showcases every facet of his vision and technique as a novelist. Shakespeare finds himself caught between his love for a golden man and his love for a black woman. Sex feeds the fires of love and possession, and from these fires grows Shakespeare's art, the passion of language. From these fires also comes syphilis, the dread disease that eventually kills him, the source of the dark vision that surfaces in his apocalyptic tragedies. Shakespeare as a writer and Shakespeare as a man battle it out, and from that dualistic confrontation emerges the perilous equilibrium of his greatest plays.

In part, Burgess's fiction is based on the theories about Shakespeare's life that Stephen Dedalus expounds in Joyce's *Ulysses*. Dedalus suggests that Shakespeare was cuckolded by his brother Richard and that Shakespeare's vision of a treacherous and tragic world was based on his own intimate experience. To this conjecture, Burgess adds the notions that the Dark Lady of the sonnets was a non-Caucasian and that Shakespeare himself was a victim of syphilis. All of these "myths" concerning Shakespeare serve Burgess's Manichaean vision: Sex and disease, art and personality are ultimately at war with one another and can be resolved only in the actual plays that Shakespeare wrote.

Nothing Like the Sun is written in an exuberant, bawdy, pseudo-Elizabethan style. It is clear that Burgess relished the creation of lists of epithets, curses, and prophecies, filled as they are with puns and his own outrageous coinings. Burgess audaciously attempts to mime the development of Shakespeare's art as he slowly awakens to the possibilities of poetry, trying different styles, moving from the sweet rhymes of *Venus and Adonis* to the "sharp knives and brutal hammers" of the later tragedies. The book is constructed in the form of a lecture by Burgess himself to his Malayan students. He drinks as he talks and explains his paradoxical theories as he goes along. His passing out from too much drink at the novel's end parallels Shakespeare's death. He puns also with his real last name, Wilson, regarding himself as in fact "Will's son," a poet and author in his own right.

ENDERBY

Enderby is prototypic of Burgess's preoccupation with the duality of forces that influence life: the struggle between society's capacity to do good and the dilemma that human nature inevitably leads to evil. Originally conceived as a whole, *Enderby* was written as two independent novels, *Mr. Enderby* and *Enderby Outside*, for the pragmatic reason that Burgess wanted to tell at least half the tale before he died from his supposed brain tumor. One of Burgess's most popular characters, the flatulent poet F. X. Enderby, was spawned in a men's room when the author thought he saw a man feverishly writing poetry as he purged his bowels. *Enderby* is teeming with opposites, juxtaposing the sublime with the ridiculous. Enderby is catapulted into life-transforming situations as the outside world continually plays on and alters the poet's sensibilities. Burgess, the writer, examines his creation, a writer, whom he happens to admire in spite of his foibles.

Mr. Enderby and *Enderby Outside* depict the difference between transformations that originate within the individual and those that society imposes on the individual. In the first novel, the very private poet is lured into marriage with Vesta Bainbridge, who leads him into a pop-art world that strips away his integrity and identity. Enderby achieves some success by prostituting his talent, but he is ultimately outraged when a rival poet gains fame and fortune by stealing his ideas, transforming them into a horror film. Enderby escapes from his wife and public life but is despondent and intellectually withered. He is taken to Wapenshaw, a psychologist, who "cures" him by destroying his poetic muse. Enderby is transmuted into Piggy Hogg, a bartender and useful citizen.

Enderby Outside is the mirror image of *Mr. Enderby*, transforming Hogg back into Enderby through a series of parallel experiences. Bainbridge has married a pop singer, Yod Crewsey, whose success is the result of poems stolen from Enderby. When the singer is shot, Enderby is accused of the murder and flees, confronting the chaos and confusion of the modern world and falling prey to another woman, the sensuous Miranda Boland. During sexual intercourse with Boland, Enderby is finally struck by inspiration. In the end, he meets a sibylline girl, Muse, who leads him to his art. Enderby is as he began, alone and free, but a poet.

In *Enderby*, Burgess shows that the master must come to peace with both his body and society before he can indulge in the intellectual. Shortly after the film version of *A Clockwork Orange* was released, Enderby returned in *The Clockwork Testament: Or, Enderby's End*, which satirizes the writer reduced to production assistant by the film industry. Enderby dies of a heart attack when he sees the violent, pornographic film made from his novel. Just as British detective novelist Arthur Conan Doyle was forced to return Sherlock Holmes to life, Burgess resurrects his antihero in *Enderby's Dark Lady*. Enderby travels to Indiana, where he writes the libretto for a ridiculous musical about Shakespeare. Burgess directs his satire at American culture, but his exploration of the poetic muse is sacrificed for the comic adventure.

EARTHLY POWERS

Earthly Powers, Burgess's longest novel, features perhaps his most arresting first sentence: "It was the afternoon of my 81st birthday, and I was in bed with my catamite when Ali announced that the archbishop had come to see me." Thus begin the memoirs of Kenneth Toomey, cynical agnostic and homosexual writer, a character based loosely on W. Somerset Maugham.

Toomey's memoirs span the twentieth century—its literary intrigues, cultural fashions, and political horrors. Toomey is seduced on June 16, 1904, that Dublin day immortalized by Joyce in *Ulysses*, and he revels in the Paris of the 1920's, the Hollywood of the 1930's, and the stylish New York of the 1940's and 1950's. His old age is spent in exotic exile in Tangier and Malta in the 1970's. During his long life, he writes plays and film scenarios, carries on with a host of male secretary-lovers, and experiences the traumas of Nazism and Communism. He abhors the state-controlled collective soul, which he sees as the ultimate product of the twentieth century.

Burgess's huge, sprawling novel displays a plot crowded with coincidence and bursting with stylistic parodies and re-creations. A priest on his way to becoming pope saves a dying child, only to see the boy grow up to be the leader of a fanatical religious cult akin to that of Jim Jones in Guyana. An American anthropologist and his wife are butchered during a Catholic mass in Africa: The natives there take the commands of the ceremony all too literally and swallow their visitors.

Toomey believes that evil lies firmly within all people and that his experiences of the twentieth century prove that the world is a murderous place. His Manichaean opposite in faith is his brother-in-law, Carlo Campanati, the gambler-gourmet priest who becomes Pope Gregory XVII. Evil remains external to humanity, the pope maintains; humankind is essentially good. In Burgess's jaundiced view of things, such misconceived idealism produces only further evils. Any similarities between Gregory and Pope John XXIII are strictly intentional.

The world of *Earthly Powers* is Toomey's world, a bright place with clipped, swift glimpses of fads and fashion. Librettos, snippets of plays, even a re-creation of the Garden of Eden story from a homosexual point of view appear in this modernist memoir. The style itself reflects Burgess's conception of the "brittle yet excruciatingly precise" manner of the gay man.

Earthly Powers wobbles. More than six hundred pages of bright wit can cloy. Verbal surfaces congeal and trail off into trivial documentation. The pope's spiritual observations impede the novel's progress, encased as they are in lectures, sermons, and tracts. Indeed, Gregory is as thin a character as Toomey is an interesting one.

The book proves that Toomey is right: Things are rotten. No amount of linguistic fun, modernist maneuvering, or Manichaean machinations can change the fact that this is the worst of all possible worlds. Chunks of smart conversation cannot hide that fact; they become stupefying and evasive in the end. The nature of free will, however, and its legacy of unquestionable evil in the twentieth century pervade Burgess's fat book and linger to undermine any "safe" position the reader may hope to find.

A CLOCKWORK ORANGE

Burgess's Manichaean nightmare in *A Clockwork Orange* occupies the center of his most accomplished book. The language of Nadsat, in its harsh, Russian-accented diction, the ongoing battle between the state and Alex the *droog*, the vision of an urban landscape wracked with violence and decay, the mysterious interpenetration of Beethoven and lust, and the unresolved issues of good and evil reflect and parallel one another so completely that the novel emerges as Burgess's masterpiece.

The issue raised is an increasingly timely one: Can the state program the individual to be good? Can it eradicate the individual's right to freedom of choice, especially if, in choosing, the individual chooses to commit violent and evil acts? Burgess replies in the negative. No matter how awful Alex's actions become, he should be allowed to choose them.

Because the novel is written from Alex's point of view, the reader sympathizes with him, despite his acts of rape and mayhem. Alex loves Beethoven; he "shines artistic"; he is brighter than his ghoulish friends; he is rejected by his parents. He is in all ways superior to the foul futuristic landscape that surrounds him. When the state brainwashes him, the reader experiences his pain in a personal, forthright manner. The violence in the rest of the book falls on outsiders and remains distanced by the very language Alex uses to describe his actions.

Burgess's slang creates a strange and distant world. The reader approaches the novel as an outsider to that world and must try diligently to decode it to understand it. Never has Burgess used language so effectively to create the very atmosphere of his fiction. The Russian-influenced slang of the novel is a tour de force of the highest order and yet functions perfectly as a reflection of Alex's state of mind and of the society of which he is a rebellious member.

The world of *A Clockwork Orange* recognizes only power and political force. All talk of free will dissolves before such a harrowing place of behaviorist psychologists and social controllers. In such a world, individual freedom remains a myth, not a reality—a matter of faith, not an ultimate truth. Everyone is in some sense a clockwork orange, a victim of his or her society, compelled to act in a social order that celebrates only power, manipulation, and control.

Even the cyclical form of *A Clockwork Orange* reveals a world trapped within its own inevitable patterns. At first, Alex victimizes those around him. He in turn is victimized by the state. In the third and final part of the novel, he returns to victimize other people once again: "I was cured all right." Victimization remains the only reality here. There are no loopholes, no escape hatches from the vicious pattern. The frightening cityscape at night, the harsh language, the paradoxical personality of Alex, the collaborationist or revolutionary tactics of Alex's "friends," and the very shape of the novel reinforce this recognition of utter entrapment and human decay. "Oh, my brothers," Alex addresses his readers, as Eliot in *The Waste Land* (1922) quotes Charles Baudelaire: *"Hypocrite lecteur, mon semblable, mon frère."*

Despite Burgess's pessimistic vision of contemporary life and the creative soul's place in it, the best of his novels still reveal a commitment to literature as a serious ceremony, as a game that the reader and the writer must continue to play, if only to transcend momentarily the horrors of Western civilization in the twentieth century.

Samuel Coale
Updated by Gerald S. Argetsinger

OTHER MAJOR WORKS

SHORT FICTION: *The Devil's Mode*, 1989.

SCREENPLAY: *Jesus of Nazareth*, 1977.

TELEPLAY: *Moses the Lawgiver*, 1976.

NONFICTION: *English Literature: A Survey for Students*, 1958 (as John Burgess Wilson); *The Novel Today*, 1963; *Language Made Plain*, 1964; *Here Comes Everybody: An Introduction to James Joyce for the Ordinary Reader*, 1965 (also known as *Re Joyce*); *The Novel Now*, 1967 (revised 1971); *Urgent Copy: Literary Studies*, 1968; *Shakespeare*, 1970; *Joysprick: An Introduction to the Language of James Joyce*, 1972; *Ernest Hemingway and His World*, 1978; *On Going to Bed*, 1982; *This Man and Music*, 1983; *Flame into Being: The Life and Work of D. H. Lawrence*, 1985; *Homage to Qwert Yuiop*, 1985 (also known as *But Do Blondes Prefer Gentlemen? Homage to Qwert Yuiop, and Other Writings*, 1986); *Little Wilson and Big God*, 1987 (partly reprinted as *Childhood*, 1996); *You've Had Your Time*, 1990; *A Mouthful of Air: Languages, Languages—Especially English*, 1992; *One Man's Chorus; The Uncollected Writings*, 1998.

TRANSLATIONS: *The Man Who Robbed Poor-Boxes*, 1965 (of Michel Servin's play); *Cyrano de Bergerac*, 1971 (of Edmond Rostand's play); *Oedipus the King*, 1972 (of Sophocles' play).

CHILDREN'S LITERATURE: *A Long Trip to Teatime*, 1976.

MISCELLANEOUS: *On Mozart: A Paean for Wolfgang*, 1991.

BIBLIOGRAPHY

Aggeler, Geoffrey. *Anthony Burgess: The Artist as Novelist*. Tuscaloosa: University of Alabama Press, 1979. The best and most accurately detailed study of work published in the first twenty years of Burgess's career. Includes analysis of *A Clockwork Orange, Napoleon Symphony, Enderby Outside, Inside Mr. Enderby, Nothing Like the Sun*, and other novels.

———, ed. *Critical Essays on Anthony Burgess*. Boston: G. K. Hall, 1986. A collection of well-regarded criticism on Burgess, with particular attention given to his "linguistic pyrotechnics." Aggeler's introduction presents an overview of Burgess's work and discussion of his novels, followed by a *Paris Review* interview with Burgess.

Biswell, Andrew. *The Real Life of Anthony Burgess*. London: Picador, 2005. Well-researched biography of Burgess explores his personal life, including his heavy drinking and sexual promiscuity. His most famous novel, *A Clockwork Orange*, is also discussed, along with Burgess's common themes of corruption, sin, and human beings' capacity for evil.

Bloom, Harold, ed. *Anthony Burgess*. New York: Chelsea House, 1987. A compilation of fine critical essays, including an essay by the eminent critic of James Joyce, Robert Martin Adams, who considers Joyce's influence on Burgess. In the introduction, Bloom presents his views on Burgess's writing, citing *Inside Mr. Enderby* as one of the most underrated English novels of the late twentieth century.

Keen, Suzanne. "Ironies and Inversions: The Art of Anthony Burgess." *Commonweal* 121, no. 3 (February 11, 1994): 9. An examination of the "Catholic quality" in Burgess's fiction and nonfiction. Focuses primarily on Burgess's novel *A Dead Man in Deptford* as well as on his autobiographies and literary criticism of James Joyce's works.

Lewis, Roger. *Anthony Burgess: A Biography*. London: Faber & Faber, 2002. This sprawling examination of Burgess's life, first published in the United States in 2004, is illuminating although sometimes chaotic. Instead of recounting the events of Burgess's life as a chronological narrative, Lewis presents a more stylized, psychodynamic interpretation of Burgess's personality and work.

Mathews, Richard. *The Clockwork Orange Universe of Anthony Burgess*. San Bernardino, Calif.: Borgo Press, 1978. An admiring monograph tracing the thematic and temporal concerns that led Burgess to write his futuristic novels, including *A Clockwork Orange*. Discusses ten novels that fit the metaphor of "clockwork universe."

Morris, Robert K. *Consolations of Ambiguity: An Essay on the Novels of Anthony Burgess*. Columbia: University of Missouri Press, 1971. This early analysis of Burgess's work discusses the thematic consistency of the Malayan trilogy, *A Vision of Battlements*, *Nothing Like the Sun*, *A Clockwork Orange*, and other novels.

Smith, K. H. "Will! or Shakespeare in Hollywood: Anthony Burgess's Cinematic Presentation of Shakespearean Biography." In *Remaking Shakespeare: Performance Across Media, Genres, and Cultures*, edited by Pascale Aebisher, Edward Esche, and Nigel Wheale. Houndmills, England: Palgrave Macmillan, 2003. Collection of essays describing how William Shakespeare has been "remade" in twentieth century screenplays, soap operas, music, documentaries, and other media. Includes analysis of Burgess's novel *Nothing Like the Sun*.

Stinson, John J. *Anthony Burgess Revisited*. Boston: Twayne, 1991. Provides valuable biographical information and critical analysis of the later works. Particular attention is given to Burgess's increasing reputation as a public intellectual and the use of language, the importance of moral choice, and the conflict between the Pelagian and Augustinian philosophies in his works.

WILLIAM S. BURROUGHS

Born: St. Louis, Missouri; February 5, 1914
Died: Lawrence, Kansas; August 2, 1997
Also known as: William Seward Burroughs II; William Lee

OTHER LITERARY FORMS

Because of their experimental techniques, the works of William S. Burroughs (BUR-ohz) are especially difficult to classify within established literary forms. *Exterminator!* (1973), for example, although published as a "novel," is actually a collection of previously published poems, short stories, and essays. Other unclassifiable works are book-length experiments, often written in collaboration and in the "cut-up, fold-in" technique pioneered by Burroughs, which might be considered novels by some. The "cut-up, fold-in" technique is similar to the picture art of collage in that text from other authors, news stories, or other works is randomly inserted and then reedited to go with the general text by the author. Examples among Burroughs's works are *Minutes to Go* (1960), written in collaboration with Sinclair Beiles, Gregory Corso, and Brion Gysin; *The Exterminator* (1960), written with Gysin; *Time* (1965), which contains drawings by Gysin; and *Œuvre Croisée* (1976), written in collaboration with Gysin and reissued as *The Third Mind* in 1978. *White Subway* (1965), *Apomorphine* (1969), and *The Job: Interviews with William S. Burroughs* (1970), written in collaboration with Daniel Odier, are additional short-story and essay collections. *The Dead Star* (1969) is a journalistic essay that contains photocollage inserts, *APO-33 Bulletin: A Metabolic Regulator* (1966) is a pamphlet, and *Electronic Revolution, 1970-71* (1971) is an essay that fantasizes bizarre political and business uses for the cut-up, fold-in technique.

Burroughs also published scores of essays, stories, and articles in numerous journals, periodicals, and short-lived magazines. One of Burroughs's most revealing publications, *The Yage Letters* (1963), collects his correspondence with Allen Ginsberg concerning Burroughs's 1952 expedition to South America in search of yage, a legendary hallucinogen. In these letters, Burroughs is Govinda, the master, to Ginsberg's Siddhartha, the disciple.

ACHIEVEMENTS

William S. Burroughs's best-known novel, *Naked Lunch*, was made notorious by American censorship attempts and consequently became a best seller. Burroughs, who wrote primarily for a cult audience, was essentially a fantasist and satirist (some of his work is also considered science fiction), and he is often misread; in these respects he has been compared accurately to Jonathan Swift. Both writers focus on the faults and evils of humankind and society, employ fantastic satire to ridicule these shortcomings, and hope through this vehicle to effect some positive change in the human condition. Burroughs's works are exceptionally vicious satires, however, "necessarily brutal, obscene and disgusting"—his own description of them—because they must mime the situations from which their recurring images and metaphors (of drug addiction, aberrant sexual practices, and senseless violence) are drawn.

Burroughs's focus on drug addiction and the paranoia and nonlinear thought processes of his characters also make his writing comparable to some of Phillip K. Dick's novels, such as *The Man in the High Castle* (1962) and *A Scanner Darkly* (1977). Burroughs's work *Blade Runner: A Movie* (1979), although unrelated to the 1982 Ridley Scott film *Blade Runner*, which is based on Dick's work *Do Androids Dream of Electric Sheep?* (1968), may have at least been the inspiration for the motion picture's title.

Superficially, Burroughs's satiric attacks are aimed at humanity's "addictions" to pleasure or power in any of the many forms either craving might take. Those who, obeying the dictates of "the algebra of need," will stop at nothing to fulfill their desires have, in the terms of the moral allegory Burroughs creates, "lost their human citizenship" and become nonhuman parasites feeding on the life essences of others. They shamelessly lie, cheat, and manipulate to attain what Burroughs's associative imagery repeatedly equates with perversion, excrement, and death. Burroughs's satire, however, cuts deeper than this. It attacks not only humankind and its addictions but also the structures of the cultures that enable these addictions to flourish and proliferate. It attacks the myths and linguistic formulas that imprison the human race, the stone walls of patriotism and religion. It demands that people first free themselves from these "word and image addictions" before they kick their more obvious habits and regain their humanity, and thus calls for nothing less than a revolution of consciousness.

The Grove Press edition of *Naked Lunch* became a national best seller and was cleared of obscenity charges in Los Angeles in 1965 and in Massachusetts in 1966. Ginsberg and Norman Mailer, who described Burroughs as "the only American novelist living today who may conceivably be possessed by genius," were among those who testified in the book's defense. While it does detail with exceptional brutality the ugly, revolting, and perverse, *Naked Lunch* is at bottom a strikingly moral but darkly comic work that employs irony and allegory, as well as more unconventional techniques, to satirize much that is false and defective in modern American life in particular and human nature in general. Especially effective as a subliminal argument against heroin abuse, the book's successful publication in the United States elevated its then practically unknown author to membership in the literary elite.

Many reviewers—some seemingly oblivious to the irony of Burroughs's works—have not been responsive or sympathetic to his themes and techniques, and none of his novels after *Naked Lunch*, with the exception of *The Wild Boys*, received comparable critical acclaim. Whereas *Naked Lunch* was lauded by Terry Southern, Mary McCarthy, Karl Shapiro, and Marshall McLuhan, as well as by Ginsberg and Mailer, the less successfully realized subsequent novels were considered by some critics, not totally inaccurately, as "language without content" and "the world's greatest put-on." Burroughs himself admitted that "*Naked Lunch* demands silence from the reader. Otherwise he is taking his own pulse."

Burroughs warned that his novels do not present their "content" in the manner the reader ordinarily anticipates. One of the triumphs of his unique style is that he has created a low-content form, a narrative near vacuum, on which unwary readers are tempted to project their own psyches, personal myths, and forgotten dreams. While they do have their own messages to convey, his works also encourage readers to develop or invent their own private fictions and to append them to the skeletal narrative structures provided by the author. Readers are thus invited to create Burroughs's works as they read them. In place of relying on the easily perceived, clearly coherent stories one might have expected, Burroughs's best works keep one reading through the hypnotic fascination of the author's flow of images and incantatory prose.

BIOGRAPHY

William Seward Burroughs II was born on February 5, 1914, in St. Louis, Missouri, to Mortimer Perry Burroughs, son of the industrialist William Seward Burroughs I, who founded the Burroughs Adding Machine company. His mother was Laura Hammond Lee, whose family claimed direct descent from Robert E. Lee, Civil War general and commander in chief of the Confederate army. Dominated by his mother's obsessive Victorian prudery and haunted by vivid nightmares and hallucinations, Burroughs led a restless childhood. He was educated in private schools in St. Louis and Los Alamos, New Mexico, where he developed seemingly disparate fascinations with literature and crime. He later studied ethnology and archaeology at Harvard University, where he encountered a group of wealthy gay men. He graduated with an A.B. in 1936, and upon his graduation, his parents bestowed on him a monthly trust of two hundred dollars that allowed Burroughs a great deal of freedom from daily concerns.

Subsequently, Burroughs traveled to Europe. He briefly studied medicine at the University of Vienna, where he met Ilse Klapper, whom he married so that she—a Jewish woman fleeing Nazi Germany—could obtain an American visa. They remained friends, but Ilse divorced Burroughs nine years later, in 1946. Burroughs returned to the United States and Harvard to resume his anthropological studies, which he soon abandoned because of his conviction that academic life is little more than a series of intrigues broken by teas. Although he attempted to use family connections to obtain a position with the Office of Strategic Services, Burroughs was rejected after he deliberately cut off the first joint of his left little finger in a Vincent van Gogh-like attempt to impress a male friend. Moving to New York City, he worked as a bartender and in an advertising agency for a year and underwent psychoanalysis. Burroughs entered the U.S. Army in 1942 as a glider pilot trainee, engineered his discharge for psychological reasons six months later, and then moved to Chicago, where he easily found work as an exterminator and a private detective, among other odd jobs.

In 1943, Burroughs returned to New York City and met Joan Vollmer, a student at Columbia University; they married on January 17, 1945. Because Burroughs's divorce from Ilse was not yet final, several sources describe Joan as his common-law wife. She introduced Burroughs to Jack Kerouac, who in turn introduced him to Ginsberg. The Beat generation was born in Burroughs's 115th Street apartment after Burroughs acquainted Kerouac and Ginsberg with the writings of William Blake, Arthur Rimbaud, and others; the three friends soon emerged as leaders of the movement. Late in 1944, Herbert Huncke, a Times Square hustler involved in criminal activity to support his drug habit, introduced Burroughs to the use of morphine and its derivatives. Burroughs was for most of the next thirteen years a heroin addict who frequently altered his place of residence to evade the police.

In 1946, Burroughs moved to Waverly, Texas, where he tried farming; he and his wife had a son, William, Jr., in 1947. Burroughs voluntarily entered a drug rehabilitation center at Lexington, Kentucky, in 1948. Returning to Waverly and already back on drugs, Burroughs was hounded by the police until he moved to Algiers, Louisiana, later that same year. To avoid prosecution for illegal possession of drugs and firearms after a 1949 raid on his Algiers farm, Burroughs relocated to Mexico City in 1950, where he began writing *Junkie*. He continued his archaeological studies at Mexico City University, pursuing an interest in the Mayan codices. On September 7, 1951, Burroughs accidentally killed his wife, Joan, while allegedly attempting to shoot a drinking glass off her head while playing "William Tell." Although Mexican authorities let the matter drop, Burroughs soon left Mexico for the jungles of Colombia.

He returned again to New York City in 1953, the year *Junkie* was published, lived for a while with Ginsberg, and then settled in Tangier, Morocco, where from 1955 to 1958 he was frequently visited by other Beat writers and worked on the manuscript that would develop into his quartet of science-fiction-like novels: *Naked Lunch*, *The Soft Machine*, *Nova Express*, and *The Ticket That Exploded*. In 1957, Burroughs again sought treatment for his heroin addiction. This time he placed himself in the care of John Yerby Dent, an English physician who treated drug addicts with apomorphine—a crystalline alkaloid derivative of morphine—a drug Burroughs praises and mythologizes in his writings. The following year, cured of his addiction, Burroughs moved to Paris, where *The Naked Lunch* was published in 1959.

In 1960, Gysin, who had helped Burroughs select the Paris edition of *The Naked Lunch* from a suitcase full of manuscript pages, introduced his experimental "cut-up" technique to Burroughs and collaborated with him on *The Exterminator* and *Minutes to Go*. Burroughs's literary reputation was firmly established with the American publication of *Naked Lunch* in 1962, and by the mid-1960's Burroughs had settled in London. He returned to St. Louis for a visit in 1965, covered the Democratic National Convention for *Esquire* in 1968, and moved again to New York to teach writing at City College of New York in 1974. In 1975, he embarked on a reading tour of the United States and conducted a writers' workshop in Denver, Colorado. After returning to London briefly, Burroughs settled in New York. In 1983, he was inducted into the American Academy and Institute of Arts and Letters.

In the late 1980's and early 1990's Burroughs did cameo roles, voice work, and writing for several movies and television shows and consulted on the film version of his book *Naked Lunch*, which was written and directed by David Cronenberg and released in late 1991. Burroughs published a number of novels and collections throughout the 1980's and 1990's, including 1987's *The Western Lands*, the last novel in the trilogy that includes *Cities of the Red Night* and *The Place of Dead Roads*. Shortly after the publication of this novel, Burroughs moved to rural Kansas, where he died in 1997.

ANALYSIS

William S. Burroughs did not begin writing seriously until 1950, although he had unsuccessfully submitted a story titled "Twilight's Last Gleaming" to *Esquire* in 1938. His first novelistic effort, *Queer*, which deals with homosexuality, was not published until 1985. Allen Ginsberg finally persuaded Ace Books to publish Burroughs's first novel, *Junkie*, which originally appeared under the pseudonym William Lee as half of an Ace double paperback; it was bound with Maurice Helbront's *Narcotic Agent*. While strictly conventional in style, *Junkie* is a luridly hyperbolic, quasi-autobiographical first-person account of the horrors of drug addiction. Of little literary merit in itself, this first novel is interesting in that it introduces not only the main character, Lee, but also several of the major motifs that appear in Burroughs's subsequent works: the central metaphor of drug addiction, the related image of man reduced to a subhuman form (usually an insectlike creature) by his drug and other lusts, and the suggestion of concomitant and pervasive sexual aberration.

In *Naked Lunch* and its three less celebrated sequels, *The Soft Machine*, *Nova Express*, and *The Ticket That Exploded*, Burroughs weaves an intricate and horrible allegory of human greed, corruption, and debasement. Like Aldous Huxley's *Brave New World* (1932) and George Orwell's *Nineteen Eighty-Four* (1949), these four works seize on the evils— or the tendencies toward a certain type of evil—that the author sees as particularly malignant in the contemporary world and project them into a dystopian future, where, magnified, they grow monstrous and take on an exaggerated and fantastic shape.

While progressively clarifying and developing Burroughs's thought, these novels share themes, metaphorical images, characters, and stylistic mannerisms. In them, Burroughs utilizes the "cut-up, fold-in" technique, which has its closest analogue in the cinematic technique of montage. He juxtaposes one scene with another without regard to plot, character, or, in the short view, theme, to promote an association of the reader's negative emotional reaction to the content of certain scenes (sexual perversion, drug abuse, senseless violence) with the implied allegorical content of others (examples of "addictions" to drugs, money, sex, power). The theory is that if such juxtapositions recur often enough, the feeling of revulsion strategically created by the first set of images will form the reader's negative attitude toward the second set of examples.

In these novels, Burroughs develops a science-fiction-like, paranoid fantasy wherein, on a literal level, Earth and its human inhabitants have been taken over by the Nova Mob, an assortment of extraterrestrial, non-three-dimensional entities who live parasitically on the reality of other organisms. Exploitation of Earth has reached such proportions that the intergalactic Nova Police have been alerted. The Nova Police are attempting to thwart the Nova Mob without so alarming them that they will detonate the planet in an attempt to destroy the evidence (and thus escape prosecution in the biologic courts) while trying to make what escape they can. The most direct form of Nova control, control that enables the Nova Mob to carry on its viruslike metaphysical vampirism with impunity, is thought control of the human population through control of the mass-communication media. Nova Mob concepts and perspectives attach themselves to and are replicated by the terrestrial host media much as a virus invades and reproduces through a host organism, a thought-control process analogous to the "cut-up, fold-in" technique itself. By the middle of *Nova Express*, the reader is caught up in a war of images in which the weapons are cameras and tape recorders. The Nova Police and the inhabitants of Earth have discovered how to combat the Nova Mob with their own techniques (of which these novels are examples) and are engaged in a guerrilla war with the Nova Criminals, who are desperately trying to cut and run. The ending of *The Ticket That Exploded* is optimistic for Earth but inconclusive, leaving the reader to wonder if Earth will be rid of the Nova Mob or destroyed by it.

NAKED LUNCH

A vividly and relentlessly tasteless fantasy-satire that portrays humankind's innate greed and lack of compassion in general and contemporary American institutions and values in particular, *Naked Lunch* immerses the reader in the impressions and sensations of William Lee (Burroughs's pseudonym in *Junkie*). Lee is an agent of the Nova Police who has assumed the cover of a gay heroin addict because with such a cover he is most likely to encounter Nova Criminals, who are all addicts of one sort or another and thus prefer to operate through human addict collaborators. Nothing of importance seems to occur in the novel, and little of what does happen is explained. Only toward the conclusion does the reader even suspect that Lee is some sort of agent "clawing at a not-yet of Telepathic Bureaucracies, Time Monopolies, Control Drugs, Heavy Fluid Addicts." The "naked lunch" of the title is that reality seen by Lee, that "frozen moment when everyone sees what is on the end of every fork." The random scenes of mutilation and depravity, bleak homosexual encounters, and desperate scrambles for drug connections into which the book plunges yield its two key concepts: the idea of addiction, the central conceit that human beings become hooked on power, pleasure, illusions, and so on much as junkies do on heroin, and that of "the algebra of need," which states simply that an addict faced with absolute need (as a junkie is) will do anything to satisfy that need.

The Nova Criminals are nonhuman personifications of various addictions. The Uranians, addicted to Heavy Metal Fluid, are types of drug addicts. Dr. Benway, Mr. Bradley Mr. Martin (a single character), and the insect people of Minraud—all control addicts—are types of the human addiction to power. The green boy-girls of Venus, addicted to Venusian sexual practices, are types of the human addiction to sensual pleasure. The Death Dwarf, addicted to concentrated words and images, is the analogue of the human addiction to various cultural myths and beliefs; he is perhaps the most pathetic of these depraved creatures. Burroughs explains: "Junk yields a basic formula of 'evil' virus: the face of evil is always the face of total need. A dope fiend is a man in total need of dope. Beyond a certain frequency need knows absolutely no limit or control." As poet and literary critic John Ciardi noted, "Only after the first shock does one realize that what Burroughs is writing about is not only the destruction of depraved men by their drug lust, but the destruction of all men by their consuming addictions, whether the addiction be drugs or over-righteous propriety or sixteen-year-old girls."

THE SOFT MACHINE

Burroughs viewed *The Soft Machine* as "a sequel to *Naked Lunch*, a mathematical extension of the Algebra of Need beyond the Junk virus." Here, the consuming addiction, displayed again in juxtaposition with scenes of drug abuse and sexual perversion, and through a number of shifting narrators, is the addiction to power over others. The central episode is the destruction by a time-traveling agent of the control apparatus of the ancient Mayan theocracy (Burroughs's primary archaeological interest), which exercises its control through the manipulation of myths; this is a clear analogue of the present-day struggle between the Nova Police and the Nova Mob that breaks into the open in the subsequent two novels.

The time traveler uses the same technique to prepare himself for time travel as Burroughs does in writing his novels, a type of "cut-up, fold-in" montage: "I started my trip in the morgue with old newspapers, folding in today with yesterday and typing out composites." Because words tie people to time, the time traveler is given apomorphine (used to cure Burroughs of his heroin addiction) to break this connection.

The "soft machine" is both the "wounded galaxy," the Milky Way seen as a biological organism diseased by the viruslike Nova Mob, and the human body, riddled with parasites and addictions and programmed with the "ticket," obsolete myths and dreams, written on the "soft typewriter" of culture and civilization. Burroughs contends that any addiction dehumanizes its victims. The Mayan priests, for example, tend to become half-man, half-crab creatures who eventually metamorphose into giant centipedes and exude an erogenous green slime. Such hideous transformations also strike Lee, a heroin addict, and other homosexuals. Bradley the Buyer, who reappears as Mr. Bradley Mr. Martin, Mr. and Mrs. D., and the Ugly Spirit, has a farcical habit of turning into a bloblike creature who is addicted to and absorbs drug addicts.

NOVA EXPRESS *and* THE TICKET THAT EXPLODED

Instances of metamorphosis are almost innumerable in *Nova Express* and *The Ticket That Exploded*. These novels most clearly reveal the quartet's plot and explore the Nova Mob's exploitation of media. Here addiction to language is investigated. As Stephen Koch has argued: "Burroughs's ideology . . . is based on an image of consciousness in bondage to the organism: better, of consciousness as an organism, gripped by the tropisms of need. Consciousness is addicted—it is here the drug metaphor enters—to what sustains it and gives it definition: in particular, it is addicted to the word, the structures of language that define meaning and thus reality itself." Thus, while in *The Soft Machine* the time traveler is sent to Trak News Agency (the motto of which is "We don't report the news—we write it") to learn how to defeat the Mayan theocracy by first learning "how this writing the news before it happens is done," in *The Ticket That Exploded* it is axiomatic that "you can run a government without police if your conditioning program is tight enough but you can't run a government without [nonsense and deception]."

Contemporary existence is seen ultimately as a film that is rerun again and again, trapping the human soul like an insect imprisoned in amber, negating any possibility of choice or freedom. In these last two novels of the quartet, Burroughs issues a call for revolt against humanity's imprisoning addiction to language. In *Nova Express*, he notes that "their garden of delights is a terminal sewer" and demands that everyone heed the last words of Hassan I Sabbah (cribbed out of context from Fyodor Dostoevski's Ivan Karamazov): "Nothing is True—Everything is Permitted." In *The Ticket That Exploded*,

Burroughs rages, "Better than the 'real thing'?—There is no real thing—Maya—Maya—It's all show business."

THE WILD BOYS

Burroughs's other notably science-fiction-like novel, *The Wild Boys*, is also composed of scenes linked more by associated images than by any clearly linear narrative framework. Here the author posits a bizarre alternative to the problematic apocalypse-in-progress depicted in his earlier quartet. In a world wrecked by famine and controlled by police, the wild boys, a homosexual tribe of hashish smokers, have withdrawn themselves from space and time through indifference and have developed into a counterculture complete with its own language, rituals, and economy. The existence of this counterculture poses a threat to those who create the false images on which the larger, repressive, external society is based, but the wild boys cannot be tamed because their cold indifference to the mass culture entails a savagery that refuses to submit to control. Although Burroughs's thinking clearly becomes more political in *The Wild Boys* and in the book that followed it, *Exterminator!*, a collection of short stories and poems that revolve around the common theme of death through sinister forces, his primary concern for freedom from the controllers and manipulators—chemical, political, sexual, and cultural—remains constant from the beginning of his literary career.

CITIES OF THE RED NIGHT

Continuing the utopian vision of *The Wild Boys*, but encompassing it into a larger, more anthropological context, Burroughs's next three works form a trilogy to expand his vision of society and its place in the natural order. The first book in the series, *Cities of the Red Night*, continues the twin themes of freedom from control and the power of mythmaking, but does so on a much larger scale. One of Burroughs's longest works, *Cities of the Red Night* is unique in that in it he sustains a rather conventional narrative voice, utilizing conventional popular genre, to achieve a re-creation of history through fantasy and myth.

The novel begins with three distinct plots that seem at first to be only tenuously related. One plot concerns a retroactive utopia founded by eighteenth century pirates, which Burroughs uses as a foundation for social criticism. A second plot, from which the title comes, depicts mythical "cities of the red night," which existed in prehistoric time and function as a dystopia through which the reader views present culture. A third plot involves a present-day investigator who traces the mystery of a deadly virus known as B-23 to its historical origins in the "cities of the red night." Each plot employs conventions from one popular genre or another: The story of the utopian pirates' colony reads very much like a boys' adventure story, the story of the advanced prehistoric cities takes its structure from science fiction, and the story of the investigation of the virus lends itself to the conventions of the hard-boiled detective story.

THE PLACE OF DEAD ROADS

In the second book of the trilogy, *The Place of Dead Roads*, Burroughs continues the process of mythmaking. His protagonist is Kim Carsons, a late nineteenth century gunslinger who utilizes a sort of "hole in time," a phenomenon introduced in *Cities of the Red Night*. Through this hole, Carsons becomes a time traveler, moving precariously across time and space, encountering different cultures and time periods in an effort to forge some sense of the whole, some sense of control over his own destiny. He seeks fulfillment in disparate, almost lonely, gay-sex encounters; in drugs; and in the sense of power he feels by manipulating others.

The story begins with a clipping from a Boulder, Colorado, newspaper that tells the reader that William Seward Hall, who writes Western novels under the pen name Kim Carsons, was shot in a gunfight in the year 1899. The story then introduces the character Carsons and, after a disjointed series of adventures and misadventures, returns the reader to that same date when Carsons loses his life, as if to say that destiny will not be averted in the end. The similarity of Carsons's true name to Burroughs's is striking here because, like Hall, Burroughs tends to fictionalize himself as author, as though authors can reach their true potential only through the lives of their characters—perhaps another way of understanding Burroughs's fascination with somehow circumventing destiny through manipulation.

THE WESTERN LANDS

In the third book of the trilogy, *The Western Lands*, the reader learns that Carsons was not shot by his opponent, Mike Chase, but by a killer from the Land of the Dead named Joe, described as a NO (Natural Outlaw), whose job it is to break natural laws. The Western land itself is a mythical place, a utopian vision of a place beyond one's images of Earth and Heaven—a land where natural law, religious law, and human law have no meaning. It is a paradise, but a paradise difficult to reach.

The intent of Burroughs's trilogy is first to create a science-fiction myth that explains all of human history, then to reveal the power of fantasy and myth to offer alternative histories, and finally, by realizing these alternative histories, to explore alternative anthropological patterns by which to organize society. The three separate plots interrelate and merge at various points throughout the trilogy, but eventually each is abandoned before completion—a technique that, Burroughs claimed, allows readers to create their own stories, to engage their own sense of mythmaking. Readers are encouraged to play a kind of "what if" game along with Burroughs: What if the Spanish had not defeated the New World into submission? What if the true foundations of liberty and individual freedom had taken hold in the Third World? What if all of our assumptions, whether religious, historical, or psychological, are wrong? This process of mythmaking in Burroughs is not a means to an end; rather, it is the object of the struggle—the great creative process of defining and redefining ourselves, which is our ultimate defense against those who would manipulate us.

QUEER

Set in Mexico and South America during the 1940's, *Queer* details in fictional guise both the author's homosexual longing and his drug addiction. Burroughs wrote, "While it was I who wrote *Junky* [*sic*], I feel that I was being written in *Queer.*" Although it was not published until 1985 because of its homosexual content, *Queer* was Burroughs's first attempt at novel writing. It is the most linear and perhaps most coherent of Burroughs's novels.

William Lee is the story's protagonist, and, though not told in first person, the novel looks at the world through his eyes. Lee shares much in common with Burroughs, as explained in the novel's introduction. Lee is a heroin addict mostly trying to kick the habit. He lusts for boys and young men, and he has an obsession with Eugene Allerton, a younger bisexual man who tolerates Lee until better circumstances happen along. Part of the story involves Lee's search, with Allerton in tow, for a plant-based hallucinogen called yage that is purported to enhance telepathic powers. In *The Yage Letters*, Burroughs's letters regarding his real-life search for yage are collected.

Queer is a short novel—only 134 pages—prefaced by a 23-page introduction by Burroughs in which he further explains Lee's motivations and actions along with some of his own. Lee is looking for an audience, a distraction from the drug addiction, and, like many addicts, becomes obsessive about a sex object in replacement. Allerton is that object, and, in order to keep his audience interested, Lee develops what he calls "Routines": entertaining, shocking, or outrageous stories to amuse and draw attention. These stories, interwoven into the love-story travelogue, provide flashes of humor that are sometimes perverse, such as the recipe for pig served cooked on the outside but still living on the inside or the story of "Corn Hole Gus' Used-Slave Lot."

Burroughs's Mexico of the 1940's is seedy and primitive. Many of the characters in the book are fellow American expatriates, and the highlight of their day is to stop in at the local bars to share the latest gossip. In the twenty-first century world of television, video games, and cell phones, younger readers may find the place descriptions more like nightmares than like historic information—especially as the switches among inner musings, location descriptions, and "Routines" are not always clearly demarcated. William Lee continues his adventures in *Naked Lunch*.

Although Burroughs's innovative, highly unconventional fiction style and often abrasive thematic preoccupations are not without their detractors, by the end of his career Burroughs had firmly established his place as one of late twentieth century fiction's most significant innovators. In fact, his "cut-up" technique has reached beyond the bounds of obscure cult fiction to influence both mainstream cinema and popular music. Burroughs played a semiautobiographical role as Tom the Priest in Gus Van Sant's 1989 film about drug addiction, *Drugstore Cowboy*; in 1991, acclaimed director David Cronenberg adapted *Naked Lunch* to the screen. In her introduction to his unprecedented reading on the popular American television show *Saturday Night Live* in 1981, actor Lauren Hutton lauded Burroughs as "America's greatest living writer," and rock music icons Lou Reed and David Bowie have both recognized Burroughs's disjointed and surreal but surprisingly moralistic approach to writing as enormously influential on their own work. The heavy metal genre of rock-and-roll music takes its name from a phrase in Burroughs's *Naked Lunch*, and the name of the popular band Steely Dan is also borrowed from his writing.

Upon his death in 1997 at age eighty-three, Burroughs was eulogized as everything from the "most dangerous" of Beat writers to the undisputed patriarch of this important movement in twentieth century American writing. Although Burroughs's lifelong penchant for the cutting edge of fiction continues to intimidate some scholars and critics, none can dispute his role as a significant innovator and catalyst for change in twentieth century fiction and popular culture.

Donald Palumbo; Gregory D. Horn
Updated by B. Diane Blackwood

OTHER MAJOR WORKS

NONFICTION: *The Yage Letters*, 1963 (with Allen Ginsberg); *APO-33 Bulletin: A Metabolic Regulator*, 1966; *The Job: Interviews with William S. Burroughs*, 1970 (with Daniel Odier); *Electronic Revolution, 1970-71*, 1971; *Letters to Allen Ginsberg, 1953-1957*, 1983; *The Adding Machine: Collected Essays*, 1985; *The Cat Inside*, 1992; *The Letters of William S. Burroughs, 1945-1959*, 1993 (Oliver Harris, editor); *Conversations with William S. Burroughs*, 1999 (Allen Hibbard, editor); *Last Words: The Final Journals of William S. Burroughs*, 2000; *Everything Lost: The Latin American Notebook of William S. Burroughs*, 2008 (Oliver Harris, editor).

MISCELLANEOUS: *The Exterminator*, 1960 (with Brion Gysin); *Minutes to Go*, 1960 (with Sinclair Beiles, Gregory Corso, and Gysin); *Time*, 1965 (drawings by Gysin); *White Subway*, 1965; *Apomorphine*, 1969; *The Dead Star*, 1969; *The Last Words of Dutch Schultz*, 1970; *Exterminator!*, 1973; *The Book of Breeething*, 1974; *Œuvre Croisée*, 1976 (with Gysin; also known as *The Third Mind*, 1978); *Blade Runner: A Movie*, 1979; *Interzone*, 1989; *Word Virus: The William S. Burroughs Reader*, 1998 (James Grauerholz and Ira Silverberg, editors).

BIBLIOGRAPHY

Burroughs, William S. *Burroughs Live*. Cambridge, Mass.: MIT Press, 2002. Collection of interviews is informative for readers hoping for a personal glimpse of the novelist. Burroughs, however, was notorious with interviewers for being a difficult subject to draw out.

Caveney, Graham. *Gentleman Junkie: The Life and Legacy of William S. Burroughs*. Boston: Little, Brown, 1998. Unconventional biography features an imaginative visual presentation that superimposes the text on reproductions of photographs, newspaper clippings, and other visual elements, all printed on multicolored pages. Considers the myths and legends surrounding Burroughs as well as his life and influence on later generations of musicians, writers, and artists.

Goodman, Michael Barry. *Contemporary Literary Censorship: The Case History of Burroughs's "Naked Lunch."* Metuchen, N.J.: Scarecrow Press, 1981. Offers a narrative history of the writing, publication, critical reception, and subsequent censorship of *Naked Lunch* in the United States. Provides much previously unpublished Burroughs material.

Harris, Oliver. *William Burroughs and the Secret of Fascination.* Carbondale: Southern Illinois University Press, 2003. Focuses on the novels *Junkie, Queer,* and *Naked Lunch,* as well as *The Yage Letters,* to trace Burroughs's creative history during the 1950's.

Hibbard, Allen, ed. *Conversations with William S. Burroughs.* Jackson: University Press of Mississippi, 1999. Collection of previously published interviews with the author spans thirty-five years (1961-1996). Includes chronology and index.

Johnson, Rob. *The Lost Years of William S. Burroughs: Beats in South Texas.* College Station: Texas A&M University Press, 2006. Discusses Burroughs's experiences during a period in his life (1946-1949) before he began publishing, when he farmed cotton (as well as marijuana and opium poppies) and socialized with Beat writers such as Allen Ginsberg and Neal Cassady. Sheds some light on Burroughs's early work. Includes illustrations and index.

Lardas, John. *The Bop Apocalypse: The Religious Visions of Kerouac, Ginsberg, and Burroughs.* Urbana: University of Illinois Press, 2001. Combines cultural history, biography, and literary criticism in examining the spiritualism and religious concerns of the three Beat writers.

Morgan, Ted. *Literary Outlaw: The Life and Times of William S. Burroughs.* New York: Holt, 1988. Standard biography remains an important source of information on Burroughs. Examines his life and career, with particular emphasis on the influence of other Beat writers on his work.

Skerl, Jennie. *William S. Burroughs.* Boston: Twayne, 1985. Attempts to provide an overview of contemporary thought on Burroughs's art and life for the general reader and literary historian. Also provides a concise analysis section.

MICHAEL CHABON

Born: Washington, D.C.; May 24, 1963
Also known as: Leon Chaim Bach; Malachi B. Cohen; August Van Zorn

The Mysteries of Pittsburgh, 1988
Wonder Boys, 1995
The Amazing Adventures of Kavalier and Clay, 2000
The Final Solution: A Story of Detection, 2004
Gentlemen of the Road, 2007
The Yiddish Policemen's Union, 2007

OTHER LITERARY FORMS

Although known primarily as a novelist, Michael Chabon (SHAY-bahn) has also distinguished himself as a writer of short fiction, publishing the collections *A Model World, and Other Stories* (1991) and *Werewolves in Their Youth* (1999). His second book, *A Model World*, helped cement Chabon's emerging reputation as a writer of emotional depth and lyrical intensity. His novel *The Amazing Adventures of Kavalier and Clay* inspired a comic-book series, published by Dark Horse Comics, based on the novel's comic-book superhero character the Escapist; Chabon has contributed but is not a primary writer for the series. He has published articles and essays in a variety of magazines such as *Esquire*, *The New Yorker*, and *The Paris Review*. He served as the editor for the anthology *McSweeney's Mammoth Treasury of Thrilling Tales* (2003) and *McSweeney's Enchanted Chamber of Astonishing Stories* (2004). He has worked on screenplays for a number of films, most notably *Spider-Man 2* (2004). A collection of Chabon's essays (largely made up of his magazine publications) titled *Maps and Legends: Essays on Reading and Writing Along the Borderlands* was published in 2008.

ACHIEVEMENTS

After having initially made a splash as a novelist, Michael Chabon was also lauded for his collections of short fiction; the story "Son of the Wolfman" won an O. Henry Award in 1999. Chabon's star climbed higher with the 2000 film adaptation of *Wonder Boys* and reached even greater heights when *The Amazing Adventures of Kavalier and Clay* won the Pulitzer Prize in 2000 and was nominated for the National Book Critics Circle Award as well as short-listed for the PEN/Faulkner Award. Chabon's subsequent foray into adolescent fantasy, *Summerland*, won the Mythopoeic Fantasy Award for Children's Literature in 2003. His further work in genre fiction has been rewarded as well; a brief version of his novel *The Final Solution* won the 2003 Aga Khan Prize for fiction for best work published in *The Paris Review* that year. Furthermore, *The Yiddish Policemen's Union* won the Edgar

Award for best mystery novel, the Nebula Award for best science-fiction novel, and the Locus Award for best science-fiction novel and was nominated for a Hugo Award for best science-fiction novel as well as the Sidewise Award for Alternate History. His historical swashbuckling novel *Gentlemen of the Road* was first serialized in *The New York Times Magazine*.

BIOGRAPHY

Michael Chabon was born on May 24, 1963, in Washington, D.C., and raised partly in Columbia, Maryland, and partly in Pittsburgh, Pennsylvania. His parents divorced when Chabon was an adolescent. During this time the young Chabon turned to comic books and works of genre fiction (such as Arthur Conan Doyle's Sherlock Holmes stories) to escape the domestic strife in his life. He attended the University of Pittsburgh, earning a B.A. in English in 1984; from there he attended the master of fine arts program at the University of California at Irvine, where he would earn his degree in 1987. More important, one of his advisers at Irvine, novelist Donald Heiney, was so impressed with Chabon's thesis that he sent the manuscript to his own agent; the novel was purchased for $155,000 (almost an unheard-of sum for a first literary novel in 1987) and was published to great advance praise. That same year, Chabon married poet Lollie Groth, a union that would end with their divorce in 1991.

For the next several years, Chabon worked on a novel that he planned to title "Fountain City," about environmental activism and a baseball park in Florida, among other things; the novel became longer and longer, until Chabon realized that it was not succeeding and put it aside to begin work on a novel about a man unable to finish a sprawling novel, *Wonder Boys*. Chabon married attorney Ayelet Waldman in 1993, with whom he would eventually have three children (Sophie, Ezekiel, and Ida-Rose). The successful adaptation of *Wonder Boys* into a film (directed by Curtis Hanson) released in 2000 combined with the author's thriving sales to make him financially independent and able to focus on his work. Chabon's second wife, Waldman has published a number of mystery novels in a series known as the Mommy-Track Mysteries; her successful work in genre fiction parallels Chabon's own interest in the field. Since his work on *Spider-Man 2* (directed by Sam Raimi), Chabon has balanced his busy life writing fiction with work on screenplays.

ANALYSIS

As might be expected of a novelist who first gained acclaim at the age of twenty-five and who has not escaped the limelight since, Michael Chabon has produced work that displays significant evolution over the succeeding two decades. While all his novels have shown Chabon's gift for fluid, lyrical prose, the tones of the works have stretched from wistful (*The Mysteries of Pittsburgh*) to wryly comic (*Wonder Boys*) to cynical and laconic (*The Yiddish Policemen's Union*). Structurally, Chabon's methods have also changed. Where his first two novels are tightly focused first-person narratives about small numbers of people over a brief time, *The Amazing Adventures of Kavalier and Clay* takes place over several years and includes an expansive cast; *The Yiddish Policemen's Union* evokes an alternative version of the world in which Sitka, Alaska, has been the Jewish homeland since World War II; and *Gentleman of the Road* is a short, quickly paced novel of historical adventure.

As Chabon's plots and style have evolved, so too have his interests and subject matter. *The Mysteries of Pittsburgh* is a book by a young man, not too long out of college, about a young man just out of college. The distance between the writer and the creation is greater in *Wonder Boys*, but at some level Grady Tripp's struggle to complete a new novel is surely based on Chabon's similar experience. With *The Amazing Adventures of Kavalier and Clay*, however, Chabon broke into new territory: The novel is set in the years before and after World War II and deals with such broad themes as art, creativity, Jewish identity, romantic happiness, and the closeted lives of gays at a time when such lives were subject to scrutiny and persecution.

Chabon's novels have often portrayed gay characters and aspects of gay lifestyle. After the success of *The Mysteries of Pittsburgh*, which is partly about a bisexual man making a choice between a relationship with a man and a relationship with a woman, Chabon became identified as an author who writes about and is sympathetic to gay characters. Similarly, although Chabon's Jewish heritage seems to have had relatively little influence on his first two novels, Jewish culture and identity are primary issues in *The Amazing Adventures of Kavalier and Clay*, *The Yiddish Policemen's Union*, and *Gentlemen of the Road*.

Chabon has also become increasingly interested in fiction genres such as detective, horror, and science fiction. In addition to editing genre collections for McSweeney's and writing a new "final chapter" to the life of Sherlock Holmes, Chabon has incorporated both science fiction and the detective story in the long consideration of Jewish identity and Zionism that is *The Yiddish Policemen's Union*. Similarly, although ostensibly a historical adventure novel, *Gentlemen of the Road* is in many ways patterned on the fantasy works of such writers as Fritz Leiber and Michael Moorcock; the primary characters are again Jewish, and the setting is an ancient Turkish city-state of Jews.

THE MYSTERIES OF PITTSBURGH

The Mysteries of Pittsburgh is primarily a coming-of-age novel. Art Bechstein is poised on the precipice of several new worlds: He is not only trying to unravel his future as a new college graduate but also coming to terms with his own troubling (to him, at first) bisexuality as well as the realization that his father is a shadowy underworld figure. Even as Art is seduced by both Arthur Lecomte and Phlox Lombardi, he is pulled between their world and his own. Both names are symbolic in their way; Arthur has more or less the same name as Art, and at some level he represents an outward manifestation of Art's previously unacknowledged bisexuality. A phlox is a kind of flower, and in truth Art's world is in flower, blooming and changing; at the same time, phlox serves as a homonym for "flux," a perfect description of Art's emotional state.

Arthur and Phlox introduce Art to Cleveland, a charming and literate aspiring young criminal who wishes to use Art to gain an introduction to Art's father. As Phlox and Arthur represent different aspects of Art's life, Cleveland represents the allure of rebellion and the thrill of unplanned and unchecked danger. By the end of the novel, the triangle of friendships that has stretched Art in different directions has fallen apart under tragedy, and Art must make his own way into adulthood.

WONDER BOYS

Wonder Boys was published seven years after *The Mysteries of Pittsburgh*. The novel tells of a middle-aged creative-writing professor, Grady Tripp, who learns that his third wife, Emily, is leaving him even as he finds out that his mistress, college chancellor Sara Gaskell (and wife to the English Department's chair, Walter), is pregnant with Grady's child. Grady has been drinking too much and smoking too much marijuana, typing away all the while at his sprawling novel *Wonder Boys*, which is seven years overdue and at this point more than two thousand pages long. The events of the novel take place over the weekend of the small fictional Pennsylvania college's WordFest literary festival. Grady's editor, Terry Crabtree, is in town to attend the festival and to inquire about Grady's novel, which Grady has implied—untruthfully—is nearing completion.

Wonder Boys is, in some ways, nominally autobiographical; like Tripp, Chabon worked on an abortive second novel ("Fountain City") for several years, watching it grow to more than fifteen hundred pages before realizing that he had to abandon it. In most ways, however, Grady Tripp is a character in his own right, and throughout the novel his name proves apt as he trips repeatedly over his own feet literally and figuratively. Even as he tries to navigate between Emily's leaving and Sara's announcement, he must also try to guide his naïve, gay, and vulnerable young wunderkind student James Leer around the pitfalls represented by Grady's lecherous gay friend Terry and James's own budding talent and vulnerabilities.

The novel becomes a kind of picaresque series of adventures, with Grady stumbling from misadventure to misadventure, accompanied by James, who stitches together lies about his background. Interposed throughout the narrative are Grady's memories of cult horror writer Albert Vetch, who died forgotten and alone. Grady eventually realizes that, unless he wants to mimic Vetch's life, he too must put away childish things and fully embrace maturity.

THE AMAZING ADVENTURES OF KAVALIER AND CLAY

The Amazing Adventures of Kavalier and Clay in many ways demonstrates Chabon's coming-of-age. Early in the novel, eighteen-year-old Jewish art student and part-time escape artist Joseph Kavalier is smuggled out of Prague; the year is 1939. Sent to the United States, he meets his distant cousin Sammy Klayman (also known as Sammy Clay). Before long, Sammy has introduced Joe to the budding medium of comic books, and together they invent their own character, the Escapist. The allure of the Escapist in their lives is obvious: Millions of European Jews are being persecuted and are unable to escape the horror of the Holocaust; conversely, the Escapist is able to escape from any trap and turn the tables on his enemies. In addition, even as Sammy fears a second kind of persecution—as a closeted young gay man—the Escapist is empowered and fearless.

As the novel progresses, Joe confronts both his fear of persecution and his fear of intimacy when he joins the war effort and is sent on a mission to Antarctica; similarly, Sammy (although involved in a marriage of convenience with Joe's lover Rosa, who becomes pregnant with Joe's child just before he leaves for the war) takes more and more chances as he seeks to live a fully integrated life. Joe, too, eventually realizes that he needs family when he rejoins Sammy, Rosa, and his son, Tommy.

THE FINAL SOLUTION *and* GENTLEMEN OF THE ROAD

Both the young adult novel *Summerland* and *The Final Solution* indicate the different directions that Chabon's interests took in the years following *The Amazing Adventures of Kavalier and Clay*. *Summerland* is a fantasy novel (similar in style to J. K. Rowling's Harry Potter series) about a boy named Ethan Feld who hates baseball, which his father makes him play. Along with his friend, Native American pitcher Jennifer Rideout, Ethan is recruited to lead a team of misfit players (from a variety of dimensions) in a series of baseball games to save the world from destruction by the mysterious Coyote, a godlike avatar of chaos. *The Final Solution* returns to where Chabon's interest in genre fiction began—Sherlock Holmes. Set in 1944 during World War II, the eighty-nine-year-old character is never named but is clearly Holmes (or based completely on Holmes). The title refers both to Adolf Hitler's plan to exterminate the Jews of Europe and to "The Final Problem" (1893), the story wherein Holmes author Arthur Conan Doyle temporarily killed off his detective hero. Like *The Amazing Adventures of Kavalier and Clay* and *The Yiddish Policemen's Union*, *The Final Solution* deals with issues of Jewish identity; the aged Holmes's last case involves a young Jewish refugee from Germany. Although Holmes can find answers to the more overt problems in the case, others are insoluble.

Like *The Final Solution*, *Gentlemen of the Road* is a short novel; it was originally serialized in *The New York Times Magazine*. Set in the tenth century C.E., this swashbuckling adventure novel follows two mercenaries, an African Jew named Amram and a long-haired Jewish Frank named Zelikman, as they work to bring the rightful heir of the Jewish Khazars back to the throne.

THE YIDDISH POLICEMEN'S UNION

The Yiddish Policemen's Union represents a culmination of Chabon's interests in Jewish identity and in genre fiction. The novel posits an alternate history: The creation of Israel in 1948 fails, and instead a temporary homeland for Jews is created in Sitka, Alaska. The novel is set at the end of the sixty-year period following establishment of that homeland, soon before the Alaskan region is to revert to American control. The language in *The Yiddish Policemen's Union* is more tightly controlled and terse than in most of Chabon's work, in keeping with its crime-novel milieu. The protagonist is a down-on-his-luck homicide detective named Meyer Landsman, who, true to his genre, drinks too much and has recently seen his marriage fall apart.

Teamed with partner and cousin Berko Shemets (half Jewish and half Tlingit native), Landsman sets out to uncover the murder of a mysterious man who has died in Landsman's own apartment building. Like his hard-boiled predecessors Philip Marlowe (the detective creation of Raymond Chandler, 1888-1959) and Sam Spade (created by Dashiell Hammett, 1894-1961), Landsman solves his crimes more through persistence and toughness than through brilliant insights; the more the various communities of Sitka try to warn him away, the deeper he digs. Chabon uses the detective-novel framework of *The Yiddish Policemen's Union* to investigate questions of Jewish American culture, Zionism, and Anti-Semitism.

Scott D. Yarbrough

OTHER MAJOR WORKS

SHORT FICTION: *A Model World, and Other Stories*, 1991; *Werewolves in Their Youth: Stories*, 1999.

NONFICTION: *Maps and Legends: Essays on Reading and Writing Along the Borderlands*, 2008.

YOUNG ADULT LITERATURE: *Summerland*, 2002.

EDITED TEXTS: *McSweeney's Mammoth Treasury of Thrilling Tales*, 2003; *McSweeney's Enchanted Chamber of Astonishing Stories*, 2004.

MISCELLANEOUS: *Michael Chabon Presents: The Amazing Adventures of the Escapist*, 2004 (2 volumes).

BIBLIOGRAPHY

Binelli, Mark. "The Amazing Story of the Comic Book Nerd Who Won the Pulitzer Prize for Fiction." *Rolling Stone*, September 27, 2001. Provides an overview of Chabon's life and career as well as brief discussion of each of his novels.

Cahill, Bryon. "Michael Chabon: A Writer with Many Faces." *Writing!* 27, no. 6 (April/May, 2005): 16-20. Presents a detailed examination of Chabon's developing interests and the inspirations behind many of his works.

Chabon, Michael. "On *The Mysteries of Pittsburgh*." *The New York Review of Books*, June 9, 2005. Brief history by the author explains the genesis of his first novel and some of the less overt autobiographical elements in the work.

_____. "Secret Skin: Superheroes, Escapism, Realism." *The New Yorker*, March 10, 2008. Examines the comic-book and superhero genres, with emphasis on the costumes as well as on the ways in which the comic-book medium differs from traditional prose fiction. Discusses the superhero motif in *The Amazing Adventures of Kavalier and Clay.*

Fowler, Douglas. "The Short Fiction of Michael Chabon: Nostalgia in the Very Young." *Studies in Short Fiction* 32, no. 1 (Winter, 1995): 75-82. Offers analysis of Chabon's *The Mysteries of Pittsburgh* and various of his short stories, with comparisons drawn to F. Scott Fitzgerald's *The Great Gatsby* (1925).

Munson, Sam. "Slices of Life." *Commentary* 115, no. 6 (June, 2003): 67-71. Focuses on Chabon's editing of the McSweeney's anthologies as well as on the development of his interests in genre fiction.

Perle, Liz. "Alternate Reality: Author Profile of Michael Chabon." *Publishers Weekly,* September 24, 2007. Discusses Chabon's creativity and interest in genre categories, as demonstrated by his novel *Gentlemen of the Road.*

JOHN CHEEVER

Born: Quincy, Massachusetts; May 27, 1912
Died: Ossining, New York; June 18, 1982
Also known as: John William Cheever

PRINCIPAL LONG FICTION
The Wapshot Chronicle, 1957
The Wapshot Scandal, 1964
Bullet Park, 1969
Falconer, 1977
Oh, What a Paradise It Seems, 1982

OTHER LITERARY FORMS

After the publication of his first fictional piece, "Expelled," in the October 10, 1930, issue of *The New Republic*, more than two hundred John Cheever stories appeared in American magazines, chiefly *The New Yorker*. Fewer than half that number were reprinted in the seven collections Cheever published in his lifetime: *The Way Some People Live* (1943), *The Enormous Radio, and Other Stories* (1953), *The Housebreaker of Shady Hill, and Other Stories* (1958), *Some People, Places, and Things That Will Not Appear in My Next Novel* (1961), *The Brigadier and the Golf Widow* (1964), *The World of Apples* (1973), and *The Stories of John Cheever* (1978); the last of these includes all but the earliest collected stories and adds four previously uncollected pieces. In 1994, a collection titled *Thirteen Uncollected Stories* was published.

Cheever's one television play, *The Shady Hill Kidnapping*, aired on January 12, 1982, to inaugurate the Public Broadcasting Service's *American Playhouse* series. Cheever, however, made a clear distinction between fiction, which he considered humankind's most exalted and intimate means of communication, and literary works written for television, film, and theater. Consequently, he remained aloof from all attempts to adapt his literary work—including the 1968 film version of his story "The Swimmer," directed by Frank Perry and starring Burt Lancaster (which he found disappointing), and the adaptations of three of his stories televised by the Public Broadcasting Service in 1979. In addition, he rarely turned his considerable energies to the writing of articles and reviews. One large and fascinating body of Cheever's writing is found in his journals, which he kept as part of a long family tradition.

ACHIEVEMENTS

Until the publication of *Falconer* in 1977 and *The Stories of John Cheever* the following year, John Cheever's position as a major American writer was not firmly established, even though as early as 1953 William Peden had described Cheever as one of the country's most "undervalued" literary figures. Despite the fact that critics, especially academic ones, frequently invoked Cheever only to pillory his supposedly lightweight vision and preoccupation with upper-middle-class life, his reputation continued to grow steadily: four O. Henry Awards between 1941 and 1964; a Guggenheim Fellowship in 1951; the University of Illinois Benjamin Franklin Award in 1955; a grant from the National Institute of Arts and Letters in 1956 and election to that organization the following year; the National Book Award for his first novel, *The Wapshot Chronicle*, in 1958; the William Dean Howells Medal for its sequel, *The Wapshot Scandal*, seven years later; election to the American Academy of Arts and Letters in 1973; and cover stories in the nation's two most widely circulated weekly newsmagazines, *Time* (1964) and *Newsweek* (1977). The overwhelmingly favorable reception of *Falconer* made possible the publication of *The Stories of John Cheever*, which in turn brought to its author additional honors: a second National Book Award; the National Book Critics Circle Award for best fiction; a Pulitzer Prize; the Edward MacDowell Medal; an honorary doctorate from Harvard University; and in April, 1982, the National Medal for Literature for his "distinguished and continuing contribution to American letters." The popular and critical success of those books and the televising of his work before a national audience brought Cheever the recognition he had long deserved and established his well-earned place in literature.

Biography

John Cheever was born in Quincy, Massachusetts, on May 27, 1912, and grew up during what he has called the "Athenian twilight" of New England culture. His father Frederick, who was forty-nine when Cheever was born, lost his position in the shoe business in the 1929 Depression and much of his self-respect a short time later when his wife opened a gift shop in order to support the family. The parents' emotionally strained relationship eventually led to their separation and caused Cheever to become very close to his brother Fred, seven years his senior. At age seventeen, Cheever was dismissed from Thayer Academy in South Braintree, Massachusetts, for smoking and poor grades; he promptly turned his experience into a story, "Expelled," which Malcolm Cowley published in *The New Republic* on October 10, 1930, and with Fred embarked on a walking tour of Europe. Upon their return, the brothers lived together briefly in Boston, where "Jon" (as he then identified himself) wrote while Fred worked in the textile business. The closeness of their relationship troubled Cheever, who then moved to a squalid rooming house on New York's Hudson Street. There, with the help of his Boston mentor, Hazel Hawthorne, he wrote synopses for Metro-Goldwyn-Mayer, subsisted on buttermilk and stale bread, associated with Cowley, E. E. Cummings, Sherwood Anderson, Edmund Wilson, Hart Crane, John Dos Passos, and Gaston Lachaise, and somehow managed to keep his art free of the political issues that dominated much of the literature of the period. It was also during that time that Cheever began three of his most enduring relationships: with Yaddo, the writers' colony in Saratoga Springs, New York; with *The New Yorker*, which published his "Brooklyn Rooming House" in the May 25, 1935, issue; and with Mary Winternitz, the daughter of the Dean of Yale Medical School, whom he married on March 22, 1941. They had three children: Susan, who became a writer; Benjamin, who became an editor at *Reader's Digest*; and Federico.

Midway through a tour of duty with the army, Cheever published his first book to generally favorable reviews, and following his discharge, he was able to support himself and his family almost exclusively, if at times precariously, by his writing. Although he liked to give interviewers and others the impression that he was something of a country squire—the heavy Boston accent, the eighteenth century house with its extensive grounds in Ossining, New York—Cheever was in fact plagued throughout much of his life by financial as well as psychological insecurity.

The 1950's was an unsettling time for Cheever. As he explained to fellow writer Herbert Gold, the decade had begun full of promise, but halfway through it "something went terribly wrong"; confused by "the forceful absurdities of life" and, like another Quincy man, Henry Adams, unprepared to deal with them, he imagined himself "a man in a quagmire, looking into a tear in the sky." The absurdities of modern life are presented, often with a comic twist, in the three novels and six collections of short stories that Cheever published between 1953 and the early 1970's—at which time the author's life took an even darker turn: a massive heart attack in 1972, acute alcoholism that eventually forced Cheever to commit himself to the Smithers Rehabilitation Center in New York, financial difficulties, and the death of his brother in 1976. In the light of this background, it is clear that the writing of his triumphant novel *Falconer* freed Cheever from the same sense of confinement that plagues his characters.

Cheever was both deeply, though not narrowly, religious (a practicing Episcopalian) and physically active (biking, walking, skiing, and sawing were among his favorite pastimes). He was also active sexually and, often feeling rebuffed by his wife, pursued numerous love affairs both with men (including the composer Ned Rorem and a number of young writers) and with women (including the actor Hope Lange). As a writer, he incorporated into his fiction the same blend of the spiritual and the worldly that marked his own character. This blend shines most strongly in *Oh, What a Paradise It Seems*, the novella Cheever published just three months before he died of cancer on June 18, 1982. In the novella, protagonist Lemuel Sears is introduced in a sentence that begins in the writing style of William Butler Yeats and ends in pure Cheever: "An aged man is but a paltry thing, a tattered coat upon a stick, unless he sees the bright plumage of the bird called courage—Cardinalis virginius in this case—and oh how his heart leapt." More than a literary work, *Oh, What a Paradise It Seems* is the gift of an enormously generous writer whose loss is, to use one of Cheever's favorite words, "inestimable."

ANALYSIS

In a literary period that witnessed the exhaustion of literature, wholesale formal experimentation, a general distrust of language, the death of the novel, and the blurring of the lines separating fiction and play, mainstream art and the avant-garde, John Cheever consistently and eloquently held to the position that the writing of fiction is an intimate, useful, and indeed necessary way of making sense of human life and affirming its worth. Cheever's ambitious and overtly religious view of fiction not only is unfashionable today but also stands in marked opposition to those critics who pigeonhole, and in this way dismiss, his fiction as social criticism in the conventional realistic mode. Certainly, there is that element of realism in his work that one finds in the fiction of John O'Hara and Anton Chekhov, writers with whom he is often compared. Such a view, however, fails to account for the various nonrealistic components of his work: the mythic resonance of William Faulkner, the comic grotesquerie of Franz Kafka, and, most important, the lyric style that, while reminiscent of F. Scott Fitzgerald's finest prose, is nevertheless entirely Cheever's own, a cachet underscoring his essentially religious sensibility.

Humankind's inclination toward spiritual light, Cheever has said, "is very nearly botanical." His characters are modern pilgrims—not the Kierkegaardian "sovereign wayfarers" one finds in the novels of Walker Percy, another contemporary Christian writer, but instead the lonely residents of Cheever's various cities and suburbs whose search for love, security, and a measure of fulfillment is the secret undercurrent of their otherwise prosaic daily lives. Because the idea of original sin is a given in Cheever's fiction, his characters are men and women who have fallen from grace. At their worst, they are narcissists and chronic complainers. The best of them, however, persevere and, as a result, attain that redemptive vision that enables them "to celebrate a world that lies around them like a bewildering and stupendous dream."

This affirmation does not come easily to Cheever's characters, nor is it rendered sentimentally. Cheever well understands how social fragmentation and separation from the natural world have eroded the individual's sense of self-worth and debased contemporary life, making humanity's "perilous moral journey" still more arduous. The outwardly comfortable world in which these characters exist can suddenly, and often for no clearly understandable reason, turn dangerously dark, bringing into sharper focus the emotional and spiritual impoverishment of their lives. What concerns Cheever is not so much the change in their fortunes as the way they respond to that change. Many respond in an extreme, sometimes bizarre manner—Melissa Wapshot, for one. Others attempt to escape into the past; in doing so, they deny the present by imprisoning themselves in what amounts to a regressive fantasy that Cheever carefully distinguishes from nostalgia, which, as he uses it, denotes a pleasurable remembrance of the past, one that is free of regret. Cheever's heroes are those who embrace "the thrust of life," taking from the past what is valuable and using it in their present situations. How a character responds to his world determines Cheever's tone, which ranges from open derision to compassionate irony. Although in his later work Cheever may have been, as Richard Schickel has claimed, less ironic and more forgiving, his finest stories and novels, including *Falconer*, derive their power from the balance or tension he creates between irony and compassion, comedy and tragedy, light and dark.

The social and moral vision that forms the subject of Cheever's fiction also affects the structure of his novels. The novel, Cheever said in 1953, is a form better suited to the parochial life of the nineteenth century than to the modern age with its highly mobile population and mass communications; but because critics and readers have continued to view the short story as inferior to the novel, the conscientious writer of short fiction has often been denied the recognition routinely awarded lesser writers who have worked in the longer form. One way out of this dilemma for Cheever was to publish a collection of stories having the unity of a novel: *The Housebreaker of Shady Hill.* Another was to write novels that had some of the fragmentary quality Cheever found at the heart of the modern age. His four novels are not, therefore, made up of short stories badly spliced together, as some reviewers have maintained; rather, they reflect—in various degrees according to the author's state of mind at the time of composition—Cheever's firm belief that wholeness of being is no longer readily apparent; instead, it is something that character, author, and reader must strive to attain. Moreover, Cheever develops his novels on the basis of "intuition, apprehensions, dreams, concepts," rather than plot, as is entirely consistent with the revelatory nature of his religious vision. Thus, although the story form is appropriate to the depiction of the discontinuity of modern life, only in the novel can that discontinuity be not only identified but also brought under some control or, as happens in *Falconer*, transcended.

THE WAPSHOT CHRONICLE

In *The Wapshot Chronicle*, Cheever's first novel, the discontinuity of modern life is apparent not only in the structure and the characterization but also in the complex relationship the author sets up between his fictional New England town and the modern world lying beyond its nineteenth century borders. The impulse to create St. Botolphs (loosely based on Quincy) came to Cheever while he stood at the window of a Hollywood hotel, gazing down on "the dangerously barbaric and nomadic world" beneath him. The strength of his novel, however, derives not from a rejection of the present or, as in the work of nineteenth century local colorists such as Sarah Orne Jewett, in a reverent re-creation of a vanished way of life, but from the way Cheever uses each to evaluate the other.

The novel traces the decline of once-prosperous St. Botolphs and the Wapshot clan and the picaresque adventures of the two Wapshot boys—the "ministerial" Coverly and his older and more worldly brother Moses—who go to seek their fortunes in New York, Washington, D.C., and elsewhere. By having the novel begin and end with an annual Fourth of July celebration, Cheever does not so much impose an arbitrary orderliness on his discursive narrative as affirm the ceremoniousness that, in his view, is necessary to spiritual and emotional well-being. The temporal frame is important for another reason: It implies that the human desire for independence equals the desire for tradition. Each must be accommodated if the individual is to prosper. If the modern world seems chaotic, even inhospitable to Leander Wapshot's sons, it nevertheless possesses a vitality and expansiveness that, for the most part, St. Botolphs lacks. While the town is to be treasured for its rich tradition and continuity, it is also to be considered a place of confinement. The burden of the novel, then, is to show that with "strength and perseverance" it is possible to "create or build some kind of bridge" between past and present.

Cheever intends this bridge to serve a larger, emblematic purpose in *The Wapshot Chronicle*, where, as in his other works, it is the distance between self and other, or, more specifically, between man and woman, that must be bridged. Although Cheever has repeatedly warned that fiction is not "cryptoautobiography," he obviously, if loosely, modeled the Wapshots on his own family and has even admitted that he wrote the novel to make peace with his father's ghost. Leander Wapshot is the book's moral center; he has the imaginative power to redeem his fallen world, to affirm what others can only whiningly negate. Lusty and romantic, a lover of nature as well as of women, he transmits to Coverly and Moses, by his example rather than by precept, his vision of wholeness. Fittingly, the novel concludes with his "Advice to my sons," which Coverly finds tucked into a copy of William Shakespeare: "Stand up straight. Admire the world. Relish the love of a gentle woman. Trust in the Lord."

Despite his affirmative stance, Leander is a diminished hero. Unlike earlier generations of Wapshot men who proved themselves by sailing around the world, Leander's sailing is limited to ferrying tourists across the bay in his barely seaworthy boat, the *Topaze*, which his wife Sarah later converts into a floating gift shop, thus further reducing Leander's self-esteem. At one point, a storm drives the boat onto some rocks, an image that captures perfectly what Leander and many other Cheever characters feel so acutely: "man's inestimable loneliness." One of Leander's friends, for example, is haunted by the knowledge that he will be buried naked and unceremoniously in a potter's field; another man sings of his "guest room blues," and a young girl who briefly stays with the Wapshots mistakenly believes that sexual intercourse will end her loneliness. Others, equally desperate, collect antiques or live in castles in a vain attempt to make themselves secure in a bewilderingly changeable world. Leander's vision and vitality keep him from the despair that afflicts these others; as a result, even his death by drowning seems less an end than an affirmation.

Leander, with his "taste for romance and nonsense," is quixotic and exuberant; his wife Sarah, with her "air of wronged nobility," her "habitual reliance on sad conclusions," and his sister Honora, who substitutes philanthropy for love, are strong-willed and sexless. He affirms life; they deny it. Sarah, the town's civic leader, and Honora, the keeper of the Wapshot fortune, uncaringly strip Leander of his usefulness and self-worth (just as Cousin Justina, the reincarnation of Charles Dickens's Miss Havisham, aggressively plots to unman Moses). To some extent they are predatory, but even more they are incomplete because they are in need of someone to love. Similarly, Leander is portrayed as a man not without flaws. He is, like many of Cheever's male characters, impractical and, at times, inattentive to his family; he can also appear childishly petulant, even ridiculous, as in the scene in which he fakes suicide in order to attract attention. More important, he loves and is loved, as the large crowd of mourners at his funeral service attests—much to Honora's surprise.

Whether his sons will fare any better in their relationships with women is left uncertain in this novel. Both marry—Coverly his "sandwich shop Venus" and Moses the beautiful Melissa Scaddon, who plays Estella to Cousin Justina's Miss Havisham. Both, after briefly losing their wives, eventually father sons, thus fulfilling the terms of their inheritance as set by Honora. Melissa and Betsey are, however, tainted, or haunted, by their pasts (in Betsey's case this is only vaguely mentioned). Moreover, most marriages in Cheever's fiction, as in life, are difficult affairs. In sum, the Wapshot boys may yet be greatly disappointed in their expectations. What is more important is the fact that Moses and, more particularly, Coverly build the necessary bridge between past and present, holding firm to what is best in St. Botolphs (as evidenced in Leander's journal) while freeing themselves from that confinement that the town, in part, represents. This optimistic view is confirmed by the novel's lively style. Straight narrative sections alternate with large portions of two Wapshot journals, humorous parodies of biblical language, and frequent direct addresses to the reader. Tragic elements are present but always in muted tones and often undercut with humor. In *The Wapshot Chronicle*, the comic spirit prevails, as well it should in a novel that twice invokes Shakespeare's Prospero, the liberator of Ariel and tamer of Caliban.

THE WAPSHOT SCANDAL

Outwardly, Cheever's first two novels are quite similar in theme, character, and structure. Like *The Wapshot Chronicle*, *The Wapshot Scandal* employs a framing device and interweaves three related stories: Honora's escape to Italy to avoid prosecution for income tax evasion and her return to St. Botolphs, where she promptly starves and drinks herself to death; Coverly and Betsey's life in yet another bland, middle-class housing development, Talifer; and Moses and Melissa's difficult existence in the affluent suburb of Proxmire Manor. Although reviewers generally responded less favorably to the second Wapshot book, finding it too discursive, Cheever has pointed out that both novels were carefully thought out in advance and has described the sequel as "an extraordinarily complex book built upon non sequiturs." Whether it is, as Samuel Coale has argued, Cheever's finest work, because it carefully balances comic and tragic elements, is open to question. More certain is that a considerably darker mood pervades *The Wapshot Scandal*. At the time he began writing it, Cheever told an audience that American life had become abrasive and debased, a kind of hell, and during its four-year composition he became severely depressed. In *The Wapshot Chronicle* the easy-to-answer refrain is "Why did the young want to go away?" but in *The Wapshot Scandal* the repeated question is Coverly's Hamlet-like "Oh, Father, Father, Father, why have you come back?"—a query that accurately gauges the extent of Coverly's and Cheever's disenchantment with a world that no longer seems either inviting or livable for men or ghosts. In the earlier book, Moses and Coverly had to escape the confinement of St. Botolphs; in the sequel, characters have too completely cut themselves off from the usable traditions, comforting stability, and vital, natural light that the town also represents. As a result, the communal center to which earlier Wapshot men had come back and, analogously, the narrative center to which *The Wapshot Chronicle* continually returned, are conspicuously absent from *The Wapshot Scandal*.

In the sequel, St. Botolphs, though by no means idealized, is rendered in less qualified terms, thus more firmly establishing Cheever's preference for its values and his impatience with the rootlessness and shallowness of the modern age. Honora, for example, is now a far more sympathetic figure endowed with two of Leander's most attractive qualities: a belief in ceremony and a love of nature. In the guise of an elderly senator, Cheever carefully distinguishes between the sentimentalizing of the past and the modern tendency to dispense with the past altogether. The modern Prometheus, the senator notes, is technologically powerful, but he lacks "the awe, the humility, that primitive man brought to the sacred fire."

Whereas earlier Wapshot men faced the terrors of the sea, Moses and Coverly face the greater terrors of daily life in the twentieth century: insecurity, boredom, loneliness, loss of usefulness and self-esteem, and the pervasiveness of death. As Cheever shows, the American Dream totters on the brink of nightmare. When one resident of Proxmire Manor suddenly finds her carefree days turn into a series of frozen water pipes, backed-up toilets, exploding furnaces, blown fuses, broken appliances, unopenable packages of bacon, and vacationing repairmen, she turns first to alcohol and promiscuity, then to suicide. The few mourners her husband can convince to attend the funeral are people they had briefly known on various sea cruises who, intuiting her disappointment and recognizing it as their own, burst into tears. Similarly, Melissa Wapshot becomes the Emma Bovary of Proxmire Manor, taking as her lover a delivery boy and eventually fleeing to Italy, where, perversely, she finds some "solace" for her disappointments in the Supra-Marketto Americano in Rome. Moses responds to his wife's infidelity by becoming a wandering alcoholic, and Betsey finds compensation for the wrongs she claims to have suffered by whittling away her husband's small store of self-esteem.

Coverly, now twelve years older than at the beginning of *The Wapshot Chronicle*, serves (as Leander did in the earlier work) as the novel's moral center. He survives, perhaps even prevails, partly because he chooses to follow the best of the past (Leander's advice to his sons) and partly because he adapts to his world without being overwhelmed by it. Trained as a computer programmer, he accepts the computer error that transforms him into a public relations man but resists the apocalyptic mood that infects nearly everyone else in the novel. Unlike Melissa, whose brief illness leads her to cultivate "a ruthless greed for pleasure," Coverly's narrow escape from a hunter's arrow prompts him to "make something illustrious of his life." His computer analysis of John Keats's poetry leads to the creation of new poetry and the realization of a universal harmony underlying not only the poems but also life itself. His brother Moses, whom he has saved for the moment from debauchery, claims to see through the pasteboard mask of Christmas morning to "the nothingness of things." Coverly, on the other hand, celebrates the "dazzling" day by romancing his wife and sharing Christmas dinner with his late aunt's blind guests, "the raw material of human kindness." Coverly's vision, as well as St. Botolphs's brand of decorum as "a guise or mode of hope," is certainly Cheever's own. Even so, that vision is tempered insofar as the author also shares Moses' pessimistic knowledge of decorum's other side: hypocrisy and despair.

BULLET PARK

The contrasting visions of Coverly and Moses reappear as Eliot Nailles and Paul Hammer, the main characters of Cheever's third novel, *Bullet Park*. Nailles is the book's comic and decidedly qualified hero. Like Cheever, he has belonged to a volunteer fire department, loves to saw wood with a chainsaw, feels a kinship with the natural world, and has a realistically balanced view of suburban living as being neither morally perfect nor inherently depraved. While both character and author are optimistic, however, the quality of their optimism differentiates them, for Nailles's is naïve and ludicrously shallow: "Nailles thought of pain and suffering as a principality lying somewhere beyond the legitimate borders of western Europe." Just as Cheever's story "The Death of Justina" satirizes a community determined to defeat death by means of zoning regulations, so *Bullet Park* satirizes Nailles's myopic optimism, which, like St. Paul's faith (Cheever quotes 2 Corinthians 11-12), is sorely tried during the course of the novel.

Beneath the appearance of respectability and comfort in *Bullet Park*, one finds the same unease that afflicts Talifer and Proxmire Manor. There is Mr. Heathcup, who interrupts his annual house painting to kill himself, claiming he could not stand "it" anymore. When Harry Shinglehouse is sucked under a passing express train and killed, only his shoe is found, an ironic memorial to a hollow life. Shaken by this and other reminders of mortality, Nailles turns to drugs. Drug addiction is one of Nailles's escapes; another is the devising of soothing explanations. When asked about his work—he sells Spang mouthwash—Nailles claims to be a chemist. When his son Tony suddenly becomes melancholy and withdraws, Bartleby-fashion, from the outside world, his father, like the lawyer in Herman Melville's tale, rationalizes his son's illness as mononucleosis rather than confront the actual cause: He tried to murder his son when Tony echoed his misgivings about the quality of his life. Neither the father's drugged optimism nor the expensive services of a doctor, a psychiatrist, and a specialist in somnambulatory phenomena effect Tony's cure. That is accomplished by the Swami Rutuola, "a spiritual cheer-leader" whose vision is not altogether different from Nailles's.

The climax of Nailles's dark night of the soul occurs when he defeats his secret antagonist, Hammer, who, as John Leonard suggests, may represent a part of Nailles's own personality. Hammer is the illegitimate son of a wealthy socialist (such ironies abound in

Cheever's fiction) and his name-changing secretary. Unloved and rootless, Hammer is haunted by a vaguely defined canard. To escape it he turns to various pursuits: aimless travel, alcohol, fantasizing, psychoanalysis, translating the pessimistic poetry of Eugenio Montale, and locating a room with yellow walls where, he believes, he will finally be able to lead "a useful and illustrious life." He finds the room, as well as a beautiful wife, but both prove disappointing, and his search for "a useful and illustrious life" continues to elude him. At this point, Hammer adopts the messianic plan formulated by his dissatisfied, expatriate mother: to live quietly in a place like Bullet Park, to single out one of its representative men, and to "crucify him on the door of Christ's Church. . . . Nothing less than a crucifixion will wake that world!" Hammer fails in this, as in his other attempts, mainly for the same reasons he turned to it. One reason is his loneliness; feeling the need for a confidant, he explains his plan to the swami, who, of course, tells Nailles. The other is his having underestimated the depth of love, even in Bullet Park, where homes are associated not with the people who live in them but with real estate: number of bedrooms, number of baths, and market value.

This "simple" book about a father's love for his son greatly pleased its author. A number of reviewers, however, were troubled by the ending, which Guy Davenport called "shockingly inept." In a review that Cheever blames for turning the critical tide against the book, Benjamin DeMott charged that *Bullet Park* was broken-backed, its "parts tacked together." In retrospect, none of the charges appear merited. Cheever's narrative method and "arch"-like form (as he called it) are entirely consistent with his thematic purpose. In part 1, the third-person narration effectively establishes both the author's sympathy for and distance from his protagonist Nailles, whose confused state of mind is reflected in the confused chronology of this section. Part 2, Hammer's journal (the third-person narrator disappears after parenthetically remarking "Hammer wrote"), is the first-person monologue of a quietly desperate madman such as one finds in works by Edgar Allan Poe and Nikolai Gogol. The return to third-person narration in part 3 enables Cheever to use as centers of consciousness each of his two main characters. At the end of the novel, Tony is saved and returns to school, Hammer is sent to a hospital for the criminally insane, "and Nailles— drugged—went off to work and everything was as wonderful, wonderful, wonderful, wonderful as it had been." By undercutting Nailles's triumph without actually dismissing it, Cheever's ending resists those simplistic affirmations and negations that the rest of *Bullet Park* has explored.

FALCONER

The prison setting is the most obvious difference between *Falconer* and Cheever's previous fiction. The more significant difference, however, is the absence of any qualifying irony in its concluding pages. Never has the author's and his protagonist's affirmation been so completely self-assured as in this, Cheever's finest achievement.

Falconer is a story of metaphoric confinement and escape. The realism here serves a larger purpose than verisimilitude; Cheever sketches the essentials of the religious experience and shows how that experience is reflected in a man's retreat from the natural world or in his acceptance of a responsible place in it. The relationship between two brothers (as in the Wapshot books) or two brotherlike figures (*Bullet Park*) is given a violent twist in *Falconer*, where the main character, a forty-eight-year-old college professor named Ezekiel Farragut, has been convicted of fratricide. Farragut's murderous act, as well as his addictions to heroin and methadone, imply his retreat into self, a retreat that is not without some justification—a narcissistic wife, a father who wanted his unborn child aborted, a mother who was hardly maternal, a jealous brother, and the violence of war—but self-pity is the sin Cheever has most frequently assailed. Farragut's task, then, is "to leach self-pity out of his emotional spectrum," and to do this he must learn inside Falconer prison what he failed to learn outside it: how to love.

Farragut's first, humble step away from self-love is the affection he has for his cat, Bandit, whose cunning he must adopt if he is to survive his time in prison and those blows that defeat Moses and Melissa Wapshot. More important is Farragut's relationship with a fellow prisoner, Jody. Neither narcissistic nor regressive, this homosexual affair is plainly shown to further Farragut's movement away from self and, in that from Jody's hideout Farragut is given an expansive view of the world he has lost, it also furthers his movement toward that world and "the invisible potency of nature." Jody teaches the professorial Farragut an important lesson concerning the usefulness of one's environment and the active role that must be assumed in order to effect one's own salvation, one's escape from the metaphoric prison. When Jody escapes from Falconer, the loss of his lover at first leads Farragut back to lonely self-love; directed by another prisoner, the Cuckold, to whose depths of self-pity Farragut could easily descend, Farragut goes to the Valley, a dimly lit lavatory where the prisoners masturbate. Here Farragut has a revelation; he suddenly understands that the target of human sexuality ought not to be an iron trough but "the mysteriousness of the bonded spirit and the flesh."

His continuing escape from useless fantasizing, from nostalgic re-creation of the past, and from passivity causes him to become more self-assured and more interested in the present moment and how to make use of it in realizing his future. The riot at nearby Amana prison (based on the September, 1971, Attica uprising, during which Cheever was teaching at Sing Sing prison) shows that Farragut is actually freer than his jailers, but it is at this point that Farragut overreaches himself. In his view, the Amana riot signals the salvation of all the dispossessed, and to aid himself in hearing the "word," that is, the news reports, Farragut begins to build a contraband radio. He hopes to get a crystal from Bumpo, who had earlier said he would gladly give up his diamond to save someone. Bumpo refuses to give up the crystal, his reason obviously being his own selfishness, yet there is something ridiculous in Farragut's vague plan for sweeping social reform when his own salvation is still in doubt. In the aftermath of his and the rioters' failures, Farragut briefly slips back into self-regarding passivity, from which he is saved by a dying prisoner. In place of the ineffectual and wholly impersonal charity of his plan to save humankind, Farragut takes upon himself the humbler and more truly charitable task of caring for a fellow human being. For the first time, Farragut, prompted by the dying man's question, faces up to the enormity of his crime, making clear to the reader, and perhaps to himself, that in murdering his brother he was unconsciously trying to destroy the worst part of his own personality. The demon exorcised, Farragut becomes spiritually free, a creature of the light.

The visible sign of this freedom is his escape from Falconer in Chicken Number Two's burial box. Borrowing freely from Alexandre Dumas, *père*'s *Le Comte de Monte-Cristo* (1844-1845; *The Count of Monte-Cristo*, 1846), Cheever treats the escape symbolically as a rebirth and a resurrection. The religious theme is effectively underscored by the novel's parable-like ending. Farragut meets a man who, although he has been evicted from his apartment because he is "alive and healthy," remains both cheerful and charitable, offering Farragut a coat, bus fare, and a place to stay. Miracles, it seems, do occur. The step from psychological retreat and spiritual darkness to freedom and light is not difficult to take, Cheever implies; it simply requires commitment and determination. As for the effect of this choice, which is as much Cheever's as Farragut's, that is summed up in the novel's final word: "rejoice."

Falconer recapitulates all of the major themes of Cheever's earlier fiction and, at the same time, evidences a number of significant changes in his art. One is the tendency toward greater narrative compression. Another, related to the first, is the inclusion of ancillary narratives, less as somewhat obtrusive sketches and more as integral parts of the main story line. The third—a more overt treatment of the religious theme—appears to have influenced the characterization, style, and structure of *Falconer*. Although Cheever always considered the novelist one who devotes himself to "enlarging" his peers rather than "diminishing" them, his two middle novels emphasize many of his characters' worst features. *Falconer* represents Cheever's return to the more certain affirmation of *The Wapshot Chronicle*; moreover, *Falconer* is Cheever's most lyrical and least bitingly humorous novel. The religious theme and the harmony it implies may also account for its being the most "novelistic" in structure of the four; this is not to say that Cheever had finally "outgrown" his earlier short-story style and mastered the more demanding form of the novel, for the structure of *The Wapshot Chronicle*, *The Wapshot Scandal*, and *Bullet Park* mirrors Cheever's vision of the 1950's and the 1960's. By the time he wrote *Falconer*, however, that sense of personal and cultural fragmentation no longer dominated his thinking, a change reflected in the relatively tight, more harmonious structure of his most affirmative work.

OH, WHAT A PARADISE IT SEEMS

Oh, What a Paradise It Seems is a slighter but in its own way no less triumphant work. The "bulky novel" that illness forced Cheever to cut short is, though brief, nevertheless remarkably generous in tone and spirit. It is also Cheever's most topical fiction yet strangely his least realistic—a self-regarding, even self-mocking fabulation, a *Walden* for the postmodern age, in which the irony falls as gently as the (acid) rain. Set in a future at once familiar (jogging, for example, has become popular) yet remote (highways with lanes in four digits)—a timeless present, as it were—the novel ends as it begins, by pretending to disclaim its own seriousness: "This is just a story to be read at night in an old house on a rainy night."

Oh, What a Paradise It Seems focuses on the "old but not yet infirm" Lemuel Sears. Twice a widower, Sears is financially well-off (he works for Computer Container Intrusion Systems, maker of "cerbical chips") and is as spiritually as he is sexually inclined. Sears's heart "leaps" in two not altogether different directions. One is toward Beasley's Pond, located near his daughter's home, where he ice-skates and in this way briefly satisfies his desire for fleetness, grace, pastoral innocence, and connectedness with the transcendental world of Emersonian Nature. When family connections (Mafia) and political corruption despoil the scene, however—transmogrifying pastoral pond into town dump—Beasley's Pond comes to symbolize for Sears not only imminent ecological disaster but, more important, the "spiritual vagrancy" of a "nomadic society" whose chief characteristics are "netherness" and "portability."

Sears's attraction to the pond parallels and in a way is offset by his physical attraction to the beautiful Renee Herndon, whose appetite for food and whose work as a real estate broker suggest that, despite the exoticism of her given name and the mysteriousness of her personal life, she represents everything that the prosaically named Beasley's, in its pristine state, does not. In his sexual pursuit of Renee, Sears is persistent to the point of clownishness. After numerous initial triumphs, Sears will eventually be rebuffed and come to see the waywardness of this attempt of his to attain what the pond, Sears's first wife, "the sainted Amelia," and even Renee in her own strange way symbolize, but not before a comical but nevertheless loving interlude with Eduardo, the elevator operator in Renee's apartment building, and a perfectly useless session with a psychiatrist named Palmer, "a homosexual spinster." The small but increasingly prominent part homosexuality plays in each of the novels reflects Cheever's ambivalence concerning his own bisexuality. Comically dismissed in the early works, it becomes in *Falconer* and *Oh, What a Paradise It Seems* viable but, as Cheever would say in a letter to one of his many male lovers, not ultimate.

As in Cheever's other fictions, the narrative here progresses along parallel fronts. Sears's dual lives, the sexual and the transcendental, become entwined in and simultaneously exist alongside those of Horace Chisholm, whose commitment to the environment evidences his longing for purity and human as well as spiritual attachment but also causes him to become estranged from his wife and family. Like Sears, he is also quixotic, which is to say both idealistic and absurd. Thanks to a number of those improbable plot complications that abound in Cheever's fiction, Chisholm, working for Sears to save Beasley's Pond, finds and returns a baby inadvertently left by the roadside after a family outing to the beach. The parents, the Logans, live next door to the Salazzos; Sammy

Salazzo presides over the pond-turned-dump. Chisholm will be welcomed into the Logan family but eventually will be killed by the mob; an angry Betsey Logan will, however, complete his work, stopping the dumping, by threatening to poison the teriyaki sauce in the local Buy Brite supermarkets. (A by-product of her action is that her hated neighbors, the Salazzos, will move away.) Sears, in turn, will utilize the latest technology to restore the pond to its original state, thus redeeming himself as well.

Cheever's ending is self-consciously "happy"—aware of its own improbability. It is, like the architecture of Hitching Post Lane where the Logans and the Salazzos live, "all happy ending—all greeting card." Cheever's satire is more than offset by his compassion, however—his recognition of and sympathy for the waywardness of the continuing human search for both home and wholeness.

Robert A. Morace

OTHER MAJOR WORKS

SHORT FICTION: *The Way Some People Live*, 1943; *The Enormous Radio, and Other Stories*, 1953; "The Country Husband," 1954; *The Housebreaker of Shady Hill, and Other Stories*, 1958; *Some People, Places, and Things That Will Not Appear in My Next Novel*, 1961; *The Brigadier and the Golf Widow*, 1964; *The World of Apples*, 1973; *The Stories of John Cheever*, 1978; *Thirteen Uncollected Stories*, 1994.

TELEPLAY: *The Shady Hill Kidnapping*, 1982.

NONFICTION: *The Letters of John Cheever*, 1988 (Benjamin Cheever, editor); *The Journals of John Cheever*, 1991; *Glad Tidings, a Friendship in Letters: The Correspondence of John Cheever and John D. Weaver, 1945-1982*, 1993.

BIBLIOGRAPHY

Bosha, Francis J., ed. *The Critical Response to John Cheever*. Westport, Conn.: Greenwood Press, 1994. Collection presents representative criticism of all of Cheever's fiction, beginning with the earliest reviews in 1943, with individual chapters devoted to each of his works. Also includes several essays written for this collection and an interview with Cheever conducted a year before he died. Supplemented with bibliography and index.

Byrne, Michael D., Dale Salwak, and Paul David Seldis, eds. *Dragons and Martinis: The Skewed Realism of John Cheever*. San Bernardino, Calif.: Borgo Press, 1993. Collection of essays focuses on Cheever's style in his fiction. Includes bibliographical references and index.

Cheever, Susan. *Home Before Dark*. Boston: Houghton Mifflin, 1984. Memoir by Cheever's daughter fleshes out what was known previously about his troubled early years and provides an insider's look at his marital and other personal difficulties (alcoholism, illnesses, sexual desires). Suffers from lack of documentation and indexing. More valuable as a synthesis of previously published material than as a daughter's intimate revelations.

Coale, Samuel. *John Cheever.* New York: Frederick Ungar, 1977. Good introductory work includes a brief biography, two chapters on selected short stories, and individual chapters on Cheever's first four novels. Focuses on the development of Cheever's style, from realism to fantasy, and concern for moral issues.

Collins, Robert G., ed. *Critical Essays on John Cheever.* Boston: G. K. Hall, 1982. Reprints an excellent sampling of reviews, interviews, and early criticism. Also presents some previously unpublished pieces, among which the most useful are Collins's biocritical introduction, Dennis Coale's bibliographical supplement, and Samuel Coale's "Cheever and Hawthorne: The American Romancer's Art," arguably one of the most important critical essays on Cheever.

Donaldson, Scott. *John Cheever: A Biography.* New York: Random House, 1988. Scrupulously researched, interestingly written, and judiciously argued biography presents Cheever as both author and private man. Fills in most of the areas in Cheever's biography that were previously unknown and dispels many of the biographical myths that Cheever himself encouraged. A sympathetic yet objective account.

_____, ed. *Conversations with John Cheever.* Jackson: University Press of Mississippi, 1987. Until his final years a rather reticent man, Cheever granted relatively few interviews. The most important ones are reprinted here, along with the editor's thorough chronology and brief but useful introduction.

Meanor, Patrick. *John Cheever Revisited.* New York: Twayne, 1995. First book-length study of Cheever to make use of his journals and letters published in the late 1980's and early 1990's. Focuses on how Cheever created a mythopoeic world in his novels and stories. Includes three chapters analyzing the Wapshot novels, *Bullet Park*, *Oh, What a Paradise It Seems*, and *Falconer.*

Waldeland, Lynne. *John Cheever.* Boston: Twayne, 1979. Introductory volume lacks the thematic coherence of Samuel Coale's work (cited above), but it has greater breadth and evidences a greater awareness of previous critical commentary.

MICHELLE CLIFF

Born: Kingston, Jamaica; November 2, 1946

OTHER LITERARY FORMS

In addition to being a novelist, Michelle Cliff is a poet, essayist, short-story writer, and literary critic. Her first writing was a response to an article about Jamaica that, in her opinion, contained inaccuracies. In her poems, short stories, and essays, she portrays the "real" Jamaica and what it is like to be Jamaican. A collection of her essays, *If I Could Write This in Fire*, was published in 2008. Cliff examines oppression, lost oral history, and sexual and racial prejudice, and she addresses the importance of revising official history. Her novels treat these same issues and concerns.

ACHIEVEMENTS

Michelle Cliff is recognized as one of the most significant writers of fiction exploring the complex issues of race, color, sexual orientation, and feminism as well as the postcolonial concerns of identity and heritage for people of mixed race. She has played a critical role in revealing the "other," or unofficial, history in her novels, and in a sense has been rewriting history. Cliff also is respected as a literary critic. In 1982, she received a fellowship from the National Endowment for the Arts and a fellowship for study at MacDowell College. In 1984, she won a Massachusetts Artists Foundation award and was named an Eli Kantor Fellow.

BIOGRAPHY

Michelle Cliff, the daughter of an American father and a Jamaican mother, was born on November 2, 1946, in Kingston, Jamaica. A light-skinned Creole, she was born into a mixed-race family that valued lightness of skin and continually insisted that she pass for white. This pressure to reject her Creole and black heritage has influenced her writing. During her childhood and adolescence, Cliff lived in Jamaica and the United States. Her family moved to the United States when she was three years old. She remained in Jamaica with other family members for some time, but she later joined the family in a Caribbean neighborhood of New York City. During the 1940's and early 1950's, Cliff often returned to Jamaica with her family for short visits; in 1956, when she was ten years old, she returned to Jamaica to attend boarding school.

After graduating from secondary school, Cliff returned to the United States and studied at Wagner College. She received a bachelor of arts degree in 1969 and then became involved in politics, including the feminist movement. She also was an active opponent of the war in Vietnam. After graduating from college, she worked in the publishing field as a reporter, researcher, and editor. She completed a master of philosophy degree in 1974 and received a doctorate from the Wartburg Institute at the University of London.

Although Cliff had been attracted to a classmate while at an all-female boarding school in Jamaica, it was during her residency in England that she realized she was lesbian. In 1976, she began a long-term relationship with American poet Adrienne Rich. That same year, Cliff began writing poetry and published her first book in that genre: *Claiming an Identity They Taught Me to Despise* (1980). From 1981 to 1983, she and Rich coedited *Sinister Wisdom*, a multicultural lesbian journal. In 1985, Cliff published another collection, *The Land of Look Behind: Prose and Poetry*.

In 1985, Cliff published her first novel, *Abeng*, which draws upon her multiracial and multicultural heritage. Her second novel, *No Telephone to Heaven*, is a sequel to *Abeng*. She began writing short stories, which were first published in *Bodies of Water* (1990). In 1993, she published her third novel, *Free Enterprise*. In 1998, she published her second collection of short stories, *The Store of a Million Items*. Cliff has had several university teaching positions as well.

ANALYSIS

Michelle Cliff writes about Jamaica and the tightly structured society of the island. She addresses problems inherent to a postcolonial culture, including prejudice, oppression, class structure, the devaluing of women, and the lost history—especially oral history—of the oppressed. Although her novels are not truly autobiographical, much of what the character Clare confronts in *Abeng* and *No Telephone to Heaven* is a reflection of her own experiences growing up in Jamaica and the United States and in living in England as a university student. Her novels display an ever-present consciousness of skin color, which is closely connected to identity, but for Cliff, the color of one's skin is both a means of identity and a means of losing identity.

Cliff's stories depict a society in which each person's place is determined by his or her skin color. This caste system is accepted simply as "the way it is." In the prejudicial thinking of her characters, skin color not only indicates certain flaws but also virtues. In *Abeng*, the character Mattie Freeman, Clare's grandmother, knows who she is. She is a Maroon, a red-skinned woman with a history that traces to Nanny, the Maroon resistor to slavery. Nanny had magical powers and spiritual insights no colonial would ever enjoy. Boy Savage, in contrast, has lost a part of his identity through his rejection of his color ancestry and his insistence on passing for white.

Language plays an important role in Cliff's novels as well. The language spoken by a character is an identifier of that character. In *Abeng*, when Clare is at her grandmother's farm with Zoe, her dark-skinned "friend," she speaks patois, which is forbidden in her middle-class existence in Kingston. For Cliff, Jamaican patois is just as viable a language as Standard English, and it is critical for readers without knowledge of patois to understand the meanings of the words. *No Telephone to Heaven* includes a glossary of patois words used in the novel.

Oral history and ethnic-specific stories, which rarely are included in the "official" accounts of the past, are integral to Cliff's novels. The novels are multilayered and create a sort of international tapestry of the history of oppressed and marginalized individuals and ethnic groups. The story of Nanny, the Maroon woman who refused to accept slavery and led her people in rebellion, is recounted or referred to in *Abeng, No Telephone to Heaven*, and *Free Enterprise*. In *Free Enterprise*, additional oral histories are told by minor characters.

Cliff extends this multilayering into the names she gives to her characters and to her novels. *Abeng* is an African word for conch shell. The conch shell served two purposes during the colonial period: It called slaves to the cane fields and was used by the Maroons to pass messages to one another. *Free Enterprise* refers both to the free enterprise of dealing in slaves in a capitalist market and to the enterprise of the main characters of the novel, resisters of slavery, and their freely entering into the fight.

Cliff writes her novels in a rich lyrical style reminiscent of her prose poems. Her descriptions of the Jamaican countryside are colorful and reflect the bond between the Maroons and nature. Jamaica becomes real for the reader with its mangoes, its tropical foliage, cane fields, and sun-drenched red earth.

ABENG

Abeng is the story of Clare Savage, a young girl growing up in a complex multicultural world. It is a world fraught with oppression, rejection, and denial. Her family belongs to the Jamaican middle class. Her father, James Arthur "Boy" Savage, is a light-skinned man of white-black ancestry who rejects his black heritage and insists upon passing for white. He takes pride in his white colonial ancestry, which traces back to Judge Savage, one of the most of brutal slave owners. Her mother, Kitty Savage, is a Maroon, or red-skinned, woman who is deeply attached to her color ancestry. Clare has one sister; she is younger than Clare and darker-skinned.

Boy and Kitty are an intriguing and often incomprehensible couple. They remain separate and contradictory. On Sunday mornings, the family goes to Boy's church, the John Knox Memorial Church. On Sunday evenings, they go to Kitty's church, the Tabernacle of the Almighty. They both consider Clare, the light-skinned daughter, to be Boy's child and the dark-skinned younger sister to be Kitty's child. The husband and wife have almost nothing in common and argue bitterly, which frightens Clare.

Clare spends summers in the country with Miss Mattie, her maternal grandmother. Although Miss Mattie was born after the freeing of the slaves, she had worked in the cane fields and remembers the harsh treatment by the overseers and how the cane cut her legs.

She no longer cuts cane, and is now a landowner. She is not of the same social class as the light-skinned Jamaicans; she is higher on the social scale as a landowner. Known for her kindness, she lets Miss Ruthie, a market woman, live on her land and raise produce to sell. Miss Ruthie has a daughter named Zoe, who becomes Clare's playmate. Miss Ruthie constantly warns Zoe not to get too involved with Clare because they are different and cannot really be friends. Clare is a *buckra*, a white-skinned person, who is not to be trusted.

The twelve-year-old Clare does not understand why so many things are the way they are. She enjoys the country, the lifestyle, and the connection with her mother's heritage. She has no comprehension of the necessity of not breaking the rules of her society. She resents the greater freedom afforded to the boys; she does not understand why she is admonished for considering Zoe her friend and equal. Then, one day, Clare breaks every rule that governs her life as a middle-class Jamaican female. She takes Miss Mattie's gun and sets out with Zoe to hunt Cudjoe, a legendary wild boar. Climbing to his lair proves too difficult, so they abandon the hunt and go for a swim in the river. Sunbathing nude, Clare is physically attracted to her forbidden friend. They are surprised by male cane cutters and become frightened. Clare fires the gun. The bullet ricochets and kills her grandmother's bull, Old Joe.

Clare admits to killing Miss Mattie's bull, but she is given no chance to explain how and why it happened. Her parents take her to Miss Beatrice, a widow who has buried all of her children. Kitty tells her daughter that Miss Beatrice will teach her how to be a "proper lady" so she can make something of herself. However, in the presence of Miss Beatrice, Clare also learns more about prejudice, oppression, and cruelty. She witnesses Miss Beatrice's harsh treatment of the elderly Minnie Bogle, a black woman who is hired to clean the dog feces from her yard. Miss Beatrice often strikes Minnie with her cane.

Miss Beatrice brings Clare to see her sister, who is considered mad. Clare is told not to talk to her, but the independent and rebellious Clare does. She learns what happens when she says "coons" and *buckras* mix. The sister tells Clare that as a young girl, she had a baby by a black man who worked for her family. She insists that what she did was wrong, and that her family was right in sending her to a convent. The sister has spent her life trying to expiate her sin.

The novel ends with Clare dreaming of fighting with Zoe, with blood trickling down Zoe's face and her apologizing and treating the wound. Awakening, Clare goes outside and discovers she is experiencing her first menstrual cycle. Clare is leaving the world of childhood and the magic of the Jamaican countryside and her summers with Zoe. In *No Telephone to Heaven*, she will deal with her fight to find her identity as an adult.

FREE ENTERPRISE

Free Enterprise is a novel of resistance and reclamation, the story of Annie Christmas and Mary Ellen Pleasant (M. E. P.), two women with black ancestry, who are dedicated to the abolition of slavery in the United States. Cliff draws upon the many stereotypes that envelop M. E. P. in official histories to present her in the novel as a powerful and determined individual who is feared by white society. She is very dark-skinned and uses her blackness to become a successful businesswoman in San Francisco. By being what white society expects her to be, a black madam catering to rich white men, she acquires money, which she uses to fund the abolitionist movement. Annie, in contrast to M. E. P., is light-skinned and is victimized by the white society she challenges.

Free Enterprise centers on the failure of John Brown's raid on Harper's Ferry, Virginia, in 1859. Through fortuitous circumstances, M. E. P., who was present at the raid, slips away from Harper's Ferry and returns to San Francisco. She remains active in the abolitionist movement and works for the rights of black citizens after the American Civil War. Annie is denied such good fortune. She is captured and put on a confederate chain gang. She disguises herself as a man but is soon discovered to be a woman. She becomes an amusement for her captors as a collar is placed around her neck. She is forced into sexual acts with male prisoners, while the captors watch. Annie is devastated. She had left the Caribbean to avoid being the mistress of a rich white man. She is emotionally and physically "broken," and she does not have the fortitude to continue actively in the fight. She retreats to Mississippi, where she lives a hermetical life.

Cliff also examines the lack of freedom of women regardless of their skin color. The secondary story of Alice and Clover Hooper, white abolitionists, elucidates the common bond of denial of freedom that unites all women. In their upper-class society, Alice and Clover are not free to speak their minds or pursue a career. They dream of going West and freeing themselves from male domination.

Shawncey Webb

OTHER MAJOR WORKS

SHORT FICTION: *Bodies of Water*, 1990; *The Store of a Million Items*, 1998.

NONFICTION: *If I Could Write This in Fire*, 2008 (essays).

EDITED TEXT: *The Winner Names the Age: A Collection of Writing by Lillian Smith*, 1978.

MISCELLANEOUS: *Claiming an Identity They Taught Me to Despise*, 1980 (prose and poetry); *The Land of Look Behind: Prose and Poetry*, 1985; *If I Could Write This in Fire*, 2008.

BIBLIOGRAPHY

Adisa, Opal Palmer. "Journey into Speech: Writer Between Two Worlds—An Interview with Michelle Cliff." *African American Review* 28, no. 2 (1994). In this special issue on black women's culture, essays explore Cliff's work on race and oppression in Jamaica and her ideas on resistance as a form of community and the significant role of women in the history of political resistance.

Browdy de Hernandez, Jennifer. *Women Writing Resistance: Essays on Latin America and the Caribbean*. Cambridge, Mass.: South End Press, 2003. Cliff is one of eighteen women whose work—including their writing—against all forms of oppression is examined in this book. The focus is on Latin American and Caribbean women who have used literature and other creative works to resist the political regimes of the countries in which they were born.

Edmondson, Belinda. "Race, Privilege, and the Politics of (Re)Writing History: An Analysis of the Novels of Michelle Cliff" *Callaloo* 16, no. 1 (1993): 180-191. A useful study of how Cliff seeks out obscure events of history and reworks those histories to include factors of race and oppression.

Elia, Nada. *Trances, Dances, and Vociferations: Agency and Resistance in Africana Women's Narratives*. New York: Garland, 2001. Examines Cliff's use of alternative and oral history, sexual disguise, and racial passing in her work. Chapter 3 is an analysis of the character Annie Christmas from *Free Enterprise*. Includes a bibliography.

Hudson, Lynn M. *The Making of Mammy Pleasant: A Black Entrepreneur in Nineteenth-Century San Francisco*. Urbana: University of Illinois Press, 2003. Contrasts Cliff's portrayal of M. E. P. with that character's portrayal in the novels of others.

MICHAEL CUNNINGHAM

Born: Cincinnati, Ohio; November 6, 1952

<small>PRINCIPAL LONG FICTION</small>
Golden States, 1984
A Home at the End of the World, 1990
Flesh and Blood, 1995
The Hours, 1998
Specimen Days, 2005

<small>OTHER LITERARY FORMS</small>

Michael Cunningham edited and wrote the introduction for *Laws for Creations* (2006), a collection of poems by Walt Whitman. Cunningham has also published short stories that have appeared in several well-known literary magazines. His story "The Destruction Artist" appeared in *A Memory, a Monologue, a Rant, and a Prayer* (2007), a collection edited by Eve Ensler and Mollie Doyle. With Susan Minot, Cunningham cowrote a screenplay adapted from Minot's novel *Evening* (1998), which subsequently became a 2007 film release. Cunningham also has written introductions or afterwords for new editions of works by such authors as Thomas Mann, Henry James, and Virginia Woolf.

<small>ACHIEVEMENTS</small>

In 1999, Michael Cunningham received the Pulitzer Prize for fiction and the PEN/Faulkner Award for his novel *The Hours*. He also received the Whiting Writers' Award (1995), a Guggenheim Fellowship (1993), a National Endowment for the Arts Fellowship (1988), and a Michener Fellowship from the University of Iowa (1982). His short fiction has been published widely, including in *The New Yorker*, *The Atlantic Monthly*, and *The Paris Review*. Cunningham's story "White Angel," taken from his novel *A Home at the End of the World*, was chosen for the Best American Short Stories series in 1989. Another short story, "Mister Brother," appeared in the O. Henry Awards' Prize Stories collection of 1999.

<small>BIOGRAPHY</small>

Michael Cunningham was born in Cincinnati, Ohio, and raised in La Cañada, Southern California. He earned his bachelor's degree in English literature from Stanford University and his master of fine arts (M.F.A.) degree from the University of Iowa. A gay man partnered for several years, Cunningham defies definition as a "gay author." While gay characters and themes are part of his novels, they do not serve as the prism through which his novels are viewed. Cunningham has taught at the Fine Arts Work Center in Provincetown, Massachusetts, and in the M.F.A. creative-writing program at Brooklyn College. He also has taught writing in formal courses and in workshops around the world.

ANALYSIS

Two of Michael Cunningham's early works, *A Home at the End of the World* and *Flesh and Blood*, focus on family, the need for community and connections, and the obligations inherent in belonging. *The Hours*, his most celebrated novel, is a well-crafted three-dimensional gem. Flawless in design, it holds up to close inspection and presents a sturdy structure, like a pyramid. Cunningham's appreciation for form helps him to reimagine Virginia Woolf's perhaps finest novel, *Mrs. Dalloway* (1925). He reconstitutes the novel into a story of three women, in three equal parts. Incidentally, *The Hours* was Woolf's working title for *Mrs. Dalloway.*

Critics wondered if Cunningham could do for Whitman with his next novel, *Specimen Days*, what he did for Woolf with *The Hours*. This question was asked and apparently answered by reviewers of *Specimen Days*, which takes its title from Whitman's autobiographical collection *Specimen Days and Collect* (1882-1883). While Lev Grossman of *Time* proclaimed Cunningham's book "one of the most luminous and penetrating novels to appear" in 2005, critic Theo Tait, writing in *New Statesman*, observed, "*Specimen Days* is as muddled, and as silly, as it sounds." *The Hours, Specimen Days*, and *A Home at the End of the World* have a common structure: limited perspectives and alternating chapters or novella-like sections that ultimately connect, often to the reader's surprise and amusement. The novels reveal a unity, a coming together, an underlying theme.

A HOME AT THE END OF THE WORLD

This work, to use the author's words, is an examination of the difference between what can be imagined and what can actually exist. *A Home at the End of the World* is the story of two men, Bobby and Jonathan, who are growing up together in Cleveland, Ohio. Their stories intermingle, and Cunningham takes turns narrating their lives, documenting their friendship, and lamenting their losses.

Jonathan is gay. His mother, Alice, is a whiz in the kitchen, and his father, Ned, operates a failing movie theater. An only surviving child, Jonathan adores his father and cherishes his mother while trying to understand his sexual feelings. His best friend and first real love is Bobby, a man-child whose older, rebellious, idolized brother died suddenly and tragically. Bobby's family was decimated by the death; his mother was driven to suicide and his father became an empty suit who drank himself into a nightly stupor. Bobby was alone, a young drug addict confused about adulthood, about sex, and about women. He loved music, especially Van Morrison and Jimi Hendrix or any artist of the Woodstock generation. Bobby inherited his dead brother's rebel mantle and his record collection. Bobby's whole life could be summed up by the lyrics of a Crosby, Stills, Nash, and Young or Buffalo Springfield song. Too young to have participated in the culture of the 1960's, his attitude and personality are frozen in tribute to its memory.

Jonathan has an active love life, relishing his freedom and sleeping with multiple partners. Living in New York City, he rooms with Clare. Clare is an older woman, once divorced and once the lover of a female celebrity, and now childless and living off a trust fund but estranged from her family. She clings to Jonathan and they joke about having a baby. Jonathan's favorite lover is a man named Erich, a would-be actor who tends bar and makes Jonathan happy. The two men share a strictly physical intimacy and never grow together emotionally. They take from one another passion without giving comfort.

In addition to Bobby and Jonathan, Alice and Clare also are narrators in the book, though they are never the center of the story. The story always revolves around the relationship between Bobby and Jonathan, even when they are apart. Alice worries about Jonathan, knowing that he is gay and not wanting to know any particulars. She wishes Jonathan would find a love of his own, not one shared with Bobby, Clare, and their daughter Rebecca.

After Ned's death, Alice moves on with her life, still hoping for a chance at happiness. Though Jonathan swears that Rebecca is as much his daughter as she is Bobby's or Clare's, Alice tells him otherwise. She knows Clare will never leave her baby to be raised by Jonathan and Bobby, even if they love Rebecca just as much as Clare does.

Erich visits Jonathan and his family. It has been several years, and Erich looks different. He is living with AIDS. The country life, a home away from the bright lights, the noise, and congestion of the city, appeals to Erich. After a weekend visit, he is invited back. Regular visits become an extended stay, and it becomes clear that Erich will eventually die in the country house.

Clare acts as a mother, protecting her child. She lies and leaves, severing her ties with her best friend Jonathan and with Bobby, the father of her child. This is the point in the story where what is imagined and what can be done part ways. It is a lovely thought to imagine that three adults and one child can be a family, and that the family can expand to accommodate a dying man with no loved ones to comfort him in his last days. While each character in *A Home at the End of the World* can achieve a measure of peace, that peace does not mean a shared vision.

THE HOURS

This novel resembles a trip to a carnival's house of mirrors. However, instead of seeing one's self, one sees multiple images of Woolf reflected everywhere. Carefully constructed, *The Hours* is, in an important way, like *A Home at the End of the World* in that they both utilize multiple narrators, each narrator providing a vital part of the book's larger story. *The Hours* features four women: Virginia Woolf, Laura Brown, Clarissa Vaughan, and Clarissa Dalloway. Only the first three characters are narrators. The fourth character, the protagonist of Woolf's novel, is represented, to some degree, by the other three women.

Each woman is living at a different time and in a different place from the others. The novel is set during a period of one day only. Woolf appears as she was in 1941, the year she killed herself. She is hoping to move from Richmond, England, where she is recovering her health, to London, where she longs to live and work. Brown is living just a few years later, in 1949, after the war and during a time when the American Dream, especially in sunny California, abounds. Finally, Clarissa Vaughan's story is set in late twentieth century New York City.

In the book's prologue, Woolf is nearing the end of her life. She is walking toward the river, loading her pockets with heavy rocks, and wading in to her death. She reappears in later chapters, alive once more, as she documents her troubled life and her work on *Mrs. Dalloway* in the early 1920's. She is visited by her older sister, Vanessa, and her children. Woolf is both mentally tough and emotionally fragile, and she hopes to convince her husband, Leonard, that her recovery is going well, and that she is strong enough to move back to London.

The first chapter of *The Hours* begins with the story of Mrs. Dalloway, though she is not Woolf's Mrs. Dalloway. In *The Hours*, she is Clarissa Vaughan, who is nicknamed Mrs. Dalloway by her former lover, Richard, who is dying from AIDS. Mrs. Dalloway is organizing a dinner party in Richard's honor; he has been recognized recently for his life's work as an author and poet. The party is set for the evening, and there are many details to attend to, including buying flowers, checking with the caterer, and dealing with last-minute uninvited guests, such as the insufferable Walter. A successful writer as well, Walter is nevertheless disrespected and disliked by Richard. Another uninvited guest is the emotional Lewis, another of Richard's former lovers, who still carries a torch for him and resents Mrs. Dalloway for "stealing" Richard from him.

The third narrator of *The Hours*, Laura Brown, is also attending to party plans. It is her husband's birthday. She is baking him a cake, and it has to be perfect. His birthday is set for today, and everything must be ready when he comes home. Laura would rather be in her bedroom reading, coincidentally, Woolf's *Mrs. Dalloway*. Laura would like her life to be more satisfying, more rewarding. Her husband and her young son Richie; her house in the suburbs; and her pregnancy all leave something to be desired by her, a hole of some sort. Her personality mirrors Woolf's own.

The Hours represents time that must be filled, whether one is happy, sad, emotionally crippled, or dying of AIDS. As long as one lives and breathes, the hours stretch on and must be endured. The uncertainty of release, the waiting for deliverance, haunts those who exist only to serve time.

SPECIMEN DAYS

If the universe were repeating patterns, if spirits were immortal, if these spirits kept finding one another over and over again through the ages, then *Specimen Days* would reflect reality and not fantasy. The novel's structure is familiar: All the characters in all the stories within the novel are tied together.

Specimen Days is divided into three stories or parts. In the first part we meet Lucas, a deformed young man who has memorized Whitman's *Leaves of Grass* and spouts lines from the poet's work at times when normal conversational give-and-take would suit him better. Lucas has recently lost his older brother, Simon, in a factory accident. He was mauled by a machine. The story is set at the dawn of the Industrial Revolution. Simon was to be married to Catherine, who works long hours as a seamstress in what would today be considered a sweatshop. Lucas, Simon, and Catherine, or versions of them, meet again and again throughout the story.

There are other common threads in the novel. Whitman appears in all the stories—as himself in the first and then through surrogates in the later stories. A china bowl with strange markings appears in all three stories, as well, and is usually sold by a woman named Gaya who also appears (or her descendants appear) in all three stories. Other than by helping to tie the three stories or parts together, Gaya and the china bowl do not seem to have greater meanings.

The second part of the novel is easily the strongest of the three. This story reads like a police procedural, with boys strapping pipe bombs to their bodies and then detonating the bombs as they hug random passersby on the streets of New York. Cat is now a police profiler, talking to the sick and twisted callers who phone her to make threats. Simon, her boyfriend, is a futures trader who collects art objects and tries to soothe Cat's frayed nerves. Cat has lost a child, Luke, to cancer. She has left her first husband and she blames herself for her son's death.

It turns out the boys with bombs have been raised by a woman they call Walt. The boys are lost, claimed by Walt as orphans. The boys have no names or identities, and no families. The home they share with Walt is pasted with pages from *Leaves of Grass*. The pages cover the ceilings and are even pasted over the windows.

Cat reaches out to the last of these three boys after finding that she is his intended target. In the process of negotiating with the boy for her life, she becomes part of his underground world. She learns there are other like-minded boys in other cities, all loosely connected and united in a cause to end civilization so that it may be started anew.

The novel's third story is set in "Old New York," a theme park located where New York City once stood. Simon is an automaton who works for a company called Dangerous Adventures. He is programmed to offer tourists lifelike experiences of the real New York City. For a price, he provides a level of terror mixed with sleaziness to the men or women who purchase his time. Simon's world is controlled by monitors, drones that fly and take pictures and come complete with laser weapons. The drones are the tools of the larger company that owns Old New York, and part of their everyday routine is to destroy faulty automatons such as Simon and his friend Marcus.

Catareen is an alien, a Nadian. The Nadians resemble reptiles, complete with narrow eyeballs, flaring nostrils, and claws. The Nadians, however, are not a warrior species. They have been transported to Earth from their native planet, where the terrain is unforgiving, the sky is perpetually dim, and the air is always dank. Catareen lives in Old New York and works as a nanny to human children.

Randy L. Abbott

OTHER MAJOR WORKS

SCREENPLAYS: *A Home at the End of the World*, 2004 (based on his novel); *Evening*, 2007 (with Susan Minot; based on Minot's novel).

NONFICTION: *I Am Not This Body: Photographs*, 2001 (photographs by Barbara Ess); *Land's End: A Walk Through Provincetown*, 2002.

EDITED TEXT: *Laws for Creations*, 2006 (by Walt Whitman).

BIBLIOGRAPHY

Hughes, Mary Joe. "Michael Cunningham's *The Hours* and Postmodern Artistic Re-Presentation." *Critique* 45, no. 4 (Summer, 2004): 349-361. Examines Cunningham's retelling, or re-presentation, of an earlier postmodern novel for his own work, *The Hours*.

Johnson, Sarah Anne. *The Very Telling: Conversations with American Writers*. Hanover, N.H.: University Press of New England, 2006. Features a frank interview with Cunningham, who discusses the craft of writing and how he came to write many of his novels, including *Specimen Days* and *The Hours*. Includes a bibliography.

Peregrin, Tony. "Michael Cunningham After Hours." *Gay and Lesbian Review Worldwide* 10, no. 2 (March-April, 2003): 30-31. Discusses Cunningham's novel, *The Hours*, the screen adaptation of the novel, and plans for future projects.

Schiff, James. "Rewriting Woolf's *Mrs. Dalloway*: Homage, Sexual Identity, and the Single-Day Novel by Cunningham, Lippincott, and Lanchester." *Critique* 45, no. 4 (Summer, 2004): 363-382. A study of three novels, including Cunningham's *The Hours*, which present variations on Virginia Woolf's novel, *Mrs. Dalloway*.

Young, Tory. *Michael Cunningham's "The Hours": A Reader's Guide*. New York: Continuum, 2003. Part of the Continuum Contemporaries series, this brief guide is especially useful for beginning readers of Cunningham's best-known novel.

JEAN GENET

Born: Paris, France; December 19, 1910
Died: Paris, France; April 15, 1986

PRINCIPAL LONG FICTION

Notre-Dame des Fleurs, 1944, 1951 (*Our Lady of the Flowers*, 1949)
Miracle de la rose, 1946, 1951 (*Miracle of the Rose*, 1966)
Pompes funèbres, 1947, 1953 (*Funeral Rites*, 1968)
Querelle de Brest, 1947, 1953 (*Querelle of Brest*, 1966)

OTHER LITERARY FORMS

Jean Genet opened his literary career with a small group of highly personal lyric poems, beginning with "Le Condamné à mort" ("The Man Condemned to Death"). His poems are collected in *Poèmes* (1948) as well as in the later collections *Treasures of the Night* (1980) and *The Complete Poems* (2001).

Genet published several plays, including *Les Bonnes* (pr. 1947, revised pr., pb. 1954; *The Maids*, 1954), *Haute Surveillance* (pr., pb. 1949, definitive edition pb. 1963; *Deathwatch*, 1954), *Le Balcon* (pb. 1956, revised pb. 1962; *The Balcony*, 1957), *Les Nègres: Clownerie* (pb. 1958; *The Blacks: A Clown Show*, 1960), and *Les Paravents* (pr., pb. 1961; *The Screens*, 1962). A so-called autobiography, *Journal du voleur* (1948, 1949; *The Thief's Journal*, 1954), contains probably more allegory than fact, but it remains an important source of information on the early years of Genet's life. Genet's nonfiction includes essays on the philosophy of art, such as "L'Atelier d'Alberto Giacometti" ("Giacometti's Studio") of 1957 and "Le Funambule" ("The Funambulists") of 1958, and essays dealing with dramatic theory, of which the most important by far is the "Lettre à Pauvert sur les bonnes," an open letter to the publisher Jean-Jacques Pauvert written in 1954 including letters to Roger Blin (collected as *Lettres à Roger Blin*, 1966; *Letters to Roger Blin*, 1969) and various prefaces to his own plays. Genet also wrote a series of sociopolitical broadsheets, beginning with "L'Enfant criminel" ("The Child-Criminal") of 1949 and leading to a sequence of pamphlets in defense of the Black Panthers (perhaps epitomized in his "May-Day Speech" of 1968) and of the Palestinians.

ACHIEVEMENTS

In any attempt to assess Jean Genet's achievement as a novelist, it is essential to separate his qualities as a writer from what might be termed the "sociological" aspect of his subject matter. Though the two interact, in the critical period between 1945 and 1965 it was the nonliterary import of his work that predominated. Genet's name came to be synonymous with the growing demand of the post-World War II generation to read what it wanted to read and to learn the truth about the less palatable aspects of the human condi-

Jean Genet
(Library of Congress)

tion, regardless of what a paternalistic censorship might decide was good for it.

In this attempt to break through the barriers of what now seems like an antiquated obscurantism but what until the late twentieth century was a powerful and deeply rooted social attitude, Genet did not stand alone. In this respect, he trod in the footsteps of James Joyce and D. H. Lawrence, of Marcel Proust and Jean Cocteau; among his contemporaries, Norman Mailer, Henry Miller, and Vladimir Nabokov were inspired by similar aims. The battle over Lawrence's *Lady Chatterley's Lover* (1928) was fought and won in 1961; behind the writers stood a small group of publishers (Grove Press in New York, Gallimard in Paris, Rowohlt-Verlag in Hamburg, Anthony Blond in London) who were prepared to fight their cases through the courts. In comparison with many of his contemporaries, Genet had one distinct advantage: He wrote in French. French censorship allowed greater latitude to "clandestine" publications (usually in the form of "limited editions," available to subscribers only) than did that of other countries. This same censorship turned a blind eye to books that, although published in France, were in languages other than French (hence the fact that Genet's earliest translator, Bernard Frechtman, lived and worked in Paris). The French magistrates presiding at censorship trials had always at the back of their minds the specter of that guffaw of disbelieving ridicule that still echoes over their predecessors, who, within the space of half a dozen years, had condemned as "immoral" both Gustave Flaubert's *Madame Bovary* (1857) and Charles Baudelaire's *Les Fleurs du mal* (1857, 1861, 1868).

As a result, Genet, who never once resorted to anonymity or sought to disguise who or what he was, was able to appear in print with material whose publication would have been inconceivable at that time in other societies or under other conditions. It was at this point that the quality, both of his writing and of his thought, became significant, for it won over to his cause a group of eminent figures who would scarcely have bothered to jeopardize their own reputations by championing a mere "pornographer." Thus, in 1950, when the prestigious firm Gallimard decided to risk publishing Genet's four novels (expurgated remarkably lightly) together with a selection of the early poems, the editors were able to call upon Jean-Paul Sartre, the leading intellectual of his generation, to write an introduction. This introduction, moreover, which appeared in 1952, constitutes what is one of the most significant treatises on ethics written in the twentieth century: *Saint-Genet: Comédien et martyr* (*Saint Genet: Actor and Martyr*, 1963).

French literature from the eighteenth century onward can boast of a long tradition of writers—from Jean-Jacques Rousseau and the Marquis de Sade, by way of Guillaume Apollinaire, to Jean Paulhan, Georges Bataille, and Monique Wittig—who have used the "pornographic" novel (that is, the novel whose principal material resides in the detailed description of extreme and violent forms of sexual experience) not merely to titillate the reader's imagination but for positive and serious purposes of their own. These purposes vary: The intention may be one of self-analysis or of "confession," it may be a concern with the absolutes of realism, or it may be a matter of denouncing the hypocrisies and the false assumptions by which the majority of "right-thinking people" choose to live. Mystics have been fascinated by the "surreal" quality of erotic experience, but so have anthropologists. The violence of sexual intensity constitutes one of the most readily accessible means of intuiting a dimension of irrational transcendentality; progressively, as European thought has moved toward a climate of materialist rationalism, the attraction of the irrational has grown more powerful. It is perhaps Genet's most significant achievement, in this quasi-sociological domain, to have brought for the first time into the full light of intellectual consciousness the role that "inadmissible" dimensions of experience may play in humankind's objective assessment of itself. To describe this, in Freudian terms, merely as "beneath the ego lies the id" is to bury it under the colorless abstractions of a Viennese-based scientific observer trained by Jean-Martin Charcot. Genet, in the characters of Divine and Mignon, of Bulkaen and Harcamone, of Jean Decarnin and of the Brothers Querelle, clothes these aspects of the human psyche in flesh and blood, illuminates them with the brilliant and torturous recall of his own experiences, and gives them an unforgettable reality.

BIOGRAPHY

The career of Jean Genet has often been compared to that of his late-medieval predecessor, the thief and poet François Villon. That Genet was a thief is undeniable; the interest lies in how he was transformed into a poet. The solid facts concerning Genet's early life are few, because, for reasons that are both literary and personal, he took great pains to transmute them into his "legend." Born on December 19, 1910, in a public maternity ward on the Rue d'Assas in Paris, the child of a prostitute and an unknown father, Genet was adopted by the Assistance Publique (the national foundling society) and, as soon as he could crawl, was sent off to foster parents in the hill country of Le Morvan, between Dijon and Nevers. There, growing up with a classic sense of insecurity, he took to petty thieving and, by the age of ten, was branded irrevocably as a thief. Many years later, probably under the influence of Sartre's philosophy of existential choice, he attributed to this critical period of his life a positive significance: His "self" was what he was for "others"; because, for others, he was a "thief," a thief was what he must necessarily be. How much of this persona is fact and how much is legend is impossible to determine.

At all events, by his early teens, Genet found himself confined to a reformatory for juvenile criminals at Mettray, a few miles north of Tours; there, he was subjected to all the most brutal forms of assault and seduction common to establishments of that type. How and when he was released, or escaped, is unknown, as is most of his career during the next ten years or more. He appears, on one hand, to have developed as a classic layabout—a male prostitute, a skilled pickpocket, a semiskilled shoplifter, and a remarkably unskilled burglar (burglary, considered as an exercise in poetic ecstasy, would not lead to the best results). His vagabond existence took him to Spain and then to North Africa, where he developed a feeling of kinship with the Arab victims of colonization that was later to emerge in *The Screens*. On the other hand, and less ostentatiously, he pursued a career as an assiduous autodidact who, on an occasion when he was arrested for stealing a volume of poems by Paul Verlaine, was more concerned with the quality of the poetry than with the commercial value of the book itself.

These two strains—criminality and poetry—would seem to have run together in not uncomfortable harness for a dozen years or more. According to one source, when Genet was sixteen, he worked as guide and companion to a blind poet, René de Buxeuil, from whom he learned at least the rudiments of French prosody, if not also the principles of Charles Maurras's fascism. Some years later, in 1936 or 1937, he deserted from the Bataillons d'Afrique (the notorious "Bat' d'Af"—the punitive division of the French army in North Africa), after having struck an officer and stolen his suitcases, illegally crossing frontiers in Central Europe and running a racket involving fake or clandestine currency. Yet, in the same period, he taught French literature to the daughter of a leading gynecologist in Brno, Moravia, writing her long letters in which explications of Arthur Rimbaud's "Le Bâteau ivre" (1883, "The Drunken Boat") alternate with laments for the fall of Léon Blum's Front Populaire in June, 1937. His next arrest, in or about 1938, was, according to some authorities, for stealing a car; according to others, it was for forging documents to save republican refugees from the Spanish Civil War.

Which crime led him to the prison at Fresnes in 1942 is again unknown. What is certain is that it was during this period of detention that Genet wrote his first published poem, "The Man Condemned to Death," and also drafted his first novel, *Our Lady of the Flowers*—according to the legend, on stolen brown paper; when the first draft was discovered and confiscated by a warder, Genet simply began all over again.

During this period there was a visitor to the prison at Fresnes named Olga Barbezat. Her husband, Marc Barbezat, owned a small press, L'Arbalàte, in Lyons, and his friends included Jean Cocteau, while she herself had for some years been acquainted with Simone de Beauvoir. Genet's manuscripts began to circulate, and it was Cocteau who first acclaimed them as works of genius. When Genet had been released and arrested yet again (the "volume of Verlaine" thievery), Cocteau himself appeared among the witnesses in court for the defense, declaring publicly that he considered Genet to be "the greatest writer in France." The outcome is again unknown, but Genet nevertheless continued his dual career as a brilliant writer and an incompetent burglar. Between 1942 and 1946, he appears to have written all four of his novels, as well as *The Thief's Journal* and the plays *Deathwatch* and *The Maids*. *Our Lady of the Flowers* was published in September, 1944, and the other novels appeared in rapid succession over the next four years. Genet's name was becoming known; in 1948, however, he was arrested again, and on that occasion was sentenced to "perpetual preventive detention."

The circumstances of this final appearance of Genet-as-criminal are, as usual, obscure. According to his supporters, he had quixotically taken upon himself the crimes of one of his lovers, Jean de Carnin (the Jean Decarnin of *Funeral Rites*), who had died heroically fighting the Germans during the liberation of Paris some three years earlier. At all events, Genet had powerful backers. On July 16, 1948, the influential newspaper *Combat* addressed an open letter (signed by Sartre, Cocteau, and the literary editors of the paper, Maurice Nadeau and Maurice Saillet) to the president of the Republic, "imploring his clemency on behalf of a very great poet." The president, Vincent Auriol, was convinced, and a free pardon was granted. From that point on, Genet was merely a writer. "I don't steal the way I used to," he told an interviewer from *Playboy* (April, 1964) nearly two decades later. "But I continue to steal, in the sense that I continue to be dishonest with regard to society, which pretends that I am not."

Genet's later work, apart from the three plays *The Balcony*, *The Blacks*, and *The Screens*, all written during the 1950's, is comparatively slight; he never repeated the great outburst of creativity that took hold of him between 1942 and 1948. His later works include a scattering of film scripts and critical essays in the 1960's, and a series of short but searingly controversial articles in defense of the Black Panthers and of the Palestinian terrorists. It is as though, having employed literature to effect his own escape from degradation, he then had little further use for it. In the main, until his death in 1986, he seemed content simply to be alive.

ANALYSIS

The elements out of which Jean Genet contrived his vision of that haunting and monstrous "other" world, which lies carefully concealed beneath the controlled and rational surface of everydayness, all belong to previously accredited literary traditions; nevertheless, the balance, and consequently the overall impact, is new. The components can be analyzed as follows.

The confession: Both *Our Lady of the Flowers* and *Miracle of the Rose*, at least as much as *The Thief's Journal*, are basically autobiographical and, in their original (perhaps subconscious) intention, would seem to have been inspired by a desire to *escape*—to escape from the intolerable degradations of existence as a petty criminal, convict, and male prostitute by externalizing these experiences through the rigorous and formal disciplines of prose and poetry, by projecting the self through words into the minds of others, thus making acceptable to them that which, without their connivance and acknowledgment, could not be acceptable to *him*. In one memorable phrase, Genet describes his pilgrimage through literature as "une marche vers l'homme": a progress toward virility—or, perhaps, simply away from dehumanization.

The "normalization" of homosexuality: To the nineteenth century mind, the homosexual was the ultimate social and moral outlaw, the criminal for whom there could exist no forgiveness. Progressively, the second half of the twentieth century saw the weakening of these strictures: The homosexual, in emotional relationships, could be as "normal" as the heterosexual lover, perhaps even more so; because of previous persecution, the homosexual became almost a "hero of the time." If this attitude is not the most original feature of Genet's work, it nevertheless constitutes a powerful motivation: the concern to portray his own emotions as something as intense and as moving as those of "normal" human beings.

The existential of the self: The intellectual relationship between Sartre and Genet is complex and awaits analysis. What is clear is that if Genet was not only influenced by Sartre's *L'Être et le néant*, 1943 (*Being and Nothingness*, 1956) but also, according to his own confession, reduced for years to silence by the devastating accuracy of Sartre's psychophilosophical analysis of Genet's creative processes in *Saint Genet: Actor and Martyr*, Sartre, likewise, at least in *Le Diable et le Bon Dieu* (pr. 1951; *The Devil and the Good Lord*, 1953), acknowledges his debt to Genet. Genet, in fact, takes the Sartrean ontology toward conclusions that Sartre himself hardly dared to explore. If the essence of the self is a void (*un néant*), then it can only "be," either what it *thinks* itself to be (according to Sartre) or what others think it to be (according to Genet). In either case, it can *know* itself to be what it is only in terms of the effectiveness of its actions (Sartre) or by looking at itself in the mirror (Genet). Yet, if a man (a negative) looks at himself and sees his reflection (a positive) in the mirror, then that which is perceived (the inanimate-positive image) is more "real" than the perceiver (the animate-negative). The image is thus more "real" than the subject, the fake more "authentic" than the genuine. For Genet, "to be" (this is also a Beckettian theme) is "to be perceived"—especially in the mirror. Hence, Genet's fiction is pervaded by the image of the mirror and of the double—from the early ballet *'Adame miroir* to the last of the novels, *Querelle of Brest*, in which the identical twin brothers, Querelle and Robert, constitute an identity only by their absolute reflection of each other.

The reversal of moral values: If the fake is more authentic than the genuine, then, in moral terms also, the evil is more authentic than the good. Genet, brought up as a Catholic believer and profoundly influenced by another Christian believer, Fyodor Dostoevski, argues as follows: Christ stated that the Kingdom of Heaven is for the humble; no man can *will* himself to be humble, any more than he can will himself to be a saint, without a degree of hypocrisy that destroys both humility and sanctity (this is, in fact, the theme of the play *Deathwatch*). Humility, the supreme virtue of the true Christian, can be achieved only involuntarily: One can be truly humble only by being *humiliated*. Consequently, the most truly meritorious acts are those that result in a total rejection or humiliation by the community—for example, murder or treason. The murderer, therefore, or the traitor (or, on a lesser level, the sneak thief) comes closer to achieving "sanctity" than the parson or the social worker. This argument is well summed up in Lawrence's vitriolic parody.

> And the Dostoyevsky lot:
> 'Let me sin my way to Jesus!'—
> And so they sinned themselves off the face of the earth.

Divine of *Our Lady of the Flowers* would agree wholeheartedly.

The attack on the establishment: Genet's existential-Dostoevskian reversal of accepted moral values is basically a rationalization of his rejection of *all* values accepted by the French establishment of his time. That does not mean, in any political sense, that he is a "revolutionary," because "the revolution" (as in *The Balcony*) implies the acceptance of a code of values as rigid as, and perhaps even more intolerant than, those that it claims to replace. In political terms, Genet is an anarchist in the most literal sense: The conformism of the Left is as repugnant to him as the conformism of the Right. Jews, blacks, criminals, Algerians, pimps, prostitutes—these are "his" people, the social outcasts, the "submerged tenth," as unwelcome to one regime as to another. From this point of view, *Funeral Rites*, while one of the weakest of Genet's novels, is at the same time one of his most significant. Ostensibly, its hero is one Jean Decarnin, a stalwart of the Resistance, Genet's lover. Yet no sooner is Decarnin dead than Genet embarks on a paean to all that is Nazi, for Adolf Hitler and for the jackbooted SS battalions that had trampled over the fair land of France. If the new establishment is to be the victorious Resistance, then Genet is as emphatic in his rejection of it as he had been in his rejection of the *grande bourgeoisie* that had preceded it. Michel Leiris once argued that the so-called committed writer can justify his calling only if, like a bullfighter, he *genuinely* exposes himself to danger. Genet accepted the challenge, in a way that Leiris himself, for all of his intelligence, seems scarcely to have envisaged. If Genet rejected the bourgeoisie, it was not so much by writing as by *being* that which no establishment can accept. Therefore, with deliberate delight, Genet, even when he was an acknowledged poet, continued to be an inefficient burglar: the last of his protests against a society that stole "in a different way."

One of the most intriguing features of the Parisian underworld of criminals, pimps, and prostitutes is its tradition of bestowing on this unlovely riffraff the most elaborate and frequently the most haunting of poetic nicknames. It is as though the highest form of human aspiration stood guard over the most debased of its activities. This is the paradox that Genet, with his passion for masks and symbols, for those moments of "mystic" revelation in which an object is perceived simultaneously to be itself and not itself, takes as the starting point of his first and, in the opinion of many critics, his best novel. The "magical" name Our Lady of the Flowers (which is also the designation of Filippo Brunelleschi's noble Florence cathedral) conceals beneath its high sonorities the sordid reality of a moronic adolescent thug, one Adrien Baillon, a former butcher boy and author of a particularly brutal and senseless murder; "Darling" (Mignon-les-Petits-Pieds) turns out to be a stereotypical muscleman, pimp, and shoplifter; and "Divine," the hero (or rather, the heroine, for that is how "she" would prefer it), is a cross-dressing male streetwalker, as are "her" companions of the sidewalk, "Mimosa II" (René Hirsch), "First-Communion" (Antoine Berthollet), and "Lady-Apple" ("Pomme d'Api," or Eugène Marceau), among others: "A host, a long litany of beings who *are* the bright explosion of their names." Half or more of these names have religious connotations, notably that of Divine herself, for surely the most beautiful of masks is that of the Son of God, even if it serves to hide a Dantesque inferno.

OUR LADY OF THE FLOWERS

There is no conventional "plot" to *Our Lady of the Flowers*, any more than there is to its successor, *Miracle of the Rose*. Because both of Genet's first two novels are, in part at least, autobiographical (the actual process of writing them was, for their author, a means of liberation, of escape from anonymous degradation, sexual abjection, and possible madness), their structure is as complex as life itself. How Louis Culafroy *became* Divine, how Divine *became* Genet-in-prison, is not told; few things interest Genet less than a coherent narrative in time. The episodes are superimposed on one another, absorbed into one another, so that the beginning is the funeral of Divine and the end is the death of Divine, and both are interwoven with the voice of Genet, who "is" Divine and who is dead and yet alive. The central figure is always Divine, who, in "her" precious dialect of a painted and decaying transvestite, pursues the unending *via dolorosa* laid down for her by her quest for the Absolute.

Divine's most terrifying characteristic is her purity, for hers is a demoniac chastity, born where good and evil meet, the purity of that hell that lies beyond Hell and that consequently drags all those who cannot follow her as far down into the depths as she herself has plunged, toward death and perdition. Her lovers are caught, one by one, in the toils of her "sanctity" and annihilated. Even Our Lady, the "sublime" adolescent strangler, becomes possessed (almost in the biblical sense) with the spirit, or rather with the gestures, of Divine, and confesses to his crime, gratuitously and needlessly—needlessly, in terms of everyday values, but *necessarily* in the context of Divine's world, where the figure has no reality without the image, nor the criminal without his punishment, and where damnation is essential to justify the ways of God to man. Confession is not repentance but defiance without repentance. If God is infinitely high above man exactly to the extent that man is infinitely far below God, then the supreme exaltation and glorification of God lies in *willing* the opposite of God, which is evil, and, with evil, its punishment. Then, and then only, are the two halves joined and the cycle completed.

In place of plot, then, *Our Lady of the Flowers* interweaves variations on a theme; this theme is the relationship between God and his most ignominious creation, man. The vision of God, for that contemporary mystic Genet, owes much to Dostoevski, something to village-church Catholicism, and most of all to post-Freudian anthropology. From Dostoevski comes Genet's obsession with the figure of the *humiliated* Christ—the Christ who, through His humiliation, bears away the sins of the world—and of the saint who achieves his sanctity through his very degradation. From village Catholicism (albeit oddly distorted) come the cherubim and the archangels, the crude plaster statuettes of the Blessèd Virgin working fake miracles. From the anthropologists comes the notion of transgression: the sophisticated equivalent of the taboo. What transforms Genet's antiheroes from subjects of psychiatric case histories, or instances in a criminologist's notebook, into symbols of a metaphysical reality is the fact that they violate not laws, but taboos.

Hence, in *Our Lady of the Flowers*, Genet is interested in crime and in criminals only insofar as they perpetrate a sacrilege, that is, insofar as they violate the laws, not of society, but of that "Other Dimension," which is God. In one of his allegories, or "parables," Genet sees himself thwarting God. Here lies the key to Genet's attitudes and, furthermore, to the significance of Divine and Darling and Our Lady. They are at death grips with God, because God offers them sanctity and salvation on *his* terms. They are tempted, but they will not be bullied. They are human beings, and they have one inalienable right: to be what they are. God would take away from them this right, so they defy God. If they are destined for sanctity, they are resolved to achieve it in their own way, not God's. They will plunge headfirst into the mire; their abjection is their dignity; their degradation is their ultimate authenticity. God has sided with society; therefore, God has betrayed them. Not for that, however, will they renounce God's kingdom, but they will get there by diving headforemost into the ditch, which reflects the stars—the mirror image of Heaven.

MIRACLE OF THE ROSE

Genet's second novel, *Miracle of the Rose*, contains at least as much, if not more, autobiographical material than the first. In *Our Lady of the Flowers*, both Divine and the child, Culafroy, are semimythical figures, all immediate reality being concealed beneath a golden mask of signs and symbols. In *Miracle of the Rose*, by contrast, Genet speaks in his own name. The "I" who endures (and endows with "magic") the sordid and stultifying brutality of the great prison-fortress of Fontevrault—now redeemed from that function and restored to its former status as a minor château of the Loire Valley—is the same "I" who earlier had been subjected to the vicious cruelty of the reformatory at Mettray, a few miles to the northeast. In neither novel is the material, in any usual sense, "romanticized." The misery and horror, the nightmarish ugliness of the life that Genet describes, is never glossed over. On the contrary, it is portrayed lingeringly in all of its nauseating detail, and the ingenious sadism by which a vengeful society deliberately sets out to reduce its victims to a level considerably below that of animals is, if anything, exaggerated. The signs and the symbols are still present and still serve to transmute prison latrines and punishment blocks into miracles and roses, but the symbolism is rather more self-conscious and therefore more self-revealing. In consequence, the reality underlying these symbols is not concealed as much as it is heightened, given a spiritual or aesthetic significance without ever losing sight of its grim and ugly materiality.

The Central Prison (Lan Centrale) of Fontevrault is an isolated community cut off from the rest of the world, cruel, intense, superstitious, hierarchical, and ascetic—not very different from the medieval abbey, with its dependent monasteries and convents, that had originally occupied the same site. The convicts of the present are simultaneously the monks and lay brothers of the long-dead past, an identification that destroys the intervening barrier of time, thus giving the whole prison a dreamlike and "sacred" quality that Genet discreetly emphasizes by setting the time of his own arrival there late on Christmas Eve: "The prison lived like a cathedral at midnight. . . . We belonged to the Middle Ages." Thus Genet establishes the basic structure of *Miracle of the Rose*, which consists in eliminating the "profane" dimension of time by superimposing different fragments of experience in time, identifying them and allowing them to interpenetrate so that the reality that survives is outside time altogether.

Undoubtedly, *Miracle of the Rose* owes something to Proust's *À la recherche du temps perdu* (1913-1927; *Remembrance of Things Past*, 1922-1931); it is understandable that Genet, comparing his own childhood with that of the wealthy, spoiled hypochondriacal young Marcel, must have felt a definite sense of alienation. *Miracle of the Rose*, however, differs from the Proustian narrative in its superimposition of a third plane of experience over and above Proust's levels of time past and time present.

That plane is the plane of the sacred, of existence that is still technically *in* life but, in fact, outside life, space, and time alike—the level of experience that is symbolized by Harcamone. Harcamone, from the mystic solitude of his condemned cell, is already "beyond life"; he lives a "dead life," experiencing the "heartbreaking sweetness of being out of the world before death." Harcamone has, in fact, through his transgression and later through his condemnation, attained that level of sanctity, isolation, and total detachment from profane reality to which Divine aspired yet failed to reach—the level at which all miracles are possible. Genet and his convict-lovers, Bulkaen and Divers, exist simultaneously on two planes, in time and space; Harcamone, on three. Consequently, it is Harcamone who dominates the rest—and not only dominates but, being himself a symbol, gives meaning to all the other symbols that compose the worlds of Fontevrault and of Mettray.

As in *Our Lady of the Flowers*, there is no plot in *Miracle of the Rose*. It is a closely woven, glittering tapestry of memories and of symbols. It is not, however, a Symbolist novel; it is, rather, a novel wherein the obsessions of memory fuse into the totality of a significant experience through the multiplicity of symbols with which they are illuminated. Frogs become princes while still remaining frogs. Murderers are changed into roses (Genet, incidentally, dislikes flowers) while still remaining murderers. Harcamone, the murderer, is the Rose of Death, yet the warden he killed was known as Bois de Rose, recalling the rosewood used for coffins. The rose is head and heart; cut off from its stem, it falls as heavily to the ground as the head beneath the knife of the guillotine; it is mourning, it is mystery, it is passion. It is beauty that symbolizes its mirror-opposite, evil and ugliness; it is paradox, blossoming simultaneously in the profane and sacred worlds. It is the Head of Christ and the Crown of Thorns. It is the Miracle and the symbol of the Miracle; it is profanation, transgression, and ultimately—in Genet's special sense—sanctity.

Once Genet began to outgrow his basically autobiographical inspiration, his novels became less impressive; after *Miracle of the Rose*, it was the drama that was destined to become his true medium of expression. *Funeral Rites*, although it contains many interesting ideas in embryo, is the weakest of his full-length published works. Its technique is uncertain: Deprived of the electrifying impulse given by the memory of his own humiliations, Genet descends to the level of the commonplace novelist struggling with the exigencies of a conventional plot.

QUERELLE OF BREST

By contrast, *Querelle of Brest* is the most technically sophisticated of Genet's novels. It is less lyric, less subjective, less poetic, and perhaps less haunting than *Our Lady of the Flowers*; on the other hand, it has a far more substantial structure, it develops its themes with a persistence in logic (or antilogic) that was missing from the earlier works; it creates a whole new range of characters, symbols, and images to replace the purely personal obsessions of *Our Lady of the Flowers*; finally, in the character of Madame Lysiane, it introduces for the first time a woman who plays an essential part in the development of the plot.

From the outset, Genet's metaphysic was based on the symbol of the mirror. The self had reality only as observed by the other (as image and reflection), but this dual self could be granted authenticity only if apprehended simultaneously by a third source of awareness. Claire and Solange in *The Maids* are reflections of each other; their "reality" depends on Madame, whose consciousness alone can embrace both. In *Querelle of Brest*, this theme of the double is worked out in greater complexity and is pushed toward its inevitable and logical conclusion. What previously was a mirror image is now literally incarnated in the double (Georges Querelle and his identical-twin brother Robert), while the "observers" are equally duplicated (Madame Lysiane and Lieutenant Seblon). To complicate the pattern, both Georges Querelle and Lieutenant Seblon—respectively a seaman and an officer in the French navy—are "doubled" by being both "themselves as they are" and the image or reflection of themselves presented to the world by the uniforms they wear. The double, with all its intricacies of significance in Genet's aesthetic, is the central theme of *Querelle of Brest*.

Genet, to begin, presents a double murder. In the everlasting fogs and granite-veiling mists of the traditional French naval base of Brest, Querelle murders Vic, his messmate, who was his accomplice in smuggling opium past the watchful eyes of the customs officers; perhaps in the same instant, Gil Turko, a young stonemason employed as a construction worker in the dockyard, goaded beyond endurance by the taunting contempt of Théo, a middle-aged fellow construction worker, fills himself with brandy to fire his courage and slashes his enemy's throat with the butt end of a broken bottle. From this moment onward, the two alien destinies begin to coincide—with this difference: Whereas Gil, terrified and hiding from the police in the ruined shell of the ancient galley slaves' prison by the Vieux Port, is the victim, Querelle is the master of his fate, or at least as near master as any mortal can hope to be. Querelle sees in Gil his own reflection, his imitator, his young apprentice who might one day grow up to be the equivalent of himself. He takes care of Gil, feeds him, argues with him, encourages him, secretly exploits him, and finally, for good measure, betrays him to the police. The relationship between Georges Querelle and Gil Turko is, however, only the central relationship in a series of doubles; not only is Georges Querelle doubled by his twin brother Robert, but Madame Lysiane, who loves Robert, also loves Querelle and at most times is unable to distinguish between them. Mario, the Chief of Police in Brest, finds his double in Norbert ("Nono"), the proprietor of the most favored brothel in the dock area, La Féria, and the husband of Madame Lysiane. Even in the absence of character pairs there are mirrors: the great wall mirrors of La Féria, against which a man can lean, propping himself against his own reflection so that he "appears to be propped up against himself."

The arguments of *Querelle of Brest*, both moral and metaphysical, are ingenious, intricate, and awkwardly paradoxical; as usual, they owe much to Dostoevski and something to the Marquis de Sade. Thomas De Quincey, writing "On Murder Considered as One of the Fine Arts," might have learned something from Querelle, just as Querelle might have learned something from Oscar Wilde's "Pen, Pencil, and Poison." The outstanding achievement of the novel, however, lies in the way in which structure, plot, argument, and symbols are integrated, forming an imaginative pattern in which every element serves to reinforce the others. The symbol of Querelle's dangerous virility is the granitic, the vertical. Querelle, on the other hand, is flexible and smiling. His symbol is transferred outside himself: It is the ramparts of Brest where he murders Vic; it is the dockyard wall over which the packet of opium must be passed; it is the walls of La Rochelle in Querelle's childhood memories. In the place of roses and angels, Genet is now using a much more abstract, sophisticated, and, in the end, powerful type of symbol. There is a geometrical precision, both of imagery and of argument, in *Querelle of Brest*, which contrasts significantly with the comparative formlessness, the viscosity, and the self-indulgent subjectivity of *Our Lady of the Flowers* or of *Miracle of the Rose*.

In his autobiographical *The Thief's Journal*, Genet refers at one point to his "decision to write pornographic books." As a statement, this is categorical; in any context (not only in that of the 1940's), Genet's novels are unquestionably and deliberately pornographic. There are passages that, even now, are difficult to read without a sickening feeling of disgust: The animality of man is unspeakable, so why speak of it?

In earlier generations, Puritans spoke with similar disgust of the "beastliness" of human appetites. The only difference, compared with Genet, is that they spoke in generalities, allegories, or abstractions. When John Milton's Comus appeared (in *Comus*, 1634), it was in the company of a "rout of monsters, headed like sundry sorts of beasts, but otherwise like men and women, their apparel glistening." The rest of *Comus*, however, is pure poetry; the "rout of monsters" is forgotten. Genet parades before us a similar rout of monsters, but he does not forget about them. Nor, in the last analysis, is he less puritanical than Milton. The exquisite ecstasy of disgust with human sexuality is something that he has known from personal experience; if he chooses to speak of it, it is at least with an authority greater than Milton's. Pushed to its ultimate indignities, pornography becomes puritanism, and puritanical pornography is instinct with poetry. Every word that Genet uses is selected with rigorous and elaborate precision. Divine and her transvestite companions are "the bright explosion [*l'éclaté*] of their names." *L'éclaté* is a rare and precious seventeenth century word, not listed in modern dictionaries, dragged by Genet out of its antique obscurity because it alone possessed the jewel-like precision of the poetic nuance he wished to convey. Genet's pornography is poetry of the highest, most rigorous, and most uncompromising order.

Richard N. Coe

OTHER MAJOR WORKS

PLAYS: *Les Bonnes*, pr. 1947 (revised pr., pb. 1954; *The Maids*, 1954); *Haute Surveillance*, pr., pb. 1949 (definitive edition pb. 1963; *Deathwatch*, 1954); *Le Balcon*, pb. 1956 (in English; pr. 1960 in French; revised pb. 1962; *The Balcony*, 1957); *Les Nègres: Clownerie*, pb. 1958 (*The Blacks: A Clown Show*, 1960); *Les Paravents*, pr., pb. 1961 (*The Screens*, 1962); *Splendid's*, pb. 1993 (wr. 1948; English translation, 1995).

POETRY: *Poèmes*, 1948; *Treasures of the Night: The Collected Poems of Jean Genet*, 1980; *The Complete Poems*, 2001.

NONFICTION: *Journal du voleur*, 1948, 1949 (*The Thief's Journal*, 1954); *Lettres à Roger Blin*, 1966 (*Letters to Roger Blin*, 1969); *L'Ennemi déclaré: Texts et entretiens*,

1991 (*The Declared Enemy: Texts and Interviews*, 2004); *Lettres au petit Franz, 1943-1944*, 2000.

MISCELLANEOUS: *Œuvres complètes*, 1951-1991 (6 volumes).

BIBLIOGRAPHY

Coe, Richard N. *The Vision of Jean Genet*. London: Peter Owen, 1968. Examines Genet's "ideas, his art, his imagery and his dreams . . . as he has chosen to give them to us in his [work]." Approaches Genet's works through the theme of solitude.

Gaitet, Pascale. *Queens and Revolutionaries: New Readings of Jean Genet*. Newark: University of Delaware Press, 2003. Uses feminist theory and gender theory to reevaluate Genet's work, exploring his representations of cross-dressing, homosexuality, and sexuality. Also reexamines the political nature of Genet's work, contradicting Jean-Paul Sartre's argument (in the work cited below) that these writings were nonpolitical.

Jones, David Andrew. *Blurring Categories of Identity in Contemporary French Literature: Jean Genet's Subversive Discourse*. Lewiston, N.Y.: Edwin Mellen Press, 2007. Analyzes how Genet's work destroys "binary oppositions," integrating opposing character traits, such as homosexuality and heterosexuality, blackness and whiteness, and masculinity and femininity. Also discusses Genet's use of language, interpreting it from the perspectives of deconstructionism, feminist theory, queer theory, and postcolonialism. Useful for advanced students or readers with a prior knowledge of Genet's works.

Knapp, Bettina L. *Jean Genet*. Rev. ed. Boston: Twayne, 1989. Excellent revision of a valuable introductory study presents chapters on Genet's life and on his individual novels. Includes chronology and annotated bibliography.

Read, Barbara, and Ian Birchall, eds. *Flowers and Revolution: A Collection of Writings on Jean Genet*. London: Middlesex University Press, 1997. Collection of essays provides discussion of many aspects of Genet's works, including analysis of how they challenged conventional ways of understanding society and personal experience and how they influenced twentieth century writers and pop-culture figures such as David Bowie and Patti Smith. Includes bibliographical references and index.

Reed, Jeremy. *Jean Genet: Born to Lose*. London: Creation Books, 2005. Brief biography recounts the details of Genet's life, including information on his novels, criminal activities, sexual relationships, friendships, and obsession with death. Includes illustrations.

Sartre, Jean-Paul. *Saint Genet: Actor and Martyr*. New York: George Braziller, 1963. Sartre was one of the earliest champions of Genet's work, and this book, which made of Genet a kind of dark saint of modernism, remains the classic biography of the author.

Thody, Philip. *Jean Genet: A Study of His Novels and Plays*. New York: Stein & Day, 1968. Explores both Genet's biography and his major themes (evil, homosexuality, sainthood, and language) and then presents in-depth discussions of his novels. Includes bibliography.

White, Edmund. *Genet.* New York: Alfred A. Knopf, 1993. Novelist and critic White has contributed a worthy successor to Sartre's influential biography. White is more scholarly than Sartre, but he writes clearly and with flair. Provides very detailed notes and an extremely thorough chronology.

JULIEN GREEN

Born: Paris, France; September 6, 1900
Died: Paris, France; August 13, 1998
Also known as: Julien Hartridge Green

<small>PRINCIPAL LONG FICTION</small>

Mont-Cinère, 1926 (*Avarice House*, 1927)
Adrienne Mesurat, 1927 (*The Closed Garden*, 1928)
Léviathan, 1929 (*The Dark Journey*, 1929)
L'Autre Sommeil, 1931 (*The Other Sleep*, 2001)
Épaves, 1932 (*The Strange River*, 1932)
Le Visionnaire, 1934 (*The Dreamer*, 1934)
Minuit, 1936 (*Midnight*, 1936)
Varouna, 1940 (*Then Shall the Dust Return*, 1941)
Si j'étais vous, 1947 (*If I Were You*, 1949)
Moïra, 1950 (*Moira*, 1951)
Le Malfaiteur, 1955 (*The Transgressor*, 1957)
Chaque homme dans sa nuit, 1960 (*Each in His Darkness*, 1961)
L'Autre, 1971 (*The Other One*, 1973)
Le Mauvais Lieu, 1977
Les Pays lointains, 1987 (*The Distant Lands*, 1990)
Les Étoiles du sud, 1989 (*The Stars of the South*, 1996)
Dixie, 1995

<small>OTHER LITERARY FORMS</small>

Julien Green first drew critical attention in the late 1920's as a writer of short fiction (*Le Voyageur sur la terre*, 1930; and *Les Clefs de la mort*, 1927) before attempting the longer narratives that became his forte. Green, however, is almost as well known for his autobiographical works as for his novels. His *Journal*, begun in 1928, has appeared in eighteen volumes published between 1938 and 2006 (partial translations in *Personal Record, 1928-1939*, 1939, and *Diary, 1928-1957*, 1964); a second series, begun in 1963, is more personal and frankly confessional in tone: *Partir avant le jour* (1963; *To Leave Before Dawn*, 1967), *Mille chemins ouverts* (1964; *The War at Sixteen*, 1993), *Terre lointaine* (1966; *Love in America*, 1994), and *Jeunesse* (1974; *Restless Youth, 1922-1929*, 1996). An additional volume, *Memories of Happy Days* (1942), was written and published in English during Green's self-imposed wartime exile in the United States.

Encouraged by Louis Jouvet to try his hand at writing plays, Green achieved moderate success as a playwright with *Sud* (pr., pb. 1953; *South*, 1955), *L'Ennemi* (pr., pb. 1954), and *L'Ombre* (pr., pb. 1956), but he soon concluded that his true skills were those of a novelist. In any case, Green's plays are seldom performed and are of interest mainly to readers already familiar with his novels.

ACHIEVEMENTS

In 1971, shortly after publication of his novel *The Other One*, Julien Green became, at the age of seventy, the first foreigner ever elected to membership in the French Academy; his election brought sudden and considerable attention to a long, distinguished, but insufficiently appreciated literary career. Green, born in France to American parents, had been writing and publishing novels in French since the age of twenty-five, attracting more critical attention in France than in the United States, despite the availability of his work in English translation. Even in France, however, his novels have not received extensive critical notice, owing in part to his work being difficult to classify.

Encouraged by the success of his earliest writings, Green lost little time in developing a characteristic mode of expression, alternately mystical and sensual, often both at once. Many critics, as if willfully blind to the erotic dimension of Green's work, sought to classify him as a "Catholic" writer in the tradition of Georges Bernanos and François Mauriac. Others, focusing on the oppressive atmosphere pervading many of his novels, sought to place Green closer to the gothic tradition. Neither classification is quite accurate, yet it was not until after Green's autobiography began to appear in 1963 that reassessment of his novels began in earnest.

Using a clear, ornament-free style that has been described as classical, Green quickly involves his readers in the solitary lives of tortured characters obsessed with the need to escape. Often, the compulsion toward escape leads to violence, madness, or death; when it does not, it produces an implied "leap of faith," which is not, however, totally satisfying to those who would see Green as a religious writer in the Catholic tradition. Even in those rare cases in which solutions are offered, it is still the problems that dominate the consciousness of author and reader alike. Endowed with keen powers of observation, Green excels in the portrayal of psychological anguish that any thoughtful reader can understand, even if he or she does not share it.

The publication of Green's autobiography beginning in the 1960's permitted at last a demystification of the novels—in Green's case, more help than hindrance. In the light of Green's frankness, many of the tortures undergone by his characters stood revealed as artistic transpositions of the author's own private anguish as he sought to reconcile his spiritual aspirations with a growing awareness of his homosexuality. Far from detracting from the power of Green's novels, such disclosures shed valuable light on his life in art, allowing critics and casual readers alike to appreciate the true nature of Green's novelistic achievement. Whatever their source, Green's novels remain powerful portraits of alienation and estrangement unmatched in contemporary French or American literature.

BIOGRAPHY

Julien Hartridge Green was born in Paris on September 6, 1900, the youngest of eight children. His father, Edward Moon Green of Virginia, had since 1895 served as European agent of the Southern Cotton Seed Oil Company. Green's mother, Mary Hartridge of Savannah, Georgia, dominated her son's early life with a curious blend of love and Puritan guilt; her death in 1914, instead of liberating the young Green from the tyranny of her moods and ideas, seems rather to have increased her hold upon his developing conscience. Green grew to adulthood torn between a strong, if repressed, sensuality and a mystical desire for sainthood, often equally strong. Converted to Catholicism within a year after his mother's death, he seriously considered entering a monastic order but deferred his plans for the duration of World War I. In 1917, he served as an ambulance driver, first for the American Field Service and later for the Red Cross; the following year, still (as he remained) a U.S. citizen, he obtained a commission in the French army by first enlisting in the Foreign Legion. Demobilized in 1919, he returned to Paris and soon renounced his monastic vocation, a loss that caused him considerable anguish.

Unable to decide on a career, he accepted with some reluctance the offer of a Hartridge uncle to finance his education at the University of Virginia. Enrolled as a "special student," Green read widely in literature, religion, and sociology; in 1921, after two years in residence, he was appointed an assistant professor of French. Still homesick for his native France, more at ease in French than in English, Green returned to Paris in 1922 to study art, gradually discovering instead his vocation as a writer and attracting the attention of such influential literary figures as Jacques de Lacretelle and Gaston Gallimard. By the age of twenty-five, already an established author with a growing reputation, Green had found his lifework.

During his thirties, Green read widely in mysticism and Eastern religions. Returning to the Catholic Church as early as 1939, Green was soon thereafter obliged to leave Paris by the onset of World War II. After the fall of France in 1940, he moved to the United States for the duration, teaching at various colleges and universities before and after brief service as a language instructor in the U.S. Army. Returning to Paris in September, 1945, he remained there, pursuing the life and career of a French man of letters until his death on August 13, 1998.

ANALYSIS

Educated primarily in the French tradition, Julien Green brought to his novels a distinctly French concern for the presentation and development of character. Whether his novels are set in France, the United States, or elsewhere, his characters are observed and portrayed with the psychological precision that has characterized French fiction from Madame de La Fayette down through Honoré de Balzac and Gustave Flaubert to Marcel Proust. With critical and seemingly pitiless exactitude, Green takes the reader inside his characters to show their thought and motivations, achieving considerable identification even when the characters tend toward violence or madness. On the surface, few of Green's characters would appear to invite identification on the part of the reader; they tend to be misfits of one sort or another, haunted by strange fears and insecurities. It is Green's singular talent, however, to present them and their thoughts in such a way that they seem almost instantly plausible and authentic, and to hold the reader's interest in what will happen to them. Life, as particularized in Green's characters, emerges as both threat and promise, most often as a trap set for the unwary.

Typically, Green's protagonists, often female with one surviving and insensitive parent, find themselves trapped in an existence that they can neither tolerate nor understand; not infrequently, they contribute to their own misfortune through a stubborn refusal to express themselves. Even so, the reader senses that to speak their minds would render them vulnerable to even greater assaults from a hostile environment. Locked within themselves, they suffer all the tortures of an earthly hell from which they yearn to escape. In his autobiography, Green observes that a feeling of imprisonment was a recurring childhood nightmare; in his novels, the theme is enlarged to archetypal proportions, assuming the authority of fable. Green's characters, for all their particularities, emerge as highly convincing exemplars of the human condition.

Escape, for all of its apparent promise, offers no relief to the suffering of Green's characters. Adrienne Mesurat, among the most convincing of Green's early heroines, gradually retreats into madness once she has achieved through an act of violence the freedom for which she has longed; Paul Guéret, the ill-favored viewpoint character of *The Dark Journey*, strikes and disfigures the young woman whose attentions he has sought, thereafter becoming a fugitive. Manuel, the title character of *The Dreamer*, retreats from the undesirable world into a fictional universe of his own making, only to die soon thereafter. Elisabeth, the protagonist of *Midnight*, seeks to escape with her lover, only to be killed with him in a fall. Clearly, the oppressive atmosphere that stifles Green's characters is internal as well as external; like Adrienne Mesurat, they remain imprisoned even when they are free to come and go as they please. Even in the later novels, such as *The Other One*, death is frequently the only means of escape available.

The power of Green's novels derives in no small measure from the author's skill in providing motivation for the behavior of his characters. In the case of Adrienne Mesurat, for example, Green quickly and convincingly shows normal desire stifled by silence until it becomes first an obsession, then true madness. Philippe Cléry, the main viewpoint character of *The Strange River*, passes the age of thirty before being obliged to examine his life; thereafter, he becomes most convincingly self-conscious, questioning his every move in an authentically ineffectual way. Sympathetic or not (and most are not), Green's characters are inescapably human and believable, commanding the reader's identification; although they seem to exist in a world of their own, they are unmistakably drawn from life, the products of Green's keen powers of observation.

It is possible, that, had Green not been reared in a time less tolerant than the twentieth century, his novels might never have come into being. Arguably, Green's expression has responded somewhat to the temper of the times, dealing more and more openly with homosexual attraction in such novels as *The Transgressor*; indeed, by the time Green wrote and published his autobiography in the 1960's, his revelations seemed less scandalous than timely and enlightening. The restraint that helped to shape his earlier works was in a sense no longer necessary. It seems likely, moreover, that the writing of the autobiographical volumes lessened the sense of creative urgency that marks the best of Green's earlier writing. In fact, Green's later novels (*Le Mauvais Lieu* in particular), while still holding the reader's attention, cover little new ground and move perilously close to self-parody.

THE CLOSED GARDEN

Green's second novel, *The Closed Garden*, written and published within a year after the success of *Avarice House*, ranks among his best and is perhaps the most memorable. Refreshingly normal at the start of the novel, eighteen-year-old Adrienne quickly erodes into madness and amnesia as a result of the stifling circumstances of her life. Recently out of school (the time is 1908), she lives in a provincial French town with her retired father and her thirty-five-year-old spinster sister, Germaine. A chronic invalid whose illness their autocratic father refuses even to recognize, Germaine rules over Adrienne with the authority of a mother but with none of the attendant love. As in Green's *Avarice House*, kinship is no guarantee of understanding or even friendship; indeed, the family emerges as perhaps the most inimical and threatening of human institutions. Using heavy irony, Green shows Adrienne's daily interaction with her hostile relatives; the reader, privy to Adrienne's innermost thoughts, looks on with horror as she is repeatedly unable to express them.

At the start of the novel, Adrienne is looking with healthy scorn at a group of family portraits to which she inwardly refers as "the cemetery," concluding with some satisfaction that her own features place her on the "strong" side of the family. Dressed as a servant, she is doing the family housework, exhibiting physical strength by moving heavy furniture with ease. It is precisely such apparent strength that will soon prove to be her undoing, as it turns inward upon herself, accomplishing in several weeks a deterioration that otherwise might take years. Deprived of normal human companionship, Adrienne becomes infatuated with a neighboring physician, Dr. Maurecourt, whom she has seen but once; such adolescent passion, harmless enough at face value, functions rather in Green's universe as an instrument of destruction. Adrienne, unable to confide to her father or sister the relatively innocent causes of her slightly irregular behavior, retreats further and further into her fantasy with each new demand for an explanation.

Steadfastly refusing to name the object of her secret passion, she soon finds herself literally locked up in the house, forbidden to leave but still dreaming of escape. Ironically, it is the nearly bedridden Germaine, rather than the healthy Adrienne, who in fact does manage to escape the father's tyranny, sneaking out of the house with Adrienne's help in order to seek refuge in a convent near Paris. Germaine's departure triggers a rare and violent dispute between Adrienne and her father, who reveals that he, like Germaine, has guessed the identity of Adrienne's lover. Overcome with shame and grief, Adrienne runs toward her father and pushes him downstairs; she is never quite sure whether she intended to kill him. In any case, he dies, and although Adrienne is never formally charged with his murder, she is eventually convicted of the crime by the tribunal of malicious gossip. Indeed, the entire village soon takes on the sinister aspect of Adrienne's now-absent family, hemming her within a circle of watchful and accusing eyes.

A brief attempt at leaving the village finds Adrienne drifting aimlessly from one provincial town to another, beset by nightmares as she sleeps fitfully in seedy hotels, imagining that she is being watched. Returning home to live among her tormentors, she falls physically ill; Dr. Maurecourt is summoned, and at the end of a lengthy and difficult conversation, she blurts out her unrequited love for him. Maurecourt, a frail widower of forty-five, is understandably nonplussed; with genuine compassion, he explains to Adrienne that he is mortally ill, having hardly more than a year left to live, while she, Adrienne, has her whole life ahead of her. For all practical purposes, however, Adrienne's life is as good as over; she again leaves the house, intending to escape but succeeding only in wandering aimlessly about the town until she is found suffering from amnesia.

Like other novels and plays of the period—John O'Hara's *Appointment in Samarra* (1934) and Jean Cocteau's *La Machine infernale* (1934; *The Infernal Machine*, 1936) come readily to mind—*The Closed Garden* is the carefully recorded history of what can happen to a human life and mind when everything possible goes wrong. Subjected to torture such as might be inflicted upon a steel rod in laboratory tests, Adrienne's mind eventually snaps. Until very near the end, however, Adrienne remains painfully lucid, aware of all that is happening to her yet powerless to stop it. Unlike such characters as O'Hara's Julian English and Cocteau's Oedipus, Adrienne seems singularly undeserving of her cruel fate; neither arrogant nor thoughtless, she seems to have been chosen almost at random by unseen forces bent upon destroying her for no good reason.

THE DARK JOURNEY

The Dark Journey, Green's third novel, breaks new ground in presenting several viewpoint characters and a number of interlocking subplots. Each of the main characters, reminiscent of Balzac's provincial "monomaniacs," is governed and identified by a ruling passion, much as Adrienne Mesurat is governed by her passion for the helpless Dr. Maurecourt. The main viewpoint character, whose life provides a link among the others, is Paul Guéret, an ill-favored and unhappily married man in his thirties who is obsessed by his passion for the young and attractive Angèle. A typical Green heroine, Angèle has been thrust by circumstances into a thankless and sordid existence from which she longs to escape, presumably in the loving company of a young man her own age. A launderer by day, she moonlights by sleeping with various gentlemen who frequent the restaurant owned and operated by the insatiably curious Madame Londe. In a sense, Angèle is less prostitute than spy, engaged by Madame Londe to supply her with useful information concerning the gentlemen's private lives. Guéret, to his consternation, is excluded from Angèle's regular clientele because he is simply not interesting enough, either as a person or because of his station in life, to warrant Madame Londe's interest. Angèle, meanwhile, is flattered and at least amused by Guéret's awkward attentions, even if she cannot bring herself to return his love in kind.

Guéret, driven nearly to distraction by Angèle's flirtatiousness and inaccessibility, becomes increasingly obsessed with his need to possess the girl, and before long his obsession leads to violence. First, after a long and painful struggle to scale the wall of Angèle's building, he breaks into her room, only to find that she is not there. The next day, unable to tolerate her taunting behavior, he beats her and goes into hiding, leaving her for dead on a riverbank. Angèle survives, although disfigured for life. Guéret, meanwhile, is in fact guilty of murder, having bludgeoned to death an old man who stumbled upon his hiding place. After several months as a fugitive, he is given asylum by the bored and sadistic Eva Grosgeorge, mother of a boy he once tutored. Eventually, Madame Grosgeorge tires of Guéret and denounces him to the police against the protestations of Angèle, still convalescent, who does her best to rescue him. Unsuccessful, Angèle lapses into a dreamlike state and, like Adrienne Mesurat before her, wanders about town in what she thinks is an attempt to escape; delirious, she dies of exposure soon after being brought back to her room. Madame Grosgeorge, meanwhile, having shot herself melodramatically at the moment of Guéret's arrest, is expected to survive.

The Dark Journey differs from Green's earlier novels in both the depth and the scope of its character development. Although both Guéret and Angèle show clear lines of descent from Green's earlier protagonists, such characters as Madame Londe and the Grosgeorge couple bear witness to a broadening of Green's psychological and social observation; Eva Grosgeorge, in particular, is a most convincing grotesque, the bored and self-indulgent younger wife of a rather bovine industrialist. Guéret, the misfit, serves unwittingly as the link between these various social types, whose paths would otherwise be unlikely to cross. As elsewhere in Green's work, interpersonal love is shown to be an unattainable illusion. Guéret's passion for Angèle, among the more normal obsessions portrayed in the book, is doomed by its own intensity. Angèle, meanwhile, is too lost in her own romantic fantasies to see beyond Guéret's ugliness to her own genuine feelings toward him until it is too late for them both.

THE STRANGE RIVER

Less sensational in subject matter and in treatment than *The Closed Garden* or *The Dark Journey,* Green's fifth novel, *The Strange River,* remains one of his least known; nevertheless, it ranks among his best. Nearly devoid of external action or incident, *The Strange River* presents social and psychological analysis of rare accuracy and power, approaching Flaubert's ambition to write a book about "nothing." To a far greater degree than in *The Dark Journey*, Green reveals his seldom-used gifts as a social satirist, here portraying in painful detail the empty existence of the idle rich. *The Strange River* is, moreover, the only one of Green's novels to be set in Paris, where he himself resided.

As in *The Dark Journey*, Green derives considerable effect in *The Strange River* from the presentation of multiple viewpoints, primarily those of Philippe Cléry and his sister-in-law, Eliane, but not excluding that of Philippe's wife, Henriette. Philippe, rich through inheritance, suffers in his own ineffectual way the double torture of being superfluous and knowing it. As titular head of a mining company about which he knows nothing and cares even less, he need only appear (and remain silent) at monthly meetings in order to do all that society expects of him. The rest of the time, he is free to remain in his elegant apartment (he owns the building) or go for long walks dressed as the gentleman he is. At thirty-one, he is aware that his marriage has long since become as meaningless and hollow as his professional title; Henriette goes out on the town without him nearly every evening and has taken a lower-class lover to occupy the rest of her time. Their only child, ten-year-old Robert, spends most of the year out of sight and mind in boarding school; his rare presence during school vacations, when he has nowhere else to go, proves irritating to his parents and aunt, as they have no idea what to say to him. Philippe, meanwhile, unless he is out walking, usually finds himself in the company of Henriette's elder sister, Eliane, who secretly loves Philippe even as she comes to despise him for what he is.

Against such a background of silence and mistrust, Green sketches in the private thoughts and feelings of his characters, expressing the pain of existence in all of its contingency. The plot of *The Strange River*, such as it is, turns upon an incident that Philippe thinks he may have witnessed in the course of one of his long walks: A middle-aged, shabbily dressed couple appeared to be struggling on the banks of the Seine, and the woman may or may not have called out to Philippe for help. In any case, Philippe went on his way, not consulting the police until hours later. As the novel proceeds, the incident often returns to haunt Philippe with its implications.

Anticipating by some twenty-five years the central incident of Albert Camus's *La Chute* (1956; *The Fall*, 1957), Philippe's experience disrupts the balance of a previously unexamined life; Philippe, however, is already too weak to do much of anything with what he has learned about himself. For months after the incident, he scans the papers for reports of bodies fished from the Seine; at length he finds one, and it is quite likely that he was in fact witness to a murder. In the meantime, another of his nocturnal walks has provided him with further evidence of his own cowardice; accosted by a stranger, he hands over his billfold at the merest threat of violence. Attending a monthly board meeting, he impulsively takes the floor and resigns his post, to the astonishment of his sister-in-law and wife, who fear that he has lost his mind; his life, however, goes on pretty much as before, closely observed by the lovesick spinster Eliane. Like Adrienne Mesurat, Eliane is both powerless and lucid in her unrequited love, increasingly attached to Philippe even as she begins to deduce his guilty secret concerning the couple on the riverbank.

Unlike all but one of Green's other novels (*The Other Sleep*), *The Strange River* is open-ended, leaving the main characters with much of their lives yet before them. The action is not resolved in violence, as in *The Dark Journey*, or in madness, as in the case of Adrienne Mesurat. Philippe, of course, is too weak to do much of anything except worry about himself.

Not until *The Transgressor*, written a quarter of a century later, did Green again try his hand at the sort of social satire so successfully managed in *The Strange River*; despite his skill in such portrayal, it is clear that Greene's true interest lay elsewhere, deep within the conscience of the individual. *The Strange River* is thus in a sense a happy accident; Green, in order to probe the inmost thoughts of a Philippe Cléry, had first to invent Philippe and place him against a social background. The result is a most satisfying work, rather different from Green's other novels but thoroughly successful in accomplishing what it sets out to do.

For a period after *The Strange River*, Green's novels tended increasingly toward fantasy, taking place in a real or fancied dreamworld fashioned by individual characters. It is perhaps no accident that these novels, atypical of Green's work taken as a whole, were written during the time of Green's estrangement from Catholicism, when he was reading extensively in mysticism and Eastern religions. Reconciled with the Church in 1939, Green was soon thereafter to leave France and his career as a novelist for the duration of World War II. *Moira*, the first of Green's true postwar novels, returns to the familiar psychological ground of his earliest work, going even further in its portrayal of the conflict between the mystical and the sensual.

MOIRA

Returning to the time and setting of his American university experience, Green presents in *Moira* the thoughts and behavior of Joseph Day, a Fundamentalist rustic who is even more of an outsider to the university life than Green himself must have been. Joseph is at odds with the school from the first day of his enrollment, horrified by the license and corruption that he sees all around him. His landlady, Mrs. Dare, smokes cigarettes and wears makeup, and his classmates discuss freely their relations with the opposite sex. His missionary zeal fueled by a truly violent temperament to match his red hair, Joseph seeks to save the souls of those around him; thus inclined, he is quite unable to see either himself or his fellows as human beings. Derisively nicknamed "the avenging angel," he burns with a white heat, quite unaware of the eroticism at its source. Early on, he unwittingly rebuffs the sexual advances of a young, male art student, who later commits suicide as a result; meanwhile, Joseph feels mysteriously drawn to the elegant, aristocratic Praileau, who has made fun of Joseph's red hair. Challenging Praileau to a fight, Joseph is so overcome by an excess of clearly sexual frenzy that he nearly kills the young man, who tells him that he is a potential murderer.

Unable to reconcile his Protestant faith with his increasingly violent feelings and behavior, Joseph confides in a fellow ministerial candidate, David Laird, whose vocation is both stronger and less temperamental than Joseph's own. David, however sympathetic, is quite unprepared to deal with the problems of his tortured friend, who proceeds toward the date with destiny suggested in the book's title. Moira, it seems, is also the name of Mrs. Dare's adopted daughter, a licentious young woman who emerges as almost a caricature of the flapper. Even before he meets the girl, Joseph is scandalized by all that he has heard about her; even so, he is quite unprepared for her taunting, loose-mouthed treatment of him.

Another apparent gay man, Killigrew, tries and fails to get close to Joseph. Joseph does, however, vividly recall Killigrew's description of Moira as a she-monster whenever thoughts of the girl invade his daydreams. At length, Joseph, having changed lodgings, returns to his room to find Moira planted there as part of a prank perpetrated upon the "avenging angel" by his classmates. Moira, of course, is a most willing accessory, her vanity piqued by the one man, Joseph, who has proved resistant to her rather blatant charms. By the time the planned seduction occurs, it is Moira, not Joseph, who believes herself to have fallen in love. In the morning, however, Joseph strangles Moira in a fit of remorse over what they have done. After burying her body without incident, he twice considers the possibility of escape but finally turns himself in to the police, who have sought him for questioning.

Despite a plot almost too tightly rigged to seem quite plausible, *Moira* ranks with the best of Green's earlier novels, showing considerable development in the depth and scope of his literary art. As in *The Dark Journey* and *The Strange River*, Green shows himself to be a shrewd and discerning observer of society and its distinctions. Characteristically, however, he remains concerned primarily with the inner workings of the human mind and emotions, and the variety of characters portrayed in *Moira* affords him ample opportunity to display his talents. Freed from taboos (both internal and external) against the depiction of homosexuality in literature, Green in *Moira* seemed to be moving toward a new, mature frankness of expression. However, the novels that he wrote after *Moira*, though explicit, fail to match that work either in suggestive power or in tightness of construction. The first novel of Green's "mature" period thus remains quite probably that period's best.

David B. Parsell

OTHER MAJOR WORKS

SHORT FICTION: *Le Voyageur sur la terre*, 1930 (*Christine, and Other Stories*, 1930).

PLAYS: *Sud*, pr., pb. 1953 (*South*, 1955); *L'Ennemi*, pr., pb. 1954; *L'Ombre*, pr., pb. 1956.

NONFICTION: *Journal*, 1938-2006 (18 volumes; partial translations in *Personal Record, 1928-1939*, 1939, and *Diary, 1928-1957*, 1964); *Memories of Happy Days*, 1942; *Partir avant le jour*, 1963 (*To Leave Before Dawn*, 1967; also known as *The Green Paradise*); *Mille chemins ouverts*, 1964 (*The War at Sixteen*, 1993); *Terre lointaine*, 1966 (*Love in America*, 1994); *Jeunesse*, 1974 (*Restless Youth, 1922-1929*, 1996); *Memories of Evil Days*, 1976; *Dans la gueule du temps*, 1979; *Une Grande Amitié: Correspondance, 1926-1972*, 1980 (with Jacques Maritain; *The Story of Two Souls: The Correspondence of Jacques Maritain and Julien Green*, 1988); *Frère François*, 1983 (*God's Fool: The Life and Times of Francis of Assisi*, 1985); *Paris*, 1983 (English translation, 1991); *The Apprentice Writer*, 1993; *Jeunesse immortelle*, 1998.

BIBLIOGRAPHY

Armbrecht, Thomas J. D. *At the Periphery of the Center: Sexuality and Literary Genre in the Works of Marguerite Yourcenar and Julien Green*. Amsterdam: Rodopi, 2007. Ambrecht compares the representation of homosexuality in the work of Green and Yourcenar, comparing their depiction of gay characters in their novels and plays. Includes a bibliography.

Burne, Glenn S. *Julian Green*. New York: Twayne, 1972. Provides a comprehensive overview of the first forty-five years of Green's career, culminating in his induction into the French Academy in 1971. Includes a bibliography.

Dunaway, John M. *The Metamorphoses of the Self: The Mystic, the Sensualist, and the Artist in the Works of Julien Green*. Lexington: University Press of Kentucky, 1978. Dunaway's study traces the sources and evolution of Green's narrative art, exploring the biographical genesis of his major fiction. Includes a bibliography and an index.

O'Dwyer, Michael. *Julien Green: A Critical Study*. Portland, Oreg.: Four Courts Press, 1997. O'Dwyer provides a biographical introduction and a critical assessment of Green's novels, short stories, plays, autobiography, journals, and other miscellaneous writings. Highlights the importance of Green's American background for a full appreciation of his work. Includes a foreword by Green.

_____. "Toward a Positive Eschatology: A Study of the Beginning and Ending of Julien Green's *Chaque homme dans sa nuit*." *Renascence* 49, no. 2 (Winter, 1997): 111-119. An analysis of *Each in His Darkness* within the context of Green's ideas about the end of the world. Examines the negative elements of Green's spiritual vision, the identical structure of the first and final chapters, and the echoes, resonances, and parallels between these two chapters.

Peyre, Henri. *French Novelists of Today*. New York: Oxford University Press, 1967. Provides a good overview of Green's career, presenting him as standing outside both the French and the American traditions from which his work derives. Includes useful readings of Green's early and midcareer fiction.

Stokes, Samuel. *Julian Green and the Thorn of Puritanism*. 1955. Reprint. Westport, Conn.: Greenwood Press, 1972. A study of Green's novels, concentrating on the various intellectual influences that help explain the spiritual background of his work. Discusses Green's use of fiction to relate the lives of individuals to the society in which they live.

RADCLYFFE HALL

Born: Bournemouth, Hampshire, England; August 12, 1880
Died: London, England; October 7, 1943
Also known as: Marguerite Radclyffe Hall

<small>PRINCIPAL LONG FICTION</small>
The Forge, 1924
The Unlit Lamp, 1924
A Saturday Life, 1925
Adam's Breed, 1926
The Well of Loneliness, 1928
The Master of the House, 1932
The Sixth Beatitude, 1936

<small>OTHER LITERARY FORMS</small>

Radclyffe Hall launched her writing career in 1906 with a collection of verse, *'Twixt Earth and Stars*. This well-received collection was followed by four more volumes of Hall's poetry, which were published between 1908 and 1915. In 1907, Hall met Mabel Veronica Batten, an amateur singer and prominent socialite, who helped her set twenty-one of the eighty poems in *'Twixt Earth and Stars* to music. With encouragement from Batten, Hall published *Sheaf of Verses* in 1908. This volume included poems on lesbian sexuality, notably "Ode to Sappho" and "The Scar."

Hall published three more volumes of verse: *Poems of the Past and Present* (1910), *Songs of Three Counties, and Other Poems* (1913), and *The Forgotten Island* (1915). The narrator in *The Forgotten Island* ruminates on her past life on the island of Lesbos and bemoans her fading love for another woman.

Aside from her collections of poetry, Hall published *Miss Ogilvy Finds Herself*, a collection of short stories, in 1934. The five stories in *Miss Ogilvy Finds Herself* mirror some of the author's own inner conflicts. Its critical reception was disappointing. Her letters are collected in *Your John: The Love Letters of Radclyffe Hall* (1997), edited by Joanne Glasgow.

<small>ACHIEVEMENTS</small>

Although *The Well of Loneliness* is Radclyffe Hall's best-known novel, she was awarded three prestigious literary prizes for another work, *Adam's Breed*. This perceptive tale portrays Gian-Luca, a food server who becomes so disgusted with watching the gluttonous people he serves stuff themselves with rich food that he eschews food and eventually starves himself.

Adam's Breed brought Hall the Eichelbergher Humane Award in 1926 for the best novel of the year, a prize that was followed in 1927 by the Prix Femina-Vie Heureuse Prize and shortly thereafter by the much-coveted James Tait Black Memorial Prize. Only once before in the history of these awards had a novel—E. M. Forster's *A Passage to India* (1924)—received both awards in the same year.

The celebrity Hall gained through the enthusiastic critical and popular reception of *Adam's Breed* made the reading public clamor for more of her writing. She devoted October and November, 1927, to beginning her next work of long fiction with the working title "Stephen," named for the novel's protagonist. This novel, renamed *The Well of Loneliness*, appeared in 1928. In this book, Hall produced the first piece of long fiction in England to explicitly explore female homosexuality, a topic Hall touched on obliquely in her earlier work. Although most critics do not consider *The Well of Loneliness* Hall's strongest novel, the notoriety that accompanied its publication established its author in feminist and lesbian and gay circles as a social and literary pioneer.

BIOGRAPHY

Marguerite Radclyffe Hall was born on August 12, 1880, to Radclyffe Radclyffe-Hall and Mary Jane Diehl Sager Radclyffe-Hall, an American expatriate from Philadelphia. Hall's father had inherited a sizable legacy from his own father, a savvy businessman who turned his tuberculosis sanitarium into a highly profitable enterprise.

Hall's father, not needing to work, left Mary Jane shortly after his daughter's birth. Mary Jane divorced him and, in 1889, married Alberto Visetti, a voice instructor at the Royal College of Music in London. Mary Jane, hoping that her first child would be a boy, raised her daughter as a boy, often dressing her in male attire and referring to her as John, a name that Hall later adopted. As her writing progressed, Hall dropped her given name and published as Radclyffe Hall.

In her teenage years, Hall inherited a substantial fortune. She entered King's College in London but left after two terms and spent the next year in Dresden, Germany. Returning to England in 1906, she bought a house in Malvern Wells, Worcestershire. In that year she published her first book of verse and met the socially prominent Mabel Veronica Batten, known as Ladye, a woman a generation older than Hall. Batten became her mentor and, in 1908, her lover.

Batten remained a major factor in Hall's life until her death from a stroke in 1916. Hall had became infatuated with Batten's niece, Una Vincenzo Troubridge, and began a sexual relationship with her, causing Batten considerable grief. Her death left Hall and Troubridge feeling terrible guilt, which haunted them until they died.

Hall died in 1943 and was buried beside Batten in Highgate Cemetery. Hall's tombstone bears the following words from Elizabeth Barrett Browning's *Sonnets from the Portuguese* (1850): "And if God Choose I Shall But Love Thee Better After Death," a testimony to the guilt that Hall suffered because of the pain she caused Batten.

Hall's reputation as a poet and novelist increased in the two decades between the publication of her first verse collection and the publication of *Adam's Breed* in 1926. She had verged on revealing her sexuality in much of her earlier writing. In 1927, however, she wrote *The Well of Loneliness*, a lesbian-themed novel in which she argued for the right of people to be different and to marry those they love, even if the "objects" of their love are of the same gender.

Although *The Well of Loneliness* is not prurient, its morality was questioned, and it soon became the subject of much controversy. On August 19, 1927, less than one month after its publication, James Douglas, editor of the *London Sunday Express*, raised questions about the book's morality and insisted that the British home secretary ban it. Hall's publisher, Cape, withdrew the novel but arranged for its re-publication in Paris.

Charges brought under the Obscene Publications Act of 1857 were lodged against the publisher and a bookseller, Leonard Hill, who had sold copies of the novel smuggled from France. Despite court testimony from numerous literary luminaries, the book was banned in England, not to be published there for twenty-two years. A lawsuit to ban the book in the United States found in Hall's favor.

In 1934, Hall became infatuated with a Russian nurse named Evguenia Souline, who was hired to care for the ailing Troubridge. Although Hall entered into an affair with Souline that lasted until shortly before Hall's death, Troubridge, much pained by the relationship, remained loyal to Hall and was at her bedside when Hall succumbed to colon cancer in 1943. In her instructions for distributing her estate, Hall trusted Troubridge to treat Souline equitably.

ANALYSIS

Lesbian sexuality and gender expression were the dominant factors in Radclyffe Hall's life, and the topics pervaded most of her writing directly or indirectly. Hall firmly believed in freedom of choice in human relationships and was ahead of her time in being an advocate for such controversial issues as same-gender marriage.

Society's disdain for homosexuality dominated Hall's thinking, and her opinions about this disdain appear in her long fiction as well as in her early poetry. She was familiar with the studies of sexologists Richard von Krafft-Ebing and Havelock Ellis, who argued that homosexuality is congenital—or genetic—rather than a matter of choice. She felt duty-bound to promote this view in her writing.

Although *The Well of Loneliness* contains Hall's most forthright sentiments regarding female homosexuality, the theme is present in a more subdued form in her first work of long fiction, *The Unlit Lamp*, in which a close relationship, covertly homosexual, exists between Joan Ogden and her governess, Elizabeth Rodney. In Victorian England, the setting of this novel, such relationships were common, but their sexual nature was overlooked in a society that shied away from acknowledging sex, especially between women.

In her next novel, *The Forge*, Hall uses the device of writing about a heterosexual couple in coded language that reveals, to those familiar with that language, that Hilary and Susan Brent are, in actuality, lesbians. The author offers veiled hints throughout the novel of a relationship other than heterosexual.

Hall's finest work of long fiction, as many critics agree, is *Adam's Breed*, in which a fully realized protagonist, Gian-Luca, is Hall's best-realized character. Although this novel does not have the homosexual overtones of much of Hall's work, it explores other important themes, those she addresses in much of her writing: isolation, alienation from family, cruelty to animals, the effects of a troubled childhood upon one's later development, and social persecution.

THE UNLIT LAMP

The Unlit Lamp is Hall's first novel, although it was published after *The Forge*. Hall got the idea to write *The Unlit Lamp* after observing a spinster caring for her demanding mother at a seaside resort. Hall was appalled by how women, especially single women, are drawn into acting gratis as servants to demanding relatives.

As *The Unlit Lamp* begins, the adolescent Joan Ogden wants to become a physician. Her governess, Elizabeth Rodney, plans to help her achieve that end by moving to London with her so that Joan can pursue medical studies. Joan has been trapped in the small town to which her mother retreated following the deaths of Joan's overbearing military father and her younger sister.

Joan and Elizabeth make one last attempt to relocate in London, but Joan's manipulative mother again draws her daughter into her trap. Elizabeth, realizing the futility of trying to fulfill her cherished dream of taking Joan to London, runs away from the small town and is married. In *The Unlit Lamp*, Hall also deals with what one might call a retreat into heterosexuality by having Elizabeth leave Joan and marry a man. Elizabeth seeks the stability and social acceptability of heterosexual marriage over a lesbian relationship.

Joan's mother dies, leaving her without options. She becomes the spinster caregiver for an old man. The frustration, isolation, and futility that pervade this novel lead to thought-provoking questions about a woman's place in society, and they articulate strong feminist sentiments long before such sentiments were common.

ADAM'S BREED

Generally considered Hall's most successful novel, *Adam's Breed* is notable for its psychologically sound character study. The story revolves around the life of Gian-Luca, who feels abandoned and alienated in unique ways. He does not know who his father is until fairly late in his life. His mother dies in childbirth. Gian-Luca's maternal grandmother, who blames him for her daughter's death, raises him.

Isolated and lonely, Gian-Luca eventually becomes headwaiter at the Doric Restaurant and marries a simple young Italian woman. Serving in World War I as a caterer for the military, at war's end he attempts to return to his former life, but the war has changed him. He cannot adjust. Working in the restaurant, he is surrounded by greedy, gluttonous patrons whose excesses disgust him to the point that the sight of food appalls him.

In the restaurant one night, he serves an Italian poet, Ugo Doria, who turns out to be his birth father. Eventually, Gian-Luca leaves his wife and goes to the New Forest to live as a recluse. Realizing that he cannot withdraw from life, he returns to his wife, but he has become so emaciated that he dies of starvation.

In this sensitively told story, Hall pursues many of the themes that interest her most. Isolation and abandonment were major factors in her own life, and she was able in *Adam's Breed* to capture the ways these two forces impinge upon a person's life; in this case, on Gian-Luca's development.

THE WELL OF LONELINESS

Although *The Well of Loneliness* is not Hall's best work of long fiction, it is the novel that reflects her deepest emotions and most pressing concerns. The leading character in the novel is Stephen Gordon, a woman whose aristocratic parents, hoping for a son, gave her a male name and dressed her in masculine clothing. As she matures, she realizes that she is a lesbian. When she receives a marriage proposal from Martin Hallam, she rejects it and then falls in love with Angela Crossby, the wife of a businessman. As Stephen's sexual orientation becomes obvious to many, her mother forces her out of the family home. Stephen goes to London and writes a novel, and even though she spends time with other gays and lesbians, she still suffers inner conflict about her sexuality.

The time is World War I, and Stephen joins the ambulance corps, where she meets and falls in love with Mary Llewellyn, an unsophisticated young woman from Wales. At war's end, the two go to Paris together and rent a house. Mary begins to feel discomfort with Stephen's activities and the people she attracts, and they separate. Stephen generously "gives" Mary to Martin, the man whose marriage proposal Stephen rejected.

The novel ends with the proclamation "Give us also the right to our existence!," a sentiment at the heart of much of Hall's writing. *The Well of Loneliness* remains the work of long fiction for which Hall is remembered. The first novel in England to broach openly the matter of female homosexuality, the book gained sufficient notoriety to ensure its sales both upon publication and after. Two years after its release in 1928, the novel brought Hall sixty thousand dollars in royalties, a princely sum at that time. In the year of Hall's death, 1943, international sales of *The Well of Loneliness* exceeded one hundred thousand copies.

R. Baird Shuman

OTHER MAJOR WORKS

SHORT FICTION: *Miss Ogilvy Finds Herself*, 1934.

POETRY: *'Twixt Earth and Stars*, 1906; *A Sheaf of Verses*, 1908; *Poems of the Past and Present*, 1910; *Songs of Three Counties, and Other Poems*, 1913; *The Forgotten Island*, 1915.

NONFICTION: *Your John: The Love Letters of Radclyffe Hall*, 1997 (Joanne Glasgow, editor).

BIBLIOGRAPHY

Castle, Terry. *Noël Coward and Radclyffe Hall: Kindred Spirits*. New York: Columbia University Press, 1996. Castle argues that although they were seeming opposites, British playwright and composer Noël Coward and Hall were friends who contributed directly to each other's work.

Cline, Sally. *Radclyffe Hall: A Woman Called John*. New York: Overlook Press, 1998. This thorough biography of Hall discusses how she assumed essentially a masculine gender identity and chronicles as well her relationships with women, many of those relationships long term.

Dickson, Lovat. *Radclyffe Hall at the Well of Loneliness: A Sapphic Chronicle*. New York: Scribner, 1975. An incisive account of Hall's literary work on the torments of being different in a society with strict gender roles and rules about sexual expression, homosexuality in particular.

Doan, Laura, and Jay Prosser, eds. *Palatable Poison: Critical Perspectives on "The Well of Loneliness."* New York: Columbia University Press, 2001. Twenty-one essays, and a perceptive introductory essay by the editors and an afterword by literary critic Terry Castle, offer excellent analyses of the critical reception of this controversial novel.

Glasgow, Joanne, ed. *Your John: The Love Letters of Radclyffe Hall*. New York: New York University Press, 1997. This collection of 576 letters Hall wrote between 1934 and 1942 to Evguenia Souline, a Russian emigre with whom she was in love, offers keen insights into Hall's character and emotions.

Souhami, Diana. *The Trials of Radclyffe Hall*. New York: Doubleday, 1999. Of particular interest in this critical biography is Souhami's discussion of the triangulated love affair that involved both Una Troubridge, Hall's lover for twenty-eight years, and Evguenia Souline, her paramour for nearly a decade.

Troubridge, Lady Una Vincenzo. *The Life of Radclyffe Hall*. New York: Citadel Press, 1961. A reminiscence by the woman who was Hall's longtime lover. A highly subjective account that is, nonetheless, interesting and informative.

PATRICIA HIGHSMITH

Born: Fort Worth, Texas; January 19, 1921
Died: Locarno, Switzerland; February 4, 1995
Also known as: Mary Patricia Plangman; Claire Morgan

OTHER LITERARY FORMS

In addition to her novels, Patricia Highsmith wrote several collections of short stories, including *The Snail-Watcher, and Other Stories* (1970), *The Animal-Lover's Book of Beastly Murder* (1975), *Slowly, Slowly in the Wind* (1979), *The Black House* (1981), *Mermaids on the Golf Course, and Other Stories* (1985), and *Tales of Natural and Unnatural Catastrophes* (1987). In 1966, she published a how-to book, *Plotting and Writing Suspense Fiction* (reprinted and expanded three times by the author), which provides a good introduction to her work. She also wrote one children's book, *Miranda the Panda Is on the Veranda* (1958), in collaboration with a friend, Doris Sanders. Although Highsmith wrote prizewinning short stories, she is best known for her novels, especially the Ripley series.

ACHIEVEMENTS

Patricia Highsmith was honored several times. For her first published story, "The Heroine," which was written while she was a student at Barnard College, she was included in the *O. Henry Prize Stories of 1946*. The novel *The Talented Mr. Ripley* was awarded the Grand Prix de Littérature Policière in 1957 and the Edgar Allan Poe Scroll from the Mystery Writers of America. For *The Two Faces of January* she received the Award of the Crime Writers Association of Great Britain.

BIOGRAPHY

Patricia Highsmith's mother, father, and stepfather were all commercial artists. She was born Mary Patricia Plangman a few months after her mother, Mary Coates, and father, Jay Bernard Plangman, were divorced, and she lived the first six years of her life with her grandmother in the house where she was born, in Fort Worth, Texas.

At the age of six, she went to New York City to join her mother and stepfather in a small apartment in Greenwich Village. She later went to high school in New York and on to Barnard College. Life with quarreling parents made her unhappy, but she did inherit from them a love of painting, and she considered it as a vocation. She ultimately decided to be a writer because she could explore moral and intellectual questions in more depth by writing novels than by painting. Highsmith enjoyed early success with a short story she wrote in college that was later published in *Harper's Bazaar* and included in the *O. Henry Prize Stories of 1946*.

Attracted to travel early, Highsmith set out for Mexico in 1943 to write a book. With only part of it written, she ran out of money and returned to New York, where she continued living with her parents and writing comics in the day and fiction at night and on the weekends to save enough money for a trip to Europe. She left for Europe in 1949, after finishing her first novel, *Strangers on a Train*, which was bought and made into a film by Alfred Hitchcock.

The next few years saw Highsmith traveling between Europe and New York and writing novels and short stories that found publishers in New York and throughout Europe. After several visits, she moved permanently to Europe, first to England for four years, then to France (to a small town near Fontainebleau, which became the setting for later Ripley stories), and finally to Switzerland in 1982. When she died in a hospital in Locarno in 1995, she left an estate of more than five million dollars. Highsmith was a solitary figure, shunning reporters and publicity. She lived alone with her favorite cat, Charlotte, working in her garden and painting. She revisited the United States but never returned to live.

ANALYSIS

Patricia Highsmith remains less a household name than other, more traditional crime novelists largely because she wrote about good men who turn bad and bad men who escape punishment. A moral compass is missing in her work, and guilt is hard to assign. She is better known and more interesting to critics in Europe, especially in England and Germany, than in her own country, which she left permanently in 1963. In a final tribute at the time of her death in 1995, critic Michael Tolkin wrote that the Hitchcock adaptation of her first published novel, *Strangers on a Train*, in which only the psychopath is permitted to kill, "is a perfect example of the kind of American cultural repression that I like to imagine as one of the reasons she left."

In Europe, too, her heroes who "kill not without feeling," says critic Susannah Clapp in *London Review of Books*, "but without fear of reprisal" have brought cries of disapproval. In a 1965 review of *The Glass Cell*, one critic declared, "There are not many nastier fiction worlds than Patricia Highsmith's and soon they sicken." Margharita Laski wrote in *The Listener*, "I used to be the only person I knew who loathed Patricia Highsmith's work for its inhumanity to man, but our numbers are growing." On the other hand, a number of respected crime writers, including Julian Symons, consider her among the best crime writers and at least one of her novels a work of true literature. American novelist and critic Gore Vidal wrote, "She is one of our greatest modernist writers."

Highsmith's killers or near killers are middle class and intelligent; they are usually artists or professionals, and they often have sophisticated tastes. In a 1980 interview with Diana Cooper-Clark, Highsmith explained why this is so. Since she believed that most criminals are not particularly intelligent, they do not interest her very much. She chose middle-class characters because she thought writers can write successfully only about their own social milieus. Since "standards of morality come from the society around," pleasant, well-mannered men often commit murder in her fictional world: "The contrast between respectability and murderous thoughts is bound to turn up in most of my books." The five novels about Tom Ripley focus on an otherwise nice young man who gets away with murder. Critics have analyzed this unlikely killer in considerable detail.

The 1980's and 1990's saw a renewed interest in Highsmith as a lesbian writer. In most of her novels women are not the active center; they do not commit murder. When asked about this, she explained that she found men more violent by nature than women. Women seemed passive to her, less likely to create action. Her women characters are among her least admirable. They often seem present only as decor or as a means of furthering the actions of the male characters. There are three novels that represent a degree of exception to this pattern. *The Price of Salt* (later published as *Carol*) is the story of two women who fall in love, and the novel—"a very up-beat, pro-lesbian book," according to its editor, Barbara Grier—has a relatively happy ending. *Edith's Diary*, the only other Highsmith novel with a woman at the center, was viewed more as a commentary of American political and social life in the 1960's than as a suspense novel. Her last book, *Small g: A Summer*

Idyll, about gays, lesbians, and the human immunodeficiency virus (HIV), could not find an American publisher and was published in England to mixed reviews. Feminists find little support in Highsmith's work. Feminist critic Odette L'Henry Evans observed in a 1990 essay that the women are not loving wives and mothers, and it is often the father who loves and cares for the child.

If Highsmith has a philosophy, it could best be described as a negative one, difficult to identify except as a rebellion against the moral status quo. In spite of the disturbing and pessimistic conclusion that readers must draw from her work—that justice is seldom truly important in human affairs, that it is a "manmade conceit," in the words of critic Brooks Peters—she is recognized as a crime writer who has important things to say about human nature and who says them uncommonly well.

Russell Harrison, in the first full-length study of Highsmith, categorized most of the best known of her novels. The early novels may generally be considered stories of American domestic life: *Deep Water, This Sweet Sickness*, and *The Cry of the Owl*. In the 1960's, according to Harrison, Highsmith began to examine U.S. foreign relations and political and social issues in *The Tremor of Forgery, A Dog's Ransom*, and *Edith's Diary*. Finally, he examines the gay and lesbian novels, *The Price of Salt* and *Small g: A Summer Idyll*. Two important novels he does not discuss are *The Glass Cell* and *The Two Faces of January*, which might be grouped with the social-issue novels.

THE TALENTED MR. RIPLEY

The Talented Mr. Ripley was the Highsmith's favorite book, and Tom Ripley is her most popular character. Highsmith once said that writing fiction was a game to her and that she had to be amused to keep writing. The game here is keeping Ripley out of the hands of the police, and much of the fun lies in allowing him to live high on his ill-gotten gains. "I've always had a lurking liking for those who flout the law," Highsmith once admitted. Critic Tolkin described Ripley aptly as "a small-time American crook who moves to Europe and kills his way to happiness." Highsmith was at odds with herself about Ripley's true value. He stands in sharp contrast to stereotypical morality, which is often hypocritical, but he also has almost no conscience and so is, in Highsmith's words, "a little bit sick in the head."

Dickie Greenleaf, a rich young man who has left home and his disapproving parents to become a painter in Italy, is Ripley's first victim. Ripley arrives on the scene, sent by the father to persuade Dickie to return. Ripley decides that he would rather stay and share Dickie's lazy expatriate life. When Dickie becomes angry about Ripley's imitation of him, Ripley decides to eliminate the real Dickie and take his place. Ripley's real talent is this imitation—he once thought of becoming an actor—and he succeeds in deceiving everyone until Freddie, an old friend of Dickie, becomes suspicious. It is necessary for Ripley to murder again in order not to be unmasked. Freddie is killed, but the police suspect Tom/Dickie of the crime. So Dickie is twice murdered, and Tom Ripley is reborn—along with a fake will in which Dickie leaves him everything. One critic finds this protean man a very contemporary type, one often found in serious literature. Ripley is indeed a classic of his kind, and while Highsmith's touch is almost playful, some readers shudder at Ripley's indifference to his own ghastly crimes. As the Ripley stories multiplied, some readers and critics alike worried that Highsmith had grown too fond of her talented but diabolical hero who is in some ways a monster.

THE GLASS CELL

The dreariness of the style of *The Glass Cell* is the dreariness of its prison atmosphere. There is very little relief from the monotony of wrongfully convicted Philip Carter's life in prison, and there are no scenes of the high life to enjoy. In *Plotting and Writing Suspense Fiction*, Highsmith provides a case history of how three versions of this novel came to be written.

The idea came from a true story, but the story changed as Philip Carter became a Highsmith protagonist. To be interesting, he had to become more active as the novel evolved, and so he kills not once but three times. The alibi he concocts for the murders is coldly calculated; prison has made a ruthless man of him. Highsmith says that she wanted Carter to go free after he commits two postprison murders because he had suffered so much in prison. He had been strung up by his thumbs by a sadistic guard, and he suffers continual physical pain in his hands. The police suspect him of murder but can prove nothing, and Carter and his wife and son are free to go on with their lives together. Highsmith delivers her own kind of justice to a once-innocent man unjustly punished by the courts.

Lucy Golsan

OTHER MAJOR WORKS

SHORT FICTION: *The Snail-Watcher, and Other Stories*, 1970 (also known as *Eleven*); *Kleine Geschichten für Weiberfeinde*, 1974 (*Little Tales of Misogyny*, 1977); *The Animal-Lover's Book of Beastly Murder*, 1975; *Slowly, Slowly in the Wind*, 1979; *The Black House*, 1981; *Mermaids on the Golf Course, and Other Stories*, 1985; *Tales of Natural and Unnatural Catastrophes*, 1987; *The Selected Stories of Patricia Highsmith*, 2001; *Nothing that Meets the Eye: The Uncollected Stories of Patricia Highsmith*, 2002.

NONFICTION: *Plotting and Writing Suspense Fiction*, 1966.

CHILDREN'S LITERATURE: *Miranda the Panda Is on the Veranda*, 1958 (with Doris Sanders).

BIBLIOGRAPHY

Bloom, Harold, ed. *Lesbian and Bisexual Fiction Writers*. Philadelphia: Chelsea House, 1997. Highsmith is one of the writers included in this overview of lesbian, gay, and bisexual fiction writers. Contains a brief biography, excerpts from reviews and criticism, and a bibliography.

Brophy, Brigid. "Highsmith." In *Don't Never Forget: Collected Views and Reviews*. New York: Henry Holt, 1966. Brophy compares Highsmith's artistic achievements to those of Georges Simenon to argue that Highsmith's crime novels, with their moral ambiguity, "transcend the limits of the genre while staying strictly inside its rules."

Cochran, David. "'Some Torture That Perversely Eased': Patricia Highsmith and the Everyday Schizophrenia of American Life." In *America Noir: Underground Writers and Filmmakers of the Postwar Era*. Washington, D.C.: Smithsonian Institution Press, 2000. In his study of underground writers and filmmakers, Cochran describes how Highsmith's amoral Mr. Ripley and other aspects of her fiction challenged the pieties of the 1950's.

Dupont, Joan. "Criminal Pursuits." *The New York Times Magazine*, June 12, 1988. Notes that although Highsmith is a celebrity in the rest of the world, she is relatively unknown in her native United States; suggests that because Highsmith has lived abroad and has never been in the United States to promote her books, she has never developed a strong link with publishers or readers. Others believe it is because her books are not clearly classifiable as thrillers, mysteries, or literature.

Harrison, Russell. *Patricia Highsmith*. New York: Twayne, 1997. This first book-length study of Highsmith in English explores the aesthetic, philosophical, and sociopolitical dimensions of her writing. Harrison focuses on Highsmith's novels, including her gay- and lesbian-focused novels.

Highsmith, Patricia. "Not Thinking with the Dishes." *Writer's Digest* 62 (October, 1983). Highsmith says she follows no set rules for story writing; she begins with a theme, an unusual circumstance or a situation of surprise or coincidence, and creates the narrative around it. Her focus is on what is happening in the minds of her protagonists, and her settings are always ones she knows personally.

Mawer, Noel. *A Critical Study of the Fiction of Patricia Highsmith—From the Psychological to the Political*. Lewiston, N.Y.: Edwin Mellen Press, 2004. An examination of Highsmith's fiction, including the Ripley novels, *The Glass Cell*, and *A Game for the Living*. Although some of Highsmith's novels can be categorized as mystery and detective fiction, Mawer argues that many of her novels explore "the mystery of character," or, how people create their own identities by interacting with others in particular situations.

Summers, Claude J., ed. *Gay and Lesbian Literary Heritage: A Reader's Companion to the Writers and Their Works, from Antiquity to the Present*. Rev. ed. New York: Routledge, 2002. This expanded edition of a book originally published in 1995 includes an excellent essay by Gina Macdonald on Highsmith's life and work to the time of her death in 1995.

Symons, Julian. *Mortal Consequences: A History from the Detective Story to the Crime Novel*. New York: Harper & Row, 1972. Symons calls Highsmith "the most important crime novelist" of her time, a fine writer whose tricky plot devices are merely starting points "for profound and subtle character studies," particularly of likable figures attracted by crime and violence. Highsmith's imaginative power gives her criminal heroes a "terrifying reality" amid carefully chosen settings, and she is at her best describing subtle, deadly games of pursuit.

Tolkin, Michael. "In Memory of Patricia Highsmith." *Los Angeles Times Book Review*, February 12, 1995. A tribute to Highsmith as "our best expatriate writer since Henry James" and an excellent analysis of why her heroes, especially Ripley, are not appreciated in the United States.

Wilson, Andrew. *Beautiful Shadow: A Life of Patricia Highsmith*. New York: Bloomsbury, 2004. The first biography of Highsmith, chronicling the author's troubled life and tracing the roots of her fiction to the works of Edgar Allan Poe, noir, and existentialism. Winner of the 2004 Edgar Award for Best Critical/Biographical Work.

ALISON LURIE

Born: Chicago, Illinois; September 3, 1926

OTHER LITERARY FORMS

In addition to writing fiction, Alison Lurie has distinguished herself in two other areas, children's literature and the semiotics of dress, and her novels reflect both concerns as well. Her interest in children's literature is reflected in *Only Children*, in which two little girls pose their fantasies against the shocking reality exposed to them by their parents, and in *Foreign Affairs*, in which one of the two central characters, Vinnie Miner, spends her sabbatical in England collecting playground rhymes. Real children's rhymes, Lurie observes, are surprisingly subversive, not like the "safe" literature written for children by adults. She develops this insight in the nonfiction work *Don't Tell the Grown-Ups: Subversive Children's Literature* (1990). Lurie's fascination with the semiotics of clothing, which she addresses in *The Language of Clothes* (1981), is reflected frequently in the novels, where she pursues the relationship between clothing and personal identity. An especially provocative example can be found in *Imaginary Friends*, where Roger Zimmern, forced by a strange religious group to abandon his normal academic dress in favor of cheap suits, loses his sense of identity.

Two literary memoirs by Lurie, published thirty-five years apart, deserve mention. The writing of the first in 1966, the memoir of a friend, an ill-fated young poet-playwright, proved life-changing. In 2001, Lurie published *Familiar Spirits: A Memoir of James Merrill and David Jackson*. She had befriended the two poets while at Amherst College during a lonely time in her life as a faculty wife. Merrill and Jackson were companions whose mercurial life together Lurie traces with compassion throughout.

ACHIEVEMENTS

Alison Lurie's fiction has received much praise from critics, and her work has been very popular with the broader reading public. Her first novel, *Love and Friendship*, appeared in 1962 and was followed by several prestigious grants and fellowships: Yaddo Foundation Fellowships in 1963, 1964, and 1966; a Guggenheim grant in 1965-1966; a Rockefeller Foundation grant in 1967-1968; and a New York State Cultural Council Foundation grant in 1972-1973. *The War Between the Tates* in 1974 brought Lurie a popular audience and more critical acclaim. An American Academy of Arts and Letters award followed in 1978, and for *Foreign Affairs* she received a Pulitzer Prize in 1985. All of Lurie's fiction displays a remarkable control of language, a style that surprises and amuses. Both for her wit and for her sharp-edged, satiric depiction of human follies, Lurie has often been compared to Jane Austen, and her following in England is among the largest of any living American novelist.

BIOGRAPHY

Alison Lurie was born September 3, 1926, in Chicago, Illinois, but grew up in White Plains, New York. Her Latvian-born father was a scholar, a teacher, and a socialist who later became the founder and executive director of the Council of Jewish Federations. Lurie's mother, also a socialist, was a former journalist for a Chicago newspaper. Lurie suffered a minor birth injury that affected the hearing in her left ear and also caused some damage to her facial muscles. An avid reader as a child, she began at about the age of thirteen to read such authors as Charles Dickens, George Bernard Shaw, and Jane Austen. In 1947, she graduated from Radcliffe College, where she had met many people who later became important literary figures, including Jonathan Peale Bishop, a teacher, critic, and essayist. She married Bishop in 1948, and they had three children. In 1975, Lurie separated from Bishop, divorcing him ten years later.

Lurie struggled with many discouraging rejections of her writing when she was in her twenties, and she regards 1966 as the turning point in her life, when she wrote and published privately a memoir of an eccentric friend, V. R. "Bunny" Lang. Thereafter came a succession of novels that garnered high praise, including a Pulitzer Prize for *Foreign Affairs*. A professor of children's literature at Cornell University in Ithaca, New York, where she began teaching in 1969, Lurie divides her time among Ithaca, Key West, and London.

ANALYSIS

Alison Lurie's novels are known for their comedy and satire, and her acute observation is most often trained on the complications of love, marriage, and friendship as they affect the lives of the upper classes, the educated, and the academic. Many of her novels take place at the fictional Convers College in New England or at Corinth University in upstate New York (based on Cornell University) or concern characters who teach at or have been associated with Corinth. These novels are not, however, all academic satire; the academics often travel to other places or become involved in issues beyond the campus.

Lurie's style is most often detached and ironic, a treatment that has won for her both blame and praise. Her novels, except for *Only Children*, explore the time in which they are written and reflect the events and culture of Lurie's own adult years. The novels typically cover a short space of time, a crisis point in the lives of the characters, but several of the characters are seen at different points in their lives because of Lurie's use of the same characters in different novels—sometimes as major characters, sometimes as minor ones. Lurie works successfully with a variety of narrative points of view: omniscient narration in *The War Between the Tates*, first-person narration in *Real People*, third-person focus narration in *Imaginary Friends* (expanded to include two focus characters in *Foreign Affairs*). She shows no penchant for either the happy or the unhappy ending, realistically leaving her characters to continue to work out their lives as best they can.

LOVE AND FRIENDSHIP

At the heart of Lurie's first two novels are couples trying to work out their relationships. Her first novel, *Love and Friendship* (a title taken from Jane Austen), draws out the main lines of the issue. What is love and what is friendship? Are they different in what is best and most enduring? In this novel, the main character, Emmy Turner, "loves" her lover more than she does her husband. In the end, however, she chooses her husband over her lover because he needs her and to him she can be a friend. Indeed, what first led her to enter into a love affair was a frustration with her husband's failure to make a friend of her, to discuss with her his work and his concerns. Ultimately, Lurie suggests, friendship is more satisfying and lasting than love; indeed, love at its best is friendship at its best.

THE NOWHERE CITY

In her second novel, *The Nowhere City*, the ending is the opposite, but the implication seems the same. Paul Cattleman rediscovers his wife at the end after much neglect and many adulteries. It is too late, however: Friendship is lost, and with it love; she tells him that she is not angry with him, but she just does not know him anymore.

REAL PEOPLE

While the love and friendship theme becomes a secondary issue in *Imaginary Friends*, the novel Lurie published after *The Nowhere City*, she makes it once again the central focus of *Real People*. In this novel, Janet Belle Spencer, a writer, has taken up residence at Illyria, a haven for writers and artists. Although she published a book of stories six months before, she is enduring writer's block, which she is unable to break out of at Illyria. She is also drawn there by her love for an artist, Ken, with whom she believes she has much more in common than with her insurance-executive husband. The artists' colony of Illyria is an unreal world, however, and Janet discovers that she and Ken are not really friends; she learns much about her writing that she resolves to change. It is at home with her husband, Clark, not at Illyria, she finally realizes, that she will be able to put to work her new understandings.

THE WAR BETWEEN THE TATES

Love and friendship in marriage are explored most intensively in Lurie's next and most celebrated novel, *The War Between the Tates*. Erica and Brian Tate, a young academic couple, are in their own eyes and in the eyes of their friends the perfect couple, but as middle age looms, Brian becomes increasingly frustrated at not being famous, and the couple's children become rebellious teenagers. True love and friendship appear to be lacking. Finally, Brian has an affair with a student whom he makes pregnant, Erica befriends the student, and both Brian and Erica, but especially Erica, wander through a bewildering maze of events that leaves their earlier sense of themselves and their marriage damaged. As the novel ends, they drift back together, confused, "out of love," but basically seeking a peace they can find only with each other.

ONLY CHILDREN

Love and friendship in marriage is the topic once again of *Only Children*, but this time the actions of the adults are seen through the eyes of two little girls, Lolly and Mary Ann, who respond to what they see in the behavior of their elders, especially their parents. In each set of parents there is one serious, deeply dedicated person (Lolly's mother, Mary Ann's father) and one shallow, egotistical, flamboyant hunter of the other sex. The two sets of parents ultimately stay together, but, lacking love based on friendship, they are merely maintaining a facade, and their example will cripple their children's ability to love. Novelist Mary Gordon has called *Only Children* "the most interior of Lurie's novels." Lurie is especially skilled at evoking the traumas that adult crimes and misdemeanors work on youngsters.

FOREIGN AFFAIRS

The love and friendship theme appears again in *Foreign Affairs*, which juxtaposes two main characters, one married and one not. Vinnie Miner, a middle-aged professor, finds love surprisingly where she had least expected it, in a friendship with a man totally unlike her, a retired sanitary engineer. The other main character, a handsome young man in Vinnie's academic department, begins the novel estranged from his wife, is temporarily dazzled and infatuated by a far more glamorous Englishwoman, but returns to his wife at the end, finding her superior in trust, honesty, and common decency.

THE TRUTH ABOUT LORIN JONES

Love and friendship are very complicated and contradictory in *The Truth About Lorin Jones*, a novel that is a departure from Lurie's earlier novels for a number of reasons. Instead of an academic setting, the setting is the contemporary art world, and the primary relationship in the novel is one that essentially exists within the mind of Polly Alter, a failed painter who is researching the life of the late Lorin Jones, an artist whose life and loves seem to speak to Polly's own situation. Lorin, who was once Lauren "Lolly" Zimmern, one of the little girls in *Only Children*, has lived a life of professional and personal frustration and is possibly still haunted by the demons of her childhood. The contemporary issues of feminism and lesbian sexuality complicate the lives of both Polly and Lorin, but Lurie adds a new twist to the feminist argument by suggesting that it was Lorin who exploited the men in her life, using them as a means to serve her own ambitions. Polly's discovery of the truth about Lorin permits her a new lease on life, as does her romance with Hugh Cameron, a onetime hippie poet who had been Lorin's first husband.

THE LAST RESORT

In Lurie's ninth novel, *The Last Resort*, Jenny Walker, formerly a subservient wife to her distinguished academic husband, faces a crisis in her marriage when she increasingly comes under the sway of the charismatic lesbian Lee Weiss. Jenny's attraction to Lee is heightened by the respect and attention Lee accords her, whereas her husband, Wilkie, is content to see her merely as a passive supporter of his plans. Wilkie himself, under the impression that he is terminally ill, begins to detach himself emotionally from his wife but has a brief flirtation with a young female admirer even as he prepares to commit suicide. Although the couple are reunited at the end of the novel, their relationship has changed. Jenny acquires greater self-confidence and feels she is now in charge of her own life. Wilkie's "greatness" is no longer allowed to dominate their relationship as it once did.

TRUTH AND CONSEQUENCES

Truth and Consequences, Lurie's tenth novel, appeared in 2005, the same year as Philip Caputo's *Acts of Faith*, a massive novel about the civil war in Sudan whose various plots turn on the disasters of unintended consequences on the well-meaning. In *Truth and Consequences*, two couples, each pairing a caregiver and a "caregetter," enact outcomes that are predictable—in other words, intended consequences. The first couple, Jane and Alan Mackenzie, until recently have been congratulating themselves on how well everything is going, how much they love each other, how respected they are in the Corinth University community—he a professor, she an administrator. However, when Alan painfully injures his back playing volleyball, Jane is forced into a caretaking role. As the book opens, Jane no longer recognizes the invalid who once was her sturdy partner. The second couple consists of Delia Delaney, a famous and narcissistic poet, and her mate, Henry Hull, a freelance editor whose only role is the care and feeding of his wife's ego. The expected happens—the caregetters are attracted to each other, as are the caregivers. What saves the story is how convincingly Lurie deconstructs what happens to love, marriages, and people when important role changes take over their lives. Her foursome, often shrill, are never cardboard cutouts of philandering husbands and wives. Just as she deepens rather than chastens the Tates in their war, Lurie adds the depth of empathy to her foursome under siege. She asks readers to see themselves in the characters.

THE ACADEMIC MICROCOSM

Lurie's novels concern themselves with relationships between people, and these rela-tionships are at the center of all of her work, but the lives of Lurie's characters are affected by more than personal forces alone. Context, temporal and physical alike, is also central to these novels, and the directions of the lives of Lurie's characters are profoundly affected by the times and the places in which they live. The most persistent context, moreover, is academic, since many of these characters, like Lurie herself, are university professors or members of their families. In this case again, *Love and Friendship* sets a pattern that later novels follow.

The academic world is also a factor in *The Nowhere City*, although the story takes place in a Los Angeles setting that dominates the novel. Paul, in the end, will retreat to the east-ern academic world that he knows (remaking his relationships with his old Harvard friends and taking a teaching post at Convers College), while Katherine, who had initially seemed the more eastern academic of the two, refuses to return there with him and seems to find a new self in Los Angeles.

The War Between the Tates again makes the academy not only a strong backdrop but also an actor in the events. Brian Tate is a highly successful sociology professor at Corinth University in upstate New York; Erica Tate is a faculty wife. Their two closest friends, who divorce in the novel, are Leonard Zimmern, an English professor, and Danielle Zimmern, Erica's closest female friend, a part-time faculty member in the French depart-ment. The convulsions of American academe in the late 1960's interfere directly in Brian's and Erica's lives. Brian, though very successful academically, has always dreamed of fame as an adviser to governments and presidents, and his middle-aged frus-tration makes him susceptible to trying to recover his lost youth by mixing socially with his graduate students, increasingly adapting his clothing and other styles to theirs, finally indulging himself in an affair with Wendy. Erica, like Katherine Cattleman in *The No-where City*, attempts to preserve her traditional moral values in the face of all this upheaval and tries not only to adapt herself to these values but also to give direction to Brian and Wendy, even to the point of insisting that Brian divorce her and marry Wendy. She be-comes peripherally involved, through her friend Danielle, in the Hens, a local feminist group, and finding the local Hare Krishna guru of the students to be an old school friend, under his guidance has her own adventure with LSD. Brian and Erica, then, experience their marital troubles amid the student rebellions of the 1960's. Though the novel does not probe as deeply as *Imaginary Friends* into the political and intellectual doubts and troubles of academe, these influences are present, shaping their reaction.

In *Foreign Affairs*, the two main characters are again college professors, both from the English department at Corinth University: the middle-aged, internationally famous expert in children's literature, Vinnie Miner, and the young specialist in the eighteenth century, Fred Turner, both on leave to do scholarly work in London. The novel for the most part tells their stories separately, their paths crossing significantly only twice. While their common background does make their lives cross in significant ways, and while both their lives are shaped by their academic backgrounds, the primary focus of the novel is on other aspects of their lives.

THE AMERICAN MACROCOSM

The university campus, then, demonstrates the importance of time and place in Lurie's novels. This is also true in a larger sense, since American culture itself, with its regional and sociological tensions, plays just as important a role as do the characters. If *Love and Friendship*, the first novel, works off a Jane Austen theme, it also echoes a peculiarly American, Fitzgeraldian theme in which the different regions and classes of the United States become important players in the conflicts of the novel. Emmy is New Jersey rich; her lover, Will Thomas, is southern shabby genteel; and her husband, Holman, is Chicago shabby-but-respectable poor. As the marital couple work out their conflicts with traditions of Convers College playing an important role, these different regional and class conflicts do much to shape their actions and reactions.

In *The Nowhere City*, 1960's America, with its new and strange customs and dress, almost overpowers its characters' ability to work out their human problems. Here, Los Angeles is the city in which "nowhere" comes to mean "present but lacking history and future." Mixed new forms of architecture in both house and public building design, styles of hair and dress, sexual lifestyles, artistic forms, even subjects being studied in the universities are all strange, macabre, and new, dividing Katherine and Paul Cattleman as they respond to them so differently. Setting plays just as important a role in *Imaginary Friends*, which brings two very traditional strongholds, the enclosed small town and the principles of academic inquiry, together with the strains of the world without.

Real People, again, though it removes its main characters to an isolated, protected, ideal world of the artists' colony, nevertheless shows that the best work cannot be done in an artificial atmosphere but only when the artists are living and writing truthfully about the world in which they are "real people." Again, too, despite all the 1960's campus shenanigans of *The War Between the Tates* (drugs; strange new lifestyles, clothes, and hairstyles), the novel presents a strong sense that the campus is only reflecting all the major movements, confusions, and displacements of the society at large.

In *Only Children*, which is set during the Great Depression, the characters reflect the concerns of that time, including its powerful economic and political conflicts. Bill Hubbard, for example, is an example of the President Franklin D. Roosevelt-type liberal Democrat, dedicated to social reforms that will lift the poor, while Dan Zimmern represents the nascent Madison Avenue type, flamboyant and driven to succeed. *Foreign Affairs*, in the experiences of both Vinnie Miner and Fred Turner, discloses the tensions of many cultural mores, especially different class and sexual expectations, complicated further by differences between Great Britain and the United States.

In her eighth and ninth novels, Lurie abandons both the international theme and academic settings, returning to the world of art and the artist that was her subject in *Real People*. *The Truth About Lorin Jones* and *The Last Resort* introduce another setting into Lurie's work—that of Key West, the southernmost point in the continental United States and the site of Lurie's second home. Lurie uses the remoteness and luxury of Key West to place her characters in a distinct setting where they can work out their problems before returning, altered and refreshed, to the "real" world. In this way, Key West operates much like the island in William Shakespeare's *The Tempest* (pr. 1611). Lurie also sketches cultural and political differences on the island, delineating the way Key West's sizable homosexual community comes under attack from wealthy, right-wing Republicans who also reside in the area. Issues such as aging and acquired immunodeficiency syndrome (AIDS) also are given extended, if sometimes lighthearted, examination.

LITERARY INFLUENCES

Lurie additionally sets the lives of her individual characters against the backdrop of the world of literature itself. In *Real People*, Janet Belle Spencer imagines Ken as the ideal reader of her fiction, largely because he recognizes every literary reference—which in turn is reminiscent of Lurie's own rich texture of literary allusion. In this regard, as already observed, she uses the "love and friendship" theme from Jane Austen. Another novelist to whom Lurie is greatly indebted is Henry James, especially in *Imaginary Friends* and *Foreign Affairs*. Indeed, *Imaginary Friends* in many ways duplicates the plot of James's *The Bostonians* (1886), in which a young woman named Verena leads a band of truth seekers through an extraordinary gift for public speaking, which seems to proceed from a trancelike ability to contact higher powers.

Foreign Affairs enlarges on the Jamesian theme not only by explicitly introducing James's work by name but also by exploring one of his most insistent themes: what happens when basically good, decent Americans encounter a far more culturally sophisticated European society. In James's novels of this type, the balance is struck in favor finally of the basic, honest decency of Americans against the more sophisticated but possibly corrupt world of the Europeans, and Lurie's novel arrives at the same resolution. This exploration is complicated by the fact that, of the two Americans, Vinnie Miner is very sophisticated in the ways of the English, knowing their ways and customs so well that she really feels more culturally at home in England than in the United States. Fred Turner, on the other hand, despite his great physical charms and handsomeness and his knowledge of eighteenth century literature, is basically a raw recruit to European culture. Both, however, have "foreign affairs": Vinnie with an almost illiterate Oklahoman whom she meets on the plane on the way over, so embarrassingly crude that she dreads presenting him to her friends; and Fred with an English aristocrat and actor so elegant and sophisticated that his American life appears crude by comparison. Despite this structural converse—in which Vinnie loves an American who is far less presentable than her European friends, and Fred loves an Englishwoman who is far more sophisticated than his American wife and friends—both find, despite all of their differences, their American loves superior after all, and their European friends, for all of their sophistication, less satisfying morally as friends and lovers than their American friends. Thus the pattern of James's international novels, in which superior American decency confronts and ultimately wins out over superior European elegance and sophistication, is repeated here in Lurie's fiction.

The influence of James can also be discerned in *The Truth About Lorin Jones*, which, like *Imaginary Friends*, recalls James's *The Bostonians*. In this case, the competition between male and female for the loyalty of a talented woman is enlarged into an exploration of the politics of lesbian feminist separatism, something only hinted at in the James novel.

CHARACTERS

If Lurie's readers often spot resonances from other fiction, they also have the pleasure of recognizing characters they have met in other Lurie novels, for Lurie frequently works with recurring characters. Emmy Turner's four-year-old boy Freddy from *Love and Friendship* is one of the grown-up main characters in *Foreign Affairs*, while Fred's wife Roo in that same novel appears as a child in the earlier *The War Between the Tates*. Sometimes Lurie will, in a later novel, go back to an earlier period in a character's life: Miranda, the grown-up, married mother of three children in *Love and Friendship*, is seen as a child in the later novel *Only Children*.

Of all the characters that recur, the most persistent one is Leonard Zimmern, first seen in *Real People* as a middle-aged, distinguished critic of American literature living in New York; later, he appears in *The War Between the Tates* as a friend of Brian and Erica. He is also the father of Roo, a child here but an adult in *Foreign Affairs*. In *Only Children*, the Depression-era story, Zimmern is a teenager, and in *Foreign Affairs* he is the father of a grown-up Roo, the famous critic whose harsh article on Vinnie Miner's work in children's literature haunts Vinnie as she goes to England.

Roger Zimmern of *Imaginary Friends* is mentioned briefly in *The War Between the Tates* as Leonard Zimmern's cousin. L. D. Zimmern also surfaces in *The Truth About Lorin Jones* as the legal owner of his half sister Lorin's unsold paintings. In addition, *The Truth About Lorin Jones* features the return of Lorin's father, Dan Zimmern of *Only Children*, and Danielle Zimmern, divorced wife of Leonard and Erica's best friend in *The War Between the Tates*. In *The Last Resort*, L. D. Zimmern returns as the cousin of Lee Weiss, the lesbian who befriends Jenny Walker. Another continuity in *The Last Resort* is the return of the character of Barbara Mumpson, who first appears in *Foreign Affairs*. This remarkable amount of recurrence suggests Lurie's strong interest in understanding how her characters have come to be who they are, despite her novels' time frames. Given that the events of each novel cover only a short period of time—one, *Only Children*, takes place in a single weekend—Lurie often spreads out characters' lives over several novels in order to continue developing the characters and to tie their lives together.

IMAGINARY FRIENDS

All the themes discussed so far are treated as well in *Imaginary Friends*. Their treatment in this novel, however, represents perhaps Lurie's broadest and deepest effort, for the academic backdrop she uses so often elsewhere is broadened here to embrace the most fundamental of human questions, questions of knowledge, of identity, of sanity, and finally of madness. The main character in this novel, sociologist Roger Zimmern—a young, brand-new Ph.D. at a large upstate New York university—goes to Sophis, a nearby small town, as the research assistant of Thomas McMann, a famous senior professor in his department whom Roger admires, despite rumors he has heard about McMann from other young faculty members and despite the realization that McMann's form of empirical sociology (the case-study method) is passé.

To investigate McMann's hypothesis that small groups can build a belief system so powerful that it can withstand, rationalize, and incorporate doubting attacks from within and without, Roger infiltrates, under the cover of a public opinion seeker, a group of religious fundamentalists called the Truth-seekers, whose young leader, Verena, leads and directs the group through automatic writing from superior beings on another planet, named Varna. Roger introduces McMann to the group as a businessman friend who is also interested in their theories. Roger's secure identity is overset by his mentor's unscientific attempt to control the experiment in the direction of his hypothesis rather than merely to observe and record. Also tormented by his sexual attraction for Verena, Roger reaches a point where he no longer knows what he believes in, no longer knows who he is, no longer knows whether there is in his discipline any objective basis for scientific inquiry. He believes that he is going mad but decides that it is, rather, his mentor who is insane, and he unwillingly becomes the primary witness whose testimony results in McMann's being committed to an asylum. The novel ends with Roger maintaining a tenuous but commonsensical hold on his own sanity. Here, Lurie touches on questions central not only to academic life but to the lives of everyone else as well: How can one truly observe and know? How real is our own sense of self?

Taken as a whole, Lurie's novels reveal a remarkable uniformity. Her own background in academe provides the most common setting for her novels, and frequently this setting is broadened to reflect the central questions with which Lurie is concerned. Her interest in clothing and identity, in the lives of children, indeed in the lives of all of her characters, is unusual. Her work is best considered not as a series of separate novels but as a continuity in which her characters' lives go on, not ceasing with the end of a particular novel but continuing as do all our lives—growing and changing through time.

June M. Frazer; Margaret Boe Birns
Updated by Richard Hauer Costa

OTHER MAJOR WORKS

SHORT FICTION: *Women and Ghosts*, 1994.

NONFICTION: *The Language of Clothes*, 1981; *Don't Tell the Grown-Ups: Subversive Children's Literature*, 1990; *Familiar Spirits: A Memoir of James Merrill and David Jackson*, 2001; *Boys and Girls Forever: Children's Classics from Cinderella to Harry Potter*, 2003.

CHILDREN'S LITERATURE: *The Heavenly Zoo: Legends and Tales of the Stars*, 1979; *Clever Gretchen, and Other Foreign Folktales*, 1980; *Fabulous Beasts*, 1981; *The Black Geese: A Baba Yaga Story from Russia*, 1999 (with Jessica Souhami).

EDITED TEXT: *The Oxford Book of Modern Fairy Tales*, 1993.

BIBLIOGRAPHY

Costa, Richard Hauer. *Alison Lurie*. New York: Twayne/Macmillan, 1992. First book-length study of Lurie's work, written with her cooperation, is an essential resource. Provides a biographical sketch as well as discussion of all her writing, including a thorough examination of her major novels through *The Truth About Lorin Jones*. Features an extensive bibliography.

Newman, Judie. *Alison Lurie: A Critical Study*. Atlanta: Rodopi, 2000. Presents a chapter of biography and then discusses in turn each of Lurie's novels through *The Last Resort*.

_____. "Paleface into Redskin: Cultural Transformations in Alison Lurie's *Foreign Affairs*." In *Forked Tongues: Comparing Twentieth Century British and American Literature*, edited by Ann Massa and Alistair Stead. London: Longman, 1994. Particularly valuable for its discussion of Lurie's theme of transatlantic cultural differences.

Rogers, Katherine M. "Alison Lurie: The Uses of Adultery." In *American Women Writing Fiction: Memory, Identity, Family, Space*, edited by Mickey Pearlman. Lexington: University Press of Kentucky, 1989. Important study of Lurie's novels through *Foreign Affairs* explores the works from a feminist perspective, focusing especially on the theme of self-examination on the part of Lurie's heroines.

Stark, John. "Alison Lurie's Career." In *Twayne Companion to Contemporary Literature in English*, edited by R. H. W. Dillard and Amanda Cockrell. New York: Twayne, 2003. Reprint of a 1989 contribution to *The Hollins Critic* discusses Lurie's career as an instance of maturation within the same fictional territory.

Stern, Carol Simpson. "Alison Lurie." In *Contemporary Novelists*. 4th ed. New York: St. Martin's Press, 1986. Argues that the usual "influence" tie-ins from Lurie to Jane Austen and Henry James are "misleading" and asserts that Lurie's long fiction is more aptly compared with the works of feminist novelists Marilyn French, Erica Jong, Doris Lessing, and Joyce Carol Oates.

Waxman, Barbara Frey. "A New Language of Aging: 'Deep Play' in Carol Shield's *The Stone Diaries* and Alison Lurie's *The Last Resort*." *South Atlantic Quarterly* 67, no. 2 (Spring, 2002): 25-51. Analyzes two novels by prizewinning authors in which beliefs and practices regarding later life have the power to change readers' attitudes toward aging and death.

YUKIO MISHIMA
Kimitake Hiraoka

Born: Tokyo, Japan; January 14, 1925
Died: Tokyo, Japan; November 25, 1970
Also known as: Kimitake Hiraoka

PRINCIPAL LONG FICTION

Kamen no kokuhaku, 1949 (*Confessions of a Mask*, 1958)
Ai no kawaki, 1950 (*Thirst for Love*, 1969)
Kinjiki, 1951 (English translation in *Forbidden Colors*, 1968)
Higyo, 1953 (English translation in *Forbidden Colors*, 1968)
Shiosai, 1954 (*The Sound of Waves*, 1956)
Kinkakuji, 1956 (*The Temple of the Golden Pavilion*, 1959)
Kyoko no ie, 1959
Utage no ato, 1960 (*After the Banquet*, 1963)
Gogo no eiko, 1963 (*The Sailor Who Fell from Grace with the Sea*, 1965)
Kinu to meisatsu, 1964 (*Silk and Insight*, 1998)
Haru no yuki, 1969 (*Spring Snow*, 1972)
Homba, 1969 (*Runaway Horses*, 1973)
Akatsuki no tera, 1970 (*The Temple of Dawn*, 1973)
Tennin gosui, 1971 (*The Decay of the Angel*, 1974)
Hojo no umi, 1969-1971 (collective title for previous 4 novels; *The Sea of Fertility: A Cycle of Four Novels*, 1972-1974)

OTHER LITERARY FORMS

In addition to serious novels and his lighter fictional "entertainments," Yukio Mishima (mee-shee-mah) wrote a number of works in a variety of genres and styles. His short stories, particularly "Yukoku" ("Patriotism"), written in 1961, are among his most sharply etched and emotionally charged works of narrative fiction. Mishima's writing for the stage earned for him an important reputation as a dramatist in Japan, both in the older forms of twentieth century drama such as *shimpa* (a hybrid between Kabuki and modern theater), for which he created a masterful melodrama of nineteenth century Japan, *Rokumeikan*, in 1956, and in the contemporary theater, perhaps most effectively for the play *Sado koshaku fujin* (pr., pb. 1965; *Madame de Sade*, 1967). He also wrote dramas specifically composed for performance by traditional *bunraku* puppet troupes. Mishima's modern versions of traditional Japanese No plays, reconceived for modern actors, were also widely admired.

In addition, Mishima earned considerable fame as an essayist, particularly for his confessional *Taiyo to tetsu* (1968; *Sun and Steel*, 1970), in which he explored his newfound commitment to and trust in his body, superseding what he had come to see as the limitations inherent in the life of the mind.

ACHIEVEMENTS

Many Japanese readers and critics, and a large number of enthusiastic readers of Yukio Mishima in translation, are willing to place him at the forefront of postwar Japanese writers, perhaps even among the best writers of the entire modern period in Japanese literature. There remains, however, a certain disparity between foreign and Japanese views of Mishima and his accomplishments. Many intellectuals in Japan view Mishima's talents and attitudes with a certain reserve. For many Japanese, Mishima's flamboyant life and death lacked the dignity appropriate to a great writer, yet his often sensational subject matter (homosexuality, right-wing patriotism, mental derangement) was not necessarily frowned upon per se. Nevertheless, the posture frequently adopted in Mishima's writings of the novelist/narrator as a kind of voyeur seemed to some critics self-indulgent and inappropriate. It should be noted, however, that the very levels of emotional and erotic life that Mishima sought to chronicle were and are a part of human, specifically Japanese, mentality, and he bears genuine witness to aspects of Japanese life that may well make his novels and other works outlive their first popularity and attain a classic status.

One Japanese critic has remarked that Japan needed Mishima in the same way that Victorian England needed Oscar Wilde: Both writers used the beauty of the perverse to reveal crucial aspects of life in their societies that were tacitly banned from examination or open discussion. In many ways, Mishima was a man living out of his time, particularly because of his seemingly total lack of interest in social and political issues. The postwar literary scene in Japan has had at its center a considerable number of distinguished writers who show a genuine social commitment, often of a Marxist orientation. To such writers, Mishima merely seemed self-absorbed and narcissistic. The fact that Mishima, toward the end of his life, combined his aesthetic responses to life with a highly charged personal sort of homoerotic militarism that resulted in his own suicide remains distasteful and disturbing to many. In other ways, however, Mishima was the very prototype of the best-educated Japanese of his period—cosmopolitan, sophisticated, and often intellectually daring.

The legend of Mishima the man will doubtless continue to fascinate the general public, but at the same time, a certain amount of his work will surely continue to find an important place in the literary history of the twentieth century, for its beautiful language, psychological insights, and the close ties many of the works show with the techniques and philosophies of the great Japanese classical masterpieces so much admired and made use of by this most artful and self-aware of modern Japanese novelists.

BIOGRAPHY

Born Kimitake Hiraoka in 1925, the eldest son of a government bureaucrat, Mishima (who took the pen name of Yukio Mishima in 1941) was reared largely by his grandmother Natsuko, a woman of artistic tastes and neurotic temperament. During his child-hood and early adolescence, Mishima, by his own admission, spent much of his time in a kind of fantasy world. He pursued his studies at the Gakushuin (Peers School), where he began to write, in a highly precocious manner, for the school literary magazine. Mishima's interest in European, particularly French, literature began during this period. Graduated from the Peers School in 1944, he was not drafted and was able to begin his studies at To-kyo University. In 1947, he began working at the Ministry of Finance but soon resigned on the strength of his early literary successes to devote his full energies to writing. As his nov-els became more and more successful, he turned as well to writing for the stage, where he met with both critical and popular success.

Mishima made his first trip abroad during 1951 and 1952, visiting the United States, Europe, and Brazil. These visits gave him both another sense of the world and an increas-ing understanding of the appeal that his works had in translation for readers outside Japan.

Mishima married in 1958 and remained close to his wife and two children until his death twelve years later. At the same time, his strenuous cult of bodybuilding and his growing association with what came to be his own private army, the Tatenokai, suggest a homoerotic side of his nature first revealed in his early writings.

Mishima embarked on the composition of his tetralogy, *The Sea of Fertility*, while en-gaging in military maneuvers with his private army. To many critics and readers in Japan, Mishima seemed to have become something of a right-wing extremist, and by 1970, he had made the decision to kill himself upon completion of the manuscript of the fourth and final novel of the series. On November 25, 1970, after making a speech to the Self-De-fense forces, he committed ritual suicide in the traditional Japanese manner.

ANALYSIS

Yukio Mishima's work covers a wide spectrum of subject matter and themes. On one hand, he drew on the first-person confessional style familiar in Japanese literature since the time of the court diaries of the late Heian period (794-1185) right up to the works of such earlier twentieth century modern Japanese masters as Shimazaki Toson (1872-1943). To that existing style, however, Mishima added a confessional eroticism seldom if ever before employed within the canon of serious literature in Japan. Mishima also ad-mired Western literature, particularly such French novelists as Raymond Radiguet and François Mauriac and the classical playwright Jean Racine, finding in them models of a style that involved an elegant surface control of language that could permit glimpses of powerful passions underneath. Mishima's often baroque style and florid vocabulary tend to flatten out in translation, but the surfaces of his works in the original are usually highly polished and, in the context of the kind of naturalism so much a part of the postwar literary scene around the world, perhaps a bit artificial. Still, in novels dealing indirectly with so-cial issues, notably in *After the Banquet*, Mishima the stylist was able to find an idiom both contemporary and altogether appropriate to his relatively public subject matter.

CONFESSIONS OF A MASK

The confessional aspects of Mishima's writing can best be seen in his early *Confessions of a Mask*, the book that made him famous and is often regarded as his masterpiece. The device of the mask and the face, a frozen image shown to society that stands in opposition to the truth of the inner psyche, is an image so often employed that it may seem merely banal. In this novel, however, the title represents a powerful and entirely appropriate symbol for the narrator as he slowly comes to grasp his profound attraction to other men, and perhaps to violence as well. The unwinding of this theme is so skillfully carried out by means of his first-person narrative technique that the structures Mishima has conceived present a cumulative effect altogether authentic, both in emotional and literary terms. Then too, while Mishima creates a narrator who is principally concerned with chronicling, understanding, and analyzing his emotional development, he was careful to include in the novel enough suggestions concerning the narrator's surroundings that the reader can gain a real sense of what it was like to have grown up as a sensitive child during the difficult years when Japan was at war.

Still, the major themes of the book are indisputably eros and (at least by occasional implication) death. The powerful vision contained in the final pages of the book, when the narrator takes full cognizance of his erotic responses to a bare-chested hoodlum, certainly represents for the author a moment of truth that cannot be emotionally denied, and any sympathetic reader will surely be drawn in to the power of that sudden and revelatory instant of self-understanding.

THE TEMPLE OF THE GOLDEN PAVILION

In *The Temple of the Golden Pavilion*, published seven years later, in 1956, Mishima again draws on the possibilities of psychological confession in the first person, but on this occasion, he uses his skill to employ newspaper accounts and trial documents as a means to penetrate the mind of another; in this sense, the book maintains a powerful objectivity. In the novel, Mishima sets out to reconstruct the psychology of a young Buddhist acolyte who, in 1950, burned down the famous Zen temple Kinkakuji, the Golden Pavilion of the title, one of the great masterpieces of traditional Japanese architecture and an important site in the ancient capital of Kyoto. In his own way, Mishima took over the techniques of such traditional writers as the great Tokugawa playwright Chikamatsu Monzaemon (1653-1724), who, particularly in his famous love-suicide plays, took an actual event for his theme and attempted to reconstruct the psychological states that might have plausibly led up to the event portrayed.

In the case of a gifted writer such as Mishima, reportage was quickly subsumed in a masterful evocation of psychological imbalance. As in *Confessions of a Mask*, Mishima limits himself to the construction of a first-person psychological and introspective narrative, in which the acolyte reveals his self-disgust, his growing obsession with beauty, and his final decision (here Mishima seems to be inadvertently imitating themes in the work of

Oscar Wilde, whom he admired) to destroy the thing he loves the most—the beautiful temple itself. Like Salomé, after she has done away with John the Baptist, the acolyte lives on, satiated and at peace, at least until traditional morality reasserts itself.

In an even more effective manner than in the earlier novel, however, Mishima took great care to include in the narrative details of setting and milieu as well as to create a series of well-sketched additional characters, thus providing the reader with both a relief and a diversion from the obsessive quality of the narrator's personality. In particular, the temple superior, a remarkably worldly and opportunistic Buddhist priest, is portrayed with shrewdness and a sardonic humor, so that he might assume the role of a kind of foil for the young acolyte, psychologically speaking. By employing such a series of delicate balances in his narrative, Mishima makes certain that the reader always has a means to look objectively at the world of the acolyte, permitting the book to stand as a disturbing artistic vision of derangement, rather than as a case history.

AFTER THE BANQUET

Reportage of another sort provides the material employed by Mishima in composing *After the Banquet*, in which the author drew on the circumstances surrounding the Tokyo mayoral elections in the late 1950's. He based his account on certain events surrounding the candidacy of a prominent Socialist politician, who, because of his attachment to the proprietress of a fashionable restaurant, suffered a good deal of criticism and, among other things, lost the election. The novel caused a considerable scandal itself because of the supposedly revelatory nature of certain details in his account, but again, Mishima used the materials he had at hand to evoke his own authentic image of a contemporary Japan, catching both crucial details of the milieu and a beautifully realized delineation of the psychology of his two main characters, the stiff politician Noguchi and the earthy, yet somehow winning, Kazu, the owner of the restaurant.

The novel offers as revealing a glimpse into the somewhat despoiled yet remarkably vigorous life of politicians in Tokyo as any postwar author has been able to manage. The success of the novel results in part from the fact that Mishima's thrust is psychological, not political; he espouses no causes but plays instead the role of a humane and astute observer. The moral of the novel lies thus within the structures of the narrative itself. The development of the relationship between the pair, in which money and opportunity signally affect the changing nature of the affection each feels for the other, make *After the Banquet* perhaps the most objectively rendered and humanly satisfying of Mishima's novels.

THE SOUND OF WAVES

Mishima's attraction to European literature is particularly apparent in his novel *The Sound of Waves*, published in 1954 after his European trip four years earlier. Here Mishima drew directly on the Greek pastoral romance of Daphnis and Chloë (used also in the twentieth century by Maurice Ravel in his celebrated 1911 ballet), couching the famous account of the antique shepherd and shepherdess in Japanese terms. Quite popular at first, and immediately a success abroad when translated into English, the work has not worn well. The style is doubtless brilliant, yet the world of classical Greece and timeless, rural Japan are too far apart to merge effectively. The result now seems a sort of artificial pastiche. On the other hand, Mishima could blend classical Japanese sources into his work with enormous skill. A work such as the modern No play *Dojoji* (pb. 1953; English translation, 1966) shows a remarkable blending of ancient form and subject matter with a thoroughly modern sensibility. In Mishima's version, a young woman, spurned in love, decides to take her revenge in a fashion that, while paying homage to the medieval play, allows a thoroughly contemporary and, for the reader or spectator, altogether intimidating moment of psychological truth.

THE SEA OF FERTILITY

Mishima's tetralogy *The Sea of Fertility*, which occupied him from the mid-1960's until his death in 1970, was to be for him the summing up of his life, art, and belief. Although the tetralogy has been widely read in the original and in translation, the critical response to these four books has remained mixed. The highest praise has been reserved for the first volume, *Spring Snow*, which begins an account of a reincarnation in four separate personalities, all to be witnessed by Honda, a subsidiary character whose own growth of self-awareness and spiritual insight stands as one of the accompanying themes of this vast fable.

In *Spring Snow*, Honda is shown as a friend and confidant of Kiyoaki, a beautiful and willful young man who only manages to fall in love with his fiancé Satoko when he finds it necessary to force his way to see her in secret. At the end of the novel, Satoko flees their difficult situation and becomes a Buddhist nun. Kiyoaki dies, with an intimation that he and his friend Honda will meet again. The novel is elegiac in its emotional tone and contains a moving re-creation of the atmosphere of late nineteenth century Japan that can surely stand among Mishima's finest accomplishments.

The three remaining volumes find Kiyoaki reborn as a young fencer turned political extremist in *Runaway Horses*, then reappearing as a Thai princess in *The Temple of Dawn*, and, in the final volume, *The Decay of the Angel*, as a selfish, and perhaps empty-spirited, working-class youth. The plan and conception of this work is surely grand, perhaps grandiose. Some readers find the series, with its increasingly powerful Buddhist references, too far removed from the realities of the present-day Japanese consciousness. Some critics have also commented on the fact that the later volumes are spottily written. In any case, it is still too soon to say whether this last and most ambitious effort on Mishima's part will take its place at the head of his oeuvre or will merely remain a last ingenious experiment in the career of this gifted, adventuresome, and sometimes perverse genius of modern Japanese letters.

J. Thomas Rimer

OTHER MAJOR WORKS

SHORT FICTION: *Kaibutsu*, 1950; *Tonorikai*, 1951; *Manatsu no shi*, 1953 (*Death in Midsummer, and Other Stories*, 1966).

PLAYS: *Dojoji*, pb. 1953 (English translation, 1966); *Yoro no himawari*, pr., pb. 1953 (*Twilight Sunflower*, 1958); *Aya no tsuzumu*, pr. 1955 (*The Damask Drum*, 1957); *Shiroari no su*, pr., pb. 1955; *Aoi no ue*, pr., pb. 1956 (*The Lady Aoi*, 1957); *Hanjo*, pb. 1956 (English translation, 1957); *Kantan*, pb. 1956 (wr. 1950; English translation, 1957); *Kindai nogakushu*, 1956 (includes *Kantan, The Damask Drum, The Lady Aoi, Hanjo*, and *Sotoba Komachi*; *Five Modern No Plays*, 1957); *Sotoba Komachi*, pb. 1956 (English translation, 1957); *Toka no kiku*, pr., pb. 1961; *Sado koshaku fujin*, pr., pb. 1965 (*Madame de Sade*, 1967); *Suzakuke no metsubo*, pr., pb. 1967; *Waga tomo Hittora*, pb. 1968 (*My Friend Hitler*, 1977); *Chinsetsu yumiharizuki*, pr., pb. 1969.

NONFICTION: *Hagakure nyumon*, 1967 (*The Way of the Samurai*, 1977); *Taiyo to tetsu*, 1968 (*Sun and Steel*, 1970); *Yukio Mishima on "Hagakure": The Samurai Ethic and Modern Japan*, 1978.

EDITED TEXT: *New Writing in Japan*, 1972 (with Geoffrey Bownas).

MISCELLANEOUS: *Hanazakari no mori*, 1944 (short fiction and plays); *Eirei no Koe*, 1966 (short fiction and essays).

BIBLIOGRAPHY

Keene, Donald. *Dawn to the West: Japanese Literature of the Modern Era, Fiction*. New York: Holt, Rinehart and Winston, 1984. Massive study of the fiction produced in Japan from the time of the Japanese "enlightenment" in the nineteenth century closes with discussion of Mishima's work.

_____. *Five Modern Japanese Novelists*. New York: Columbia University Press, 2003. Keene devotes a chapter to Mishima in this examination of five Japanese novelists with whom he was acquainted. Provides his personal recollections of the writers as well as literary and cultural analyses of their works.

_____. *Landscapes and Portraits: Appreciation of Japanese Culture*. Tokyo: Kodansha International, 1971. Devotes a section to Mishima and his writings, commenting on a variety of his works but especially on *Confessions of a Mask*, because, atypically, this novel is autobiographical and so provides insight into the author's thinking and his relation to his own work. Mishima's preoccupation with death also is explored.

Miyoshi, Masao. *Accomplices of Silence: The Modern Japanese Novel*. Berkeley: University of California Press, 1974. Chapter 6 in part 2, "Mute's Rage," provides studies of two of Mishima's major novels, *Confessions of a Mask* and *The Temple of the Golden Pavilion*, as well as comments on other works. Includes notes and an index.

Nathan, John. *Mishima: A Biography*. 1974. Reprint. Cambridge, Mass.: Da Capo Press, 2000. Classic biography includes a new preface in this reprint edition. Nathan knew Mishima personally and professionally, and he presents a detailed and balanced portrait.

Piven, Jerry S. *The Madness and Perversion of Yukio Mishima*. Westport, Conn.: Praeger, 2004. Psychological study of Mishima traces the events of his life—most notably his early childhood, spent largely in his grandmother's sickroom—to provide a better understanding of the author and his works.

Scott-Stokes, Henry. *The Life and Death of Yukio Mishima*. Rev. ed. New York: Noonday Press, 1995. Following a personal impression of Mishima, presents a five-part account of Mishima's life, beginning with its last day, then returns to his early life and the making of the young man as a writer. Part 4, "The Four Rivers," identifies the rivers of writing, theater, body, and action, discussing in each subsection relevant events and works. Supplemented by glossary, chronology, bibliography, and index.

Starrs, Roy. *Deadly Dialectics: Sex, Violence, and Nihilism in the World of Yukio Mishima*. Honolulu: University of Hawaii Press, 1994. Critical and interpretive look at Mishima's work focuses on its elements of sex, violence, and nihilism. Examines Mishima's intellectual background, including the influences of Thomas Mann and Friedrich Nietzsche, and describes the quality of Mishima's thought. Includes bibliography and index.

Yourcenar, Marguerite. *Mishima: A Vision of the Void*. 1986. Reprint. Chicago: University of Chicago Press, 2001. Yourcenar, herself a novelist, analyzes Mishima's works and his role as a suicide in a film to argue that his life was "an exhausting climb" toward what he perceived as its proper end.

GLORIA NAYLOR

Born: New York, New York; January 25, 1950

OTHER LITERARY FORMS

In 1986, Gloria Naylor wrote a column, *Hers*, for *The New York Times*. She is also the writer of a number of screenplays, short stories, and articles for various periodicals. She is known primarily, however, for her novels.

ACHIEVEMENTS

Enjoying both critical and popular acclaim, Gloria Naylor's work has reached a wide audience. *The Women of Brewster Place* won the 1983 American Book Award for best first novel and was later made into a television miniseries. Naylor's other awards include a National Endowment for the Arts Fellowship in 1985 and a Guggenheim Fellowship in 1988.

Surveying the range of African American life in the United States, from poor ghetto to affluent suburb to southern offshore island, Naylor's work examines questions of black identity and, in particular, celebrates black women. In the face of enormous problems and frequent victimization, black women are shown coping through their sense of community and their special powers. Male readers might find less to cheer about in Naylor's early works, as she writes from a feminist perspective. Later works, however, recognize the plight of black males, acknowledging their struggles and celebrating their achievements. Though Naylor's focus is the black experience, her depictions of courage, community, and cultural identity have universal appeal.

BIOGRAPHY

The oldest child of parents who had migrated from Mississippi, Gloria Naylor was born and reared in New York City, her parents having left the South the year before her birth. An avid reader as a child, Naylor seemed to have inherited her passion for reading from her mother, a woman who would go to great lengths to purchase books to which she was denied access in Mississippi libraries because blacks were not allowed inside. The year Naylor graduated from high school, Martin Luther King, Jr., was assassinated, and the shock of this event caused Naylor to delay her college education. She chose instead to become a missionary for the Jehovah's Witnesses in New York, North Carolina, and Florida. She eventually found missionary life too strict, but her zeal apparently carried over into her later feminism. Although her writings are not religious, a fundamentalist pattern of thinking pervades them. She tends to separate her characters into the sheep and the goats (the latter mostly men), the saved and the damned, with one whole book, *Linden Hills*, being modeled on Dante's *Inferno* (c. 1320).

In high school Naylor read widely in the nineteenth century British novelists, but later in a creative writing course at Brooklyn College she came across the book that influenced her most—*The Bluest Eye* (1970), by the black American novelist Toni Morrison. The example of Morrison inspired Naylor to write fiction and to focus on the lives of black women, who Naylor felt were underrepresented (if not ignored) in American literature. Naylor began work on *The Women of Brewster Place*, which was published the year after her graduation from Brooklyn College with a bachelor of arts degree in English. By that time, Naylor was studying on a fellowship at Yale University, from which she received a master of arts degree in African American studies in 1983.

Naylor's background and literary achievements won for her numerous invitations for lectureships or other appointments in academia. She held visiting posts at George Washington University, the University of Pennsylvania, Princeton, New York University, Boston University, Brandeis, and Cornell. Diverse in her pursuits, Naylor wrote a stage adaptation of *Bailey's Café*. She founded One Way Productions, an independent film company, and became involved in a literacy program in the Bronx. She settled in Brooklyn, New York.

ANALYSIS

White people do not appear often and are not featured in the work of Gloria Naylor, yet their presence can be felt like a white background noise, or like the boulevard traffic on the other side of the wall from Brewster Place. White culture is simply another fact of life, like a nearby nuclear reactor or toxic waste dump, and the effects of racism and discrimination are omnipresent in Naylor's work. Against these stifling effects her characters live their lives and try to define their sense of black identity, from the ghetto dwellers of Brewster Place to the social climbers of Linden Hills to the denizens of Willow Springs, a pristine southern island relatively untouched by slavery and segregation.

Naylor writes about these settings and characters in a romantic mode that sometimes verges on the melodramatic or gothic. The influence of her earlier reading—such authors as Charlotte Brontë and Emily Brontë, Charles Dickens, William Faulkner, and Morrison—is apparent. The settings have heavy but obvious symbolic meanings, some derived from literary references: Brewster Place is a dead-end street, Linden Hills is a modern version of Dante's Hell, and Willow Springs recalls the magical isle of William Shakespeare's *The Tempest* (1611). The weather and numerous details also carry symbolic freight, almost as much as they do for such an emblematic writer as Nathaniel Hawthorne. In addition to literary influences, the symbolism seems to draw on Hollywood, particularly Hollywood's gothic genre, horror films; for example, in *Linden Hills* the character Norman Anderson suffers from attacks of "the pinks"—imaginary blobs of pink slime—while the rich undertaker Luther Nedeed locks his wife and child away in the basement.

These two examples also show, in an exaggerated fashion, how Naylor's characters fit into the Romantic mode. Her characters tend to go to extremes, to be emotional and obsessive, or to have a single trait or commit a single act that determines their whole life course. While rather one-dimensional and melodramatic, they nevertheless linger in the memory. Such is the case with Luther Nedeed, who represents Satan in *Linden Hills*, and with the old conjure woman Miranda "Mama" Day, who represents Satan's usual opposition in the scheme of things.

In Naylor, this scheme of things illustrates how she has transferred her former missionary fervor, along with the framework of religious thought, to her feminism. Luther Nedeed's behavior is only the most sensational example of men's cruelty to women in Naylor's work; he has a large following. On the other hand, the mystical ability of Mama Day, the Prospero of women's rights, to command the forces of nature and the spirit world is only the most sensational example of women's special powers in Naylor's thinking. Even the women of Brewster Place demonstrate these powers through their mutual love and support, enabling them to triumph over devastating personal tragedies and demeaning circumstances.

Naylor's men are another story: If not outright demons or headed that way, they seem to lack some vital force. Even the best men are fatally flawed—they are subject to the pinks, are addicted to wine, or have weak hearts. Failing at key moments, they are useful only as sacrifices to the feminine mystique. A prime example is the engineer George Andrews of *Mama Day*, who, for all his masculine rationality and New York smarts, does not know how to handle (significantly) a brooding hen. A close reading of Naylor's works reveals the men's victimization, along with the women's; however, Naylor is concerned with the women in her earlier novels. Naylor's later works indicate that she has expanded her vision to include men.

THE WOMEN OF BREWSTER PLACE

Naylor began fulfilling her commitment to make black women more prominent in American fiction with *The Women of Brewster Place: A Novel in Seven Stories*. The seven stories, featuring seven women, can be read separately, but they are connected by their setting of Brewster Place and by characters who appear, or are mentioned, in more than one story. The women arrive on the dead-end street by different routes that exhibit the variety of lives of black women, but on Brewster Place they unite into a community.

The middle-aged bastion of Brewster Street is Mattie Michael, who over the course of her life was betrayed by each of the three men she loved—her seducer, her father, and her son. She mothers Lucielia Louise Turner (whose grandmother once sheltered Mattie) when Ciel's abusive boyfriend destroys her life. In addition, Mattie welcomes her close friend Etta Mae Johnson, who also once gave Mattie refuge. Etta Mae is a fading beauty who has used men all of her life but is now herself used by a sleazy preacher for a one-night stand. The other women featured are the young unwed Cora Lee, a baby factory; Kiswana Browne, an aspiring social reformer who hails from the affluent suburb of Linden Hills; and Lorraine and Theresa, two lesbians seeking privacy for their love.

Few men are in evidence on Brewster Place, and these few inspire little confidence. C. C. Baker and his youth gang lurk about the alleyway and, in the novel's brutal climax, rape Lorraine. The crazed Lorraine in turn kills the wino Ben, the old janitor who earlier had befriended her. Naylor acknowledges the plight of the men, however. In her description of the gang members, she says,

> Born with the appendages of power, circumcised by a guillotine, and baptized with the steam of a million nonreflective mirrors, these young men wouldn't be called upon to thrust a bayonet into an Asian farmer, target a torpedo, scatter their iron seed from a B-52 into the wound of the earth, point a finger to move a nation, or stick a pole into the moon—and they knew it. They only had that three-hundred-foot alley to serve them as stateroom, armored tank, and executioner's chamber.

As these scenes suggest, Brewster Place is located in a ghetto plagued by social ills. The women must face these on a daily basis in addition to their personal tragedies and dislocations. Instead of being overcome by their sufferings, however, the women find within themselves a common fate and a basis for community. They gain strength and hope from their mutual caring and support. In addition to their informal support system, they form a block association to address larger problems. The ability of women to unite in such a community inspires admiration for their courage and their special powers.

LINDEN HILLS

The community feelings of Brewster Place, from which the women gain a positive sense of identity, somehow make the ghetto's problems seem less awesome, paradoxically, than those of Linden Hills, an affluent suburb. If Brewster Place is a ghetto, Linden Hills is a hell. Naylor underlines this metaphor by deliberately modeling *Linden Hills* after Dante Alighieri's *Inferno*. Linden Hills is not a group of hills, but only a V-shaped area on a hillside intersected by eight streets. As one travels down the hill, the residents become richer but lower on the moral scale. Lester and Willie, two young unemployed poets who perform odd jobs for Christmas money (they are the modern counterparts of Vergil and Dante), take the reader on a guided tour.

Lester's sister Roxanne deems black Africans in Zimbabwe unready for independence; one young executive, Maxwell Smyth, encourages another, Xavier Donnell, no longer to consider Roxanne as a prospective corporate bride; and Dr. Daniel Braithwaite has written the authorized twelve-volume history of Linden Hills without making a single moral judgment. Other sellouts are more personal: The young lawyer Winston Alcott leaves his gay lover to marry, and Chester Parker is eager to bury his dead wife in order to remarry.

Significantly, Linden Hills is ruled by men. The archfiend is Luther Nedeed, the local undertaker and real estate tycoon who occupies the lowest point in Linden Hills. Speaking against a low-income housing project planned for an adjacent poor black neighborhood, Nedeed urges outraged Linden Hills property owners to make common cause with the racist Wayne County Citizens Alliance. Most damning of all, however, is that Nedeed disowns his own wife and child and imprisons them in an old basement morgue; the child starves, but the wife climbs up to confront the archfiend on Christmas Eve.

MAMA DAY

It is clear that, while examining problems of middle-class black identity in *Linden Hills*, Naylor has not overlooked the plight of black women. In *Mama Day*, Naylor returns to a more celebratory mood on both subjects. The setting of *Mama Day* is a unique black American culture presided over by a woman with even more unique powers.

The coastal island of Willow Springs, located off South Carolina and Georgia but belonging to no state, has been largely bypassed by the tides of American history, particularly racism. The island was originally owned by a white person, Bascombe Wade, who also owned slaves. Bascombe married Sapphira, one of his slaves, and they had seven sons. In 1823, Bascombe freed his other slaves and deeded the island to them, his sons, and their respective descendants in perpetuity (the land cannot be sold, only inherited). Bascombe was more or less assimilated, and a black culture grew up on the island that was closely tied to the land, to the culture's beginnings, and to African roots. In other words, Willow Springs is definitely a mythical island—a tiny but free black state flourishing unnoticed under the nose of the Confederacy. Naylor underlines the island's mythic qualities by drawing parallels between it and the magical isle of *The Tempest*.

If Prospero presides over Shakespeare's island, then Prospero's daughter, Miranda "Mama" Day (actually a great-granddaughter of the Wades), presides over Willow Springs. Known and respected locally as an old conjure woman, Mama Day is a repository and embodiment of the culture's wisdom. In particular, she is versed in herbs and other natural phenomena, but she also speaks with the island's spirits. Mama Day uses her powers to heal and aid new life, but other island people who have similar powers are not so benevolent. One such person is Ruby, who stirs her knowledge with hoodoo to kill any woman who might take her man.

Unhappily, Mama Day's grandniece, Cocoa, down from New York on a visit with her husband, George, arouses Ruby's jealousy. By pretending to be friendly, Ruby is able to give Cocoa a deadly nightshade rinse, scalp massage, and hairdo. Just as a big hurricane hits the island, Cocoa begins to feel the effects of the poison. George, an engineer, native

New Yorker, and football fan, works frantically to save Cocoa, but he is overmatched. With his urbanized, masculine rationality, he cannot conceive of what he is up against or how to oppose it. Suffering from exhaustion and a weak heart, he is eventually killed in an encounter with a brooding hen.

Meanwhile, Mama Day has been working her powers. She confronts Ruby in a conjuring match, good magic versus bad magic, just as in Mali's oral epic tradition of the thirteenth century ruler Sundjata and in other traditions of modern Africa. Ruby is destroyed by lightning strikes, and Cocoa is saved. It is too late for George the doubter, however, who learns about the mystical powers of women the hard way.

BAILEY'S CAFÉ

In each of Naylor's first three novels, clear links to the work that follow it are evident. The character Kiswana Browne in *The Women of Brewster Place* serves as the connection to *Linden Hills*, having moved from that bourgeois community to Brewster Place to stay in touch with the struggles of her people. Willa Prescott Nedeed, the imprisoned wife in *Linden Hills*, points the way to *Mama Day*, since she is grandniece to Mama Day and first cousin to Cocoa. It is George, Cocoa's husband, who provides the link to *Bailey's Café*, Naylor's fourth novel.

In perhaps her most ambitious work yet, Naylor moves her readers from the magical island of Willow Springs to an equally intriguing site, for Bailey's Café is both nowhere and everywhere. It is sitting at the edge of the world yet is found in every town. As the café's proprietor, Bailey (though that is not his real name), tells readers,

> Even though this planet is round, there are just too many spots where you can find yourself hanging onto the edge . . . and unless there's some place, some space, to take a breather for a while, the edge of the world—frightening as it is—could be the end of the world.

Bailey's Café offers that breather, though some who enter the front door decide not to take it, instead going right through the café out the back door and dropping off into the void.

Like the inhabitants of Brewster Place, the customers in Bailey's Café are marginalized people. Their lives have taken them beyond the poverty and hard times of their urban sisters and brothers to the very edge of despair. However, for the women who people this extraordinary novel, Bailey's is simply a place to get directions to Eve's boardinghouse. Sweet Esther, abused to the point that she will receive visitors only in the dark; Peaches, whose effect on men drives her to mutilate her face with a can opener; Jesse, whose loss of marriage, child, and good name lead her to female lovers and heroin; and the pregnant virgin Mariam, ostracized from her village and bearing the effects of female circumcision— all find at Eve's a haven for their battered souls.

Throughout the individual stories of these women, Naylor uses unifying imagery: flower imagery, since each woman is associated with a particular bloom; musical imagery, jazz mostly, though the chords of the broken lives suggest the blues; and religious imagery, figuring heavily in Eve and her garden, but most noticeably in the virgin birth at the end of the novel. This birth is where the connection to *Mama Day* is made clear. Explaining the circumstances of his birth to Cocoa, George told of being left as an infant outside Bailey's Café by his mother, who was later found drowned. The last few pages of *Bailey's Café* reveal George as the drowned Mariam's child, recursively pointing back to *Mama Day*.

Similar to Naylor's other novels in its concentration on the diverse lives of black people, *Bailey's Café* nonetheless marks a shift for Naylor. This shift is evident in her inclusion of Mariam, from Ethiopia, who broadens the depiction of the black experience by encompassing an African one. Mariam is also Jewish, a fact that links her to the Jewish shopkeeper, Gabriel, in the novel. The coming together of the characters in celebration of the baby's birth—a celebration that intermixes different cultural and religious beliefs—brings a multicultural component to the novel absent in Naylor's other works.

Another notable change is Naylor's foregrounding of male characters. Bailey himself, the novel's narrator, is an example. His running commentary on the customers who find themselves in his establishment, his knowledge of Negro Leagues Baseball, and his narration of his courtship of his wife, Nadine, make him a central and engaging figure throughout the book. Another example is Miss Maples, the cross-dressing male housekeeper at Eve's boardinghouse. His rather lengthy individual story is included with those of the women; it points to Naylor's intention to portray a different kind of male identity as well as her desire to cultivate a different relationship with her male characters. This shift links *Bailey's Café* to *The Men of Brewster Place*, Naylor's fifth novel.

THE MEN OF BREWSTER PLACE

Naylor's return to Brewster Place gives readers the opportunity to revisit the male characters introduced in the first book (generally portrayed negatively) and see them in a different light. No longer assuming background roles, they are up front, giving an account of their actions in the first book. In *The Women of Brewster Place*, Mattie's son Basil skipped town while awaiting sentencing, causing his mother to lose the property she had put up for his bail. Here Basil does return, check in hand, to repay his mother for her loss; however, she is dead, and his unfulfilled desire to make amends leads him into a detrimental relationship and a prison sentence. Eugene, absent from his daughter's funeral in the first book, is in fact on site. His grief compels him to undergo a harsh punishment, one that has much to do with the fact that he could never tell Ciel that he is gay. C. C. Baker, responsible for the vicious gang rape of Lorraine, executes another heinous crime in this book but gives the reader insight into his tragic character. When he squeezes the trigger to kill his brother, he does so with eyes closed, thanking God "for giving him the courage to do it. The courage to be a man."

In *The Men of Brewster Place*, Naylor seems to be acknowledging that there is after all more than one side to a story and that she is ready to let the whole story be known. Passages from the first book provide continuity between the two works, as does the resurrected voice of Ben, the janitor killed by Lorraine. Reminiscent of the character Bailey in *Bailey's Café*, Ben is both character and narrator.

However, Naylor brings some new voices to Brewster Place when she introduces Brother Jerome and Greasy. These characters link together the lives of the men living in Brewster Place. Brother Jerome is a retarded child with an ability to play the piano that speaks of genius. The blues that pour from his fingers speak to the lives of each man, rendering their conditions tangible. Greasy makes his brief but memorable appearance in the story called "The Barbershop," leaving the men to carry the burden of his self-inflicted demise. Naylor's portrayals of these two characters are perhaps the most moving of the book. These characterizations, along with the complexity of all the male characters, point to a Naylor who is taking a broader view. She had prefaced *The Women of Brewster Place* with a poem by Langston Hughes that asked the question, "What happens to a dream deferred?" In *The Men of Brewster Place*, she seems ready to acknowledge that deferred dreams are not only the province of women.

Harold Branam
Updated by Jacquelyn Benton

OTHER MAJOR WORKS

NONFICTION: *Conversations with Gloria Naylor*, 2004 (Maxine Lavon Montgomery, editor).

EDITED TEXT: *Children of the Night: The Best Short Stories by Black Writers, 1967 to the Present*, 1995.

BIBLIOGRAPHY

Braxton, Joanne M., and Andrée Nicola McLaughlin, eds. *Wild Women in the Whirlwind: Afro-American Culture and the Contemporary Literary Renaissance*. New Brunswick, N.J.: Rutgers University Press, 1990. This wide-ranging collection of critical articles brings the cultural history of black women's writing to the 1980's. Barbara Smith's article "The Truth That Never Hurts: Black Lesbians in Fiction in the 1980's" discusses the section of *The Women of Brewster Place* entitled "The Two," but other articles also bear indirectly on Naylor's important themes.

Felton, Sharon, and Michelle C. Loris, eds. *The Critical Response to Gloria Naylor*. Westport, Conn.: Greenwood Press, 1997. A collection of essays analyzing four of Naylor's novels—*The Women of Brewster Place*, *Linden Hills*, *Mama Day*, and *Bailey's Café*—from a wide variety of perspectives.

Fowler, Virginia C. *Gloria Naylor: In Search of Sanctuary*. New York: Twayne, 1996. Fowler analyzes Naylor's first four novels; she also explains how Jehovah's Witnesses, of which Naylor was a member until she was twenty-five years old, and Naylor's feminism have influenced her fiction. Includes an interview that Fowler conducted with Naylor, a bibliography, and a chronology of Naylor's life.

Gates, Henry Louis, Jr., and K. Anthony Appiah, eds. *Gloria Naylor: Critical Perspectives Past and Present.* New York: Amistad, 1993. Focuses on Naylor's first four novels, with reviews of each book and essays analyzing her work. Two of the essays examine the role of William Shakespeare and of black sisterhood in Naylor's novels.

Kelley, Margot Anne, ed. *Gloria Naylor's Early Novels.* Gainesville: University Press of Florida, 1999. A collection of essays analyzing Naylor's first four novels, with several essays examining her work from a feminist perspective. Includes bibliographical references and an index.

Montgomery, Maxine Lavon. "Authority, Multivocality, and the New World Order in Gloria Naylor's *Bailey's Café.*" *African American Review* 29, no. 1 (Spring, 1995): 27. Montgomery discusses *Bailey's Café* as a woman-centered work that draws on black art forms and biblical allusions. Though she fails to recognize the true identity of Mariam's child (George of *Mama Day*), Montgomery otherwise provides a valid reading of *Bailey's Café,* commenting on the "more mature voice" with which Naylor addresses the concerns of her earlier novels.

_____, ed. *Conversations with Gloria Naylor.* Jackson: University Press of Mississippi, 2004. A compilation of previously conducted interviews and conversations with Naylor, in which Naylor addresses a wide range of topics. Includes Naylor's conversations with writers Toni Morrison and Nikki Giovanni.

Puhr, Kathleen M. "Healers in Gloria Naylor's Fiction." *Twentieth Century Literature* 40, no. 4 (Winter, 1994). Puhr discusses the healing powers of Naylor's female characters, principally Mattie Michael (*The Women of Brewster Place*), Willa Nedeed (*Linden Hills*), and Miranda (*Mama Day*), as well as Naylor's healing places, particularly the café and Eve's garden in *Bailey's Café.* She also discusses Naylor's works in terms of African American ancestry, generational conflicts, and broken dreams.

Stave, Shirley A., ed. *Gloria Naylor: Strategy and Technique, Magic and Myth.* Newark: University of Delaware Press, 2001. A collection of essays focusing on *Mama Day* and *Bailey's Café.* Stave argues that Naylor deserves an elevated position in the American literary canon.

Whitt, Margaret Earley. *Understanding Gloria Naylor.* Columbia: University of South Carolina Press, 1998. A thoughtful examination of Naylor's novels, through *The Men of Brewster Place,* that discusses major themes, symbolism, character development, Naylor's critical reputation, and her literary influences.

Wilson, Charles E., Jr. *Gloria Naylor: A Critical Companion.* Westport, Conn.: Greenwood Press, 2001. An analysis of Naylor's first five novels, with a separate chapter devoted to an examination of each book. The first chapter chronicles the events of Naylor's life, including information obtained in an interview conducted for this book, while another chapter establishes Naylor's place within African American literature.

DAVID PLANTE

Born: Providence, Rhode Island; March 4, 1940
Also known as: David Robert Plante

PRINCIPAL LONG FICTION
The Ghost of Henry James, 1970
Slides, 1971
Relatives, 1972
The Darkness of the Body, 1974
Figures in Bright Air, 1976
The Family, 1978
The Country, 1981
The Woods, 1982
The Francoeur Novels, 1983 (includes previous 3 novels)
The Foreigner, 1984
The Catholic, 1985
The Native, 1987
The Accident, 1991
Annunciation, 1994
The Age of Terror, 1999
ABC, 2007

OTHER LITERARY FORMS

In addition to his novels, David Plante has published short stories and essays as well as two memoirs. He has been a frequent contributor of short fiction to *The New Yorker* magazine, including stories such as "Mr. Bonito" (1980), "Work" (1981), "The Accident" (1982), and "A House of Women" (1986). He has also served as a reviewer and features writer for *The New York Times Book Review* and has contributed essays and introductions to works such as *Wrestling with the Angel: Faith and Religion in the Lives of Gay Men* (1995), edited by Brian Bouldrey. Plante's *Difficult Women: A Memoir of Three* (1983) is an account of his relationships with Sonia Orwell, George Orwell's widow, and writers Jean Rhys and Germaine Greer. *American Ghosts* (2005) is a personal memoir in which Plante focuses on how writing has served to link his past to his present by helping him to come to grips with his lineage as a French Canadian in New England, his Catholic upbringing, and his sexual orientation.

ACHIEVEMENTS

Although David Plante has never enjoyed a large readership, he has achieved considerable recognition among his peers, winning the acclaim of Philip Roth and other prominent contemporaries. Plante began his career with several self-consciously artistic novels, but in his later works he fashioned a spare, radically simplified style with a deceptive look of artlessness. In contrast to the minimalist writers to whose works his fiction bears a superficial resemblance, Plante uses this pared-down style as a vehicle to explore the consciousness of his protagonists, which he presents in a manner that differs sharply from the involuted style of most novels of consciousness. This is Plante's distinctive achievement in contemporary American fiction.

Plante's sixth novel, *The Family*, was nominated for the National Book Award in 1979. In 1983, while teaching writing at the University of Tulsa in Tulsa, Oklahoma, Plante received a Guggenheim grant, and in the same year he won the Prize for Artistic Merit from the American Academy and Institute of Arts and Letters. He also received an award from the British Arts Council Bursary and was named a fellow of the Royal Society of Literature.

BIOGRAPHY

David Plante was born in Providence, Rhode Island, on March 4, 1940, the son of Anaclet Joseph Adolph Plante and Albina (Bison) Plante. In 1959-1960, he attended the University of Louvain in Belgium, and in 1961 he earned a B.A. from Boston College. After graduation, Plante taught at the English School in Rome, Italy, at the Boston School of Modern Languages, and at St. John's Preparatory School. He also worked for two years (1962-1964) as a researcher for *Hart's Guide to New York* in New York City. In 1966, inspired, in part, by the example of the Anglo-American novelist Henry James, Plante settled in England, where he met Nickos Stangos, who would become his life partner.

Although he became a British citizen, Plante continued to spend time on both sides of the Atlantic; he was a writer-in-residence at the University of Tulsa (1979-1983) and at King's College, Cambridge (1984-1985). The first Westerner allowed to teach at the Gorky Institute of Literature in Moscow, Plante also served as writer-in-residence at the University of East Anglia (1977-1978), Adelphi University (1980-1989), and L'Université du Quebec à Montreal (1990). In 1998, he was named professor of writing at Columbia University. He divides his residency between New York and London.

ANALYSIS

David Plante's work is significant primarily for its contribution to the genre of the modernist novel of consciousness. His early experimental novels, although static and highly derivative, adumbrate the techniques Plante would later refine in novels that artfully explore the self-consciousness of individuals as they strive to understand their relationship with the external world. Plante succeeds in creating, through an often masterful command of language, a powerful synesthesia, blending paintings of the mind with the art of storytelling.

The dominant themes in Plante's novels concern the nature of relationships and the efforts of the individual to break out of self-consciousness in order to participate in these relationships. He explores the forces that unite people, whether family members, friends, or lovers, and the ability of these forces to bind as well as alienate, create as well as destroy.

Plante's method of narration in his early works reveals unconventional techniques that he later incorporated into his more traditional novels. In his earliest works, such as *The Ghost of Henry James*, *Slides*, *Relatives*, *The Darkness of the Body*, and *Figures in Bright Air*, Plante experiments with an almost plotless structure with an emphasis on language and the expression of consciousness, echoing Henry James, Nathaniel Hawthorne, James Joyce, and Gertrude Stein. Instead of a narrative of progression and movement within a defined space and time, these novels present random associations from constantly changing perspectives. Plante often creates snapshots of consciousness in the form of numerous brief narrative sections that flash in front of the reader, revealing not concrete images but glimpses of various characters' impressions, perceptions, and emotions. Through this technique, Plante attempts to use a character's consciousness to define and describe meaning, leading many critics to observe that these early novels are not novels at all but rather collections of psychological fragments that, though often powerful, ultimately confuse and disappoint the reader.

THE FRANCOEUR NOVELS

With the publication of his largely autobiographical trilogy *The Francoeur Novels* (which includes *The Family*, *The Country*, and *The Woods*) in 1983, Plante continued to develop his theme of relationships between family members through the perspective of subjective consciousness and fragmented images, but he integrated these experimental techniques into a more traditionally defined narrative. The first book of the trilogy, *The Family*, introduces Daniel Francoeur, Plante's autobiographical counterpart in the trilogy, and his six brothers, born to a Catholic, working-class French Canadian couple, Jim and Reena Francoeur. The novel is set primarily in Providence, Rhode Island, at the Francoeurs' newly acquired lake home. Plante traces the emotional struggle of the nine family members to remain unified, communicative, and productive in the face of internal tension and external threat. Because of their ethnic background and unsophisticated social orientation, the family members feel alienated from the Providence community, and when Jim loses his job through union pressure, the internal problems within the family are magnified at the same time the bonds of love and dependence between individual members are tested.

Although most of the narrative is seen and evaluated through Daniel's consciousness, the focus of the novel is not on him or on any one character; rather, it is on the Francoeur family as a single living organism trying to support and nurture all of its parts for the survival of the whole. The dependence of each family member on the well-being of the others is exemplified by the hysterical disintegration of the family unit when Reena experiences a recurrence of an emotional illness.

Plante develops Reena's character more fully than he does the others in *The Family*, and he examines her closely through Daniel's eyes, making her the touchstone for the novel's major theme: the fragility of the seemingly indestructible. Reena possesses the objectivity to see quite clearly the flaws in the character of each of her sons while simultaneously loving each totally; she is unable, however, to acknowledge her husband's inability to cope with his unemployment. Her failure to deal with her husband as a fallible human being forces her sons to take sides against their father and ultimately to question their familial duties.

Despite her strength and authority as the Francoeur matriarch, Reena remains a child-wife, puzzled and victimized by an uncommunicative, brooding husband. She confides frequently in Daniel, who comes to see his mother's position in the family as isolated and vulnerable. The only woman in a world full of men, an interloper in a fraternity house environment, Reena has tried to remain as unobtrusive as possible in her husband's and sons' world, from avoiding bringing into the house flowers and lacy decorations that might intrude on their male starkness to suppressing her fears and anger. She has created, literally, seven times over, a world that she can never enter. When her emotional breakdown occurs and Jim resists getting medical help for her, afraid she might come back from the sanatorium as something other than his submissive wife, the family organism suffers a shock and responds with violence: sons against father, mother against sons, brothers against brothers. The novel concludes with a semblance of unity, but the organism has been damaged.

The damage is subtly revealed in the second (although last-written) book of the trilogy, *The Woods*. Peace has returned to the Francoeur home, but only because Jim and Reena have surrendered to a self-imposed isolation and stagnant existence. They appear only peripherally in the novel, and the focus remains on Daniel, who visits his parents' home during a vacation from college. An extremely self-conscious adolescent, Daniel finds himself facing terrifying indecision and overwhelming freedom. Though little action takes place in the novel's three brief chapters, Plante conveys in simple yet intense language Daniel's need to belong, to anchor himself somewhere, to overcome his apathy and lack of ambition. Daniel's first sexual experience brings him no closer to what he wants as he becomes increasingly obsessed with the maleness of his own body. His decision to file with the draft board as a conscientious objector, despite the influence of his older brother Albert, a lifelong military man, role model, and major source of financial support for the Francoeurs, does give Daniel a sense of definition, though it is mixed with shame. In *The Woods*, Plante creates in Daniel a representation of the time in adolescence when passivity is the safest action, when any other action seems too great a risk, and when even one's own body appears strange and threatening.

This period in Daniel's life has long passed when *The Country* opens. Once again, Daniel, now a writer living in London, returns to his parents' home in Providence, where he joins his six brothers, not for any holiday or family celebration but as a response to the final assault on the family unit: the slow, degrading physical and mental deterioration of Reena and Jim Francoeur. Now in their eighties, they are weakened to the point of partial immobility and senility. The sons, some with wives and children, gather to take care of their parents' basic needs as well as to attempt, in quiet desperation, to restore the bonds of familial understanding and love. Reena's mental problems have intensified with age, and Daniel listens, as always, to her frightened and often bitter ramblings about her sacrifices for her husband and family. In more tender moments, however, Reena shows her devotion to her dying husband, frequently enveloping his withered body in her arms, grasping his hands in silence, and kissing his cheek. Reena is also still able to express love toward her sons, sharing their secrets and laughing at the jokes whispered to her in French.

The Country does not, however, use Reena as a symbol for the state of the Francoeur family as the first novel did. Except for a brief flashback to twenty years earlier at a tense family gathering at the lake house, the last book of the Francoeur trilogy explores the character of Jim, who in the earlier works receives uneven and ambiguous treatment. Through a first-person narrative, Daniel attempts to understand the complexities of a man who once seemed so simple. In moments of lucidity, Jim expresses to Daniel his doubts about having been a good father, husband, and worker, and Daniel realizes that, despite his father's domination over his mother and the unrelenting sense of social and familial duties imposed on his sons, Jim loved his family in every way that his Old World cultural background permitted, limited greatly by an inability to express his emotions.

As Daniel witnesses the pathetic deterioration of his once hearty and active father, he frantically tries to reestablish communication and a sense of tradition. In response, his father awkwardly attempts to understand his son's life as a writer in a foreign country. Ultimately, the father, drifting in and out of the present in a cloudy mind, leaves his son the only wisdom he knows: "Work hard. . . . And be a good boy." When his father dies, Daniel is able to grieve honestly for a man who, he now realizes, "could not think of himself, but had to think of his duty to the outside world." Reena, after an initial feeling of emancipation from her husband's authority, reacts to his death by retreating into incessant speech and fearful imaginings, once again alone among the men she created.

In *The Country*, the strongest work in the trilogy, Plante achieved what he had been working toward since his first novels: the subordination of plot with an emphasis on emotion and perception. The only significant action in *The Country* is the observation of time and death, but the helplessness of every member of the Francoeur family is a haunting and consistent echo throughout the novel. This echo gives *The Country* a power not realized in Plante's earlier works.

THE FOREIGNER

In the two novels succeeding the Francoeur trilogy, Plante's protagonist continues to narrate in the first person, though he is never mentioned by name in the earlier work, *The Foreigner*; only through allusions to the hero's family background does the author identify him as a member of the Francoeur family, probably Daniel once again. Adam Mars-Jones has suggested in a review of *The Foreigner* that the narrator may be Daniel's older brother Andre, noting that at the end of *The Family* the Francoeurs receive a postcard from Andre, who is in Europe, the same postcard that is mentioned in *The Foreigner.* This connection does exist, but the narrator of *The Foreigner* undeniably possesses the same history, voice, and sensibility as the protagonist of *The Francoeur Novels*, whatever name the reader gives him.

The Foreigner does not relate to the trilogy in any other way, nor does it follow the previous work chronologically. In this novel, the hero is twenty and leaving his Rhode Island home in 1959 to travel to Europe, hoping to shed his "Americanisms" and experience the expatriate lifestyle in the fashion of Ernest Hemingway, whose epigraph, "In Spain you could not tell anything," introduces the book. Instead of the romance and rebirth he expected, the narrator discovers loneliness and alienation from the environment and the people, even his American college friends who meet him in France. Wanting to get as far away as possible from what these friends represent, he is grateful to find a mysterious black woman he met previously on his crossing from America. From the moment he links himself with Angela Johnson and her emotionally disturbed lover Vincent, the strangeness and danger he craved are never far from him, though never fully defined.

Angela and Vincent demand all of their new friend's money, leaving him totally dependent on them by the time he realizes that they are possibly involved in illegal activities. The narrator's odd relationship with Angela and Vincent is revealed in the Hemingway style of terse dialogue and matter-of-fact description blended with Plante's characteristically fragmented narrative and vivid images of consciousness. *The Foreigner* is a unique work for Plante, however, in that it does make some attempt, though sporadic and uneven, to provide a climactic scene, the street-dance suicide of Vincent. No previous Plante novel uses this traditional narrative element. The circumstances that lead up to the story's climax, however, remain subordinate to Plante's interest in the objective correlatives of his protagonist's consciousness, the means of representing his thoughts and emotions as concrete objects or communicable expressions. Many of these thoughts reflect the narrator's voyeuristic, homosexual obsession with Vincent and the total sense of alienation brought about by this attraction.

THE CATHOLIC

Daniel's homosexuality, only implied in *The Francoeur Novels*, is made explicit in *The Foreigner* and becomes the major focus of *The Catholic*. Early in the Francoeur trilogy, Daniel becomes obsessed with the figure of the nude, crucified Christ, a ubiquitous presence in his Catholic home. As he grows older, Daniel develops strange correlations between the body of Christ and the power of male sexuality. In *The Catholic*, Daniel decides that the only way for him to overcome his intense self-consciousness and escape from his body's prison is to surrender himself physically and spiritually to another man. Women, in Daniel's perception, have no spirituality: They are fixed, concrete, earthbound objects and therefore can only give him back to himself as a mirror does, thus increasing his awareness of himself. Although Daniel turns to women as confidants and advisers, sexually they cannot provide the transcendental experience he seeks.

When Daniel falls in love with Henry, he mistakes sexual obsession for heightened consciousness. They spend only one night together, and Daniel immediately realizes that Henry wants to maintain his autonomy and selfhood as desperately as Daniel wants to lose his. The novel becomes little more than an explication of Daniel's frightening sexual compulsions and the aftermath of grief and guilt. *The Catholic* does not develop the narrative structures attempted in *The Francoeur Novels* and *The Foreigner*; it resembles more closely Plante's earlier novels in its extremely obscure language and disturbing images.

ANNUNCIATION

Plante's thirteenth novel, *Annunciation*, represents a culmination of many of the themes and images of the earlier novels as well as something of a departure from their terseness and almost plotless structure. Intertwining the tale of art historian Claire O'Connel and her teenage daughter Rachel with that of art editor Claude Ricard, Plante examines the darkness that envelops and threatens to overwhelm the characters. Attempting to shelter her daughter from the truth of her husband's suicide, Claire brings Rachel to England, where she is raped and becomes pregnant. The already tenuous relationship between the mother, sensual and with a survival instinct, and the daughter, ethereal and painfully like her father, is strained even more when Claire becomes engaged. Ironically, Claire's fascination with the subject of her thesis, Baroque artist Pietro Testa, and her quest to find a previously uncataloged painting titled, once again ironically, *Annunciation* eventually brings mother and daughter together.

Along the way other characters are able to touch the enigmatic Rachel in a way her mother has not been able to, including Belorussian Maurice Kurigan and Claude Ricard, a young art editor of Russian descent. Although he is still stinging from a physical but unfulfilling relationship with an Englishwoman and the suicide of a distant cousin, Claude finds that his depression and rage abate when he and Maurice throw themselves into helping Claire. To do so they travel to Moscow, where Maurice's contacts, the Poliakoffs, are unhelpful, Maurice dies, and Claude is stricken with fever before Claire's arrival. In a climactic scene, Rachel, even more determined than her mother to find the painting, walks away from her mother, who has finally told her of her father's suicide. Overwrought, Claire, led to the ailing Claude by Poliakoff, asks him to take her to the picture, which he had previously discovered. Stricken by the purity of the angel and the Virgin in the painting, Claire falls to her knees, overwhelmed with tears. In the final scene the Americans are together in the Poliakoff apartment as the Russians try to imagine the West. The novel ends with Claude's reverie on God—"No, I don't believe in God, but I can imagine him. . . . That vast dark space behind the image of a sunlit glass of water is the only way I can imagine God"—an ending that brings the novel a redemptive full circle from the eight-word opening chapter: "A glass of water in a dark room—."

THE AGE OF TERROR

More experimental in form than *Annunciation* and set almost exclusively in the Soviet Union during its final days, *The Age of Terror* traces a spiritual journey of sorts for twenty-three-year-old Joe, which begins the moment he sees an archival photograph of Russian partisan Zoya Kosmodemyanskaya, who had been hanged and mutilated by invading German troops during World War II. Impotent and without faith but hoping nonetheless to rekindle his dormant idealism, Joe quits college in New England and travels to Leningrad, where he encounters a modern Zoya, a former KGB operative now engaged in a joint venture with the American expatriate Gerald in selling people into prostitution under the guise of helping them flee the country. Interspersed with bleak, wintry scenes of life during the breakup of the Soviet Union are surreal vignettes inspired by the Russian past, all of which prophesy a "different world," one beyond imagination, that will replace this "terrible" world.

Joe is both beckoned and repulsed by the soulless landscape of Leningrad and Moscow in the last days of the Soviet Union and by the innate despair of the native population as they go about their daily struggle for existence. His ambivalence is counterpointed by Gerald's certainty: "The truth, which makes men of boys, is that no one will be saved, that we're all bad." No matter how much one wants to feel "something beyond the age of terror," there is nothing. Befuddled, in part, by a persistent low fever, Joe eventually succumbs to the strength of Gerald's cynical conviction, and, against Zoya's express wishes, he confirms to Gerald the existence of her beautiful son Yura, whose desire to be a ballet dancer is an ironic consequence of the many years that his mother secretly monitored the movements of the ballet company's artists and their contacts with foreigners.

This betrayal is the turning point of the book. Later, Zoya belatedly embraces the nationalism of her namesake, whose photograph attracted both Joe and Gerald to Russia as if it were a place that embodied all of their personal suffering and longing; she announces to Gerald that she has taken a job with the publications department at the Bolshoi Ballet and that their partnership is at an end. Zoya decides that she will no longer be Gerald's willing accomplice in the hope that he will get her out of the country; instead, she has thrown in her lot with her fellow citizens. In revenge and perhaps in an effort to bind Zoya solely to him, Gerald has both Yura and his dance partner Larissa kidnapped and sold into the sex trade.

The novel concludes as Joe, still hallucinating from a fever, accompanies the now-devastated Zoya into the midst of a snow-covered forest, the forest he had once worshiped in his dreams. As he follows her into a snowdrift, Joe glimpses over Zoya's shoulder the brown clapboard house that had been his childhood home. Thus, the final vision of *The Age of Terror* is of two individuals bound by and reconciled through their sorrow.

ABC

Plante's next novel, *ABC*, published eight years after *The Age of Terror*, provides yet another exploration of one of the author's favorite themes in both his fictional and his autobiographical works: how vividly the lingering presence of the dead informs the experience of the living. In this case, the principal character, Gerard Chauvin, is so traumatized by the accidental death of his six-year-old son, Henry, in a deserted house near the family's summer residence that he abandons his wife, Margaret, and his career and sets out on an international quest to make some sense of the senselessness of his loss. Gerard's search is triggered by the fact that he was distracted from keeping an eye on his son by his presumably accidental discovery of a scrap of paper on which was written the alphabet in Sanskrit; his subsequent struggle to contend with his guilt and grief becomes inextricably tied to his newfound obsession with patterns of arrangement, such as the disposition of objects on the shelf in his son's room or the ordering of the letters of the alphabet.

A college teacher of French Canadian extraction, much like Plante himself, Chauvin becomes incrementally drawn to other individuals who have experienced similar personal tragedies: a Chinese woman named Catherine, whose daughter Susan committed suicide with a drug overdose; a Sephardic Jew named David Sasson, whose wife, Dirouhi, an Armenian art historian, is murdered by Greek terrorists; and a Chechen woman named Aminat, whose daughter is raped and murdered by Russian troops during Chechnya's ongoing struggle for independence. The unbearable suffering felt by each of these characters is translated into an irrational but compelling desire to discover why the letters of the alphabet are arranged as they are. It is as if all four characters believe that by finding the answer to why "a" comes before "b" and "b" before "c," they will discover that there is some ordering principle to the apparent randomness of life.

The momentum of Gerard's philological inquiry, impelled both by the chronological nature of the subject matter and by the consecutive narratives of his compatriots, takes him from his hometown of Manchester, New Hampshire, across the Atlantic to England and eventually to the Eastern Mediterranean. His journey and eventually that of the whole group, like the study of the origins of written language, propels them farther and farther east toward the traditional geographic cradle of ancient civilization. In particular, after Gerard meets Catherine on the second floor of the central public library on Copley Square in Boston, the two travel, by her invitation, to her flat in London and then to Cambridge University, where Catherine's daughter Susan had studied philology with an eccentric don named Charles Craig. In the latter's rooms at King's College, they encounter David Sasson, himself in search of whether there might be some prototype of all Indo-European alphabets, some original system of written symbols from which all other languages evolved. David, in turn, invites Gerard and Catherine to his houses in Athens and on the island of Paros, where they all find on the beach the distracted Aminat, who has hitched her way illegally from Chechnya in an effort to reach the site of ancient Ugarit in present-day Syria. Grief is the tie that binds these "abecedarians" together.

Each stage of their progressive journey comes with commentary on the attempts by generations of scholars to trace the origin of the Roman alphabet. In fact, some critics have compared the novel, in this regard, to Dan Brown's immensely popular *The Da Vinci Code*

(2003) in that both can be read as historical detective stories. This injection of academic research is applauded by some critics, who find that such didacticism adds texture to the narrative; at various points in their travels, for example, Gerard and the others find copies of James Février's seminal text *Histoire de l'écriture* (1948; history of writing), the primary source Plante uses for most of the linguistic discoveries of his characters. Every time the book resurfaces, someone reads a passage from the text, which adds another piece to the philological puzzle. Other critics, however, find such instructional moments inexpertly handled, and they cite Plante's inclusion of Charles Craig in his cast of characters apparently only for the purpose of having someone deliver a lesson on how all letters most likely originated as pictograms, representing physical objects.

Beyond any knowledge of language formation, Gerard, Catherine, David, and Aminat are looking for the organizing principle behind all verbal communication and, thus, trying to find the answer to a question that no one has answered before. In so doing, they hope to end their feeling of helplessness by discovering some ultimate meaning. Perhaps, in this regard, their quest is essentially spiritual. In a trailer park near the site of Gerard's son's death, for example, a young Indian girl links the letters of the alphabet to humanity's sense of the divine when she recites a line from the ancient Hindu sacred text the Bhagavad Gita in which the god Krishna asserts: "Of sounds I am the first sound, A."

In the final analysis, it could be said that, like Plante himself in his memoir *American Ghosts*, Gerard is simply seeking some form of transcendence, some link to the universal as embodied, in this instance, in the concept of the alphabet. Perhaps by studying history the members of the group will find the answers that they seek; David, spokesman for this perspective, argues that "the history of humankind is the history of gods" and that historical study may ultimately prove the existence of God or the gods who revealed the first alphabet to humankind.

Several aspects of *ABC* have attracted the most critical comment. The novel's first chapter has been praised consistently for its emotional impact, particularly Plante's vivid evocation of a family's impromptu summer "adventure" gone terribly wrong. Disagreement has arisen, however, over the relative success of the rest of the book, with some critics annoyed by the plot's many improbable coincidences and what they see as the ending's formless mysticism; still others find the book a lyrical record of the mysteries of human life and applaud the dreamlike conclusion, which is reminiscent of the ghost-haunted walk in the forest at the end of *The Age of Terror.*

Penelope A. LeFew; Jaquelyn W. Walsh
Updated by S. Thomas Mack

OTHER MAJOR WORKS

NONFICTION: *Difficult Women: A Memoir of Three*, 1983; *American Ghosts: A Memoir*, 2005.

BIBLIOGRAPHY

Dukes, Thomas. "David Plante." In *Contemporary Gay American Novelists: A Bio-bibliographical Sourcebook*, edited by Emmanuel S. Nelson. Westport, Conn.: Greenwood Press, 1993. Provides a brief biography and then presents a discussion of Plante's major works and themes.

Plante, David. "Creating the Space for a Miracle." Interview by Suzi Gablik. In *Conversations Before the End of Time*. New York: Thames and Hudson, 1995. Interview with Plante is part of a collection of interviews with philosophers, writers, and other artists that aims to address the meaning of art in culture at the end of the twentieth century.

_____. "My Parents, My Religion, and My Writing." In *Catholic Lives, Contemporary America*, edited by Thomas J. Ferraro. Durham, N.C.: Duke University Press, 1997. Plante discusses the influence of Catholicism on his fiction.

_____. "Portrait of the Artist: Interview with David Plante." Interview by Aaron Hamburger. *Lambda Book Report* 13 (April/May, 2005): 6-8. Plante, an avowed atheist, argues for the existence of some collective consciousness that connects not only the living but also the dead.

_____. "Seeing Through a Glass, Darkly: David Plante." Interview by Paul Baumann. *Commonweal* 121 (August 19, 1994): 14, 21-22. Plante discusses the significance of religious themes in his work, the influence of Ernest Hemingway on his writing, the importance of his French Blackfoot Indian heritage to his style, his fears about the lack of redemption in masterpieces of American literature, and his belief that writing can lead one outside oneself.

Summer, Claude J, ed. *The Gay and Lesbian Literary Heritage*. Rev. ed. New York: Routledge, 2002. Includes a short article focusing on Plante's place in the tradition of gay literature and argues that in his fiction he covers a wide range of homosexual identity, from the overt to the underdeveloped and the ambiguous.

MANUEL PUIG

Born: General Villegas, Argentina; December 28, 1932
Died: Cuernavaca, Mexico; July 22, 1990
Also known as: Juan Manuel Puig

PRINCIPAL LONG FICTION

La traición de Rita Hayworth, 1968 (*Betrayed by Rita Hayworth*, 1971)
Boquitas pintadas, 1969 (*Heartbreak Tango: A Serial*, 1973)
The Buenos Aires Affair: Novela policial, 1973 (*The Buenos Aires Affair: A Detective Novel*, 1976)
El beso de la mujer araña, 1976 (*Kiss of the Spider Woman*, 1979)
Pubis angelical, 1979 (English translation, 1986)
Maldición eterna a quien lea estas páginas, 1980 (*Eternal Curse on the Reader of These Pages*, 1982)
Sangre de amor correspondido, 1982 (*Blood of Requited Love*, 1984)
Cae la noche tropical, 1988 (*Tropical Night Falling*, 1991)

OTHER LITERARY FORMS

Although he is best known for his novels, Manuel Puig (pweeg) was also an author of nonfiction, a playwright, and a screenwriter. His screenplays for his own *Boquitas pintadas* (1974) and for José Donoso's novel *El lugar sin límites* (1978) both won prizes at the San Sebastián Festival. His plays include *El beso de la mujer araña* (pb. 1983; *Kiss of the Spider Woman*, 1986), an adaptation of his novel, and *Misterio del ramo de rosas* (pb. 1987; *Mystery of the Rose Bouquet*, 1988).

ACHIEVEMENTS

Manuel Puig established himself both as a Latin American novelist and as a writer capable of providing insight into contemporary American society. For many years, Puig was a highly mobile exile from Argentina, spending considerable stretches of time in New York City and also favoring other cosmopolitan centers, such as Rio de Janeiro. In the process, he became a cross-cultural writer, exploring such phenomena as the effects of mass communications and culture, the issues of changing gender roles and variant sexualities, and the need to establish new types of bonds in an impermanent and rapidly changing social environment.

In addition to the university audience that is likely to gravitate toward Latin American authors, Puig's work appeals to various subcultures such as those found in New York. Film enthusiasts are understandably drawn to this novelist, who used a storehouse of cinematic knowledge in his fiction. Film critic Andrew Sarris, among others, has directed his readers toward Puig's novels and followed Puig's career with interest. The growth of the gay people's liberation movement and the general interest in alternative sexualities also increased Puig's readership, and he, in turn, was willing to learn from this movement, with its stress on the validation of nonstandard sexual expression. The author was receptive to the idea that some readers would come to his works, lectures, and public readings specifically attracted by this content, and he discussed his thoughts about sexuality in the magazine *Christopher Street* and other gay forums. Puig also became a figure admired by many members of another subculture, science-fiction readers and writers, who feel drawn not only to Puig's *Pubis angelical*, with its unmistakable borrowings from science fiction, but also to the author's overall production, for its critique of culture and society.

Puig's work thus reaches an audience more diverse than the literary sophisticates who are the only audience for many experimental writers. The excellent relationships the author established with cultural subgroups in the United States reveal his profound willingness to reach out to many types of readers, including the special enclaves that may be considered marginal or bizarre by the literary establishment.

Biography

Juan Manuel Puig was born on December 28, 1932, in General Villegas, Argentina. His early life, however confusing it may have been to him, provided him with excellent insight into the problems of mass-media saturation and contemporary uncertainties about sexuality and sex-role definition. As the author reported it, his almost daily filmgoing began before he had reached the age of four. The boy favored films with a strong element of glamour and fantasy, especially the extravagantly mounted musical comedies and dramas imported from the United States. His attention, he recalled, was directed almost exclusively to the female lead performers; male actors failed to provoke an empathetic response.

At the age of ten, Puig suffered a traumatic experience: an attempted rape by another male. Because Puig chose to make public this very troubling incident in his early life, one may assume that it is associated with his later literary interest in showing the effects of formative experiences in the shaping of one's identity, particularly in the emergence of a conflicted or uneasy sense of one's sexual self.

Puig's hometown was severely limited in its cultural and educational opportunities, but U.S. films provided continual reminders of the larger, cosmopolitan world. Puig's mother was an urban woman who had gone to the pampas to work in the provincial health services and ended up staying there and marrying a local man. This woman stood out from her surroundings in many ways; with her great passion for reading and filmgoing, she seems to have had a streak of Gustave Flaubert's Madame Bovary in her character. At any rate, the provincial's longing for a cosmopolitan environment became powerfully represented in Puig's first two novels.

A secondary factor in Puig's development was the disjunction between his Spanish-language environment and the English-language film world. The language used in Hollywood films, as conventionalized as it often is, cannot be considered representative of any spontaneously occurring form of expression, but Puig nevertheless identified the English language with Hollywood (indeed, as he later explained, it made him feel close to Hollywood), and he sought to bridge the gap between his world and the cinematic world by mastering English. The idea of English as the language of film persisted with Puig, to the extent that his first few writing efforts were film scripts in English. He was an active consultant in the translation of his novels into English, and he actually wrote the first version of *An Eternal Curse on the Reader of These Pages* in English, later composing a Spanish equivalent; the published English version of the novel was based on both the unpublished English original and the Spanish "translation."

Puig's early career was marked by various unsuccessful attempts to find an outlet for his special love and knowledge of film and other popular forms. From 1955 to 1962, Puig sought to break into screenwriting and directing but was consistently unable to make progress in the film industry. A scholarship in 1957 to the Experimental Film Center permitted him to study filmmaking in Rome; later, he tried Spanish-language script work in Argentina, but he seemed to be insufficiently attuned to national realities. To become comfortable with an Argentine Spanish suitable for screenwriting, Puig worked at reproducing the voices he had heard around him in his hometown. The re-creation of these voices from a long-ago small-town world proved more absorbing than the task of screenwriting and allowed Puig to begin writing novels.

The sets of concerns referred to above are, essentially, the crucial issues of Puig's first two novels. In 1963, the restless Puig moved to New York, took a fairly undemanding job as an airline employee, and set about writing narrative, the literary form that would eventually prove his most successful medium. The author was soon able to obtain praise for his work, but it was 1968 before *Betrayed by Rita Hayworth* was published, and then without attaining a wide readership. *Heartbreak Tango* followed, as popular and readable as a soap opera, which it resembled. It drew readers to his earlier novel, and Puig became a celebrated feature of the Buenos Aires scene, which during those "boom" years tended to make celebrities of innovative writers.

In 1973, however, his third novel, *The Buenos Aires Affair*, was confiscated by authorities. After the impounding of the copies of this work, Puig published with the Barcelona firm of Seix Barral. Well established as a novelist with an international reputation, Puig traveled widely, spending considerable time in New York. He died in Cuernavaca, Mexico, on July 22, 1990.

ANALYSIS

Although Manuel Puig took pains to introduce new variants on his favored thematic issues and to seek new solutions to the formal problems of organizing a novel, he has tended to remain identified in many minds with his first work. The highly memorable title of this novel would seem to make actor Rita Hayworth a character in the plot, and, indeed, this implication is in a sense accurate, though the action takes place far from Hollywood.

BETRAYED BY RITA HAYWORTH

In *Betrayed by Rita Hayworth*, Hayworth and other luminaries of the late 1930's and early 1940's figure as vivid presences in the decidedly unglamorous lives of a group of small-town Argentine children growing into a troubled adolescence, continually turning to the films to supply satisfactions that are missing in their existence.

Betrayed by Rita Hayworth also introduced a type of character common throughout Puig's writings: the young person confused about sex. Here, the protagonist Toto is particularly prominent in this role. Toto's early stream-of-consciousness narratives reveal his inability to make the standard distinction between male and female; he identifies himself with Shirley Temple and his unreliable father with the treacherous Rita Hayworth. As is evident from the beginning, his uncertain notions about sexuality and sex roles are entwined with his popular-culture fantasy vision of life. The two themes come together in Toto's essay about the 1938 film *The Great Waltz*. Attempting to convey the film's ambience of a rapturous, waltz-mad Old Vienna, Toto inadvertently signals his conflict-filled view of sex. Among other things, he expresses the idea that heterosexual sex, even in the form of simple embracing and kissing, is physically harmful to women; he inserts his own element of voyeurism not found in the original film; and he dwells on the theme of insecurity about one's sexual attractiveness.

Betrayed by Rita Hayworth shows with extraordinary vividness the ability of a popular medium to bedazzle and distract consumers, particularly when audience members lack other sources of stimulation. The novel, however, does not constitute simply a lovingly nostalgic evocation of a filmgoer's paradise, for Puig also offers a critique of popular culture. It becomes clear that his characters are suffering the effects of the acritical and unquestioning consumption of a mass-culture product.

As well as including material on the sexual lives of very young characters (both real and imaginary), this first novel was unusual enough in its approach to appear risky to publishers. The small, daring Buenos Aires firm of Jorge Álvarez launched the work but then was forced to close. Later, a more prestigious house, Editorial Sudamericana, reprinted it, but only after the publication of Puig's second novel, the playfully nostalgic appeal of which convinced the public that Puig was readable. Although *Betrayed by Rita Hayworth* subsequently became a best seller, it remains a difficult work to assess and to characterize. Perhaps most difficult of all the issues involved is that of establishing the work's relation to the phenomenon of popular culture.

Sudamericana's publicity for *Betrayed by Rita Hayworth* characterized the text as a "pop novel," certainly an attractive and catchy phrase. Along with the merrily kitsch cover, which showed a tawdry Art Deco fantasy vision of Hollywood-style glamour, the publicity surrounding the work suggested that Puig had produced either an item of pop culture or a denunciatory satire of the Hollywood culture. As Puig noted, these two options seem to account for most of the readings of his works, although neither is especially accurate. *Betrayed by Rita Hayworth*, for example, cannot be critically restricted to a mere part of pop culture, for the simple reason that it evinces complex new structures characteristic of the twentieth century novel. The narration is not undertaken by a recognizable and reliable narrative voice, as it typically is in the easy-to-read formula best seller; rather, one must discover what is happening to the characters by extracting information from a variety of types of narration. These include a babble of neighborhood voices discussing the hero's birth and his mother's situation, extracts from a young girl's diary, diverse forms of stream-of-consciousness writing, a prizewinning school essay by the protagonist, letters, and other modes, all designed to look like transcriptions from the flow of thought and language. Because the novel is so strikingly anomalous, with its paradoxical joining of sophisticated novelistic form and popular culture, it conveys the impression of a somewhat uneasy synthesis.

HEARTBREAK TANGO

Heartbreak Tango is much easier to read than its predecessor. It was an immediate best seller when it appeared and, in effect, served to draw readers to Puig's more complex early novel. *Heartbreak Tango* takes the form of an old-fashioned installment novel, with each chapter revealing a new, tantalizing glimpse of a fairly intricate but banal plot. The reader is drawn along by two major lines of development: how a wondrously handsome young man of fairly good family came to an impoverished, tubercular end, and how the tense relations between a housemaid and her upwardly mobile seducer culminated in the latter's murder. Further interest comes from following the fates of three other young women: the handsome young rake's scheming sister; a local cattle baron's daughter, who rendezvouses with the rake while waiting to marry into the landed aristocracy; and another of the hero's conquests, an ambitious blond who can never manage to rise above the lower middle class.

The characters, however sympathetic they may be at moments, are satirized for their obsession with status and standing. Puig warned against placing too great an emphasis on the satiric element. While well-educated urban readers might see the book as turning the members of the provincial middle class into figures of fun, such a reading fails to take into account the great amount of material dedicated to the exploration of Puig's twin themes of popular culture and concepts of sexuality.

One of the most telling indicators of the extent to which the media have saturated the culture is the language used by the characters to speak of their own lives. So enthralled are they by the commercially standardized language of sentimental and romantic films, advertising copy charged with mass-appeal allure, and other popular subgenres (song lyrics, sportscasting, "tearjerker" novels, and so on) that this language becomes second nature to them. The problem is the lack of correlation between their own existence and the rapturous, adventurous, or "macho" language they employ. The incongruity is especially acute in the area of courtship mores. The reader sees a small society in which both marriage and informal liaisons are heavily governed by questions of prestige and economic power, while the characters see love and sexuality through a haze of dreamily romantic or aggressively Don Juanesque phrases.

The presentation of popular culture in *Heartbreak Tango* is much more diverse than it is in *Betrayed by Rita Hayworth*. The characters, no longer children growing into adolescence, are young adults moving toward an early, disaffected middle age. Their patterns of pop-culture consumption reflect this shift. They have lost the child's ability to be enraptured by a film, and they turn to the cinema house as a meeting place, a distraction in which they indulge by ingrained habit. Concerned with presenting themselves impressively, they rely on advertising and magazine materials in order to master style. The artifacts of mass culture—photo albums, commercial art, decorative product packaging, dance-hall decor, and household bric-a-brac—surround them. They are living in the "golden age" of radio, and the airwaves are full of gimmicky programs, including variety shows, serial dramas, and musicals.

On one hand, the young people present the classic picture of "junk-culture addicts"; they show many signs of a virtual dependence on their pop culture. (One young woman, for example, cannot forgo her daily radio soap opera, even when a long-absent friend shows up at her house.) Despite this constant consumption of media, however, their satisfaction with it lessens. The rakish hero reports attending the cinema without feeling any interest in the film shown, while an observant heroine notices that her town is being shipped films that are too out-of-date to screen elsewhere. These expressions of ennui with the homogeneous mass media do not, however, entail a critical questioning of mass culture. The young people are not moved by their boredom and dissatisfaction with certain pop-culture artifacts to ask whether the massive standardization of this culture might be unwarranted and intellectually unhealthy, nor do they attempt to find alternative forms of diversion. The young men and women remain fixed in their accustomed patterns.

The focus on sexuality is less concerned with individual cases than it is with the social codes that govern the expression of sexual feelings. The small-town young people try to satisfy various conflicting sets of standards. On the surface, the unmarried women are expected to remain chaste, while men are given more leeway, although they are required to satisfy conditions of respectability. Overlapping this Victorian standard, and at times in conflict with it, is the code of machismo, which demands of the young men a constant effort to conquer numbers of women, to cultivate a swaggering style, and to appear unconcerned with their own well-being. An additional set of factors has to do with the intense and widespread desire for upward mobility.

Apart from the inherent passion between the sexes, the desire for prestige is the most powerful force in determining the characters' involvements with one another. The Don Juanesque hero's sister continually schemes to link him with the cattleman's daughter and to steer him away from the blond social climber, while the stockbroker seeks to guide his daughter toward a landowning customer. Meanwhile, the blond attempts to minimize a loss of status incurred by an earlier seduction, hoping to charm her Casanova-lover into marriage. In a subplot, the hero masterminds the amorous life of a lower-class friend. Under this tutelage, the aspiring policeman seduces a servant, avoiding any lasting commitment that might impede his rise in society.

Of the various liaisons contracted during the novel, all are somehow colored by the dream of acquiring an advantageous match in marriage. The schemes uniformly come to nothing, for the hero dies without marrying any of his lovers; the wealthy landowner rejects the stockbroker's daughter, along with a shipment of diseased cattle; the policeman's brief enjoyment of middle-class status is ended by his spurned girlfriend's violence. In an ironic turnabout, the vision is realized only by the servant girl, who stands at the very bottom of this hierarchy. After being seduced, impregnated, and abandoned—even after murdering her lover—she somehow succeeds in obtaining for herself a stable and provident mate.

Puig is unmistakably critical of this scenario, in which sex and courtship are made part of the politics of class standing. He offers a condemnatory portrait of this system, making his attitude clear by portraying popular culture as stressing the acquisition of an impressive lover or spouse. (At the height of the cross-class tangle of sexual alliances, the local movie theater is running a Hollywood film centered entirely on the concept of marrying for wealth and security.) The criticism is clear, but Puig has not begun to look at alternative arrangements that would remove sexuality from this very politicized framework. This missing factor does, however, appear in Puig's later work, when he turns to utopian speculations about the future of sex.

THE BUENOS AIRES AFFAIR

If Puig's first novel was substantially patterned on the modern "serious" novel and his second novel derived playfully from the serialized soap opera, his third work, *The Buenos Aires Affair*, offered a renovated version of the detective novel. Puig remained manifestly faithful to the idea of simplifying his novelistic form enough to allow easy reading, although this accessibility did not preclude subtlety and complexity.

The novel was confiscated in Buenos Aires and deemed obscene, although it contains little in the way of overwhelming erotic content. *The Buenos Aires Affair* would seem to have hit a sensitive spot because the pair of lovers, an art critic and an aspiring sculptress, clearly form a sadomasochistic team, and the man bears the burden of a very troubled homosexual past. In short, the theme of nonstandard sexuality, indirectly alluded to in the confusion of Toto in *Betrayed by Rita Hayworth*, now emerges as an overt theme.

The "affair" of the title refers to both a police case, in the sense of a mysterious set of circumstances requiring investigation, and a liaison between the protagonists. The two meanings of the word coalesce, for the police are called in to resolve an out-of-control situation between the lovers. The man, having lost his ability to keep his sexual expression from interfering with society, has kidnapped his girlfriend and is holding her in bondage. This disruptive act, reported at the very beginning of the novel, eventually turns out to be merely the culmination of a torturous relationship that came to have such a grip on the hero that he was no longer able to refrain from destructive and self-destructive actions. The novel reconstructs the pressures that led this man, an educated and influential member of the arts community, to burst out in reckless, antisocial behavior. Intertwined is the story of the sculptress. The woman's history is less dramatic, for she does not succumb to any wild outbreak of deranged behavior; rather, she has gradually reached a point where she finds any purposeful action difficult to plan or execute, so that even her sculpting is largely the passive activity of presenting and "conceptualizing" found objects. A third direction in the novel's development is the unfolding of the events caused by the kidnapping. The police, far from solving the tangle of disturbing evidence, essentially go through various standard procedures until the hero brings the matter to an end by destroying himself in his panic; the ever-passive heroine is befriended by a sane, motherly neighbor woman. In effect, the total contribution of the authorities is to report as properly as possible on a set of circumstances that they can neither influence nor understand. If any detective work is accomplished, it is that performed by the reader in attempting to obtain some degree of insight into this disordered tale of unhappy sexual alliances and cultural fashions.

To provide an understanding of the protagonists' problems, Puig employs a number of narrative procedures that tend to place the characters on the psychiatric couch. Transcriptions of the hero's exchanges with his psychotherapist are included, as well as "case histories" of both the man and the woman. The histories of both characters' troubles are couched in a language of pseudoscientific objectivity, again evoking concepts of psychiatric investigation of the past.

In utilizing these "psychoanalytical" narratives, Puig would seem to be lampooning classical psychotherapy yet making use of its theories. The man's psychiatrist is, in effect, as confused and helpless as any layperson as he watches his patient display increasingly muddled thinking and erratic behavior. The woman, though not undergoing any type of psychiatric treatment that is directly presented to the reader, has recently fallen into the hands of the medical establishment as a result of her sudden inability to function, with similarly unhelpful results. It is worth remarking that the two people in the novel who are best able to counsel and soothe the frantic protagonists are simply laypersons who have a calm and stable outlook. The hero enters into a series of telephone exchanges with an older, tradition-steeped sculptress who, unlike the classically trained psychiatrist, is willing to speak to the disturbed man in commonsense terms. Her ability to carry on a sensible, reasonable conversation with the man stands out in a novel full of fatuous, jargon-filled talk. Reinforcing this theme that steady, ordinary people can function successfully as therapists is the appearance of the neighbor woman who, at the end, cares for the heroine. This neighbor, a young woman clearly satisfied with her husband and baby, asks the heroine as little as possible about the circumstances leading to her current beleaguered state, instead concentrating on getting her to rest and feel comfortable.

While the novel shows professional therapists being outdone by concerned lay-persons, it is essentially favorable to the notion, heavily associated with psychiatry, that early-childhood experiences may underlie troubles faced in adulthood. At the same time, Puig is concerned with expanding the narrowly psychological and individualistic view of childhood development. He moves beyond the particular—the workings of the child's family—to look at factors that potentially affect all children reared in a particular society. The effects of mass media and culture are, once more, subjected to detailed scrutiny. The heroine, for example, carries a permanent sense of unease as a result of constantly being compared with the media-propagated images of perfect womanhood.

Her case history dwells on her father's attempts to remake his daughter into a conventionally attractive, vivacious young woman and her resulting unhappiness over her failure to match this standard. The father's favored reading matter, the popular 1940's magazine *Rico tipo* (fancy guy), is singled out for particular denunciation for its tendency to promote a single image of acceptable femininity and to deride women who fail to adhere to this highly conventional pattern of attractiveness. Another spotlighted aspect of popular culture is the system of recreational clubs for young women. In *The Buenos Aires Affair*, these social organizations are seen as essentially concerned with questions of prestige and "connections." The heroine's childhood is further marred by her ambitious mother's attempts to attain upward mobility through this supposedly leisure-providing system.

In *The Buenos Aires Affair*, Puig is most critical of the distortion of artistic activity that allows conformity to the capitalist society's patterns of "product marketing." For example, although the hero is well read in the field of art criticism, he is seldom observed analyzing artistic work. His essential function is that of a publicist and impresario. His friends, with their incessant festival-going, see themselves as marketable commodities that must be kept in the art public's eye. In this unattractive panorama of self-packagers and self-promoters, only one exception stands out: the extraordinarily sane older woman who is able to counsel the troubled hero. All evidence points to her conscientious and principled practice of assemblage art; her steadfast and workmanlike approach strikes the art critic in his professional conscience. It is his realization that he has awarded a prize to his heavily "hyped," but inconsequential, sculptress-lover, rejecting the well-conceived work of the older woman, that precipitates his final round of deranged behavior.

Culture consumption as a search for prestige is another of the novel's motifs. An amusing example occurs on the night of the heroine's conception. Her parents have just seen a performance of a play by Eugene O'Neill that affords them theatergoing satisfaction, but they are inhibited in their later discussion of it by their extreme desire not to be "one-upped" by each other. Within the dynamics of this marriage, the wife can lay claim to some degree of superiority to her husband; while he tends to favor "easy reading" material, she has the time to maintain at least a superficial knowledge of the arts. The daughter continues this pattern of competence in the arts as a way of maintaining status. In addition, Puig points to the fact that the characters live in a mass-media culture by using excerpts from old Hollywood melodramas as epigraphs to the chapters. These film dialogues do not comment directly on the issue treated in the chapter, but rather suggest a world in which the hyperbolic "Hollywoodization" of life situations has altered people's expectations about the drama, suspense, and romance they should find in their own lives.

The Buenos Aires Affair thus continues the examination of mass culture, but it is also a study in the attitudes and actions of fine-arts consumers. In earlier Puig novels, the characters can be seen as suffering from cultural deprivation, because of their lack of education, their isolation, or both. *The Buenos Aires Affair* presents characters who are of a cultural level comparable to that of an educated reader of novels; Puig thereby holds up a mirror to his reader that reflects criticism of the characters onto the reader himself. The heroine, Gladys, reads fashionable serious authors and spends time as a prizewinning, if docile and eager-to-please, art student. Her choices as a consumer of culture are typically those of a trend-conscious, informed viewer or reader, from a preference for starkly functional decor to her favorite television fare, relatively "classy" examples of Hollywood cinema. The hero is an influential art critic. What is amiss is their approach to culture. The heroine's artistic career offers an extreme example of a creator so uncertain of her own expression that she depends slavishly on the academic standards of competence that will win praise and awards for her. Leaving the structured world of the art school, she is unable to produce and becomes so distraught over her relation to art that even going to museums becomes unbearably painful.

If Gladys represents the constraints of academically institutionalized art, her lover reveals the same pattern in antiestablishment art. He is a leading figure on the experimentalist scene. His favored artists use approaches originally designed to defy and astound the art orthodoxy—found objects, assemblages, works with a strong random element, and so on. The creators of this work, however, are not rebels but dedicated careerists, obsessed with the notion of making a name for themselves. Among the ridiculous, petty actions attributed to this cliquish group, the worst is its treatment of Gladys. The woman is clearly going through a period of instability, but the avant-garde group chooses to perceive her as wildly innovative rather than unbalanced. Her debris sculptures, more pathological indications than works of art, are gaudily exploited as the last word in assemblage art. The group's disregard for the well-being of the disoriented woman at the center of all this promotional hoopla is the surest indictment of a type of high culture wholly dominated by the need to market and sell novelties to a jaded public.

The overall effect is to bring home the problem of passive cultural consumption and production by featuring characters and settings not likely to be far removed from the readers' own set of experiences. Particularly in Gladys, the bright, industrious young person who finds both modern culture and sex perpetually mind-boggling, Puig has created a figure capable of reflecting the reader's and the author's own difficulties amid the confusions of the current cultural scene.

The transition from the early, literarily complex Puig to the more accessible author of the later novels is not even. *Betrayed by Rita Hayworth* is set apart from the subsequent novels by its structural complexity and the amount of work the reader must perform to extract a sense of what is going on in the work. *Heartbreak Tango* was deliberately written for a broad audience, and Puig has expressed disappointment that the novel did not reach a wider public than it did. While the work does not require laborious reading, its commentary on the phenomenon of mass culture is by no means simplistic. *The Buenos Aires Affair*, relatively accessible despite a degree of narrative experimentation, introduced a new set of issues as Puig turned his critical scrutiny to the fine-arts culture, its consumers and practitioners, and the author's concern with nonstandard forms of sexuality.

KISS OF THE SPIDER WOMAN

Kiss of the Spider Woman, although a fascinating work in many respects, marks a certain repetition of themes and structures already familiar to Puig's readers. Without denigrating this work, one may describe it as lending itself less to critical consideration than do others of Puig's works, for it appears designed for readers who are not literary analysts. To give only one example of this phenomenon, long citations from essays on homosexuality are included as footnotes, an inclusion having very little to do with the literary texture of the work and a great deal to do with Puig's desire to convey to lay readers a consciousness of this misunderstood phenomenon. The same process of "laicization"—of writing more and more for the reader who is not a literary specialist—was the most notable aspect of the evolution of Puig's writing after that time.

Puig accepted the courtship of such determinedly "lay" reader groups as science-fiction aficionados and cultural workers concerned with the presentation of alternatives in sexuality; at the same time, many academic readers were baffled by the evolution of Puig's work. It has yet to be determined whether Puig actually moved away from the typical high-culture, "literary" reader or whether this variety of reader simply learned new reading strategies to follow Puig.

Naomi Lindstrom

OTHER MAJOR WORKS

PLAYS: *Bajo un manto de estrellas*, pb. 1983 (*Under a Mantle of Stars*, 1985); *El beso de la mujer araña*, pb. 1983 (*Kiss of the Spider Woman*, 1986; adaptation of his novel); *Misterio del ramo de rosas*, pb. 1987 (*Mystery of the Rose Bouquet*, 1988).

SCREENPLAYS: *Boquitas pintadas*, 1974 (adaptation of his novel); *El lugar sin límites*, 1978 (adaptation of José Donoso's novel).

BIBLIOGRAPHY

Bacarisse, Pamela. *Impossible Choices: The Implications of the Cultural References in the Novels of Manuel Puig*. Calgary, Alberta: University of Calgary Press, 1993. Excellent critical study of Puig's work focuses on the references to American films and to other elements of popular culture in his work. Includes bibliography and index.

_____. *The Necessary Dream: A Study of the Novels of Manuel Puig*. Totowa, N.J.: Barnes & Noble Books, 1988. Provides a useful introduction to Puig's literary career and the themes of his work, with individual chapters devoted to the major novels. Includes notes and bibliography.

Colas, Santiago. *Postmodernity in Latin America: The Argentine Paradigm*. Durham, N.C.: Duke University Press, 1994. Puig is included in this study of postmodern literature, which also examines the writings of Julio Cortázar and Ricardo Piglia. Devotes two chapters to *Kiss of the Spider Woman*, placing the novel within the context of Argentine politics.

Craig, Linda. *Juan Carlos Onetti, Manuel Puig, and Luisa Valenzuela: Marginality and Gender*. Woodbridge, England: Tamesis, 2005. Presents analysis of works by Puig and two other Latin American writers. Asserts that these authors express a shared sense of "postcolonial emptiness" and continually question realism.

Kerr, Lucille. *Suspended Fictions: Reading Novels by Manuel Puig*. Urbana: University of Illinois Press, 1987. Explores the themes of tradition, romance, popular culture, crime, and sex in Puig's major novels and examines the design of the author's career. Includes detailed notes.

Lavers, Norman. *Pop Culture into Art: The Novels of Manuel Puig*. Columbia: University of Missouri Press, 1988. Provides a concise discussion of the close relationship between Puig's life and the themes, techniques, and materials of his first seven novels. Includes bibliographies.

Levine, Suzanne Jill. *Manuel Puig and the Spider Woman: His Life and Fictions*. Madison: University of Wisconsin Press, 2001. Biography by one of Puig's translators draws on personal knowledge of Puig as well as on research in examining the intersections of his life and his art.

Magnarelli, Sharon. "Betrayed by the Cross-Stitch." In *The Lost Rib: Female Characters in the Spanish-American Novel*. Toronto, Ont.: Associated University Presses, 1985. Close reading and feminist analysis of Puig's novel *Betrayed by Rita Hayworth* is included in a larger examination of how female protagonists are portrayed in Spanish American fiction.

Mobili, Giorgio. *Irritable Bodies and Postmodern Subjects in Pynchon, Puig, Volponi*. New York: Peter Lang, 2008. Discusses works by Puig and other postmodern writers, focusing on their representations of wounded, torn, or deformed bodies and how they employ these depictions to address societal issues.

Tittler, Jonathan. *Manuel Puig*. New York: Twayne, 1993. One of the best introductions to Puig's work available in English. Begins with an introduction that provides a useful survey of Puig's career and then devotes separate chapters to the novels. Includes detailed notes and an annotated bibliography.

JAMES PURDY

Born: Fremont, Ohio; July 17, 1914
Died: Englewood, New Jersey; March 13, 2009
Also known as: James Amos Purdy

OTHER LITERARY FORMS

In addition to his novels, James Purdy wrote in a variety of genres, including poetry, the short story, and drama. The most important of these other works are *Sixty-three: Dream Palace* (1956); *Color of Darkness: Eleven Stories and a Novella* (1957); *Children Is All* (1961), a collection of ten stories and two plays; and a volume of poetry, *The Running Sun* (1971).

ACHIEVEMENTS

James Purdy is considered one of the most important of the postmodern American writers. Along with Thomas Pynchon, John Barth, and John Hawkes, Purdy is acknowledged as one of the best of the generation of post-Joycean experimental writers. His writing is unique and powerful, and his vision remains etched in the reader's mind. Like other postmodern writers, Purdy took delight in experimenting with the texts and subtexts of narratives and treated his themes with humor and irony. In essence, Purdy's characters are motivated by irrationality; his style is ornate and complex, and his themes are surreal. Purdy is a writer whose works must be examined if the textures and ideas of the postmodern novel are to be appreciated.

BIOGRAPHY

James Amos Purdy was born on July 17, 1914, near Fremont, Ohio. He attended the University of Chicago and the University of Puebla in Mexico. Later, he worked as an interpreter in Spain, Latin America, and France. From 1949 until 1953, he taught at Lawrence College in Appleton, Wisconsin. In 1953, he decided to devote himself to writing full time. Purdy received Guggenheim Fellowships in 1958 and 1962 and a Ford Fellowship in Drama in 1961. He took a teaching post at New York University and settled in Brooklyn Heights, New York. On March 13, 2009, Purdy died in New Jersey.

ANALYSIS

Because James Purdy was so hesitant to make public the details of his private life, it is impossible to correlate any of his works with his personal experiences. His works are hermetically sealed from his life and must be examined as entities in themselves. Purdy's themes, styles, and ideas change, develop, and expand from novel to novel, so it is not possible to delineate any one particular aspect of his work that is found consistently throughout. Certain preoccupations, however, are found, in varying degrees, in most of his works, and certain characteristics that are typical of postmodern fiction.

The characters in Purdy's novels are bizarre, grotesque, and governed by abnormal impulses and desires. Purdy uses his characters for purposes of symbolic manipulation rather than for the purpose of character development in the traditional sense. Many of his characters are physically or mentally mutilated, or both: They are tattooed, wounded, stabbed, raped, and, in one case, crucified. One of the major characteristics of all of his novels is his use of "unreal" characters whose thinking processes are "nonrealistic."

A primary concern of Purdy is the relationship of children to their parents; most of his novels include a domineering phallic woman, the search for a father, and the interrelationships within a family matrix. Many of his characters are orphans, illegitimate children, or children who have been abandoned by their parents. Along with these motifs, Purdy is preoccupied with the idea of being "grown-up" or mature. Within the quest for a father figure, the idea of becoming mature is interwoven into the text, and within this framework Purdy usually parodies the search for identity and its resultant ambivalence.

The interplay of sex, love, and violence occurs frequently throughout Purdy's writing. Virtually no love between man and woman appears in Purdy's novels—male-female relationships are either those of a prostitute and a man or a man who rapes women. Purdy does include a number of sexual affairs between men in his works, but these usually end in obsession and violence. In addition, many of the novels involve incest.

Also interwoven in the stories are themes of tyranny, freedom, dominance, and obsessive love. Frequently, the female characters are aggressive and domineering, and often the male characters are passive and dominated. Many of the characters are attempting to find their "freedom" from dominance, but the nature of obsessive love does not permit this.

Finally, in some manner or another, Purdy's novels all involve a writer within the narrative. In some books, this figure takes on more importance than in others; this device, typical of self-conscious "metafiction," serves to emphasize the autonomous reality of the fictive world.

MALCOLM

Many of the themes, motifs, and preoccupations of his subsequent novels are found in Purdy's first novel, *Malcolm*. The orphan motif that occurs so frequently in Purdy's works plays a vital part in *Malcolm*. Malcolm (no last name given), the reader is told, belongs nowhere and to nobody. His father has disappeared, and Malcolm's search for him forms the central psychological structure of the book. The fifteen-year-old Malcolm is sitting on a park bench outside the hotel where he is staying when Mr. Cox, an astrologer, takes an interest in him. He gives Malcolm a series of addresses in order to interest him in "things," and the ensuing visits to the people who live at the respective addresses form the core of the action in the novel. Malcolm becomes a parody of the picaro, for instead of acting he is acted upon. His main concern is to find his father, but his actions are governed by the tyrannical Mr. Cox and his circle of friends.

Within Mr. Cox's circle are Madame Girard and Girard Girard, an eccentric billionaire. At one point in the novel, Malcolm is offered a chance to be Girard Girard's son, but Malcolm tells him he has only one father and Girard Girard cannot take his place. Later, after Malcolm marries Melba, a famous black singer, he believes that he sees his father at a restaurant. Malcolm follows this man into the restroom. The man, however, denies that he is Malcolm's father and throws Malcolm down, causing Malcolm to hit his head. After this incident, Malcolm, who has deteriorated physically since his marriage, becomes too weak to get out of bed and eventually dies.

Thus, in this first novel, Purdy reveals many of his recurring preoccupations. In addition to the orphan's search for the father (paralleling the search for identity), Purdy explores the topic of tyranny and the theme of the fatality of a loveless marriage. A concern with the maturation process is also found in *Malcolm*. Gus, one of Melba's former husbands, is chosen to help Malcolm mature before his marriage. Gus's solution to helping Malcolm "mature" is to have Malcolm tattooed and to have him visit a prostitute.

In *Malcolm*, the characters are constantly questioning the substantiality of their existence; they are two-dimensional, almost comic-book figures. Malcolm is given addresses, not names, and consequently, places and events take primacy over the development of the personality. Malcolm himself has no last name, and when he dies there is no corpse in his coffin. All that is left of Malcolm are three hundred pages of manuscript that he had written, which Madame Girard attempts to organize.

THE NEPHEW

In *The Nephew*, Purdy turns to the small town of Rainbow Center for his setting and tells a story that superficially resembles a slice of small-town life. Underneath the seemingly placid exterior of Rainbow Center, however, as beneath the surface of the novel, much is happening. The text is surcharged with meanings, and the experience of reading this novel is similar to that of watching a film with the sound track slightly off.

The plot is simple and straightforward. Alma Mason and her brother, Boyd, receive news that their nephew Cliff is missing in action during the Korean War. Cliff, another of Purdy's orphans, had lived with the Masons. In order to alleviate some of the grief of his death, Alma decides to write a memorial honoring Cliff. The novel focuses on Alma's attempts to gather material for the writing of Cliff's memorial. During this process, she discovers many facets of Cliff's existence of which she had been unaware—particularly that Cliff had hated the town and that he had had a homosexual affair—which lead her to some revelations about herself and her relationship to Boyd and others in the community.

One of Purdy's concerns that can be noted throughout the novel is the inadequacy of judging people by their actions and their words. Communication is always inadequate and misinterpreted. Alma never does finish her memorial to Cliff, another indication that one can never fully understand another person. By the end of the story, however, Alma does become much more tolerant in her attitude toward what she considers the foibles of others.

CABOT WRIGHT BEGINS

Like *The Nephew*, *Cabot Wright Begins* concerns the attempt to write about another person—in this case, a businessman and rapist named Cabot Wright. Instead of one narrative voice, as in *The Nephew*, many emerge in *Cabot Wright Begins*, and this blending and confusion of narrative voices further demonstrate the impossibility of learning the true story about another person.

Purdy's third novel is an extremely pessimistic indictment and extended meditation on modern American culture. In *Cabot Wright Begins*, people are controlled by media-think, big business, and popular culture and by all the superficial aspects of modern existence. Feelings, emotions, and actions are all superficial, and even the rape scenes involving Cabot Wright are narrated in a dispassionate manner—much like secondhand violence seen on television or in the cinema. People exist on the screen of the text, and their ability to function in normal human terms is questioned.

Cabot Wright, another orphan, is twenty-six years old during the time of the novel. He is a stockbroker turned rapist. Bernie Gladhart, a used-car salesman, has been cajoled by his wife into writing the great American novel and has decided that a life history of Cabot Wright would be the perfect subject matter. In fact, the tentative title of Bernie's novel is "Indelible Smudge," which indicates Purdy's judgment about American culture at this time. Princeton Keith, the owner of a large publishing house, however, has commissioned Zoe Bickle to write the story in terms of popular fiction. Through a skylight, Zoe literally falls upon Cabot Wright himself, and Cabot offers to help her ghostwrite his biography. In the process of turning his life into popular fiction, however, he becomes alienated from himself. To him, the story does not portray his real self.

Cabot Wright seems to symbolize the attempt of modern men and women to assert their identity through violence. Only through the act of rape can Cabot penetrate the surface of another, but even then he becomes increasingly alienated and less alive. For Cabot, there are no answers.

EUSTACE CHISHOLM AND THE WORKS

In *Eustace Chisholm and the Works*, Purdy presents his concept of the sacrificial, violent, and grotesque aspects of love. In many horrific scenes he shows the results of obsessional love. The story revolves around the sexual love Daniel Hawes has for seventeen-year-old Amos Ratcliff. Amos, an illegitimate son, has been rejected by his father and has had incestuous relationships with his cousin (later revealed to be his mother). Daniel attempts to repress his feelings for Amos, but they finally become so overwhelming that he reenlists in the Army to escape. Instead of escaping, however, he permits his love for Amos to be brought to the surface and projected upon his commanding officer, Captain Stadger. During the affair between these two, Captain Stadger becomes increasingly more sadistic until finally he kills Daniel by disemboweling him, then commits suicide. This incident is the first in a series of homosexual blood sacrifices found in Purdy's novels.

Once again, as in all of Purdy's previous works, there is an author involved in an attempt to write the story. In this case, Eustace Chisholm is the writer who is attempting to incorporate the story of Amos and Daniel within the context of a larger epic poem that he is writing.

JEREMY'S VERSION

Purdy's next novel, *Jeremy's Version*, was written as part 1 of a projected trilogy called *Sleepers in the Moon-Crowned Valleys*. Although Purdy had dealt with orphans, the search for a father figure, and interrelationships within families in his previous works, this was his first novel in which the family matrix formed the basis for the entire work.

Again, there is a writer—in this case, Jeremy Cready—narrating the story being told to him by Uncle Matt. The basic story (which actually occurred more than fifty years before) involves the battle of wills between two strong women, Elvira Summerlad and Winifred Fergus; a divorce case; and the interrelationships of the three sons with one another and with their mother and father. Elvira Summerlad and Wilders Fergus were married, much against the wishes of his sister, Winifred, who thought the marriage was doomed. In a sense, Winifred was right, because Wilders abandoned Elvira and their sons. Winifred, however, goes to Wilders and tells him that since his sons are almost grown, he is needed at home. When he arrives, Elvira starts divorce proceedings against him.

The basic conflict is between Elvira and Winifred for custody of the children. Wilders is indifferent to the whole affair. One of Purdy's major themes—that of the son confronting the father—occurs during the divorce proceedings, when the gay oldest son, Rick, confronts Wilders. Rick demands that Wilders tell him the reason for his existence since his father has never been around before to teach him—he has only had his mother, who, he claims, has emasculated him. After Elvira wins the divorce case, her second son, Jethro, attempts to shoot her, but Matt saves her and is wounded. A similar shooting scene, between mother and son, occurs again in *The House of the Solitary Maggot.*

I AM ELIJAH THRUSH

I Am Elijah Thrush is a dreamlike, ornate, and highly stylized book, populated with strange characters and filled with unusual events. More than any of Purdy's other novels, this book exists in the realm of allegory and symbols. Among the major characters are a famous mime, Elijah Thrush; his great-grandson, a mute, called the Bird of Heaven; Millicent De Frayne, a tyrannical old dowager who retains her youth by drinking the seminal fluid of young men; and Albert Peggs, the black memoirist who tells the story and who, himself, has a bizarre "habit." In addition, the novel incorporates many elements of mythology in a comic manner, suggesting the debasement of culture in modern America.

As in many of Purdy's previous novels, the plot in *I Am Elijah Thrush* involves a person (in this case, Albert Peggs) being hired by someone to write the story. Millicent De Frayne hires Albert to recount the story of Elijah Thrush. Once again, this story involves a clash of wills between two strong people—Millicent and Elijah. For more than fifty years, she has been trying to gain control of Elijah and marry him. Eventually, she succeeds by manipulating Albert, the Bird of Heaven, and Elijah onto her boat, where she finally marries him. Late in the novel, Albert's "habit" is discovered: He sustains the life of a golden eagle by permitting the eagle to feed upon him. At the wedding feast of Millicent and Elijah, the eagle is served as the entree. After this incident, Albert "becomes" Elijah Thrush.

One of Purdy's major themes is that of confirming, or finding, an identity. In his novels, there is a plethora of name-changes, mistaken identities, disguises, masquerades, and other such motifs. The dreamlike structure of the narrative suggests that Albert Peggs is attempting to discover his identity by telling this story.

THE HOUSE OF THE SOLITARY MAGGOT

The House of the Solitary Maggot is part 2 of the series called *Sleepers in Moon-Crowned Valleys.* The story is reconstructed—this time on a tape recorder—by one of the characters, and, as in part 1 of the series, *Jeremy's Version*, the family matrix is the psychological focus in the novel. The story involves Mr. Skegg, the magnate (the "solitary maggot"); Lady Bythewaite; and their three illegitimate sons: Clarence, who is legally "acknowledged" by the father; Owen, who is acknowledged by the mother; and Aiken, who is not acknowledged by either parent until later in the book.

The novel takes place in a dying community called Prince's Crossing. Owen, the youngest son, hero-worships his brother, Clarence, who goes to New York to become a famous silent-film star. After Clarence leaves, Owen turns to the other older brother, Aiken, whom he also worships. The two become inseparable. Aiken, who himself has no acknowledged father or mother, serves as a father figure to Owen, helping him "mature" by giving him his first shave and taking him to visit a prostitute. After visiting her, Owen loses his sight. Aiken, who has finally been acknowledged by Lady Bythewaite as her long-lost son, buys the Acres, the showplace of the community. When Clarence returns and refuses to accept Aiken as his brother, Aiken, whose pride is hurt, burns down the house and marries the prostitute. This marriage is a failure, and Aiken decides to leave.

Although Aiken has been estranged from Owen, he loves him obsessively. When Aiken goes to say good-bye to Owen and their mother, Owen shoots him. Lady Bythewaite, one of Purdy's typical strong-willed, castrating women, then shoots Owen. In another of Purdy's characteristically grotesque scenes, Owen's eyeballs fall out and Aiken swallows them. While Aiken remains unconscious in the hospital, Clarence returns and wants to be acknowledged as Aiken's brother. When the unconscious Aiken cannot comply, Clarence slits his own throat. Eventually, Aiken comes to live with his mother. Mr. Skegg acknowledges him as his son and takes care of him in his illness. The story concludes with the death of Aiken, who, in a dreamlike sequence, tries to ride off on a horse with the dead Owen.

In a Shallow Grave

The protagonist of Purdy's next novel, *In a Shallow Grave*, is Garnet Montrose, a war hero who has been so badly wounded that he is turned almost inside-out and is the color of mulberry juice. Garnet seeks "applicants" to take messages from him to the Widow Rance, whom he wishes to court, but the applicants are so appalled by Garnet's appearance that they cannot accept the job. Finally, Quintus, a black adolescent, shows up by accident at Garnet's house and accepts the position. Quintus's responsibilities are to read to Garnet and to rub his feet. Later, a man named Daventry shows up. Even though he is not an applicant, he takes the position of messenger to the Widow Rance. Within this narrative structure, Purdy pursues many of his recurring themes.

One of the primary scenes involves a communion among Garnet, Quintus, and Daventry. Garnet is about to have his property taken away, but Daventry says that he will save Garnet's land and property if Garnet will commune with him. Daventry takes his knife, slits open his chest, and the three of them drink his blood. Later, they discover that Garnet's property has been saved by the Veterans Administration, who heard of his plight and paid the mortgage. The wounding and shedding of blood, along with the religious connotations of the scene, seem to indicate that language is inadequate for portraying emotions, that the only way to "love" another person is to shed blood for him or her.

Again, homosexual love appears in the novel, for Daventry and Garnet fall in love. They consummate their love in the dance hall where Garnet goes to dance by himself and relive the moments in the past when he was "normal." With Garnet's permission, Daventry marries the Widow Rance, but on his wedding night, he is swept up by a strong wind, smashed against a tree, and killed.

Narrow Rooms

Narrow Rooms is a story about the love-hate relationship between Roy Sturtevant (the renderer) and Sidney De Lakes. Roy Sturtevant had been in love with Sidney since the eighth grade, until Sidney slapped him publicly and humiliated him; from that time, Roy has been planning his revenge. The story opens after Sidney has returned from prison, where he served time for killing Brian McFee. He finds a job as keeper of Gareth Vaisey, who has been injured in a fall from a horse. Sidney and Gareth fall in love and have an affair, but Roy Sturtevant still exercises a strange power over them.

In the central scene in the novel, after Roy and Sidney have a sexual encounter, Roy commands Sidney to crucify him on the barn door and then bring the body of Brian McFee to view the crucifixion. Roy, still alive, is taken down from the barn door and carried into the house. Sidney and Roy then pledge their love for each other, and Gareth, jealous, shoots them both. Subsequently, Gareth also dies. Though the subject matter of *Narrow Rooms* is largely sensational, the novel continues Purdy's exploration of the destructive nature of obsessive love.

Mourners Below

In *Mourners Below*, Purdy returns to the theme of hero worship. Seventeen-year-old Duane Bledsoe is mourning the death of his two half brothers, Justin and Douglas, who have been killed in the war. Eugene Bledsoe, the father, with whom Duane lives, is aloof and psychologically distant. The central episode in the novel occurs when Duane goes to a fancy-dress ball at the mansion of Estelle Dumont (who had been Justin's lover), and Estelle seduces him. After the ball, another of Purdy's rape scenes occurs when Duane is sexually assaulted by two men along the roadside. During the brief affair between Duane and Estelle, Estelle conceives a child, also named Justin. At the end of the story, Duane is given the child to rear, and Eugene states that it is Duane's destiny to rear a son.

Although this novel incorporates many of Purdy's familiar conceptions, it appears to be much more optimistic about the human condition than his previous novels. For example, Eugene and Duane do become reconciled in many ways, and there are many indications that Duane will make a good parent for the child. Furthermore, many of the grotesque and sadistic aspects of love are absent in this book. The men and the women in the story are not the tyrannical types found in previous works; they exhibit much more normal motivation. *Mourners Below* seems to indicate a new phase in Purdy's development, for in this novel he emphasizes the hopeful qualities of love and human existence.

On Glory's Course

The search for a lost son plays a crucial role in *On Glory's Course*. Adele Bevington, the main character in the novel, has had an illegitimate son taken away from her and placed for adoption. The rest of the novel revolves around her quest for her lost son. One of the wounded veterans living in Fonthill, the location of the novel, believes that he knows the identity of Adele's son—he is a soldier who has been gravely wounded in the war and is now residing at the Soldiers' Home, barely alive and unable to respond to any communication. Adele attempts to prove that this soldier, Moorbrook, is her son, but by the end of the novel, neither Adele nor the reader is certain about Moorbrook's identity. Once again, Purdy's recurring motif of the search for a father figure is woven into the text of the novel.

IN THE HOLLOW OF HIS HAND

In the Hollow of His Hand relates the kidnapping of a boy, Chad Coultas, by Decatur, an Ojibwa Indian. Decatur is actually the father of the boy and wishes to rear him as an Indian; however, Lew Coultas, the man who has brought up Chad, wishes to recapture him and take him "home." The mother of Chad, Eva Lewis, had not even realized that Decatur was the father until he returned home from the military and began taking Chad on rides after school. She then remembered that she had, indeed, had a one-day affair with Decatur years before the action in the novel begins.

During the attempt to find Chad, the town of Yellow Brook is awakened to its small-town foibles and provincial attitudes, and once again Purdy reveals the darker side of small-town life and values. This novel is darkly satiric and deals with Purdy's attempts to create an almost mythological construct of his obsession with the search for an identity within the context of the family. Yet *In the Hollow of His Hand* is also an extremely humorous novel, delving into the souls of small-town America and American culture.

GARMENTS THE LIVING WEAR

Set in Manhattan, *Garments the Living Wear* opens with Jared Wakeman, an actor and organizer of a theater group facing a desperate situation. Not only has his benefactor, Peg Shawbridge, almost run out of money, his actors have been decimated by acquired immunodeficiency syndrome (AIDS), which Purdy's characters refer to simply as the Plague. Even Des Cantrell, whom Jared refers to as his soul mate, shows the first signs of the illness. The situation radically changes when Edward Hennings, an aged financial wizard and Peg's former lover, arrives with his young androgynous bride, Estrallita. Edward desires Jared, luring him with the dual attractions of money for his theatrical endeavors and the mysterious Estrallita.

Purdy imbues the novel with an aura of myth and mystery as Edward seemingly cures Des. This atmosphere is reinforced by the appearance of Jonas Hakluyt, an ex-convict turned evangelist with messianic overtones. The novel combines humor and psychological realism, myth, and magic as Purdy's characters struggle to survive in a world where both people and events are unpredictable and reality is frequently overshadowed by illusion.

OUT WITH THE STARS

Out with the Stars revolves around a group of socially intertwined figures. Abner Blossom, with the support of his talented protégé, Val Sturgis, has emerged from his retirement to compose an opera based on a mysterious libretto that was found in a "parlor" where young men indulge in orgies. The libretto is based on the life of Cyrus Vane, a photographer who specialized in nude studies of young African American men. Vane's wife, Madame Petrovna, is bitterly opposed to production of the opera and will go to any lengths to stop it. A secondary theme in the novel deals with corruption and the loss of innocence of Sturgis and his roommate, Hugh, as they drift deeper into the exotic world of Vane and Blossom. Purdy vividly explores both racial and sexual prejudice in *Out with the Stars*.

GERTRUDE OF STONY ISLAND AVENUE

In *Gertrude of Stony Island Avenue*, Carrie Kinsella, an elderly woman who has lived a dull and uneventful existence, attempts to understand the life and death of her daughter, Gertrude, a famous and flamboyant artist. During this search, she encounters a series of eccentric characters who influenced and were influenced by Gertrude. Purdy explores the nature of love and relationships as Carrie struggles to accept the fact that she and Gertrude failed to love each other. Like most of Purdy's novels, *Gertrude of Stony Island Avenue* presents a shadowy world full of pretense and ambiguity. Purdy's language and symbolism mirror this world, which is often distorted, hiding more than it reveals.

Earl Paulus Murphy
Updated by Mary E. Mahony

OTHER MAJOR WORKS

SHORT FICTION: *Don't Call Me by My Right Name, and Other Stories*, 1956; *Sixty-three: Dream Palace*, 1956; *Color of Darkness: Eleven Stories and a Novella*, 1957; *The Candles of Your Eyes*, 1985; *The Candles of Your Eyes, and Thirteen Other Stories*, 1987; *Sixty-three: Dream Palace—Selected Stories, 1956-1987*, 1991; *Moe's Villa, and Other Stories*, 2000.

PLAYS: *Mr. Cough Syrup and the Phantom Sex*, pb. 1960; *Cracks*, pb. 1962; *Wedding Finger*, pb. 1974; *Clearing in the Forest*, pr. 1978; *True*, pr. 1978; *A Day After the Fair*, pb. 1979; *Now*, pr. 1979; *Two Plays*, 1979 (includes *A Day After the Fair* and *True*); *What Is It, Zach?*, pr. 1979; *Proud Flesh: Four Short Plays*, 1980; *Strong*, pb. 1980; *The Berry-Picker*, pb. 1981; *Scrap of Paper*, pb. 1981; *In the Night of Time, and Four Other Plays*, 1992 (includes *In the Night of Time*, *Enduring Zeal*, *The Paradise Circus*, *The Rivalry of Dolls*, and *Ruthanna Elder*); *The Rivalry of Dolls*, pr., pb. 1992.

POETRY: *The Running Sun*, 1971; *Sunshine Is an Only Child*, 1973; *She Came Out of the Mists of Morning*, 1975; *Lessons and Complaints*, 1978; *The Brooklyn Branding Parlors*, 1986.

MISCELLANEOUS: *Children Is All*, 1961 (stories and plays); *An Oyster Is a Wealthy Beast*, 1967 (story and poems); *Mr. Evening: A Story and Nine Poems*, 1968; *On the Rebound: A Story and Nine Poems*, 1970; *A Day After the Fair: A Collection of Plays and Stories*, 1977.

BIBLIOGRAPHY

Adams, Stephen D. *James Purdy.* New York: Barnes & Noble Books, 1976. Adams examines Purdy's major work from the early stories and *Malcolm* up through *In a Shallow Grave.* Of particular interest is Adams's discussion of the first two novels in Purdy's trilogy *Sleepers in Moon-Crowned Valleys.*

Canning, Richard. *Gay Fiction Speaks: Conversations with Gay Novelists.* New York: Columbia University Press, 2000. This book's extensive interview focuses primarily on Purdy's identity as a gay novelist. Purdy also discusses his plays, acknowledging his interest in and debt to the Jacobean theater of early seventeenth century England.

Chupack, Henry. *James Purdy.* Boston: Twayne, 1975. This introductory overview contains a biography, an introductory chapter on what Chupack terms the "Purdian trauma," and analyses of Purdy's works. Includes a bibliography and an index.

Guy-Bray, Stephen. "James Purdy. In *The Gay and Lesbian Literary Heritage: A Reader's Companion to the Writers and Their Works, from Antiquity to the Present,* edited by Claude J. Summers. New York: Henry Holt, 1995. In this short article, Guy-Bray tries to identify some of Purdy's most pervasive themes, including the betrayal of love, the use of violence to resolve inner conflict, and the malevolence of fate.

Lane, Christopher. "Out with James Purdy: An Interview." *Critique* 40 (Fall, 1998): 71-89. Purdy discusses racial stereotypes, sexual fantasy, political correctness, religious fundamentalism, gay relationships, and the reasons he has been neglected by the literary establishment.

Schwarzchild, Bettina. *The Not-Right House: Essays on James Purdy.* Columbia: University of Missouri Press, 1968. A collection of Schwarzchild's incisive essays on Purdy's work, primarily focusing on his novels.

Tanner, Tony. Introduction to *Color of Darkness* and *Malcolm.* New York: Doubleday, 1974. Tanner's introductory essay discusses Purdy's novel *Malcolm* and the short-story collection *Sixty-Three: Dream Palace.* It also compares Purdy's effects with those achieved by the Russian realist Anton Chekhov.

Whitaker, Rick. "James Purdy." In *The First Time I Met Frank O'Hara: Reading Gay American Writers.* Photographs by Iannis Delatolas. New York: Four Walls Eight Windows, 2003. Whitaker examines the lives and works of Purdy and other gay writers, focusing on how their literary styles and perspectives were influenced by their sexuality.

Woodhouse, Reed. "James Purdy's *Narrow Rooms.*" *Unlimited Embrace: A Canon of Gay Fiction, 1945-1995.* Amherst: University of Massachusetts Press, 1998. Woodhouse devotes a chapter to Purdy in his evaluation of fifty years of fiction written for, by, and about gay men. He views Purdy's works as an exploration of the ethics of gay life.

MARY RENAULT
Mary Challans

Born: London, England; September 4, 1905
Died: Cape Town, South Africa; December 13, 1983
Also known as: Mary Challans

PRINCIPAL LONG FICTION

Purposes of Love, 1939 (also known as *Promise of Love*, 1940)
Kind Are Her Answers, 1940
The Friendly Young Ladies, 1944 (also known as *The Middle Mist*, 1945)
Return to Night, 1947
North Face, 1948
The Charioteer, 1953
The Last of the Wine, 1956
The King Must Die, 1958
The Bull from the Sea, 1962
The Mask of Apollo, 1966
Fire from Heaven, 1969
The Persian Boy, 1972
The Praise Singer, 1978
Funeral Games, 1981
The Alexander Trilogy, 1984 (includes *Fire from Heaven*, *The Persian Boy*, and
  Funeral Games)

OTHER LITERARY FORMS

All but two of the works published by Mary Renault (rehn-OHLT) are novels. *The Lion in the Gateway: Heroic Battles of the Greeks and Persians at Marathon, Salamis, and Thermopylae* (1964) is a children's history of ancient Greek battles. *The Nature of Alexander* (1975) is a heavily documented biography placing the charismatic leader in the context of his time and customs, a book that also defines the two abiding preoccupations of Alexander's life and Renault's art. "Outward striving for honor," the Greek *to philotimo*, balances *arete*, the profound inward thirst for achievement knowingly made beautiful. Together, as Alexander himself wrote, they win immortality: "It is a lovely thing to live with courage,/ and die leaving an everlasting fame."

ACHIEVEMENTS

Critics praised Mary Renault's first five novels, written and set around World War II, for their realism, psychological depth, and literary technique. In 1946, one year prior to its publication, *Return to Night* won the MGM Award, $150,000, then the world's largest literary prize. Although this novel was never made into a motion picture, the award brought Renault American acclaim, augmented later by the success of her Greek novels, but her work has never gained the academic attention it deserves. Renault received the National Association of Independent Schools Award in 1963 and the Silver Pen Award in 1971, and she was a fellow of the Royal Society of Literature.

BIOGRAPHY

Mary Renault (the pen name of Mary Challans), a physician's daughter, was born on September 4, 1905, in London. At eight, she decided to become a writer, and she read English at St. Hugh's College, Oxford, from 1924 to 1927, where she preferred to study the Middle Ages, the setting of an attempted historical novel she destroyed after several rejections. She had once thought of teaching, but after graduation she entered nurses' training at Radcliffe Infirmary, Oxford, where she received her nursing degree in 1937. She dated her literary career from 1939, though she continued as a neurosurgical nurse at Radcliffe Infirmary throughout World War II, writing in her off-duty hours. Her first novels were widely popular, but she claimed, according to Bernard F. Dick, that "if her early novels were destroyed irrevocably, she would feel absolutely no loss."

Renault's postwar travels in the eastern Mediterranean provided the impetus for a new literary phase marked by her emigration to South Africa in 1948. After this move, her exhaustive self-taught knowledge of ancient Greek history and philosophy made her a mesmerizing novelist able to re-create a lost world. In the estimation of Dick, Renault was "the only bona fide Hellenist in twentieth century fiction." Renault remained a resident of South Africa until her death on December 13, 1983.

ANALYSIS

Mary Renault's novels celebrate and eulogize people's potential but transitory glory, a combination difficult for a world that has relinquished its acquaintance with the classics. Critic Peter Wolfe has described Renault's first five novels as her literary apprenticeship, "1930's novels" marked by then-fashionable themes of political engagement and sexual liberation. Bernard F. Dick has argued that her early fiction was influenced by the restrictive, pain-filled atmosphere of a World War II surgical hospital. Both are partly correct; Renault's early work deals with the individual's freedom from contemporary power structures and stifling social conventions.

Such topical concerns, however appealing to modern readers, are nevertheless peripheral to the core of Renault's art, the Platonism that she followed to the mythic depths in her later novels. When she began to write, Renault was already familiar with the Theory of Ideas developed in Plato's dialogues, wherein everything perceptible by human senses is imitative of changeless perfect Ideas beyond time and space. Each Idea corresponds to a class of earthly objects, all of which must inevitably change, leaving the Ideas the only objects of true knowledge in the universe. A transitory earthly object, however, may remind people of the Idea it represents. Plato theorized that before entering the body, the soul had encountered the infinite Ideas, and that, once embodied, the soul might vaguely remember them. Renault often convincingly incorporates Plato's anamnesis, the doctrine that "learning is recollection," in her fiction. Plato also believed that human recognition of such natural truths as the mathematically perfect circle could lead people stepwise to the contemplation of Absolute Truth, which he equated with Absolute Goodness and Absolute Beauty. He taught that the immortal human soul may be reborn through metempsychosis, or transmigration, another concept found throughout Renault's work.

Renault's novels are also informed by Plato's theory of love as defined by Socrates in *The Symposium* (c. 388-368 B.C.E.): Love is the desire for immortality through possession of or union with the Beautiful. Love manifests itself on its lowest levels by human sexuality, proceeds upward through intellectual achievement, and culminates in a mystical union of the soul with the Idea of Beauty. That Renault's heroes aspire to such union is their glory; that being mortal they must fail is the fate she eulogizes.

Plato, like most classical Greeks, allowed heterosexual love only the lowest rung on his ladder of love, as the necessary element for reproduction. Only the homosexual relationship was considered capable of inspiring the lifelong friendships that offered each partner the ideal of *arete*. All of Renault's novels illustrate some aspect of Platonic love; in the first, *Promise of Love*, she shows Vivian, a nurse, and Mic, who loves her because she resembles her brother Jan, achieving self-knowledge not through sexual passion but by affection, the ultimate stage of Platonic love, which at the close of the novel "recalls the true lover of [Plato's dialogue] the *Phaedrus* who is willing to sleep like a servant at the side of his beloved."

Renault's other early novels also have strong Platonic elements. *Kind Are Her Answers* foreshadows her interest in theater as mimetic form, Plato's first literary love, which she realized more fully in *The Mask of Apollo*. Her third novel, *The Middle Mist*, concludes with references to Plato's *Lysis*, his dialogue on friendship that claims that erotic satisfaction destroys *philia*, the more permanent nonphysical union promised by Platonic love, a theme to which Renault returned more successfully in *The Last of the Wine*. Renault attempted unconvincingly in *Return to Night* and *North Face* to state the *amor vincit omnia* tradition of "women's fiction" in mythological metaphors, and found that she had to develop a new fictional mode capable of expressing her archetypal themes with Platonic concepts.

THE CHARIOTEER

Not published in the United States until 1959 because of its forthright treatment of homosexuality, *The Charioteer* is the only Renault novel to incorporate a systematic development of Platonic philosophy as the vehicle for commentary on contemporary life. In the *Phaedrus* (c. 388-368 B.C.E.), Plato depicted reason as a charioteer who must balance the thrust of the white horse of honor against the unruly black horse of passion. The image unifies Renault's tale of Laurie Odell, wounded at Dunkirk, who must come to terms with his homosexuality. After his friendship with the sexually naïve conscientious objector Andrew Raines dissolves, Laurie finds a lifelong partner in Ralph Lanyon, who brought him back wounded after they had fought at Dunkirk. Laurie attains an equilibrium between the two conflicting halves of his nature in a Platonic denial of sexual excess. As Renault comments in the epilogue, a Greek device she favors, "Now their [the horses'] heads droop side by side till their long manes mingle; and when the charioteer falls silent they are reconciled for a night in sleep."

In the ideal Platonic pattern, the older man assumes a compassionate responsibility for the honor of the younger, altogether transcending physical attraction and cemented by shared courage in battle. Renault's efforts at an entirely convincing presentation of such friendship are hindered by the intolerance with which homosexual relationships were usually viewed in the society of her time and the often pathetic insecurity it forced upon them. Despite these handicaps, Renault sympathetically portrays Laurie as "a modern Hephaestus, or maimed artist," as Wolfe notes, a character who wins admiration through striving to heal his injured life and nature and make of them something lasting and beautiful.

From roots far deeper than Plato's philosophy, Renault developed the vital impulse of her eight Greek novels, her major literary achievement. Central is the duality of Apollo and Dionysus, names the Greeks gave to the forces of the mind and of the heart, gods whose realms the mythologist Walter F. Otto has described as "sharply opposed" yet "in reality joined together by an eternal bond." In Greek myth, Zeus's archer son Apollo, wielder of the two-sided weapon of Truth, endowed people with the heavenly light called Art, by which he admonished humankind to self-knowledge and moderation through his oracle at Delphi. Paradoxically, Apollo shared his temple and the festival year at Delphi with his mysterious brother Dionysus, god of overwhelming ecstasy, born of mortal woman and all-powerful Zeus, torn apart each year to rise again, offering both wine's solace and its madness to humankind. Thought and emotion were the two faces of the Greek coin of life—in Otto's words, "the eternal contrast between a restless, whirling life and a still, far-seeing spirit."

Each of Renault's Greek novels focuses on a crucial nexus of physical and spiritual existence in Greek history. The age of legendary heroes such as Theseus of Athens, subject of *The King Must Die* and *The Bull from the Sea*, was followed by the Trojan War, 1200 B.C.E., the stuff of classical epic and tragedy and the harbinger of Greece's Dark Age, when only Athens stood against the Dorian invasion. By the sixth century B.C.E., the setting of *The Praise Singer*, Athens, under the benevolent tyrant Pisistratus, had become the model *polis* of the Greek peninsula, building a democracy that repelled imperial Persia and fostered the world's greatest tragedies in their Dionysian festivals. *The Last of the Wine* treats the fall of Athens to Sparta in the Peloponnesian Wars, 404 B.C.E., torn by internal strife and bled by foreign expansion. The restored Athenian democracy of a half-century later is the milieu of *The Mask of Apollo*. Shortly after Plato's death, his pupil Aristotle taught a prince in Macedon who dreams of Homeric deeds in *Fire from Heaven*, accomplishes them in *The Persian Boy*, and leaves an empire to be shattered by lesser men in *Funeral Games*—Alexander the Great.

THE LAST OF THE WINE

The Last of the Wine, like most of Renault's Greek fiction, is ostensibly a memoir, a form favored by classical authors. Its fictional narrator, a young and "beautiful" Athenian knight named Alexias, endures the agonizing aftermath of Athens's ill-fated Sicilian venture under Alkibiades, the magnetic but flawed former student of Sokrates. With Lysis, the historical figure on whom Plato modeled his dialogue on ideal friendship, Alexias begins the idealistic attachment they learned together from Sokrates, but physical passion, handled with sensitivity by Renault, overcomes them, and they ruefully must compromise their ideal. Sacrificing his honor for Lysis during the famine caused by the Spartan siege of Athens, Alexias models for sculptors, at least one lascivious, to feed his wounded friend, and in the battle to restore Athenian democracy, Lysis falls gloriously with Alexias's name upon his lips.

The novel's title, an allusion to the Greek custom in which the wine remaining in a cup is tossed to form the initial of a lover's name, metaphorically represents Athens's abandonment of the ideals of its Golden Age. Renault poignantly shows Lysis, a gentleman athlete in pursuit of *philotimo*, the hero's struggle for outward glory to emulate his ideal, beaten sadistically in the Isthmian Games by a monstrous professional wrestler, just as Athenian democracy is becoming warped by politicians such as the vicious Kritias and the cold-blooded Anytos, who will help condemn Sokrates. Alkibiades' personal disaster, abandoning Athens for its Spartan enemies, is an exemplary case of a leader who cannot resist abusing his charismatic gifts.

The Greek ideal of democracy learned at Sokrates' side and based on individual *arete*, inward pursuit of honor, still allows Lysis a moral victory often overlooked in this splendidly elegiac novel of the death of an era. "Men are not born equal in themselves," Lysis tells Alexias over wine one evening in Samos. "A man who thinks himself as good as everyone else will be at no pains to grow better." Lysis fights and dies for "a City where I can find my equals and respect my betters . . . and where no one can tell me to swallow a lie because it is expedient." At the end of the novel, as he listens to the distorted minds of bureaucrats, Alexias remembers the lamps of Samos, the wine-cup on a table of polished wood, and Lysis's voice: "Must we forsake the love of excellence, then, till every citizen feels it alike?"

THE KING MUST DIE *and* THE BULL FROM THE SEA

Renault analyzes the ideal of kingship in *The King Must Die* and *The Bull from the Sea*. In the earlier novel, she traces Theseus's early life from Troezen and Eleusis, where with the bard Orpheus he establishes the Sacred Mysteries, to the labyrinthine palace of Crete, where he destroys the brutal son of King Minos, who oppresses Athens. In the second, she pursues Theseus's progressive rule in Athens through his abandonment of Ariadne to Dionysus's bloody cult and his capture of the Amazon Hippolyta to the great tragedy of his life, his fatal curse on their son Hippolytus. Stylistically more evocative of Homer's mighty simplicity than the Attic cadences of *The Last of the Wine*, Renault's Theseus novels treat kingship as a manifestation of the divine inner voice that chooses the moment of willing consent when the monarch sacrifices himself for his people.

Both novels discuss a past so dim that its events have become the raw material of myth. Theseus's birth meshes the earthly with the supernatural, since it results from the divinely inspired compassion of the Athenian King Aigios for the stricken land of Troezen; the reader is left, as is customary in Renault's fiction, to decide where history ends and metaphysics begins. Until his son's death, Theseus practices the lesson learned from his grandfather's ritual sacrifice of the King Horse, one of the shocking joys hidden in pain that opens much of Renault's fiction: "The consenting . . . the readiness is all. It washes heart and mind . . . and leaves them open to the god."

By closing himself to the speaking god, however, obeying not his reason but his emotional reaction to his wife Phaedra's false accusations of Hippolytus, Theseus is lost. Only two bright moments remain to him: an anamnetic dream of Marathon where he fights beside the Athenians defending their city, his name their stirring war cry, and a glimpse before he dies of the boy Achilles, "as springy and as brisk as noonday, his arm round a darkhaired friend." Prescient, Theseus watches tragedy in the making: "The god who sent him that blazing pride should not have added love to be burned upon it," but—consoled that his own reputation has become Achilles' "touchstone for a man"—Theseus for the last time consents to the god of the sea.

THE MASK OF APOLLO

By the mid-fourth century B.C.E., late in Plato's life, sophisticated Athenians had accepted the gods as metaphysical forces within the human personality. In *The Mask of Apollo*, Renault poses the primal duality of Apollo and Dionysus in Greek culture, the calm, farseeing force of reason and art balanced against the irresistible force of ecstasy. An old mask of Apollo, reputedly from the workshop of the Parthenon's architect Phidias, accompanies Renault's narrator Nikeratos through his successful acting career, the fascinating backdrop to the political career of Dion of Syracuse, Plato's noble friend, who might have become the ideal philosopher-king Plato postulated in *The Republic*.

Though Dion is a model soldier and a principled statesman, circumstances force him to abandon his philosophical ideals to save Syracuse from devastation. Renault parallels his fall with Nikeratos's performance in Euripides' *The Bacchae* (405 B.C.E.), the enigmatic masterpiece named for the followers of Dionysus. As he meditates before Apollo's mask, Nikeratos hears his own voice: "With *The Bacchae* he [Euripides] digs down far below, to some deep rift in the soul where our griefs begin. Take that play anywhere, even to men unborn who worship other gods or none, and it will teach them to know themselves."

Plato's tragedy, acted out by Dion, was the "deep rift" that made people unable to follow him with united minds and hearts: "No one would fight for Dion, when he gave, as his own soul saw it, his very life for justice." By serving Apollo and Dionysus equally, however, Nikeratos the artist earns his gifts, one a Platonic dream of acting in a strange revenge drama, speaking lines beside an open grave to a clean skull in his hand. Through his love for his protégé Thettalos, whom he frees for achievements he knows will be greater than his own, Nikeratos plays Achilles in Aeschylus's *The Myrmidons* in a performance viewed by Alexander, a boy for whom men will fight and die, "whether he is right or wrong," a prince who "will wander through the world . . . never knowing . . . that while he was still a child the thing he seeks slipped from the world, worn out and spent." Had he encountered Plato's Ideals, which he instinctively sought, Renault proposes as the curtain falls on *The Mask of Apollo*, the Alexander of history might have made the philosopher-king Plato's Dion never could have been; but Nikeratos observes that "no one will ever make a tragedy—and that is well, for one could not bear it—whose grief is that the principals never met."

FIRE FROM HEAVEN

Renault's Alexander grows from boy to king in *Fire from Heaven*, in which she abandons the memoir form for more objective narration, as though no single point of view could encompass Alexander's youthful ideals, fired by the blazing Homeric *philotimo* in Achilles' honor he learned at the epic-conscious Macedonian court. Modern archaeology supports Renault's conviction that Alexander deliberately patterned his actions, even his father Philip's funerary rites, on the *Iliad* (c. 750 B.C.E.; English translation, 1611), which he read as though returning home, recognizing in his mutual love with Hephaistion the tragic bond of Achilles and Patroclus, the basis of the Western world's first, perhaps greatest, poem.

Arete, which cloaks the heavenly Idea of excellence in earthly beauty, came to Alexander less from Aristotle than through his instinctive attraction to Sokrates through Plato's works, which he read as a boy in Macedon. After defeating Thebes's Sacred Band at Cheironeia, where Philip's Macedonians secured the domination of all of Greece, Alexander stands "with surmise and regret" at Plato's tomb in Athens, listening to his disciple Xenokrates: "What he [Plato] had to teach could only be learned as fire is kindled, by the touch of the flame itself."

THE PERSIAN BOY

The novel in which Renault most precariously treats the question of homosexuality, *The Persian Boy*, is narrated by Bagoas, the handsome eunuch once King Darius's favorite and now the lover of Alexander. Renault's choice of Bagoas's point of view reflects her belief that Alexander was not corrupted by Persian luxury and imperial power, as many historians from classical times to the present have asserted, but that he sought to assimilate Eastern ways as a means of uniting his realm in spirit as well as military fact. Just as Alexander's "passionate capacity for affection" could allow him to accept affection wherever it was sincerely offered from the heart and yet remain wholly true to Bagoas's "victor now, forever," Hephaistion (who Renault feels is the most underrated man in history), Alexander felt "Macedon was my father's country. This is mine"—meaning the empire he had won for himself.

Renault believes that Alexander's eventual tragedy was that he was humanly unable to achieve equilibrium between his followers' personal devotion to him and their pragmatic selfish desires. Through Alexander's complex relationship with his dangerous mother Olympias, herself a devotee of Dionysus, Renault exemplifies the peril of neglecting the god of ecstasy basic to *The Bacchae*, in which Olympias herself had acted during Alexander's youth as a shocking challenge to Philip's authority. Toward the end of Alexander's own life, Dionysus's cruelty touches even him. Renault shows his purported deterioration as less his own fault than his men's when he must hold them by force as well as by love, even violating Macedon's dearest law, killing before their Assembly had condemned a man to death. The powerful god leads Alexander to excess; Bagoas sees that "his hunger grew by feeding." The Roman historian Arrian, following the memoir of Alexander's only faithful general Ptolemy, commented, "If there had been no other competition, he would have competed against himself."

Bagoas better than any also sees that "great anguish lies in wait for those who long too greatly." Alexander loses Hephaistion and with him nearly abandons his own senses, emerging only after his friend's funeral, in which he watches Thettalos, without Nikeratos for the first time, perform *The Myrmidons* one last time; "'Perhaps,' Bagoas thought, 'the last of the madness had been seared out of him by so much burning.'"

At the close of *The Persian Boy*, Renault notes in her afterword, "When his [Alexander's] faults (those his own times did not account as virtues) have been considered . . . no other human being has attracted in his lifetime, from so many men, so fervent a devotion. Their reasons are worth examining." In her two novels of Alexander's life, Renault not only examines the reasons but also brilliantly probes to the heart of one of the greatest human mysteries: how one person can ask, as did Homer's Achilles, "Now as things are, when the ministers of death stand by us/ In their thousands, which no man born to die can escape or even evade,/ Let us go"—and how other people, with all their hearts, can answer.

Such "true songs are still in the minds of men," according to the aged bard Simonides, narrator of *The Praise Singer*, recalling the "lyric years" when tragedy was being born of song and Athens was becoming the center of the earth. "We die twice when men forget," the ghosts of heroes seemed to tell him as a boy, and he has spent his life in "the bright and perilous gift of making others shine." In this novel, where Renault's heroic epitaph for *philotimo* and her noble elegy for people's hope of *arete* have given place to a gentler, less exalted nostalgia, she recognizes that "praising excellence, one serves the god within it." Renault also notes in her afterword that "the blanket generalization 'absolute power corrupts absolutely' is a historical absurdity," and she demonstrates that the respected rule of Pisistratus, nominally a "tyrant," formed the solid foundation on which Pericles erected Athenian democracy, even presaging through a discredited seer "a lightning flash from Macedon."

In Alexander's time, Renault observed, "the issue was not whether, but how one made [war]." At his death, brought about at least in part by his self-destructive grief for Hephaistion, Alexander's generals embarked on a cannibalistic power struggle—only Ptolemy, his half brother, emerging with any of the dignity Alexander had worn so easily in conquering his empire. Renault's *Funeral Games* is "the ancestral pattern of Macedonian tribal and familial struggles for his throne; except that Alexander had given them a world stage on which to do it."

FUNERAL GAMES

The most violent of Renault's Greek novels, *Funeral Games* contains a darkness that is alleviated only by flashes of Alexander reflected through the decency of the few who knew him best—Ptolemy, Bagoas, and Queen Sisygambis, who looked upon Alexander, not Darius, as her son. In them, something of Alexander's flame lingers a little while, a heavenly light extinguished at last in the wreckage of his empire in human depravity that Alexander could not prevent nor Renault fail to record.

In her eight novels of ancient Greece, Renault far surpasses conventional historical fiction. She achieves a mythic dimension in her balance of Apollonian and Dionysian psychological forces and philosophical precision in her treatment of Platonic doctrines. Her style is adapted to the Greek literature of each period she delineates, Attic elegance for *The Last of the Wine* and *The Mask of Apollo*, Hellenic involution counterpoised against Alexander's Homeric simplicity of speech. Renault links all eight novels with a chain of works of art, a finely crafted touch the classical Greeks would have applauded: The great tragedies, *The Myrmidons* and *The Bacchae*, Polykleitos's sculpture of Hermes modeled on Alexias, and the bronze of the liberator Harmodios in Pisistratos's day all serve as shaping factors in the portrait of her ultimate hero, Alexander. Mastering time, space, and modern ignorance of the classical world, Renault captures the "sadness at the back of life" that Virginia Woolf so aptly cited as the essence of Greek literature, the inevitable grieving awareness of people at the impassable gulf between their aspirations and their achievement. In the face of the eternal questions of existence, Renault's novels offer a direction in which to turn when, in Woolf's words, "we are sick of the vagueness, of the confusion, of the Christianity and its consolations, of our own age."

Mitzi M. Brunsdale

OTHER MAJOR WORKS

NONFICTION: *The Nature of Alexander*, 1975.

CHILDREN'S LITERATURE: *The Lion in the Gateway: Heroic Battles of the Greeks and Persians at Marathon, Salamis, and Thermopylae*, 1964.

BIBLIOGRAPHY

Abraham, Julie. "Mary Renault's Greek Drama." In *Are Girls Necessary? Lesbian Writing and Modern Histories*. New York: Routledge, 1996. Chapter on Renault's work is part of a larger study of lesbian writers. Discusses *The Last of the Wine*, *The Mask of Apollo*, *The Charioteer*, and other works.

Conrath, Alan Brady. "Something About Mary." *Gay and Lesbian Review Worldwide* 11, no. 3 (May/June, 2004): 15-17. Discusses why Renault is not considered a top-rank writer, attributing her literary reputation to the current critical bias against historical fiction and the fact that Renault was a woman writer in the 1950's and 1960's.

Dick, Bernard F. *The Hellenism of Mary Renault*. Carbondale: Southern Illinois Press, 1972. Excellent introduction to Renault's work examines her entire literary output through *Fire from Heaven*. Dick places Renault in the mainstream of fiction and applauds her as one of the most creative historical novelists of the twentieth century.

Hoberman, Ruth. *Gendering Classicism: The Ancient World in Twentieth-Century Women's Historical Fiction*. Albany: State University of New York Press, 1997. Presents a feminist interpretation of historical fiction set in ancient Greece and Rome. Examines works by Renault and five other women writers, describing how these writers challenged the misogynist classical tradition.

Moore, Lisa L. "Lesbian Migrations." *GLQ: A Journal of Lesbian and Gay Studies* 10, no. 1 (2004): 23-46. Discusses Renault's place within gay and lesbian literature, evaluating the work of the pioneer lesbian writer, who disavowed gay rights, deemed male artists to be superior to women, and benefited from South African apartheid.

Sweetman, David. *Mary Renault: A Biography*. New York: Harcourt Brace, 1993. Explores Renault's life in England, including her education at Oxford, and then describes her years in South Africa. Offers a fascinating study of Renault's sexuality as it relates to her historical novels. Includes bibliography.

Wolfe, Peter. *Mary Renault*. New York: Twayne, 1969. First book-length examination of the writer is both a plea for Renault's recognition by the critics as an important twentieth century writer and a critical analysis of her work.

Zilboorg, Caroline. *The Masks of Mary Renault: A Literary Biography*. Columbia: University of Missouri Press, 2001. Analyzes Renault's novels from the perspective of queer theory, arguing that the depiction of transgressive sexual identities is a common feature of Renault's fiction. Includes bibliography and index.

MAY SARTON

Born: Wondelgem, Belgium; May 3, 1912
Died: York, Maine; July 16, 1995
Also known as: Eléanore Marie Sarton

OTHER LITERARY FORMS

A poet as well as a novelist, May Sarton published a considerable number of volumes of verse. Her *Collected Poems, 1930-1973*, appeared in 1974 and *Collected Poems, 1930-1993*, appeared in 1993. She also wrote a fable, *Miss Pickthorn and Mr. Hare*; an animal fantasy story, *The Fur Person: The Story of a Cat*; several volumes of autobiography, including *I Knew a Phoenix: Sketches for an Autobiography* (1959), *Plant Dreaming Deep* (1968), and *A World of Light: Portraits and Celebrations* (1976); and several journals of her life in Nelson, New Hampshire, and York, Maine.

ACHIEVEMENTS

It was after World War II, with the novel *The Bridge of Years* and the poems collected in *The Lion and the Rose* (1948), that May Sarton's reputation began to grow. Her novels met with a mixed response from critics and reviewers, sometimes condemned for awkward or imprecise style, an odd charge against a practicing poet. Even Carolyn Heilbrun, Sarton's defender, admitted that confusing shifts of viewpoint occur in her fiction. On the other hand, Sarton's honesty in presenting human problems, seeing them from varied perspectives, has generally been acknowledged. In some ways, novels such as *Mrs. Stevens Hears the Mermaids Singing* and *Crucial Conversations* are dramatized debates about art, feminine culture, interpersonal relationships, tradition, and memory.

Sarton also was accused of sentimentality and preciousness, and she tried to shift her style to a more direct, less self-conscious one after the early 1970's, perhaps answering critics of *Mrs. Stevens Hears the Mermaids Singing*, who saw it as too arch, too knowing. She tended to take current issues or fashions such as the Vietnam War, death-and-dying, feminine consciousness, and Jungian psychology as material for her novels. Autobiographical material frequently enters into her fiction, particular characters being reinvoked in various works and especially types such as authoritarian women, supportive women, and rebellious young people.

Sarton complained of the lack of serious critical scrutiny of her work and expressed disappointment as well at her failure to achieve a large popular success. She has been stereotyped as a woman's writer, presumably creating slick plot situations, overdramatic dialogue, and conventional characters in romantic duos or trios. Some of these charges are true; she herself, noting the difficulty of supporting herself by her work even as late as the 1970's, although she was a prolific and well-established writer, spoke of the difficulties of being a single woman writer not sustained by a family or a religious community. Nevertheless, she affirmed the possibility of self-renewal, commenting, "I believe that eventually my work will be seen as a whole, all the poems and all the novels, as the expression of a vision of life which, though unfashionable all the way, has validity." The surge of interest in her work at the end of the twentieth century, particularly among feminist scholars, would seem to confirm Sarton's hopes.

BIOGRAPHY

May Sarton was born Eléanore Marie Sarton in Wondelgem, Belgium, on May 3, 1912. Her mother, Mabel Elwes Sarton, a designer who worked at Maison Dangette, Brussels, was a determined craftsperson and an uncompromising seeker of high standards. Her father, George Sarton, pampered by his Belgian upper-middle-class family after losing his mother early, was an active socialist who did mathematical studies at the University of Brussels before settling into his life's work as a major historian of science; he founded the leading journal in the field, *Isis*, in 1912. He was a methodical scholar who even after his day's scholarly labors would make notes in the evening concerning recent research by other scholars. May's mother compromised her talents for her husband's career, but her gift of "refashioning things magically" inspired her daughter's own verbal artistry.

One close friend of Sarton's mother was Céline Dangotte Limbosch, or Mamie, whose home near Brussels Sarton has recalled as the one place in the world that would not change and whose traits appear in the heroine of *The Bridge of Years*. Mamie's husband, Raumond Limbosch, a poet who never published his poems, also figures in that novel as a philosopher.

Sarton's earliest years were spent in Belgium, but with the coming of World War I, the family fled to England. In 1915, the Sartons went to the United States, staying briefly in New York before settling in Washington, D.C., where the Carnegie Institute gave support to George Sarton's projected history of science. Mabel Sarton founded Belgart, specializing in handmade fashion apparel. Sarton's father's somewhat informal appointment at Harvard University led the family to Cambridge, Massachusetts, in 1918. There, young Sarton attended Shady Hill School, a Spartan institution run by an educational innovator, Mrs. Hocking, wife of a well-known philosopher, who combined the study of philosophy with poetry. Miss Edgett, an imaginative math teacher, inspired Sarton to be a poet, but Sarton also received encouragement from a family friend in Cambridge, Edith Forbes Kennedy. Kennedy was the inspiration for a character, Willa MacPherson, in *Mrs. Stevens Hears the Mermaids Singing*, whose friendship and encouragement push young Hilary Stevens along on her poetic career. School plays also awakened Sarton's interest in drama.

In 1919, the family briefly returned to settle their affairs in Belgium. For a short time, Sarton attended the Institute Belge de Culture Française, which she later attended for a year at age twelve. The institute was presided over by Marie Closset, who published poetry as Jean Dominique, and two other women. Literature was taught from great works, and memorization was required. Sarton spent that year with the Limbosches while her parents were in Beirut, Lebanon, so that her father could learn Arabic for his research. The literary atmosphere and general culture that she encountered there influenced Sarton greatly.

A 1926 graduate of Cambridge Latin High School, Sarton recalled attending Boston Repertory Theater, reading poems with friends, and feeling revolutionary about Henrik Ibsen during these years. Her parents had settled into Channing Place, Cambridge, which was the center of Sarton's life until her parents' deaths. Sarton spent two years wanting to be an actor, doing summer stock in Gloucester before joining Eva LeGallienne's Civic Repertory Theater in 1929. She spent three years with the theater company; from 1931 to 1932, Sarton was in Paris working as director of the company's apprentices. While in Paris, she became friends with Aurélian-Marie Lugné-Poë, a founder of Théâtre de L'Œuvre, a theater that brought many new plays to France. Lugné-Poë appears as a director in *The Bridge of Years*. Although he thought Sarton had more talent as a writer, he was willing to help her improve her acting skills. Their unsuccessful romantic relationship parallels that which occurs in *A Shower of Summer Days*, whose heroine goes to a country home in Ireland to overcome a love affair.

When LeGallienne ran out of money, Sarton, together with Eleanor Flexner and Kappo Phelan, kept the Apprentices Theater going, settling in Dublin, New Hampshire, and appearing elsewhere on tour. That venture failed after two years, a considerable shock for Sarton that turned her in the direction of writing fiction. In the following year, she wrote several short stories, none of which sold. In June, 1936, she went to Cornwall, England, first staying with Charles Singer, the historian of science, and then moving to London. She met Elizabeth Bowen, who was to become a friend over the next several decades and was the subject of passionate feelings; Juliette and Julian Huxley, at whose apartment over the London Zoo she spent a month; and Virginia Woolf. She also met James Stephens, the Irish poet, and became a particular friend of S. S. Koteliansky, editor and mentor of various writers, including Katharine Mansfield.

From 1936 to 1940, Sarton visited Belgium each spring, and for decades she could not decide whether she was European or American. She began writing poetry at the age of twenty-six. Needing funds and having no settled career, she returned to the United States in 1939 to read her poetry at various colleges. Despite feeling "the inward disturbance of exile," she felt the love and friendship of many different people.

During the years of World War II, Sarton worked for the U.S. Office of War Information in the film department. In 1943, she set up poetry readings at the New York Public Library to provide cultural experience for wartime workers. She returned to England in 1944 to visit her friend Bowen, who also visited Sarton whenever she was in the United States. With *The Bridge of Years*, Sarton's novel writing began again in earnest. Novels and other fiction and volumes of poetry have appeared at close intervals since. Her early poetry won her the Gold Rose for Poetry and the Edward Bland Memorial Prize (1945).

Sarton supported herself by teaching, serving as Briggs-Copeland instructor in composition at Harvard from 1950 to 1952, poet-in-residence at Bryn Mawr from 1953 to 1954, and lecturing on poetry at Harvard, the University of Iowa, the University of Chicago, Colorado College for Women, and Wellesley and Beloit colleges. In 1953, she met Louise Bogan, whose calm and order she valued considerably, though Bogan, poetry editor of *The New Yorker*, did little to advance Sarton's career. Other novels appearing in the early 1950's earned Sarton a Guggenheim Fellowship from 1954 to 1955. Her reputation had grown with *A Shower of Summer Days*, though the critical reception, as with later novels, was mixed.

The Birth of a Grandfather came at a turning point in Sarton's life: Her mother had died in 1950 after a long illness and her father died quite suddenly in 1956. The family home in Cambridge was sold, and Sarton moved in October, 1958, to an old house equipped with a barn and thirty-six acres in Nelson, New Hampshire, a small village. Sarton then settled briefly in Ogunquit, Maine, and then in York, Maine, in an old house on the coast, writing further volumes of poetry, autobiographical sketches, and journals. Her love for animals is reflected in *The Fur Person*, a story about a gentleman cat's adventures.

Sarton's career reflected her conviction that "art must become the primary motivation, for love is never going to fulfill in the usual sense." Increasingly, she took her stand as a feminist: "We [women] have to be ourselves." Her understanding of her own sexual orientation seems to have grown partly out of her isolation as a woman and as a writer and her sense that marriage and family would detract from her creativity. She died in Maine in 1995.

ANALYSIS

The Small Room, a novel dealing with women training women as intellectual disciples in the atmosphere of a small women's college, was written while Sarton lived in Nelson. The novel also introduced a lesbian love affair between Carryl Cope, a brilliant but flinty scholar, and Olive Hunt, a benefactor of the college. *Mrs. Stevens Hears the Mermaids Singing*, which Sarton wrote at a time of gloom because of worries over her financial situation, was at first refused publication because it depicted a lesbian relationship, and the publishers required excisions before the book was accepted. *Kinds of Love, As We Are Now, Crucial Conversations*, and *A Reckoning* explore various marital or amatory dilemmas along with the problem of being a woman and an artist. *The Bridge of Years* is, perhaps, Sarton's most complex work. This is partly because the prototypes of the main characters were close to Sarton's own experience and the themes were motivated by intellectual friendships established in Europe prior to World War II.

THE BRIDGE OF YEARS

Based on Sarton's student years in Belgium and memories of her own family, *The Bridge of Years* centers on a Belgian family, Paul and Melanie Duchesne, and their three daughters, during four segments of their lives. These periods, besides accounting for personal growth in the major characters, also demarcate the stages of political change after World War I: optimism in the immediate postwar period; the decline of public morale and search for political solutions to the Depression of the 1930's; the fear of renewed European conflict attendant upon the rise of Adolf Hitler; and the outbreak of that conflict as liberal, humanitarian values come under attack with World War II.

Melaine Duchesne, a designer of furniture, a stickler for fine craftsmanship, a courageous and optimistic woman whose country home is a model of stability, is based on Sarton's mother and her longtime friend Céline Limbosch. Paul, the temperamental philosopher who cannot express his thoughts, is partly based on Raymond Limbosch and partly on George Sarton, May's father, especially in his need for an ordered existence and exact routine. Paul's breakthrough into true philosophical statement under the pressure of the war is, as much as anything, Sarton's own search for authentic expression. Her father's leftist socialism and critical intelligence are reflected in Pierre Poiret, the university student son of close friends of the Duchesne family. The immemorial Bo Bo, the stiff but protective Teutonic nursemaid, is a portrait of Sarton's childhood governess.

Of the daughters, Colette, the youngest, is the poet, a romanticist living in a fairy world, Sarton's view of herself as a child. Solange, who becomes a veterinarian, has the patient skill with animals that Sarton herself possessed. The eldest daughter, Françoise, with her long affection for Jacques Croll, a fatigued soldier from World War I, believes that art is everything, turning herself inward when Jacques, maneuvered by Melanie, marries a local girl. Françoise feels compromised when Jacques tips her a wink as he walks down the church aisle with his bride. Her resulting emotional breakdown, and the awareness that art cannot be everything when "life [is] lived near the point of conflict," reflect Sarton's own emotional turmoil in the 1930's as she sought to become an artist.

Paul Duchesne's skepticism about the perfectibility of the human spirit is tempered by his German friend, the intellectual Gerhard Schmidt, who sees the need for individual effort to resist tyranny. After escaping from his homeland during Hitler's purge of intellectuals, he goes to fight with the Loyalists in Spain while his son, Hans, hypnotized by the Nazis, becomes a storm trooper. This opposition of father and son is repeated in the case of Emile Poiret, a pious Catholic floral illustrator with a sense of cosmic presence in things, and his antireligious son, Pierre. The novel presents facets of the European response to the breakdown of democratic civilization in the 1920's and 1930's and, at a more personal level, reflects the idea that some persons must extend themselves in love if civilization is to continue.

THE BIRTH OF A GRANDFATHER

The question of who one is, especially in the context of generations and of change, was a continuing concern of Sarton. It is presented through the dramatic, carefully staged scenes of *The Birth of a Grandfather*, in which the omniscient author moves among the characters, heightening the effect by the questions they ask themselves. The interior speculation is in the style of Henry James, though the consciousness attributed to a given character does not always seem consistent with his personality or inner life. This novel begins at the Maine island retreat of the wealthy and established Wyeth family. Tom Dorgan, a Boston Irish Catholic, is romantically involved with Betsy Wyeth, Frances and Sprig Wyeth's daughter. In contrast to these young lovers, Lucy, Frances's sister, is undergoing a divorce. It is Frances, the major character, and her husband, Sprig, from the middle-aged generation, whose painful readjustment to marriage and to age form the basis of the plot.

The older generation includes Uncle Joe, an urbane retired diplomat, Aunt Jane, a wise old woman capable of immersing herself in others, and Gran-Quan, Sprig's father, a man consumed by dramatic self-pity over the death of his wife and constantly supported by his sister, Jane. The Wyeths' son, Caleb, is reluctantly in the heart of family matters, biding his time until he gains independence from them. Appropriately enough, a major scene is the family's Fourth of July celebration on a nearby island. The fireworks are, for Frances, like moments of purity amid darkness, but they also herald the sudden death of Aunt Jane and the breaking up of Gran-Quan's private world and descent into insanity. Betsy and Caleb see their parents in new ways: Frances represents human frailty, and Sprig is seen as one sheltered from the pains of life.

The second part of the novel, "Ice Age," set in Cambridge, Massachusetts, shows the threat that tension and obligation bring to family unity. Tom and Betsy have married, and a child is on the way. This potentially joyful event threatens Sprig, who cannot accept the loss of direction in his life, which has settled into traditional philanthropy and conservation of the family wealth. By contrast, his friend Bill Waterford, who treats life with saving grace, calmly announces his impending death from cancer. Bill's life has had a sense of purpose. Two dinner scenes set forth two perspectives: In one, Hester, Sprig's sister, sees Sprig and Frances trying vainly to avert the emotional threat of Caleb's demand to be allowed to go alone to Greece for a year. In another, Tom Dorgan, innocently holding forth on the coming prospect of family life, exacerbates the conflict of generations, but he also sees that the Wyeths can admit to being wrong and remain loyal to each other. Caleb puts aside his immediate demand for independence, recognizing his father's own imprisonment in his reticence and sense of responsibility.

Coming to terms with Caleb leaves Sprig uncertain about his love for his wife, and a visit to Bill provokes the question of what real life is. Bill's wife, Nora, warns him that one may fail to exercise one's talents out of fear of freedom and power, a question that Sarton explored in various ways in probing the nature of the artist. Caleb's destination, Greece, awakens other echoes in Sprig, reminding him of the Greek scholarship for which he had once wished; Sprig then realizes his potential for continued growth.

In the third part, the grandfather is reborn, both in the sheer physical sense of the new grandchild and in meeting the meaning of his own life. Sprig must surrender his friendship with Bill, and he must test his own talent, no longer relying on Bill's support. Frances wonders whether she has not turned self-detachment into a prison; the answer comes with the realization that birth and death, the march of ongoing generations, has significance. This insight strikes her when, while visiting Bill, she encounters his nearly exhausted wife, Nora; a seemingly unsuitable marriage has worked because Bill was able to give of himself. Upon the departure of Caleb, to whom Sprig has given financial independence so that Caleb may try what he has wanted, Sprig himself turns to translating Greek plays as a self-imposed test. He acknowledges also that he has loved himself rather than Caleb in their relationship. With new honesty and willingness to assume self-defined responsibility, Sprig reconnects to the exuberance of his youth. He and Frances reaffirm their faithfulness, and love wins out as absolute value.

Sarton uses imagistic motifs, such as the current in the Charles River and the isles of Greece, to suggest important ideas in the novel. The shifting omniscient viewpoint highlights dramatic intensities, but it is used at times without strong motivation or without a careful build-up of character. It also can turn into undisguised narrative commentary. Moral implications do come through in catchwords such as "escape" and "freedom," which reverberate through the novel. Occasionally, moral judgments become banal. The novel has shown Sprig's life as empty of personal demands on himself and his resistance to his children as a fearful reaction to his own aging, but the moral tends to blunt the focus.

MRS. STEVENS HEARS THE MERMAIDS SINGING

Coming roughly at the middle of Sarton's career, *Mrs. Stevens Hears the Mermaids Singing* is the author's most intense study of the female artist. Here, too, the style received mixed reviews, one critic praising the music of the prose, another objecting to the fussiness and humorlessness of the writing. What one critic found to be a well-done presentation of the mystery of the creative impulse a second found to be "an embarrassing probing of art" and "acute self-consciousness," and a third found the novel's characters "muse-chasers who believe themselves to be delicate vessels of talent." Scholar Heilbrun, in noting that the novel deals with the poet Hilary Stevens's escape from the passivity of a feminine destiny, sees Sarton as aware that "the real artist is not the fantasy creature imagined by women trapped in domesticity." Art comes, as Hilary insists, at the expense of every human being, the self and the self's ties with other people.

The plot interweaves Hilary's initiation of Mar Hemmer, a potential poet recovering from an intense relationship with a man, with her reveries as she is being interviewed about her own poetic development. Mar, despite his lack of emotional proportion, helps her to see her own life in perspective. Married to an unstable war veteran in England, Hilary began to write poetry after his sudden death. An intellectual friend, Willa MacPherson, encourages her to continue writing poetry and provides one night of passionate sexual exploration. Another friend, however, creates self-doubt, which Hilary identifies with the masculine force in herself. She knows that she can preserve her artistry only by caring about life, which does not necessarily mean sparing others from pain. As Hilary later points out to Mar, poetry and feeling are connected only if the poet understands that "true feeling justifies whatever it may cost." One cannot be anesthetized against the pain of life.

Philippa Munn, Hilary's proper girlhood governess with whom she is infatuated, plays the role that Sarton's own teachers did in her youth. Poetry diffuses sensuality, Hilary learns; it creates a moment of revelation, not simply of indulgence. As Hilary's wise physician tells her as she lies in the hospital recovering from a breakdown over her husband's death, she must write poems about objects and about a person to whom she can fasten herself deeply, but she should not confuse love for someone with poetry. Poetry can become "passionate decorum" in which love is presented as a mystique; what gives strength to poems is form.

Mrs. Stevens Hears the Mermaids Singing mixes the Platonic tradition of poet as maker whose creations surpass his or her own conscious understanding with an Aristotelian stress on the formal artifact that has its own laws of being and is autonomous. The notion of the poet as rapt by emotional experience lies also within the Platonic tradition of poetry as ecstasy. The events making up the life of Hilary Stevens have parallels with Sarton's own life, and the novel is a justification of that life. The presentation of the poet as a solitary individual misunderstood by the world also reflects Sarton's romanticism.

A Reckoning

As the heroine of *A Reckoning*, Laura Spelman, resident of an upper-middle-class Boston suburb, faces terminal cancer, she interprets her growing "death-wish" as a return to the Jungian "house of gathering." It is a world of timeless personages; Sarton had been reading Jung before writing the book. She had also become more concerned with feminism and more open about lesbian sexuality. As Laura is alienated from her own body, she works to resolve her unexamined passions by assessing her life. She comes, according to one critic, to an "understanding of life as an amalgam of human relationships, culture, and the natural world."

The novel also shows Harriet Moors, a budding novelist and lesbian, trying to put her life into art, an issue complicated by the opposition of her lover to any fiction that might hint at the truth of their liaison. It seems that not only marriage but also a binding lesbian attachment is fatal to art: Harriet Moors will have to suffer the loss of her lover as the price of continuing with her art.

Laura has to sort out her feelings for her mother, Sybille, a woman of dazzling power whose beauty and charm have oppressed her daughters. Jo, Laura's sister, after her mother had interrupted Jo's passion for a woman, had fled into the sterile intellectuality of academic life. Daphne, Laura's other sister, has become insecure and emotionally dependent. Laura has found escape in marriage. The destructive Sybille is a less flattering version of Céline Limbosch, of whom Sarton has said that she forced friends into decisions they did not wish to make and attacked their authentic being. Even in her senility in a nursing home, Sybille is someone about whom her daughter treads warily. Earlier in her life, Laura had had an intense friendship with Ella; the reader may strain, in fact, to realize it was a lesbian relationship. Harriet Moors's visits for advice on her novel rekindles in Laura her memories of Ella. She comes to realize that if love is painful, then art is mutilating. Yet in dying, Laura finds positive answers in music and in poetry.

The final reckoning is instigated by Laura's warm and helpful Aunt Minna, whose reading aloud to Laura forces her to consider that "journey into being a woman" and what women are meant to be. Women are locked away from one another in a man's world, she decides. Marriage may be normal destiny, but for those living intensely, a mystical friendship is the hope—of women for women, of men for men. Sybille, according to Ella, feared "the tenderness of communion."

Laura's loss of lonely autonomy is convincingly presented, but the master image, that of weaving a pattern, is imposed rather than dramatized. Ella's appearance at the end does not really complete the final weaving of the pattern by mystical friendship; the scene reminds the reader of sentimental fiction often found in women's magazines. Clearly, too many issues have come within the compass of the heroine's last months. Death may force its victims to focus their lives and aspirations, but the last days of Laura Spelman are not deeply and plausibly linked to her life as a married woman and parent or even to her efforts to approach art. As in *Mrs. Stevens Hears the Mermaids Singing*, reminiscence plays a key role. Whole scenes are recalled in dramatic form, but the very selectivity of memory and its often self-serving quality may raise questions about the honesty and sheer structural relationship between what Laura recalls and what she really was—a Boston upper-middle-class housewife with delusions of creativity, the kind of thing against which Sarton herself warned. *A Reckoning* lacks the strengths of Sarton's best work: thematic depth, balanced characters, organic use of imagery, adequate plot development, and motivated action.

Roger E. Wiehe

OTHER MAJOR WORKS

PLAY: *The Underground River,* pb. 1947.

POETRY: *Encounter in April,* 1937; *Inner Landscape,* 1939; *The Lion and the Rose,* 1948; *The Land of Silence, and Other Poems,* 1953; *In Time Like Air,* 1958; *Cloud, Stone, Sun, Vine: Poems, Selected and New,* 1961; *A Private Mythology,* 1966; *As Does New Hampshire, and Other Poems,* 1967; *A Grain of Mustard Seed: New Poems,* 1971; *A Durable Fire: New Poems,* 1972; *Collected Poems, 1930-1973,* 1974; *Selected Poems of May Sarton,* 1978 (Serena Sue Hilsinger and Lois Byrnes, editors); *Halfway to Silence,* 1980; *Letters from Maine,* 1984; *The Silence Now: New and Uncollected Earlier Poems,* 1988; *Collected Poems, 1930-1993,* 1993; *Coming into Eighty,* 1994.

NONFICTION: *I Knew a Phoenix: Sketches for an Autobiography,* 1959; *Plant Dreaming Deep,* 1968; *Journal of a Solitude,* 1973; *A World of Light: Portraits and Celebrations,* 1976; *The House by the Sea,* 1977; *Recovering: A Journal,* 1980; *Writings on Writing,* 1980; *May Sarton: A Self-Portrait,* 1982; *At Seventy: A Journal,* 1984; *After the Stroke: A Journal,* 1988; *Honey in the Hive: Judith Matlack, 1898-1982,* 1988; *Endgame: A Journal of the Seventy-ninth Year,* 1992; *Encore: A Journal of the Eightieth Year,* 1993; *At Eighty-two,* 1996; *May Sarton: Selected Letters, 1916-1954,* 1997 (Susan Sherman, editor); *Dear Juliette: Letters of May Sarton to Juliette Huxley,* 1999; *May Sarton: Selected Letters, 1955-1995,* 2002 (Sherman, editor).

CHILDREN'S/YOUNG ADULT LITERATURE: *Punch's Secret,* 1974; *A Walk Through the Woods,* 1976.

MISCELLANEOUS: *Sarton Selected: An Anthology of the Journals, Novels, and Poems of May Sarton,* 1991 (Bradford Dudley Daziel, editor); *May Sarton: Among the Usual Days,* 1993 (Sherman, editor); *From May Sarton's Well: Writings of May Sarton,* 1994 (Edith Royce Schade, editor).

BIBLIOGRAPHY

Evans, Elizabeth. *May Sarton, Revisited.* Boston: Twayne, 1989. Updates the 1973 Twayne series volume on Sarton by Agnes Sibley. A revaluation of Sarton's lifetime achievements, offering careful analysis of her work in four genres. Includes a helpful chronology of Sarton's life and accomplishments.

Fulk, Mark K. *Understanding May Sarton.* Columbia: University of South Carolina

Press, 2001. Consciously avoids assuming that Sarton is of interest only to students of feminist or lesbian writers, attempting to come "closer to the spirit of Sarton's work as she saw it."

Hunting, Constance, ed. *May Sarton: Woman and Poet*. Orono, Maine: National Poetry Foundation, 1982. Twenty-four essays on Sarton's novels, journals, and poetry, including analyses of her journals and memoirs and the French influences on her writing style. Includes a bibliography and an index.

Peters, Margot. *May Sarton: A Biography*. New York: Alfred A. Knopf, 1997. In this first full-length biography, Peters examines why Sarton inspired such a devoted following among readers and discusses her uncertainty about the literary value of much of her work.

Sarton, May. *May Sarton: Selected Letters, 1916-1954*. Edited by Susan Sherman. New York: W. W. Norton, 1997.

_____. *May Sarton: Selected Letters, 1955-1995*. Edited by Susan Sherman. New York: W. W. Norton, 2002. A collection of correspondence that offers invaluable insight into Sarton's life and work. Includes indexes.

Sibley, Agnes. *May Sarton*. New York: Twayne, 1972. An early book-length treatment of Sarton's novels, and her poetry, through the 1960's. Groups the novels under two themes: "detachment" for the early novels and "communion" for the later ones.

Swartzlander, Susan, and Marilyn R. Mumford, eds. *That Great Sanity: Critical Essays on May Sarton*. Ann Arbor: University of Michigan Press, 1992. Thoughtful essays on Sarton's works, including discussions of Sarton and contemporary feminist fiction and of art and lesbian sexuality in her novel *Mrs. Stevens Hears the Mermaids Singing*.

Whitelaw, Lis. "The Education of May Sarton: Love Between Women in Four Novels by May Sarton." In *Beyond Sex and Romance? The Politics of Contemporary Lesbian Fiction*, edited by Elaine Hutton. London: Women's Press, 1998. This analysis of Sarton's novels from the perspective of queer theory is included in a collection of essays in which lesbian feminist critics examine works by lesbian authors.

CHRISTINA STEAD

Born: Rockdale, New South Wales, Australia; July 17, 1902
Died: Sydney, New South Wales, Australia; March 31, 1983
Also known as: Christina Ellen Stead

OTHER LITERARY FORMS

Christina Stead began her career with a volume of short stories, *The Salzburg Tales* (1934), and she contributed short stories to both literary and popular magazines. A posthumous collection, *Ocean of Story: The Uncollected Short Stories of Christina Stead*, was published in 1985. Her volume *The Puzzleheaded Girl* (1967) is a collection of four novellas. Her other literary output includes reviews and translations of several novels from the French. She also edited two anthologies of short stories, one with her husband, William Blake.

ACHIEVEMENTS

Christina Stead is considered to be in the first rank of Australian novelists; in 1974, she received Australia's Patrick White Award. One of Stead's novels, *The Man Who Loved Children*, received particular critical acclaim. Stead resisted critics' attempts to represent her as a feminist writer, but she has received attention from feminist critics for her depictions of women constricted by their social roles.

BIOGRAPHY

Christina Ellen Stead was born in Rockdale, New South Wales, on July 17, 1902. Her parents were David George Stead, a naturalist and fisheries economist, and Ellen Butters Stead. After her mother died of a perforated appendix when Christina was two years old, her father married Ada Gibbons, a society woman, and they had six children to whom Stead became big sister. Stead trained at the Sydney Teachers College, where she became a demonstrator in experimental psychology. As a public school teacher, she taught abnormal children and administered psychological tests in the schools. Stead suffered voice strain, however, and she later saw this as a symptom of her being unfit for the work. Like Teresa Hawkins in *For Love Alone*, Stead studied typing and shorthand to embark on a business career.

In 1928, Stead left Sydney, sailing on the *Oronsay* for England. She worked as a grain clerk and as a bank clerk in London and Paris, experiences that became background for her novel about finance, *House of All Nations*. By that time, Stead had met the economist and writer William Blake (born William Blech), whom she married in 1952. Stead settled in the United States from 1937 to 1946, publishing several novels and working for a time as a writer with the Metro-Goldwyn-Mayer film studio in Hollywood. At the end of World War II, Stead returned to Europe with Blake, living in various places on the Continent and returning to England when she feared that she was losing her feel for the English language. In 1968, Stead's husband died, and a few years later, in 1974, she returned to live with one of her brothers in Australia. She died in Sydney on March 31, 1983, at the age of eighty.

ANALYSIS

Christina Stead was preeminently a novelist of character. She identified herself as a psychological writer, involved with the drama of the person. Her stories develop out of the dynamics of characters asserting their human energy and vigor and developing their wills. Stead established personality and communicated its energy and vitality through her creation of a distinctive language for each character. This individuating language is explored in the characters' dialogues with one another (Sam Pollit talking his fantastic baby talk to his children), in their interior monologues (Teresa Hawkins, walking miles to and from work, meditating on her need to find a life beyond the surface social conventions), and in letters (the letter to Letty Fox from her former lover, who wants his money back after she has had an abortion). The language establishes the sense of an individual person with obsessions and characteristic blindnesses. One gets to know the quality of the mind through the texture of the language. As Christopher Ricks has noted of Stead's accomplishment, she re-creates the way people talk to themselves "in the privacy of [their] skulls." Ricks's phrase gives a sense of how intimately and deeply the language belongs to the person: It is in the skull and the bone.

In her novel *Letty Fox*, Stead has Letty sum up her adventures to date by saying, "On s'engage et puis on voit." The statement (roughly translated as "one gets involved and then one sees") is an existentialist one that reconciles what critics see as two forces in Stead's fiction: a preoccupation with character that links Stead to nineteenth century novelists and an analysis of social, psychological, and economic structures behind individual lives that links her to her contemporaries.

The phrase "On s'engage et puis on voit" also sums up Stead's method. First, she immerses the reader in the particular atmosphere of the character's mind and world; only then does she lead the reader to see a significance behind the individual passion. The phrase implies that one cannot see clearly by being disengaged, looking down on the human spectacle with the detachment of an objective physical scientist. Instead, one must become part of the experience, seeing it as a participant, in order to understand its reality. Some of the constant preoccupations of Stead's characters include family, love, marriage, money, and individual power.

THE MAN WHO LOVED CHILDREN

Stead's masterpiece, most critics agree, is her larger-than-life depiction of a family, *The Man Who Loved Children*. Out of print for twenty-five years, the book enjoyed a second life because of a partly laudatory review by the poet Randall Jarrell; Jarrell's review was included as an introduction when the novel was reissued in 1965. *The Man Who Loved Children* immerses its readers in the life of the Pollit family, in its swarming, buzzing intimacy. The father, Sam Pollit, is a garrulous idealist who advocates eugenics for the unfit but who fantasizes for himself babies of every race and a harem of wives who would serve his domestic comfort. On the surface, Sam's passions are his humanitarian ideals and his love for his children, but his underlying passion is what Geoffrey Chaucer said women's was—his own way or his own will. Sam is an egotistical child himself; he sees only what he wants to see. His characteristic talk is his overblown, high-sounding rhetoric expressing schemes to right the world and the fanciful, punning baby talk, whining and wheedling, that he uses with the children.

Henny, wife to Sam and stepmother to Louisa, is Sam's compulsive antagonist, worn down with childbearing and the struggle to manage her overextended household. Henny's passion is to survive, to fight dirt and debt and the intermittent sexuality that involves her in continual childbearing. Henny's characteristic talk is insult and denunciation, castigating with graphic details and metaphors the revolting sights, sounds, smells, tastes, and touches that assault her. Stead emphasizes Henny's eyes in descriptions of the fierce eyeballs in her sockets and her mouth in descriptions of her incessantly drinking tea and mouthing insults.

Stead's way of explaining the unbridgeable gap between the minds and sensibilities of the marriage partners is to say that they have no words in common. Sam's abstraction can never communicate with Henny's particularity. They have no words that they understand mutually, and so for most of the book the two characters communicate with each other only through messages relayed by the children or by terse notes concerning household necessities. In spite of that essential gap, a sixth child is conceived and born to the couple during the course of the novel, and the resources of the household are further strained, finally to the breaking point.

What brings the family to destruction is a complex of causes, many of which are fundamentally economic. The death of David Collyer, Henny's once rich father, is a blow to the family's fortunes. The Pollits lose their home, and Henny's creditors no longer expect that her father will pay her debts. Collyer's death also leaves Sam without a political base in his government job, and Sam's enemies move to oust him. The money crisis is intensified by Sam's refusal to fight for his job. Instead, he retires to their new ramshackle home to do repairs and to play with the children. Sam grandly waits to be exonerated while Henny struggles to keep the family fed and clothed.

Another cause of the breakup of the family is the birth of Sam and Henny's newest baby. Part of the trouble is economic: The new child means more expenses when Henny had promised her money-conscious eldest son Ernie that there would be no more children. The birth also brings an anonymous letter charging falsely that the child is not Sam's because Sam has been away in Malaya for several months. The letter, filled with spite, probably has been sent by one of Henny's disappointed creditors, but it exacerbates the mutual resentment of the couple and drives them closer and closer to serious violence against each other. (The pregnancy not only invades Henny's body and multiplies her worries but it also costs her her lover, who deserts her when he hears of the pregnancy. Henny is more than ever in Sam's power.)

A pivotal character in the fierce struggle between the parents is Louisa, eldest daughter of Sam and stepdaughter of Henny. Louisa's emergence from childhood upsets the hierarchy of the household. The "man who loved children" does not love them when they question his authority and threaten his position as "Sam the Bold," leader of the band of merry children. In retaliation, Sam calls Louisa names from "Loogoobrious" to "Bluebeak." In disputing Sam's ability to make it rain (his cosmic power), Louisa and Ernie—who is quick to jump in with what he has learned in school about evaporation—introduce norms from the world outside the family.

By the end of the novel, the family tears itself apart. Sam is unconsciously comparing himself to Christ and seeing Nature as his bride, while he says that women are "cussed" and need to be "run" and that he will send Henny away and keep the children. When Louisa asks for freedom to be sent to her dead mother's relatives in Harpers Ferry, Sam says that he will never let her leave, that she must not get married but must stay and help him with the children and his work. The quarreling between the parents increases until Louisa thinks that they will kill each other. The quarrels become physical battles, and Henny screams to the children to save her from their father. In despair, Ernie makes a dummy out of his clothes and hangs himself in effigy. Sam teases and humiliates the children, insisting that they stay up all night and help him boil down a marlin, an image that is reminiscent of Henny, with its staring eye, deep in its socket, and the wound in its vitals.

Louisa sees the two parents as passionate and selfish, inexorably destroying each other and the children, completely absorbed in their "eternal married hate." To save the children, Louisa considers poisoning both parents. Sam provides both the rationale, that the unfit should make room for the fit, and the means, cyanide that he ghoulishly describes as the bringer of death. Louisa succeeds in getting the grains of cyanide into only one large cup of tea when Henny notices what she has done and drinks it, exonerating Louisa and saying "damn you all." Even with Henny dead and Louisa's confession of her plan and its outcome, Sam refuses to believe her and refuses to let her go. Louisa's only escape is to run away, thus seizing her freedom.

The power of *The Man Who Loved Children* derives in part from the archetypal nature of the conflicts—between parents and children for independence; between man and woman, each for his or her own truth and identity; and between parents for their children, their objects of greatest value. The power also results from the particularity of the characterization, the metaphors that Stead employs to communicate the nature of each family member, and the astounding sense of individual language mirroring opposed sensibilities.

LETTY FOX *and* FOR LOVE ALONE

The epigraph to another Stead novel, *Letty Fox*, says that one can get experience only through foolishness and blunders. The method that Letty follows in her adventures puts her in the stream of picaresque heroes; the novel's subtitle, *Her Luck*, makes more sense with reference to the notion of a submission to experience, to one's fate, than it does with reference to the common meaning of "luck" as "good fortune." Letty's "luck" is that she survives and learns something about the ways of the world.

Stead once said that in *For Love Alone*, the novel that preceded *Letty Fox*, she wrote about a young girl of no social background who tries to learn about love, and readers did not understand the story. In *Letty Fox*, she thus gave American readers a story that they could understand: the story of a modern American girl searching for love and trying to obtain status through marriage.

In both novels, the social structure tells young women that they have no valid identity except through the men they marry. In *For Love Alone*, Teresa Hawkins, like her friends, fears becoming an old maid. Even though Letty Fox has had a series of lovers and a series of responsible, interesting jobs, she does not feel validated without the security of marriage. This firmly held conventional belief is belied by Letty's own family situation. Her beloved father, Solander, has a mistress, Persia, with whom he has lived faithfully for many years. The family women wonder how Persia can hold Solander without a paper and without a child. On the other hand, Mathilde, Letty's mother, has the marriage title but little else. She has three daughters—Letty, Jacky, and the much younger Andrea, conceived in a late reconciliation attempt—but Persia has Solander.

Like the picaresque hero, on her own, Letty learns the ways of the world. She truly loves Luke Adams, who tantalizes her with pretended concern for her youth and innocence and fans her fascination with him. She lives for a summer with a married man and has an abortion for which she must repay him. Originally confused by Lucy Headlong's interest in her, Letty refuses a lesbian affair with her. Letty sees a range of choices in the lives of the women around her: from her sister Jacky, in love with an elderly scientist, to her younger sister

Andrea, sharing the early maternal experience of her friend. Letty wants the security of marriage, but the men she knows do not want to make serious commitments. In *For Love Alone*, Teresa remarks on the short season for the husband hunt, with no time for work or extended study. In the marriage market for the comparatively long season of seven years, Letty does not catch a husband, even when her vicious cousin Edwige does.

Except in the matter of marriage, Letty trusts her own responses and takes credit for her own integrity. When her lover Cornelius is about to leave her for his mistress in Europe and his wife, Letty faces him with the truth of relationships from a woman's point of view. She tells Cornelius that she has ambition and looks. She works for men, and she is their friend. She suffers without crying for help and takes responsibility for her life. She sees men run after worthless, shiftless women and honor the formality of marriage when there is no substance to their relationships with them. All these facts might be just part of the injustice of the world, but Cornelius and many other men Letty knows also expect that she should be their lover and yet admit that there is no love involved but only a relationship of mutual convenience. Like the British poet William Blake, Letty sees prostitution as an invention of men who have tried to depersonalize the most intimate relationship between people. Letty affirms the reality of the sexual experience in its intimacy and its bonding.

With all her clear sight and all her independence, however, Letty does not feel safe and validated until she is married to her longtime friend Bill Van Week. Ironically, Letty marries Bill when he has been disinherited by his millionaire father, so the security Letty attains is not financial. In summing up her life to date, Letty does not claim total honesty, but—like a typical picaresque hero—she does claim grit. She says that with her marriage, her journey has begun. Here Stead limits the awareness of her character. At the end of the novel, Letty says that marriage gives her not social position but self-respect. In this retreat, Letty joins the social mainstream but denies her individual past experience. Self-respect is not an award; it is not issued like a diploma or a license. Letty, who may stand up very well to the practical problems of real life with Bill, is by no means liberated, and her awareness is finally limited.

DARK PLACES OF THE HEART

Dark Places of the Heart, which was published in Great Britain as *Cotter's England*, is an exploration of the influence of Nellie Cotter Cook on the people around her—her family, friends, and acquaintances. A central concern is the relationship between Nellie and her brother Tom, a jealous relationship with which Nellie seems obsessed. Like Michael and Catherine Baguenault, the brother-sister pair in *Seven Poor Men of Sydney*, Nellie and Tom seem too close to each other, too intimately attuned to each other's sensibilities. In their battles, Nellie calls Tom a man out of a mirror who weaves women into his life and then eats their hearts away. Tom calls Nellie a spider who tries to suspend a whole human being on a spindly thread of sympathy. Tom also criticizes Nellie's bent for soul saving, saying that it gets people into trouble.

The motif of hunger and starvation runs through the novel. When Tom brings a chicken to the family home in Bridgehead, no one in the family knows how to cook it. When George goes away to Italy, he writes that Nellie should buy cookery books, a suggestion that she scorns. Seemingly exhibiting a strange kind of hunger, Nellie craves followers who will make her destiny.

Nellie and Tom's battles often center on Tom's relationships with women, which precipitate a tug-of-war between Nellie and Tom for the love of the woman in question. Many allusions and incidents in the novel suggest that Nellie's interest is lesbian. Nellie begins her luring of these women by demanding their friendship and, ultimately, by forcing them to prove their loyalty through death. Such demands literalize the existentialist definition of love, that the lover puts the beloved beyond the value of the world and his or her life, making that beloved the standard of value, the absolute. The demand is messianic, and in this novel the cost is the suicide of Caroline Wooler: After witnessing what seems to be a lesbian orgy, Caroline climbs a building under construction and jumps to her death.

Nellie views Caroline's death as a personal triumph. At the end of the novel, with her husband dead, Nellie goes with the window washer Walter to a temple, a "Nabob villa," where she explores "problems of the unknowable." Like Sam Pollit, who at his worst compared himself to Christ, Nellie Cook is drawn finally to outright mysticism, an interest that combines, in Nellie's case at least, a fascination with death, a craving for a high destiny, and an uncontrollable urge to manipulate other people. It seems that for Stead, the "dark places of the heart" make people dissatisfied with their humanity.

Kate Begnal

OTHER MAJOR WORKS

SHORT FICTION: *The Salzburg Tales*, 1934; *The Puzzleheaded Girl*, 1967; *Ocean of Story: The Uncollected Short Stories of Christina Stead*, 1985.

TRANSLATIONS: *Colour of Asia*, 1955 (of Fernand Gigon's travelogue); *In Balloon and Bathyscaphe*, 1956 (of Auguste Piccard's science memoir); *The Candid Killer*, 1956 (of Jean Giltène's novel).

EDITED TEXTS: *Modern Women in Love*, 1945 (with William Blake); *Great Stories of the South Sea Islands*, 1956.

BIBLIOGRAPHY

Adie, Mathilda. *Female Quest in Christina Stead's "For Love Alone."* Lund, Sweden: Lund University Press, 2004. Examines the quest of Teresa Hawkins in *For Love Alone*, analyzing the character from the perspectives of feminism, postcolonialism, and myth criticism. Also discusses Stead's other novels to trace the development of the female quest theme throughout the author's fiction.

Blake, Ann. *Christina Stead's Politics of Place*. Nedlands: University of Western Australia Press, 1999. Analyzes Stead's novels and short stories in order to describe how the writer creates a sense of place in her work. Includes bibliography and index.

Brydon, Diana. *Christina Stead*. New York: Macmillan, 1987. Provides a thorough examination of all of Stead's novels and discusses the critical reception of Stead's fiction. While admitting that she presents Stead's work from an essentially feminist perspective, Brydon qualifies this stance by examining Stead's fiction as about both sexes in varied social relationships. Includes an extensive bibliography.

Harris, Margaret, ed. *The Magic Phrase: Critical Essays on Christina Stead*. St. Lucia: University of Queensland Press, 2000. Collection of sixteen essays includes some that review Stead's entire career and others that concentrate on individual works. Among the novels discusses are *Seven Poor Men of Sydney* and *The Man Who Loved Children*.

Jarrell, Randall. "An Unread Book." Introduction to *The Man Who Loved Children*, by Christina Stead. New York: Holt, Rinehart and Winston, 1965. Randall, an American poet, provides the first serious and thorough critical examination of Stead's work, incorporating many of the themes on which subsequent critics would enlarge.

Lidoff, Joan. *Christina Stead*. New York: Frederick Ungar, 1982. The earliest full reading of Stead's fiction from a feminist perspective, this book concentrates on *The Man Who Loved Children* and *For Love Alone*. Includes an interview with Stead, a chronology, and an extensive bibliography.

Pender, Anne. *Christina Stead: Satirist*. Altoona, Vic.: Common Ground, 2002. Focuses on Stead's attempt to interpret the history of her own period through satire. Shows the ways in which Stead both uses and reinterprets the conventions of the genre.

Peterson, Teresa. *The Enigmatic Christina Stead: A Provocative Rereading*. Melbourne, Vic.: Melbourne University Press, 2001. Closely examines five novels and a collection of short stories to argue that Stead's work contains a subtext of lesbian sexuality and male homosexuality.

Rowley, Hazel. *Christina Stead: A Biography*. New York: Henry Holt, 1994. Transcends Stead's penchant for privacy to provide a detailed and incisive account of the writer's troubled life and contentious personality. Includes bibliographical references and index.

Williams, Chris. *Christina Stead: A Life of Letters*. Melbourne, Vic.: McPhee Gribble, 1989. Admirable study, the first full-length biography of Stead, depends in large part on previously unpublished materials, including Stead's letters and early drafts of stories, as well as on interviews with Stead's friends and family members.

GORE VIDAL

Born: West Point, New York; October 3, 1925
Also known as: Eugene Luther Vidal; Edgar Box

<small>PRINCIPAL LONG FICTION</small>
Williwaw, 1946
In a Yellow Wood, 1947
The City and the Pillar, 1948 (revised 1965)
The Season of Comfort, 1949
A Search for the King: A Twelfth Century Legend, 1950
Dark Green, Bright Red, 1950
Death in the Fifth Position, 1952 (as Edgar Box)
The Judgment of Paris, 1952 (revised 1965)
Death Before Bedtime, 1953 (as Box)
Death Likes It Hot, 1954 (as Box)
Messiah, 1954 (revised 1965)
Julian, 1964
Washington, D.C., 1967
Myra Breckinridge, 1968
Two Sisters: A Memoir in the Form of a Novel, 1970
Burr, 1973
Myron, 1974
1876, 1976
Kalki, 1978
Creation, 1981
Duluth, 1983
Lincoln, 1984
Empire, 1987
Hollywood: A Novel of America in the 1920's, 1990
Live from Golgotha, 1992
The Smithsonian Institution, 1998
The Golden Age, 2000

<small>OTHER LITERARY FORMS</small>

Gore Vidal (vuh-DAHL) has written short stories as well as novels, and he is known as a master essayist, having regularly published collections of essays. Vidal also wrote and adapted plays for the small screen during the so-called golden age of television, and he wrote screenplays during the last days of the Hollywood studio system.

Achievements

Gore Vidal is considered a leading American literary figure. While primarily a novelist, he has mastered almost every genre, except poetry. He has won success in films, in television, and on Broadway. Many readers consider him a better essayist than novelist, though Vidal emphatically rejects that judgment.

While many of his contemporaries have focused their writings on mundane details of everyday life, Vidal has continued to write the novel of ideas. He has maintained his focus on the largest questions: What is the nature of Western civilization? What flaws have prevented the United States from achieving its democratic promise? How does a free individual live an intellectually fulfilling and ethically proper life in a corrupt society? These concerns are reflected not only in his writing but also in his political activities, including a bid for the U.S. Senate in 1982. Vidal won a National Book Award in 1993 for his collection of essays *United States: Essays, 1952-1992*, and his books are routinely included in "best" lists and course syllabi.

Biography

Gore Vidal was born Eugene Luther Vidal on October 3, 1925, at West Point, where his father, Eugene Vidal, taught aeronautics at the military academy. His father helped to establish civil aviation in the United States and later became the director of air commerce in Franklin D. Roosevelt's presidential administration. His mother, Nina, was a beautiful socialite, the daughter of Thomas P. Gore, the powerful U.S. senator from Oklahoma, and soon after Vidal's birth, the family moved to Senator Gore's mansion in Washington, D.C. He began using the name Gore Vidal when he was fourteen years old.

One of the most learned of contemporary writers, Vidal never went to college. His education began at the home of Senator Gore: The senator, who was blind, used his grandson as a reader and in return gave him free run of his huge library. In 1935, Nina and Eugene Vidal were divorced, and Nina married Hugh D. Auchincloss, a member of a prominent family of bankers and lawyers. Gore Vidal then moved with his mother to the Auchincloss estate on the Potomac River in Virginia, where his education included rubbing shoulders with the nation's political, economic, and journalistic elite.

Vidal was brought up removed from real life, he has stated, protected from such unpleasant realities as the effects of the Great Depression. He joined other patrician sons at St. Albans School, after which he toured Europe in 1939, then spent one year at Los Alamos School in New Mexico before finishing his formal education with three years at Phillips Exeter Academy in New Hampshire.

In 1943, Vidal joined the U.S. Army and served on a transport ship in the Aleutian Islands. His military service gave him subject matter and time to write his first novel, *Williwaw*. He finished his second book, *In a Yellow Wood*, before he left the Army. In 1946, he went to work as an editor for E. P. Dutton and soon published *The City and the Pillar*. Good critical and popular response brought him recognition as one of the nation's best young authors. He used Guatemala as his home base from 1947 to 1949 and then bought an old estate, Edgewater, on the Hudson River in New York. He wrote five more novels before he was thirty years old.

Meanwhile, a controversy engulfed Vidal and shifted his life and career. *The City and the Pillar* deals with homosexuality, and because of this, the literary establishment removed him from its list of "approved" writers and critics largely ignored his next few novels. To earn money in the 1950's, Vidal wrote mysteries under the name Edgar Box and wrote scripts for the major live television dramatic series. He also became a successful screenwriter, with such films as *The Catered Affair* (1956) and *Suddenly Last Summer* (1959, with Tennessee Williams). In addition, he wrote plays. He achieved major Broadway successes with *Visit to a Small Planet: A Comedy Akin to a Vaudeville* (pr. 1957) and *The Best Man: A Play About Politics* (pr., pb. 1960).

Vidal has called these his years of "piracy," aimed at gaining enough financial security to allow him to return to his first love, novels. His years in Hollywood and on Broadway established Vidal's public reputation for sophisticated wit and intelligence. He ran for Congress in 1960, supported by such famous friends as Eleanor Roosevelt, Joanne Woodward, and Paul Newman. Although he was defeated, he ran better in his district than did the Democratic presidential candidate, John F. Kennedy. Vidal shared a stepfather with Jacqueline Kennedy and had become friends with the Kennedy family; this connection pulled him further into public affairs. In 1964, Vidal published *Julian*, his first novel in ten years. It was a major critical and public success. Many best sellers followed, including *Myra Breckinridge*, *Burr*, *Creation*, and *Lincoln*.

Conflicts over civil rights, the Vietnam War, and the Watergate scandal made the 1960's and 1970's one of the most tumultuous periods in American political history. Vidal's essays, published in major journals, established his reputation as an astute and hard-hitting social critic. His acid-tongued social commentary brought him to many television talk shows, where he made many friends and enemies. He had spectacular public feuds with members of the Kennedy family and with such fellow celebrities and authors as William F. Buckley, Jr., Norman Mailer, and Truman Capote. In 1968, Vidal was a cofounder of the New Party, and in 1970-1972 he was cochair of the People's Party. In 1982, he ran for the U.S. Senate in California and, out of a field of eleven in the Democratic primary, came in second, behind Governor Jerry Brown.

The range and breadth of Vidal's interests showed in *United States*, a thousand-page collection of his essays that won the National Book Award for 1993. Here one finds literary discussions ranging from readings of Henry James and William Dean Howells to attacks on those of his contemporaries (John Barth, Thomas Pynchon) whom he calls "the academic hacks," novelists writing only for an audience of literature professors. He also attacks what he calls the "heterosexual dictatorship" and the increasingly grandiose and imperial self-image of the United States.

Palimpsest: A Memoir (1995) is a book that Vidal said he had sworn never to write, a personal memoir. In it he reveals his family background and tells of his struggles with establishments literary and political, concluding with his view of his quarrel with the Kennedy family. In a lyrical passage, he writes of the great love of his teenage years, a classmate named Jimmie Trimble, who died in World War II. In the 1990's, Vidal added a new aspect to his public persona by appearing as a character actor in several films, including *Bob Roberts* (1992), *With Honors* (1994), *The Shadow Conspiracy* (1997), and *Gattaca* (1997).

In 1998 Vidal became embroiled in further public debate as a member of the committee that selected the Modern Library's one hundred best twentieth century English-language novels. One of many controversial aspects of the list was the absence of those writers he called academic hacks. Vidal insisted that his role was only to make recommendations and that he bore no responsibility for the final selections.

In *Point to Point Navigation: A Memoir, 1964 to 2006* (2006), Vidal updates *Palimpsest*. In this work he bids farewell to Howard Auster, his companion of fifty-three years, who died in 2003. Following Auster's death, Vidal moved from his Italian villa to the Hollywood Hills of Los Angeles, where, he says, he is graciously edging toward the door marked Exit.

ANALYSIS

In an age and country that have little room for the traditional man of letters, Gore Vidal has established that role for himself by the force of his writing and intelligence and by his public prominence. He is a classicist in writing style, emphasizing plot, clarity, and order. Iconoclastic wit and cool, detached intelligence characterize his elegant style.

Because Vidal knows most contemporary public figures—including jet-setters, Wall Street insiders, and Washington wheeler-dealers—many readers comb his writing to glean intriguing bits of gossip. *Two Sisters: A Memoir in the Form of a Novel*, for example, is often read as an account of the lives and loves of Jacqueline Kennedy Onassis and her sister, Lee Bouvier. Some people search Vidal's writing for clues to his own life and sexuality.

Vidal draws from his own rich experience as he creates his fictional world, yet he is a very private person, and he resists people's urge to reduce everyone to a known quantity. He refracts real people and events through his delightfully perverse imagination. The unwary gossipmonger can easily fall into Vidal's many traps.

If readers can learn little of certainty from Vidal's fiction about such famous people as the Kennedys, they can learn much about his major concern, the nature of Western civilization and the individual's role within it. He is interested in politics—how people make society work—and religion, the proper perspective on life as one faces death. In his early novels, one can see Vidal's interest in ideas. Vidal's young male protagonists find themselves entering a relativistic world in which all gods are dead. A "heterosexual dictatorship" and a life-numbing Christian establishment try to impose false moral absolutes. Society tempts the unwary by offering comfort and security and then removes the life-sustaining freedom of those who succumb to the temptation.

THE CITY AND THE PILLAR

In writing his third novel, Vidal probed the boundaries of society's sexual tolerance. The result, *The City and the Pillar*, affected the rest of his career. To Vidal, the book is a study of obsession; to many guardians of moral purity, it seems to glorify homosexuality. In American fiction up to that point, either homosexuality had been barely implied or the homosexual characters had been presented as bizarre or doomed figures. In contrast, Vidal's protagonist is an average young American man, confused by his homosexuality and obsessed with the memory of a weekend encounter with another young man, Bob Ford. While Bob regards the weekend as a diversion to be enjoyed and forgotten, Jim enters the gay world. If he is doomed, it is not because he prefers men to women but because he is obsessed with the past. When he finally meets Bob again and tries to revive the affair, Bob rejects him. Enraged and humiliated, Jim kills Bob. Vidal later issued a revised edition in which Jim forces Bob to submit sexually; in the emotional backwash from the confrontation, Jim realizes the sterility of his obsession.

Vidal later said that he could have been president of the United States had it not been for the homosexual label applied to him. Readers assumed that Vidal must be the character he invented. Vidal is a sexual libertarian who believes that sex in any form between consenting adults is a gift to be enjoyed. He believes, furthermore, that a "heterosexual dictatorship" has distorted human sexuality. "There is no such thing as a homosexual or a heterosexual person," Vidal says. "There are only homo- or heterosexual acts. Most people are a mixture of impulses if not practices, and what anyone does with a willing partner is of no social or cosmic significance." In 1948, people were not ready for that message. Although *The City and the Pillar* was a best seller, such powerful establishment journals as *The New York Times* eliminated Vidal from their lists of "approved" writers. His next few books were failures, critically and financially.

THE JUDGMENT OF PARIS

Two of the books ignored after *The City and the Pillar*, *The Judgment of Paris* and *Messiah*, later found admirers. In these novels Vidal began to develop the style that is so recognizably his own. Moreover, it is in these two books that Vidal fully expresses his philosophy of life: "I have put nearly everything that I feel into *The Judgment of Paris*, a comedic version, and *Messiah*, a tragic version of my sense of man's curious estate."

In *The Judgment of Paris*, Vidal retells the ancient myth of Paris, who was asked by Zeus to choose the most beautiful of three goddesses: Hera (power), Athena (knowledge), and Aphrodite (love). In the novel, Philip Warren, an American innocent, meets Regina Durham (Hera) in Rome, Sophia Oliver (Athena) in Egypt, and Anna Morris (Aphrodite) in Paris. Regina and Sophia offer him, respectively, political power and the life of the intellect. To Philip, political power rests on the manipulation of people, and intellectual life requires the seclusion of the scholar from humanity. He chooses love, but he also leaves Anna Morris. His choice implies that one must accept no absolutes; nothing is permanent, not even love. One must open oneself to love and friendship and prepare to accept change as one moves through life.

MESSIAH

Many readers consider *Messiah* an undiscovered masterpiece. Religion, the human response to death and nothingness, has been a major concern in Vidal's fiction, especially in *Messiah, Kalki,* and *Creation. Messiah* is narrated by Eugene Luther, an old man secluded in Egypt. He is a founding member of a new religion that has displaced Christianity and is spreading over the world. Luther, who has broken with the church he helped build, scribbles his memoirs as he awaits death. The movement was built around John Cave, but Cave was killed by his disciples and Cave's word was spread by an organization using modern advertising techniques. One can readily find in *Messiah* characters representing Jesus Christ, Saint Paul, the Virgin Mary, and Martin Luther. The process by which religious movements are formed interests Vidal. *Messiah* shows, by analogy, how the early church fathers manipulated the Gospels and the Christ figure for their own selfish needs.

JULIAN

With *Julian*, Vidal again examines the formation of a religious movement, this time looking directly at Christianity. Julian the Apostate, Roman emperor from 361 to 363 C.E., had long been the object of hatred in the West because he had tried to reverse the Christianization of the empire. In the nineteenth and twentieth centuries, Julian began to attract admirers who saw him as a symbol of wisdom and of religious toleration.

Julian, reared as a Christian, lived in an age when the modern Christian church was taking shape. Warring prelates conducted abstract debates that robbed religion of its mystery and engaged in persecutions that ignored Jesus' message of love and peace. Julian was trained as a philosopher. His study of ancient wisdom awakened in him love and respect for the gods of the ancient world and for the Eastern mystery religions then being suppressed by Christianity. When he became emperor, Julian proclaimed religious toleration and tried to revive "paganism."

Like Paris before him and Philip Warren after, Julian was offered the worlds of intellect, love, and power. Julian chose power, but he tempered the absolute authority of emperor with love and wisdom. He was also a military genius who, like Alexander the Great, was tempted by the dream of world conquest. He was killed during an invasion of Persia.

Vidal constructs his novel as a fictive memoir written by Julian and presenting Julian's own view of himself and his world. The novel opens in 380 C.E., seventeen years after Julian's death. Two friends of Julian, the philosophers Libanius of Antioch and Priscus of Athens, correspond as they prepare Julian's memoirs for publication. Their letters and comments on the manuscript provide two other views of the events described by Julian. Because they are writing as the Emperor Theodosius is moving to destroy the ancient religions, Julian's life takes on a special poignancy. Vidal's major point, says biographer Ray

Lewis White, is that modern people of the West are the descendants of the barbarians who destroyed the classical world, and that the modern world has yet to be civilized. If Julian had lived, Vidal believes, Christianity might well have remained only one of several Western religions, and Western civilization might now be healthier and more tolerant than it is.

CREATION

In 1981, Vidal took readers even further back into history in *Creation*. In 445 B.C.E., Cyrus Spitama, an elderly Persian diplomat to Athens and grandson of the Persian prophet Zoroaster, begins to dictate his memoirs to his nephew, the philosopher Democritus. Cyrus is angry after hearing the historian Herodotus give his account of the Persian-Greek war, and he decides to set down the truth.

Here Vidal traces the earliest foundations of Western civilization and the formation of major world religions. Cyrus, a diplomatic troubleshooter for the Persian court, takes the reader on a tour of the ancient world. He knows Persian emperors Darius and Xerxes; as a traveler to China and India, he meets the Buddha and Confucius, and he remembers his own grandfather, Zoroaster. In Athens he talks with such famous figures as Anaxagoras and Pericles and hires Socrates to repair his wall. In *Creation*, Vidal shows the global interaction of cultures that goes back to the ancient world. He rejects the provincialism that has allowed historians to wall Western civilization off from its Asian and African sources.

BURR

This master of historical fiction also turned his attention to the United States. Starting with *Washington, D.C.*, Vidal began a sequence of novels covering U.S. history from its beginning to the post-World War II era. In chronological sequence, the novels are *Burr*, *Lincoln*, *1876*, *Empire*, *Hollywood*, *Washington, D.C.*, and *The Golden Age*. Vidal's iconoclastic view of the past may have shocked some readers, but in the turmoil of the Vietnam and Watergate era, many people were ready to reexamine U.S. history. At a time when many Americans held that the old truths had failed, Vidal said that those truths had been hollow from the start.

Burr is one of the most widely admired of Vidal's novels. Aaron Burr, the preeminent American maverick, appealed to Vidal personally. *Burr* is narrated by Charlie Schuyler, who in 1833 is a twenty-five-year-old clerk in Burr's law office. He is an aspiring author who writes for William Leggett and William Cullen Bryant, editors of the *New York Evening Post*. Disliking Martin Van Buren, President Andrew Jackson's heir apparent, Leggett and Bryant set Charlie to work running down the rumor that Van Buren is the illegitimate son of Burr; if the rumor is true, they can use the information to destroy Van Buren. The seventy-seven-year-old Burr responds warmly to Charlie's overtures to write about his life. In the next few years, Burr gives the young writer copies of his journal and dictates to him his memories of the past.

Although Vidal's portrait of the Founding Fathers shocks some readers, his interpretation is in line with that of many of the nation's best historians. Vidal reminds the reader that Burr was one of the most able and intelligent of the Founding Fathers. Vidal allows Burr, from an insider's viewpoint, to demystify the founders of the republic. George Washington, Alexander Hamilton, Thomas Jefferson, and the other Founding Fathers created the republic, Burr says, because it satisfied their personal economic and political interests to do so.

Burr admires some of his contemporaries, especially James Madison and Andrew Jackson, but he detests Thomas Jefferson. Jefferson is a ruthless man who wants to create a nation "dominated by independent farmers each living on his own rich land, supported by slaves." What Burr cannot excuse is Jefferson's cant and hypocrisy:

> Had Jefferson not been a hypocrite I might have admired him. After all, he was the most successful empire-builder of our century, succeeding where Bonaparte failed. But then Bonaparte was always candid when it came to motive and Jefferson was always dishonest.

What are the motives of the Founding Fathers? Burr tells Alexander Hamilton: "I sense nothing more than the ordinary busy-ness of men wanting to make a place for themselves. . . . But it is no different here from what it is in London or what it was in Caesar's Rome." The Founding Fathers write the Constitution because it suits their purposes, and they subvert it when it suits their purposes.

Burr makes no secret of his opportunism, although he does regret his mistakes. He should have realized that the world is big enough for both Hamilton and himself, he says. Instead, Vice President Burr kills Hamilton in a duel and is then accused by Jefferson of heading a plot to break up the United States and establish himself as the king in a new Western empire.

Charlie does find evidence that Van Buren is Burr's son, but Charlie, having come to love the old man, refuses to use it. Van Buren rewards him with a government position overseas.

LINCOLN *and* 1876

With *Lincoln*, Vidal surprised those who expected him to subject the Great Emancipator to the same ridicule he had directed at Washington and Jefferson. Vidal's Lincoln is a cold, remote, intelligent man who creates a unified, centralized republic that is far different from the one envisioned by the Founding Fathers. In *1876*, Charlie Schuyler returns to the United States from Europe, where he has lived since 1837. He left in the age of Jackson and returns in the age of Ulysses S. Grant to a booming industrializing, urbanizing nation. He watches, in the American centennial year, as the politicians steal the presidential election from Democrat Samuel J. Tilden. He sees members of the ruling class using the rhetoric of democracy but practicing it as little as they had in the days of Washington and Jefferson.

EMPIRE

In *Empire*, Vidal paints wonderful word portraits of Henry Adams, Henry James, William Randolph Hearst, John Hay, and Theodore Roosevelt, along with the fictional characters of newspaper publishers Caroline and Blaise Sanford and Congressman James Burden Day. The creation of the internal empire, begun by Jefferson's Louisiana Purchase, had already made a shambles of the American democratic promise. Now Roosevelt and other American leaders begin to look overseas for new areas to dominate. Their creation of the overseas empire lays the groundwork for the increasingly militarized republic that emerges in the twentieth century.

HOLLYWOOD

Many of these same figures appear in *Hollywood*, set a few years later, in the administrations of Woodrow Wilson and Warren Harding. While the forging of the American empire continues, Vidal turns his gaze on a new force that is corrupting the democratic promise, the mass media. Newspaper publisher Hearst and the Sanfords have long understood the power of the press, but Hearst and Caroline Sanford see that the new medium of film has potential power beyond the printed page. Instead of reporting events, film could create a new reality within which newspapers and politicians would have to work.

WASHINGTON, D.C.

In *Washington, D.C.*, Blaise Sanford, his son Peter, Senator James Burden Day, and his assistant, Clay Overbury, are locked in a political and moral drama. Senator Day, a southern conservative, much like Senator Gore, opposes the new republic being created by Franklin D. Roosevelt, Harry S. Truman, and Dwight D. Eisenhower. He has a chance to be president but lacks money. Burden Day gives in to temptation and takes a bribe; his presidential bid fails, and later Clay Overbury, using his knowledge of the bribe, forces Day out of the Senate and takes his seat. Overbury is a young man who cares nothing for friends or ideas or issues. Winning personal power is the only thing that interests this politician, who is modeled on John F. Kennedy.

As Day is dying, he says to the spirit of his unreconstructed southern father: "You were right. . . . It has all gone wrong." Aaron Burr would have understood what he meant.

THE GOLDEN AGE

The Golden Age opens on November 4, 1939, when the U.S. Congress amends the Neutrality Act, allowing the United States to sell weapons to England and France, which are at war with Nazi Germany. Vidal places on center stage those who dominated national life when he was growing up in Washington, D.C., including Presidents Franklin Roosevelt and Harry Truman, Eleanor Roosevelt, Franklin's alter ego, Harry Hopkins, and Vidal's grandfather, Senator Thomas Gore. Peter Sanford, founder of *American Idea*, a political and cultural journal, meets these political leaders, as well as such artists and writers as Leonard Bernstein, Dawn Powell, Tennessee Williams, and a promising novelist named Gore Vidal.

Franklin Roosevelt is a mystery even to those closest to him. Is he a devious political genius scheming relentlessly to create a global empire, even at the cost of war? Or is he improvising, desperately trying to placate an isolationist, antiwar public while scrambling to help Great Britain and France hold off the Nazi onslaught? One thing is clear, Hopkins says: Washington now rules a world empire. The United States, offspring of the Enlightenment, sees itself as a democratic, peace-loving Athens but is actually a warlike, imperial Rome.

Roosevelt believes that the American future lies in Asia. He ruthlessly squeezes and humiliates Japan, deliberately provoking an attack. Senator Gore says that Roosevelt keeps attention riveted on Hitler while he prods Japan into attacking so he can live up to his promise that no American will fight in a foreign war—unless we are attacked first. If attacked, Hopkins says, then we go for the big prize: for global domination. The attack on Pearl Harbor surprised no one, one insider muses, except the American people.

In 1945, Roosevelt dies and Truman takes over. Roosevelt had helped destroy German and Japanese power and had shoved aside the spent empires of Britain and France. Truman now tries to impose his will on the Soviet Union, the one remaining obstacle to American global hegemony. The Soviets resist American pressure, and Truman divides the world into two camps, with Washington at the head of the so-called Free World. The Americans begin their long quest to impose their version of democracy on a restive world. Only the United States, says Secretary of State Dean Acheson, has the power to bend history to its will. In pursuit of that illusion the United States transforms itself into a militarized global empire.

The novel jumps forward to the night of New Year's Eve, 1999. Peter Sanford awaits the new millennium, just hours away. He is amused now at his youthful illusion that in 1945 the United States was entering a cultural Golden Age. The Golden Age lasted five years, just a flare that briefly lit the darkness. Peter and author Gore Vidal meet, both now old men, so old, they say, that they can remember back to when the United States was still a democracy. Peter challenges Vidal: You made me up, he says, and placed me in a book filled with American imperial wars—you should have given me a better world to live in.

MYRA BRECKINRIDGE

If most scholars approved of Vidal's well-researched historical fiction, many readers were shocked at *Myra Breckinridge*. Myra opens her book with the proud proclamation, "I am Myra Breckinridge whom no man will ever possess." She maintains her verve as she takes readers on a romp through popular culture. Because the novel is dead, she says, there is no point in writing made-up stories; the film of the 1940's is the high point of Western artistic creation, although it is being superseded by a higher art form, the television commercial. Myra has arrived in Hollywood to fulfill her destiny of reconstructing the sexes.

She has a lesson to teach young would-be stars such as Rusty Godowsky and old cowboy stars such as Buck Loner:

> To be a man in a society of machines is to be an expendable, soft auxiliary to what is useful and hard. Today there is nothing left for the old-fashioned male to do, . . . no physical struggle to survive or mate. . . . only in travesty can he act out the classic hero who was a law unto himself, moving at ease through a landscape filled with admiring women. Mercifully, that age is finished. . . . we now live at the dawn of the age of Women Triumphant, of Myra Breckinridge!

Beneath the gaiety of Myra's campy narrative, a serious purpose emerges. Her dead gay husband, Myron, had been abused and humiliated by many males. Myra carries out her plan to avenge Myron, and to revive the Female Principle, by forcing Buck Loner to submit to her demands to take over his acting studio and by raping with a dildo the macho, all-American stud Rusty.

Myra is brought down by an automobile accident, which upsets her hormonal balance. Her breasts vanish, and she sprouts a beard; she is, in fact, Myron, after gender reassignment surgery. As the book ends, Rusty is gay and Myron/Myra is married and living happily with Rusty's former girlfriend. In a sequel, *Myron*, Myron and Myra struggle for domination of the single body and again have much to say about popular culture, the mass media, and human sexuality.

Perhaps as respites from the scrupulous historicity of the American history novels, Vidal interspersed them with fantasies in which reality is plastic and ever changing. In *Myron*, characters are likely to find themselves in the midst of the old films they are watching. *Duluth* represents a deliberately postmodernist interpenetration of an actual Duluth with a serial television show also called *Duluth*.

LIVE FROM GOLGOTHA

Live from Golgotha continues the motif of a reality subject to random change. It is set in 96 C.E., but the first century is being manipulated by forces from the twentieth, operating through psychic channelers and the Hacker, whose computer manipulations apparently can destroy not only records of the past but even memories of those records. Indeed, there is a plan afoot to return to the Crucifixion, televise it live, and perhaps even change the events. Timothy, the narrator, is the biblical Timothy to whom Saint Paul wrote epistles. He has been chosen to preserve the Gospel story in the face of these computerized depredations, though his knowledge of the event is at best secondhand, coming from Paul, who knows it only through a vision. The story departs radically from the standard biblical story. Timothy and Paul are bisexual, as are most of the first century people depicted. Jesus is thought to have been morbidly obese. Anachronistic terms such as "Mossad" and "intifada" abound. Future figures such as Mary Baker Eddy and Shirley MacLaine make appearances.

Timothy eventually learns that the actual Jesus was a Zealot, a political revolutionary. With electronic assistance, Jesus framed Judas, the fat man Paul saw in the vision, and fled to the twentieth century. There he became the Hacker in order to clear out images of "gentle Jesus meek and mild." He plans to start Armageddon through a nuclear attack on Arab capitals. Timothy uses more advanced technology to prevent Jesus' escape from arrest. The Crucifixion takes place, with the real Jesus, but Japanese technicians add to the image a rising sun and the mother goddess Amaterasu. *Live from Golgotha* has been condemned for its irreverence and blasphemy as well as for the outlandishness of its central conceit, but many readers have nevertheless enjoyed its wit and its lusty portrayal of the first century Roman world.

THE SMITHSONIAN INSTITUTION

Vidal's next novel, *The Smithsonian Institution*, also deals with retroactive time change, but of a political rather than a theological sort. T., a thirteen-year-old mathematics prodigy in 1939, is summoned to the Smithsonian Institution to take part in a secret scientific experiment. He soon learns that the apparent wax dummies that are part of the project are actually living people. Indeed, T. is seduced by Mrs. Grover Cleveland. T. has an Einstein-like ability to visualize equations dealing with time. Anxious to ward off the coming of World War II because it would lead to the development of terrifying new weapons, the scientists secretly in charge of the Smithsonian (with the assistance of the supposed wax dummies of political leaders) plan to use T.'s ideas to construct a time machine and change the past so that the war will not occur. After one trip that only makes things worse, T. returns to a war in which he saves an alternate version of himself and enables the war to be concluded more quickly, without the weapons development.

Some commentators have said that the audience Vidal created for himself with his highly regarded historical novels was destroyed by *Myra Breckinridge* and *Myron* and by his later campy fantasies *Kalki* and *Duluth*. Vidal continued to write one best seller after another, however, and his books have steadily gained critical admirers. Vidal's books, essays, and television appearances stimulated, intrigued, and angered a large part of his audience, yet his appeal as a writer and public figure remained compelling. As long ago as 1948, with *The City and the Pillar*, Vidal made a decision to live his life and conduct his artistic career in his own way. To many admirers, he is a symbol of freedom. The turmoil of the modern age makes his civilized voice of reason seem more necessary than ever before. Often accused of cynicism, Vidal has responded that he is a pessimist and a realist who also believes that people can, or must act as if they can, take action to make the world better.

William E. Pemberton
Updated by Arthur D. Hlavaty

OTHER MAJOR WORKS

SHORT FICTION: *A Thirsty Evil: Seven Short Stories*, 1956; *Clouds and Eclipses: The Collected Short Stories*, 2006.

PLAYS: *Visit to a Small Planet: A Comedy Akin to a Vaudeville*, pr. 1957; *The Best Man: A Play About Politics*, pr., pb. 1960; *Romulus: A New Comedy*, pr., pb. 1962; *An Evening with Richard Nixon*, pr. 1972.

SCREENPLAYS: *The Catered Affair*, 1956; *Suddenly Last Summer*, 1959 (with Tennessee Williams); *The Best Man*, 1964 (adaptation of his play); *Last of the Mobile Hot-Shots*, 1969; *Caligula*, 1977.

TELEPLAYS: *Visit to a Small Planet, and Other Television Plays*, 1956; *Dress Gray*, 1986.

NONFICTION: *Rocking the Boat*, 1962; *Reflections upon a Sinking Ship*, 1969; *Homage to Daniel Shays: Collected Essays, 1952-1972*, 1972; *Matters of Fact and of Fiction: Essays, 1973-1976*, 1977; *The Second American Revolution, and Other Essays, 1976-1982*, 1982; *At Home: Essays, 1982-1988*, 1988; *Screening History*, 1992; *The Decline and Fall of the American Empire*, 1992; *United States: Essays, 1952-1992*, 1993; *Palimpsest: A Memoir*, 1995; *Virgin Islands, A Dependency of United States: Essays, 1992-1997*, 1997; *Gore Vidal, Sexually Speaking: Collected Sex Writings*, 1999; *The Last Empire: Essays, 1992-2000*, 2000; *Dreaming War: Blood for Oil and the Cheney-Bush Junta*, 2002; *Perpetual War for Perpetual Peace: How We Got to Be So Hated*, 2002; *Imperial America*, 2004; *Point to Point Navigation: A Memoir, 1964-2006*, 2006; *The Selected Essays of Gore Vidal*, 2008 (Jay Parini, editor).

MISCELLANEOUS: *The Essential Gore Vidal*, 1999 (Fred Kaplan, editor); *Inventing a Nation: Washington, Adams, Jefferson*, 2003; *Conversations with Gore Vidal*, 2005 (Richard Peabody and Lucinda Ebersole, editors).

BIBLIOGRAPHY

Altman, Dennis. *Gore Vidal's America*. Malden, Mass.: Polity, 2005. A longtime friend of Vidal and a careful student of his thought and career, Altman explores Vidal's dissection of the gap between the professed American dedication to peace and democracy and its practice of war and imperialism.

Baker, Susan, and Curtis S. Gibson. *Gore Vidal: A Critical Companion*. Westport, Conn.: Greenwood Press, 1997. Presents biographical information as well as criticism and interpretation of Vidal's works, which are divided into his historical novels and his "inventions." Includes bibliographical references and index.

Frank, Marcie. *How to Be an Intellectual in the Age of TV: The Lessons of Gore Vidal*. Durham, N.C.: Duke University Press, 2005. While many critics mourn the death of the public intellectual in America, Frank shows Vidal playing that role with intellectual vigor and astute exploitation of his celebrity to gain access to opinion-shaping media.

Harris, Stephen. *The Fiction of Gore Vidal and E. L. Doctorow: Writing the Historical Self.* New York: Peter Lang, 2002. Discusses Vidal's strong identification with history, as reflected in his writing.

Kaplan, Fred. *Gore Vidal: A Biography.* New York: Doubleday, 1999. Comprehensive work describes the events that shaped the life and career of this important novelist, playwright, scriptwriter, essayist, and political activist.

Kiernan, Robert F. *Gore Vidal.* New York: Frederick Ungar, 1982. Seeks to assess Vidal's place in American literature by exploring his major writings up to the early 1980's. Presents astute descriptions of the Vidalian style and manner.

Parini, Jay, ed. *Gore Vidal: Writer Against the Grain.* New York: Columbia University Press, 1992. Vidal's distaste for much of the academic study of contemporary fiction has been mirrored in a lack of academic study of his work. Parini sought to redress the balance by compiling this work, which deals with both Vidal's fiction and nonfiction.

Peabody, Richard, and Lucinda Ebersole, eds. *Conversations with Gore Vidal.* Jackson: University Press of Mississippi, 2005. Collection of interviews extending over nearly forty-five years reveals in Vidal's own words how he has tied history, politics, and literature together into one tight intellectual bundle.

Stanton, Robert J., and Gore Vidal, eds. *Views from a Window: Conversations with Gore Vidal.* Secaucus, N.J.: Lyle Stuart, 1980. Compilation of interviews is arranged according to themes. Vidal comments on his and other authors' works, on sexuality, and on politics. Vidal edited the manuscript and made corrections, with changes noted in the text.

PATRICK WHITE

Born: London, England; May 28, 1912
Died: Sydney, New South Wales, Australia; September 30, 1990

OTHER LITERARY FORMS

Patrick White first attempted to achieve literary success as a playwright in London in the 1930's. His work was largely rejected, partly, he implies in his memoir *Flaws in the Glass: A Self-Portrait* (1981), because of his lack of connections in the theatrical world (although he did not deny that his talent was immature at that time). In particular, White believed that his effort to dramatize *The Aspern Papers* (1888), Henry James's famous novella based on an incident in the life of Lord Byron's mistress, might have succeeded, thanks to James's dialogue, had it found a sponsor. Later, however, White successfully published a number of plays, mostly in the 1960's and 1980's; one play, *The Ham Funeral* (pr. 1961), received much attention.

White's collections *The Burnt Ones* (1964), *The Cockatoos: Shorter Novels and Stories* (1974), and *Three Uneasy Pieces* (1987) bring together the best of his shorter fiction published originally in Australian literary journals (for the most part); White also published in *The London Magazine*, where, among others, the fine stories "Clay" and "A Cheery Soul" appeared. White experimented with writing film scripts; one was filmed and received some mildly favorable reviews. His autobiographical memoir, already mentioned, mixes poetic impressionism with trenchant satire.

ACHIEVEMENTS

Patrick White's stature as a novelist was already considerable among discerning critics and discriminating readers in the English-speaking world before it was confirmed by his

Patrick White
(The Nobel Foundation)

reception of the Nobel Prize in Literature in 1973. The books that established White's reputation after World War II were *The Aunt's Story*, which has been widely recognized as a masterpiece; *The Tree of Man*; and the virtually unforgettable *Voss*. At the same time, White's fiction, though accessible to the general reader, unlike the work of such modernist masters as James Joyce and William Faulkner (or contemporary "experimental" fiction), never achieved a wide readership. It is uncompromisingly addressed to the same discerning public that respects Joyce, D. H. Lawrence, Thomas Mann, and Marcel Proust.

If rather philistine criticism of White's work from intellectual readers as well as from the general public in Australia and elsewhere began in the 1960's, after *Riders in the Chariot*, *The Aunt's Story* is almost universally admired, and *The Tree of Man*, *Voss*, *Riders in the Chariot*, *The Vivisector*, *The Eye of the Storm*, and *A Fringe of Leaves* all have admirers who regard them as virtual classics. White's transformation of Australian history into epic and tragic vision in *The Tree of Man*, *Voss*, and *A Fringe of Leaves* is brilliant, and his vision of the fragmented world of the twentieth century is equally impressive, especially in *The Vivisector* and *The Eye of the Storm*. White's major successes ultimately assure their author a place beside the masters of prose fiction in English, including Joyce, Lawrence, and Graham Greene.

BIOGRAPHY

Patrick Victor Martindale White was born in Wellington Court, London, on May 28, 1912, of parents whose affluence allowed them the opportunity to travel and enjoy the social pretensions available to prosperous Australians able to play the role of landed gentry. White's father, Victor (Dick) White, was one of several brothers who enjoyed prosperity in the family grazier business. Although the Whites could trace their lineage to respectable yeoman stock in Somerset, it was only in Australia that they achieved such success. Ironically, their social aspirations so far as the mother country was concerned were forever tainted by their status as "colonials" and Australians, the former penal colony being one of the least prestigious of the British dominions. White's mother was a Withycombe, and it is to the maternal connection that White attributed most of his imaginative and poetic gifts. At the same time, White disliked his strong-willed and socially ambitious mother, Ruth. Toward his father White was more ambivalent; he pitied Victor White for his weakness but found him impossible because he hid his emotions behind his social role as a landed gentleman. Resenting and distrusting his parents as he did, and contemptuous of their social ambitions and their inclination to conceal their humanity behind public personae, White felt as much an outsider and rebel against the class to which he was born as is his painter hero, Hurtle Duffield, in *The Vivisector*, a working-class child adopted by a prosperous Sydney family.

White tended as a child to identify with his nanny and her working-class husband, a circumstance that helps to account for the persistent scorn and irony in his fiction directed toward the assumptions and manners of the Australian upper class. In addition to being an "outsider" in his relationship to the Australian affluent class, White found that his status in English boarding schools, and later at Cambridge, was that of an outsider by virtue of his Australian citizenship and accent. Hence, throughout his career, White as artist played the role of an outsider in a double sense, a condition intensified by his frequent alternation of residences between Australia and England in childhood and youth.

White's major concentration at Cambridge was modern languages, primarily German, an interest augmented by time spent on the Continent, in the Germany of the Weimar Republic in its waning days and in the early years of Adolf Hitler's rule, during summer vacations from 1932 to 1935. One German city, Hanover, is depicted in White's fiction as the archetypal German cathedral town from which White's characters Voss and Himmelfarb both originate.

After he left Cambridge, White spent a bohemian period in London in the middle and late 1930's, lodging mainly in Ebury Street, where he wrote three unsatisfactory novels and attempted without success to begin a career in the theater as a playwright. During this time, White fell under the influence of various intellectual friends and apprentice artists, the most important being the Australian expatriate Roy de Maistre, who was, like White, gay. (White seems to have accepted his homosexuality in his boarding school adolescence, and to have had little difficulty over it at Cambridge and in the London of the 1930's.)

In 1939, White's unsatisfactory first novel, *Happy Valley*, was published, and soon White voyaged to the United States to try his hand in New York literary circles and to begin a period of dissipation that lasted for several months. During this New York period, he completed his strong second novel, *The Living and the Dead*, a book that shows him mastering and exorcising some of the literary and cultural influences of his youth. The decision of White's working-class hero, Joe, to go to Spain to fight on the Loyalist side is a symbol of commitment; it reflects White's own decision, reached after much guilt and self-analysis, to return to England (unlike some other English expatriates, such as W. H. Auden) and offer himself to the campaign against Hitler.

After receiving a commission in the Royal Air Force's intelligence division, White spent the majority of his war years in North Africa, Alexandria, the Middle East, and Greece. It is clear that his years in the war were a significant rite of passage for him. He gained decisiveness and self-reliance as well as maturity. Equally important, he met Manoly Lascaris, a Greek whose mother had been British; Lascaris was to become White's lover and life partner. Eventually, White and Lascaris decided on permanent residence in Australia, and White arrived there in 1947 with the manuscript of *The Aunt's Story* as a kind of "talisman." Hence, White was an Australian by a conscious choice, however reluctant the choice may have been. At the same time, his country was not always overwhelmed by White's decision, for although White used the Australian heroic past extensively in his fiction, he continued to be an outsider whose work did not always display clear relationships with Australian literary traditions.

White's long career in Australia flourished primarily at two residences, one of which was the small "farm" called Dogwoods, really only a house, some outbuildings, and a few acres at Castle Hill, just outside Sydney and later incorporated into it. In 1963, White moved to Martin's Road in Sydney. In the Castle Hill period, White and Lascaris kept some cattle and tried to support themselves, partially, by some gardening. In later years, White's writing provided some support.

After he had published numerous novels and a book of short stories, White was awarded the Nobel Prize in Literature in 1973. He used the money to establish a fund for struggling Australian writers of some talent and literary ambition. His later life was marked by increasing fame and some travel and by considerable attention from the mass media and from academic critics and scholars. He died in Sydney on September 30, 1990.

ANALYSIS

Patrick White's fiction is concerned with the psychological depth and the emotional density of experience, and with the perceptions of the solitary self. This obsession with the isolated self in its search for fulfillment, its quest for an experience of unity and the divine, and its attempts to resolve the contradictions of its social heritage and its sexual nature provides the central drama in White's fiction. On one hand, White's fiction is rich in its command of the nuances of dialogue and social intercourse; it is possible to discuss these works in terms primarily of the novel of manners and social comedy. On the other hand, White's fiction is the work of an author obsessed with tragic vision and a religious quest. After *The Aunt's Story*, White's novels contain characters who struggle and overcome obstacles to understanding and vision, and whose lives culminate in visionary or mystical affirmation. Stan Parker in *The Tree of Man* testifies to the unity of holiness of being; Elizabeth Hunter finds the eye of God in the center of her storm; Rod Gravenor in his final letter to Eddie Twyborn asserts the reality of love and faith in God. Such affirmations, though they represent White's own beliefs, if his autobiographical statements are to be accepted, are nevertheless to be seen as dramatic statements, paradoxical assertions aimed at overcoming doubts and confusion, and ultimately as aesthetically correct as the statements of faith in the poetry of the seventeenth century metaphysical poets. Despite all the parallels with Victorian novelists who write family novels with complicated plots, White was essentially a religious visionary akin to poets such as T. S. Eliot and W. H. Auden, and one very much at odds with the dominant spirit of his age.

HAPPY VALLEY

White's first published novel, *Happy Valley*, is regarded by most critics as a failure, and the judgment is accurate. The novel deals with the passions and defeats of a group of characters in an Australian rural setting, but White is not entirely in control of his characters and plot, nor of his own style. The characters are mostly flawed romantics, somewhat obsessed by sex and erotic entanglements, and their emotions are often operatic and even Wagnerian in scope. The novel lacks the saving grace of White's magisterial and sophisticated irony, which tends to control the style in the later books and prevent both author and characters from lapsing into the excesses of emotion. White, however, does use the Australian landscape effectively as a dramatic backdrop for human drama played out under the eye of an inscrutable cosmos.

THE LIVING AND THE DEAD

The Living and the Dead, the second published novel of White's prewar apprenticeship, shows considerable improvement. The novel, set in England, primarily London, casts a critical and retrospective look at the 1930's, but like many novels of the period by English and American writers, it displays a movement from empty intellectualism and social snobbery to political and ideological commitment on the part of some characters. The central figures in the book are Elyot and Eden Standish and their feckless and snobbish mother. Elyot and Eden provide an ironic contrast: Elyot is a skeptical rationalist who wants to withdraw from experience, while Eden is a romantic who accepts life with its attendant suffering. Each finds a suitably ironic reward: Eden gains love with a working-class hero only to lose him when he departs to join the Loyalist cause in the Spanish Civil War; Elyot, fearing involvement with others, is doomed to a life of loneliness until he finds himself exposed to the suffering he has tried to avoid, through the death of his mother and the departure of his sister for Spain. Ironically, the experience of tragedy helps to heal Elyot's loneliness and alienation; at the end of the novel, he finds a satisfying release from the prison of himself.

Literary scholar Brian Kiernan has pointed out that many influences of T. S. Eliot's early poetry are evident in the novel; London is Eliot's "Unreal City" of *The Waste Land* (1922), for example. It might be added that Elyot Standish is White's most Prufrockian character; he represents the same kind of paralyzed and life-evading intellectual that Eliot satirized in his early poetry, and White's portrayal indicates his own aversion to such a figure.

If Elyot is skillfully drawn, his mother, with all her vulgarities and superficialities, is equally effective, and her final spasmodic affair with an English jazz musician is poignant, as is the description of her final illness. Less effectively depicted, but still successful, are Eden, Elyot's romantic sister, and Wally Collins, the itinerant jazz musician just back from America, who is presented as representative of the rootless and uncommitted modern urban person. The weakest figure of all is Joe Barnett, the working-class hero, who is too obviously inspired by the abstraction of the virtuous proletarian that afflicted much of the fiction of the 1930's.

The emphasis on commitment and release from alienation with which the novel concludes is handled with much aesthetic tact and restraint. The adoption of the Loyalist cause in Spain is portrayed as more of a humanist commitment than an acceptance of an ideological or religious imperative, although no doubt White's sympathies were leftist. While White's characters find an exit from the modern wasteland through tragic self-sacrifice, the novel does not provide any assurance that the solution found is an enduring one, either for the characters who accept it or for the author.

THE AUNT'S STORY

With his next novel, *The Aunt's Story*, White established himself as a novelist of stature with a mature tragic vision. One of the most difficult things for a novelist to do, White believed, is to make a "virtuous woman" an interesting character. White accomplished this feat with Theodora Goodman, the aunt, who to all outward appearances lives an uneventful life, save for its tragic denouement. The real "story" of the spinster aunt is rendered through White's depiction of her inner life; despite Theodora's apparently barren existence, her experience is rich indeed.

Theodora's tale is told in three economically narrated sections: an Australian sequence titled "Meroe"; a European interlude, "Jardin Exotique"; and a climactic American adventure, "Holstius." In these sections, Theodora's childhood, youth, and maturity are portrayed. She has a strong, rather masculine sensibility, and an imaginative nature with deep psychological insight, in an unprepossessing feminine body.

In part 1, Theodora's journey from innocence to the experience of young adulthood is chronicled. The contrast between the heroine's strong desire for individuality and the conventional femininity and conformity of her sister is strongly marked. At boarding school in adolescence, Theodora develops one of her strongest relationships, a friendship with the sensitive Violet Adams, who, like Theodora, is fascinated by art and poetry. Theodora here reveals her intense and rather hard inner nature: She would like to be a poet, but her chosen subject would be landscapes and studies of rocks.

In her childhood and youth, too, Theodora shows more love for her father's country estate than for the city: Meroe is the "Abyssinia," or happy valley of innocence, which provides a romantic metaphor for her years of growth and maturation. Later, following World War I, when Australia, after a brief emergence from its provincial slumber, relapses into a comfortable vacuous middle-class existence, Theodora lives in Sydney and cares for her mean-spirited and snobbish mother in the latter's failing years. In this period, the mysterious murderer Jack Frost provides some excitement and titillation for a bored middle-class population, and serves as a symbol of the mysterious Jungian shadow she longs to encounter. Her major chance for the conventional felicity of marriage and children occurs when she is courted by the apparently strong and manly Huntly Clarkson. In a role reversal typical of many later White novels, however, Huntly soon is revealed as weak and somewhat feminine in his relationship with the resolute Theodora. Her skillfulness and strength strike a deathblow to their courtship.

Released from an unrewarding life by the death of her mother, Theodora finds herself free to seek her destiny abroad, and her journey of initiation to Europe constitutes the central action in part 2, "Jardin Exotique," where she encounters a group of European eccentrics in a "grand hotel" setting on the French Riviera. Here Theodora exercises her talent for living, which had been suppressed and frustrated in Australia. She enters imaginatively into the lives of her companions, identifying with them and living their exotic histories vicariously. Her friends, a seedy group of expatriates, have all built up myths of romantic pasts. Theodora not only is a responsive and sympathetic consciousness for them but also is able to enrich their illusions by her own imagination. Ironically, however, each fantasy life proves to have been an artful lie near the end of part 2, leaving Theodora with the sense of having been cheated when the pathetic reality of a character's past is revealed. The final irony occurs when the Hotel du Midi is destroyed by fire, probably a symbol of the coming war.

This section, rich in fine characterizations and virtuoso stylistic divertissements, is White's portrait of the Europe of the 1930's and his moral evaluation of it. Theodora, at first seduced by Europe and its illusions of a glamorous past and then disillusioned by the emptiness of its reality, emerges from the experience morally tested and unscathed, but still an unfulfilled and psychologically incomplete personality. It is not until part 3, "Holstius," that Theodora confronts her own tragic destiny.

Part 3 takes place in the United States, where Theodora is overwhelmed by a sense of the vastness of the American continent and her own sense of isolation. A chance encounter with a traveling salesman on a train near Chicago results in a conversation that is symbolic: The salesman boasts of America's size and population in the best Babbitt or booster style, while Theodora is impressed with the abstractness of the individual self in a country where enormous numbers—of square miles, people, and sums of money—seem to dominate.

Leaving the train in the mountains of Colorado, Theodora wanders into a lonely canyon, driven by an urge to confront the unknown side of her inner self at last. Alone, at night, she hallucinates an experience of mythic force: a meeting with a stunted little man, almost like a folklore dwarf, who informs her that his name is Holstius (a name that perhaps both combines and caricatures the Jungian "animus," or male self in a woman, and the idea of "wholeness"). In Theodora's encounter with the imaginary Holstius, the masculine side of her nature emerges and speaks to her at last, and her inner conflicts appear to be resolved. The confrontation is traumatic, however, and the cost of it is the loss of Theodora's sanity, for the next day a nearby farmer and his family are forced to take charge of her, regarding her as mad.

The Aunt's Story is an expression of mature tragic vision, a novel that explores the possibilities and anguish of the solitary self in search of wholeness and fulfillment, in a more assured manner than White's first two published novels. Unlike *The Living and the Dead*, it envisions self-discovery and self-fulfillment as a private quest, to which the changing political and social winds are incidental, almost irrelevant. In this respect, and in its hints of a symbolism drawn partly from Jungian psychology, as well as in its masterful weaving of a subtle texture of imagery, *The Aunt's Story* marks the beginning of White's maturity as an artist.

THE TREE OF MAN

White's next three novels were much larger in scope and intention, epic in length at least. They also project a vision of the Australian past and of the middle twentieth century present influenced by that past. The first, *The Tree of Man*, tells the saga of Australia's pioneer past, as seen through three generations, but mainly through the experience of Stan and Amy Parker, homesteaders who wrest a farm from the wilderness. Stan and Amy are attractive characters, although rather conventional, and their lives are given a depth not found in most novels of pioneer life. Moreover, White provides splendid comic relief through their foils, the irresponsible O'Dowds, so that despite its length, the novel has considerable popular appeal, unlike much of White's fiction. While Stan and Amy's life as lonely settlers in the outback often possesses a beauty and quiet dignity, their later lives are frustrating, and their sense of progress and achievement is dissipated in the disappointing lives of their children, and in Amy's later estrangement from her husband.

A brilliant reversal of perspective occurs in the closing pages. Here, the aged Stan Parker, apparently a neglected and forgotten failure living in a suburb of Sydney, rises to heights of tragic dignity. Accosted by an annoying fundamentalist evangelist, Parker rejects the easy formula for salvation the latter offers and asserts his own faith: He identifies

God with a gob of spittle. To the evangelist, this is a blasphemous comment, and some have tended to treat it as a defiant and rebellious one, but, as William Walsh and some other critics have claimed, Parker's statement is a confession of faith in the ultimate goodness of life and of the holiness of being. This event marks the beginning of the paradoxical but assured religious affirmation that surfaces at crucial moments in most of White's subsequent novels.

Voss

The sense of an impressive tragic vision is heightened and intensified in White's next novel, *Voss*, which is, like *The Aunt's Story*, one of his better-known works. It describes its hero's Faustian ambition to be the first to conquer the Australian continent by leading an exploratory expedition across it. Voss's noble failure (based on an actual expedition led by the explorer Ludwig Leichhardt) is counterbalanced by his mystical love for Laura Trevelyan, which transforms him from an exponent of the heroic and resolute will (like that celebrated by Friedrich Nietzsche in the late nineteenth century) to a more chastened and forgiving spirit. At the end, Voss is ready to accept his failure and death with a sense of Christian (or at any rate, religious) resignation.

Although a humorless and often exasperating character, Voss is a dynamic force who entices stolid Australian businessmen into financing his enterprise. His nature, however, is more complex than most of the unimaginative bourgeois Australians realize; only Laura, a complicated young woman who privately rebels against conventional Christianity and the age's worship of material progress, perceives the hidden sensitivities and beauty of Voss's character.

In the early stages of the novel, Laura and Voss seem to be in conflict, as their opposed but complementary natures seem to strike sparks from each other. Once Voss and his companions embark on their heroic journey in the Australian desert, however, Laura and Voss appear to communicate through a mystical or telepathic bond. Jungian psychology would consider each a person who has partially suppressed a hidden self: Voss has repressed his feminine qualities by devotion to the ideals of the masculine will; Laura has suppressed her masculine alter ego in the service of femininity. Their mystic communication enlarges and fulfills both their natures.

Defeated by the Australian climate and landscape, the treachery of his companions, and his own miscalculations, Voss meets a tragic end. The heroic grandeur of Voss's failure is impressive, however; White's hero has a strength and ambition beyond that of the protagonists of many modern novels, and in his defeat and death he gains some of the humanity that he had so obviously lacked.

RIDERS IN THE CHARIOT

Voss's acceptance of the Southern Cross as a symbol of his transformation from Nietzschean ideals to a more humane and forgiving outlook prompted some to assume that White himself was espousing doctrinal and institutional Christianity in *Voss*. This is not so, but White does affirm his personal religious vision—a synthesis of Jungian thought, Christian and Jewish mysticism, and poetic vision. His next novel, *Riders in the Chariot*, is perhaps his most ambitious attempt to present the religious vision that undergirds all of his fiction after *The Tree of Man*. *Riders in the Chariot* draws its title from Ezekiel's biblical vision of the chariot, but its prophetic and at times apocalyptic tone comes partially from William Blake, whose visionary conversation with Isaiah and Ezekiel in *The Marriage of Heaven and Hell* (1790) provides an epigraph. The four main protagonists, two men and two women (one black or "abo" painter, one Jewish mystic, one evangelical Christian, and one nature mystic) are all outcast visionaries, who combine to make a gigantic and impressive human mandala.

Himmelfarb is a scholar who turns from enlightened rationalism to the dense but powerful mystical images of the Kabbala, including the "blue fire" of some Kabbalist treatises. White's other seekers in the novel are religious questers who follow different and perhaps equally valid paths to their epiphanies and revelations. Miss Hare's nature mysticism is a naïve affirmation of being that resembles the kind of mysticism preached and celebrated by Ralph Waldo Emerson and Walt Whitman. By contrast, Mrs. Godbold's way is that of orthodox Christian piety, and Alf Dubbo's path is that of the romantic transcendentalist vision, as proclaimed by Blake and others.

Riders in the Chariot asserts the primacy of mystical search over conventional life, and it is also Blakean in its harsh indictment of evil in the modern world and in modern history. Evil is seen in various forms in this novel: in the anti-Semitism and later the Nazism that Himmelfarb encounters; in the smug self-righteousness of decaying puritanism in Miss Hare's tormentor, Mrs. Jolley; in the narcissistic upper-class arrogance and contempt for the less fortunate shown by Mrs. Chalmers-Robinson; and in the feeble and thwarted religiosity of the Reverend Pask and his sister. Above all, it is seen in the working-class bigotry and mule-headed chauvinism, with its suspicion of outsiders, of the Australian workmen, who reenact the Crucifixion as a blasphemous joke on Himmelfarb on Good Friday. Primarily, White is inclined in this novel to see evil as a kind of spiritual blindness or lack of vision "of the infinite," as Blake's epigraph says, although the malice demonstrated by Mrs. Jolley and White's laborers is hard to explain in such simple terms. Nevertheless, White's sense of the overwhelming presence of evil in the modern world, especially "moral evil," or evil for which humans are responsible, is one of the most convincing features of the book. Equally strong is the sense of moral goodness or innocence in his four central characters, however much they may occasionally surrender to their flaws. Whether one is interested in White's attempt to portray the different paths of mysticism, it is hard to forget the strength of his portraits of four characters who remain admirable while enduring great suffering.

THE SOLID MANDALA

White devoted the early and middle years of the 1960's to works that were smaller in scale. In *The Solid Mandala*, which White considered one of his three best novels, his idiosyncrasies emerge more noticeably than in earlier works. This novel affirms White's Jungian religious vision more strongly than ever, and to underscore the theme for the obtuse reader, the noble example of Fyodor Dostoevski is invoked by Arthur Brown, the inarticulate visionary who is in part a spokesman for White. Arthur is set in contrast with his tragic brother, Waldo, a minor fiction writer and critic hampered by excessive rationalism and rendered creatively impotent by fear of his emotions and imagination. Ironically, after failing as a writer and ruining his life by aloofness from humanity, Waldo is ambushed by his repressed sexuality near the end: He becomes a pathetic cross-dresser wearing his late mother's discarded dresses, and thus expressing the thwarted feminine side of his nature.

Arthur Brown's life also ends pathetically in a lonely old age, yet Arthur, one of White's holy simpletons or divine fools, lives a spiritually fulfilled, if obscure and misunderstood, existence. Arthur has a mystical sympathy with animals and nature and with some of the other less articulate characters, especially Dulcie Feinstein, a rich young woman to whom both brothers are attracted. A close communion also exists between Arthur and Mrs. Poulter, a working-class woman who is a kind of surrogate mother and wife to him. Arthur finds meaning in existence through his apprehension of mandalas, the Jungian symbol for the unity and holiness of all being, and of all innocent and life-enhancing forms of existence. Two major mandala symbols dominate Arthur's experience: a large green marble, or "solid mandala," which appears to him to be symbolic of the holiness toward which humanity should strive; and a mystic dance in the shape of a mandala he performs with Mrs. Poulter.

Arthur and Waldo both lead tragic lives, if judged by conventional human standards, and each is an incomplete person: Arthur, the mystic and visionary, lacks a well-developed rational mind; while Waldo, the rationalist, is dead to all spiritual and transcendental existence. The story is thus a fable about the tragic split in humanity between the rational and the mystical faculties of the mind, between—if some psychologists, such as Robert Ornstein, are to be believed—the left and the right sides of the human brain. Despite the tragic nature of the novel, however, White makes Arthur much the more attractive of the two brothers and reaffirms once more one of the themes of *Riders in the Chariot* and other novels: If a choice must be made between reason and mysticism, the path of the mystic, however despised in a rationalistic and technological age, is the more rewarding and redemptive road.

Although beneath the rough and grainy surface of *The Solid Mandala* there are surprising riches and pleasures, its sometimes crabbed and eccentric nature might have suggested to some that White had fallen into a creative decline in the 1960's. The three remarkable novels that followed, however, proved that the converse was true: *The Vivisector*,

The Eye of the Storm, and *A Fringe of Leaves* not only testify to an impressive sustained surge of creative power but also show White in more masterful control of his material and of his artistic form than ever before.

THE VIVISECTOR

The Vivisector describes the life of a rebellious and obsessed painter, Hurtle Duffield, who triumphs over enormous obstacles—an obscure background, a stultifying upper-class education, the cultural sterility of the Australian environment, numerous unhappy love affairs—to achieve triumph as a modern artist, a master of the techniques of Impressionism, Surrealism, and abstract Impressionism, who successfully shapes Australian material into a solid series of enduring works.

In terms of form, *The Vivisector* is one of White's more daring gambles, for it ostensibly follows the shapeless biographical narrative mode of some of the most primitive works of fiction, tracing Duffield's development from his childhood to his death through a series of selected incidents and periods. Close inspection of *The Vivisector* shows, however, that White has made sophisticated use of a naïve narrative form in his treatment of Duffield's struggle. For example, Duffield's experience is rendered in terms of his relationship to a series of Jungian anima figures who serve as lovers, supports, and muses. These range from his crippled foster sister, Rhoda Courtney, a childhood rival but a supporter of his old age; through Ponce Nan, a vital but tragic prostitute; and Hero Pavloussi, the wife of a Greek businessman with whom he enjoys a brief, passionate, but unsatisfying romance.

As a painter, Duffield is a tireless worker and committed visionary whose paintings recapitulate many motifs familiar to White's readers. At one point, Duffield perfects his craft by painting rocks; the action suggests the need to come to terms with the intractable and substantial nature of the visible and phenomenal world. In his early stages, Duffield is a rebellious and defiantly blasphemous painter who charges God with being the great "vivisector," an unfeeling and cruel being who experiments with human suffering as a scientist dismembers animals—or as Duffield and other artists approach human life, seeing it as raw material for art. Guilt over the suicide of Nan, however, for which he feels partially responsible, and compassion for the frustrated gay grocer Cutbush, whom he paints as a Surrealist figure machine-gunning lovers, work in Duffield a more tolerant and forgiving nature, and his work at last becomes more a kind of worship than blasphemy. In his last period, weakened by strokes, he becomes obsessed with painting in indigo and is characterized by a wry humility and kindness. Duffield thinks of his final, fatal stroke as a moment when he is "indiggodd," or departing "into God."

THE EYE OF THE STORM

If *The Vivisector* is rich in vital characterizations and frequently possesses the exuberance of Duffield's raw energy, *The Eye of the Storm* is a splendidly controlled performance that demonstrates once more that when he chose, White could display a sure mastery of the techniques of the English novel of manners as practiced by such writers as E. M. Forster. *The Eye of the Storm* is constructed around the social comedy of the last days of Elizabeth Hunter, a regal but selfish matriarch of Sydney society who at eighty-six is slowly dying in her home on Moreton Drive while her son and daughter scheme to have her removed from the care of her nurses and placed in a nursing home. As is usual with White, however, the social comedy of the novel's surface masks tragedy and religious vision: in this case, the Learesque tragedy of Mrs. Hunter and her two children, and the crisis of faith suffered by her remarkable nurse, Sister Mary de Santis. Although the present time of the novel amounts to only a few days, White's narration re-creates, through the memories of the characters, the spiritual and psychological histories of their entire lives. Elizabeth Hunter, like White himself the talented offspring of a grazier, has during her life grown from a grazier's wife with social aspirations into a lady of poise and charm. At the same time, this majestic woman is portrayed as a dominating and selfish mother whose poise and beauty have given her untalented and unattractive daughter, Dorothy, an inferiority complex and driven her talented but narcissistic son to become both a successful London actor and a pathetic womanizing failure in private life.

Mrs. Hunter in later life, however, has been transformed during a hurricane on Brumby Island, when, abandoned and alone, she experienced a numinous epiphany in the still of the eye of the storm. As a result, she has become a compassionate, understanding, and deeply religious woman, although her piety is of the unchurched kind. This transformation lends a Lear-like poignancy to her last days, when the poorly concealed malice of Basil and Dorothy is embodied in their effort to move her to a nursing home. The irony in this situation is heightened by the fact that Basil Hunter longs to play Lear himself, as the capstone of his career. Another tragic irony is Dorothy's idolizing of the Duchess Sanseverina in Stendhal's *The Charterhouse of Parma* (1839): Longing to be a masterful woman like the duchess, Dorothy resents her mother, whose social poise and personality recall that Stendhal heroine. The tragic irony in the actions of the children comes to a climax in their sentimental journey to their home ranch, where they finally surrender to their loneliness and huddle together in an act of incest during the night.

In contrast to the bleak and loveless lives of Basil and Dorothy, Mrs. Hunter finds solace in the loving care of Mary de Santis, her nurse and a reluctant believer in Greek Orthodox Christianity. Sister de Santis's care aids Mrs. Hunter in her final days, and in turn, Sister de Santis finds her own provisional faith reaffirmed by an epiphany of numinous divine immanence at the end of the novel in a mystic moment of water, birds' wings, and morning light, recalling biblical images of Revelation.

An interesting and partially comic minor plot in *The Eye of the Storm* involves another of Elizabeth Hunter's nurses, the youthful Flora Manhood, who finds herself caught between resentment of her male lover and a temptation to join her cousin in a lesbian affair. Despite White's obvious sympathy for Flora and her lesbian inclinations, the matter is resolved by her decision to remain heterosexual, while lesbian sexuality is treated with a touch of comic irony. It is curious that White, himself gay, was able to treat homosexuality with enormous sympathy yet finally imply the desirability of a traditional heterosexual identity.

Without a doubt, *The Eye of the Storm* is one of White's most carefully crafted and formally satisfying novels, and the one that most closely approximates the Jamesian ideal of complete mastery of novelistic form. This novel, which might have been considered the crowning work of a lesser career, was followed by other equally challenging works.

A FRINGE OF LEAVES

A Fringe of Leaves has many impressive strengths. Like *Voss*, this epic tale is inspired by the Australian past, specifically the experience of Eliza Fraser, a heroic woman who survived shipwreck, the loss of husband and companions, and captivity by Aborigines to return to civilization and become a legendary heroine. White's heroine, Ellen Gluyas Roxborough, is a woman of enormous appetite for living who undergoes numerous metamorphoses on her road to destiny. At first an imaginative Cornish farm girl who longs to journey to some mystical or fabled sacred place such as Tintagel, Ellen marries a dry country squire, Austin Roxborough, and is made over, on the surface at least, into a polished eighteenth century lady and a dutiful adornment to her husband's estate near Winchester. As Ellen takes a sentimental journey to Australia (or "Van Diemen's Land") to visit her husband's rakish brother, Garnet, her inner self emerges, first in a brief affair with Garnet, then in the ordeal of survival of shipwreck and capture by "savages."

The shipwreck and the captivity sections form the heart of the narrative. In the shipwreck, Ellen gradually has her civilized self stripped from her, along with her clothing, which is removed layer by layer. Later, after losing her husband and becoming a captive of the Australian natives, Ellen is obliged to confront her own authentic humanity. Her will to survive is indomitable; to cling to her sense of being human, she weaves a "fringe of leaves" as a kind of primitive clothing and an assertion of her belonging to a human realm above the world of nature. A central question for her, however, is that of her relationship to her captors. Is she of the same order as the dark-skinned Aborigines? The question is answered when she participates in a ritual feast at the center of the novel; it is a rite of cannibalism that provides not only physical nourishment but also, ironically, a sense of religious fulfillment. At the center of her "heart of darkness," Ellen finds her essential humanity.

The captivity section—which one critic has compared to the captivity narratives of prisoners of the American Indians—is followed by an idyllic interlude that represents a return to innocence for Ellen. In this episode, Ellen meets an escaped convict, murderer Jack Chance, who in London had brutally murdered his wife; Jack atones for that by falling in love with Ellen. With Jack, Ellen enjoys her most satisfying sexual relationship, but this edenic experience, like all others, must end when Ellen crosses the Brisband River (likened to a snake) that separates the Australian wilderness from the settled country.

In the resolution of the novel, Ellen is both a heroine to other pioneers, especially the women, and a penitent. In her own eyes, her guilt over her participation in the cannibal rite and the betrayal of Jack is great, but her will to live triumphs over her sense of unworthiness and self-immolation. At the close of the novel, it is clear she will return to routine and ordered life by marrying a pleasant, but somewhat inarticulate, Australian settler.

In its depiction of the indestructible will to survive, *A Fringe of Leaves* is a masterpiece, perhaps White's finest novel. Its central character, Ellen Roxborough, may well become one of the unforgettable heroines of literature.

THE TWYBORN AFFAIR

Although *A Fringe of Leaves* has received much favorable comment, White's subsequent novel, *The Twyborn Affair,* was the object of a different reception, especially in the United States. This work is one of White's most controversial, for it attempts to deal with homosexual experience more candidly than ever before in White's fiction. Moreover, the novel is an interesting experiment in technique because it is constructed of three sections that are essentially self-contained units, yet it also attempts to form a greater unity of a lengthy novel covering several decades.

Eddie Twyborn, the hero (and sometimes heroine) of the novel, is presented as a feminine personality in the body of a handsome male: an unusual "prisoner of sex" whose incarceration is indeed tragic. In part 1, Eddie Twyborn appears as the transvestite lover of a likable older man, a somewhat decadent Greek living in France in the pre-World War I period. The couple are spied upon by Joanie Golson, a friend of Eddie's upper-class, overbearing Australian mother, and there is a certain amount of rather strained social comedy here until the affair ends with the death of Twyborn's Greek lover. In part 2, Twyborn returns to Australia after the war as a decorated hero and tries living in the outback as a worker on a sheep ranch. There he becomes emotionally entangled with the brutal foreman, Don Prowse, who finally rapes him, and with the owner's wife, who falls in love with him, misunderstanding his sexual nature while beguiled by his charm and sensitivity.

The failure to live peacefully as a man in part 2 is followed by Twyborn's life in London in part 3, where he surfaces in the late 1930's in female dress. This time, he is the madam of a brothel patronized by the rich and fashionable, and he becomes something of a celebrity. During this period, he suffers from a thwarted love for his patron, Lord Gravenor, who is finally revealed as gay also. A touching reconciliation with his selfish mother, now humbled by age and living in London alone, provides a kind of tragic recognition scene at the novel's end. This is followed by Twyborn's death in the London blitz.

Undoubtedly, Eddie Twyborn—the name is an obvious pun on "twice-born"—is one of the most interesting gay heroes in literature, and perhaps White's theme, the irony of a feminine nature in a male body, has never been treated with such insight. The novel's eccentricities, however, are pronounced, and the social comedy in parts 1 and 3 often becomes tiresome. Like White's other major novels, the work achieves a kind of tragic dignity, despite its flaws, yet it appears vastly inferior to his other novels published in the 1970's.

White's strengths as a writer are many. He is a masterful stylist, and his characterizations are psychologically complex and memorable. His skill at social comedy is complemented by contempt for the arrogance of wealth and power. Beyond these gifts, however, White sought to create tragic fictional works on the Greek or Shakespearean scale in an age of irony and a diminished or disappearing tragic vision. White's fiction also, in the works following *The Aunt's Story*, articulates the author's own prodigious mythology and majestic religious vision. It is a vision drawing on numerous disparate sources—Blake and the Kabbala, Carl Jung, Dostoevski, and the Bible—but it forms a synthesis that affirms the importance of a search for transcendence and the significance of mystical experience. Both his vision and his novels are likely to stand the test of time.

Edgar L. Chapman

OTHER MAJOR WORKS

SHORT FICTION: *The Burnt Ones*, 1964; *The Cockatoos: Shorter Novels and Stories*, 1974; *Three Uneasy Pieces*, 1987.

PLAYS: *Return to Abyssinia*, pr. 1947; *The Ham Funeral*, pr. 1961 (wr. 1947); *The Season at Sarsaparilla*, pr. 1962; *A Cheery Soul*, pr. 1963; *Night on Bald Mountain*, pr. 1963; *Four Plays*, 1965 (revised as *Plays*, 1985-1994; 2 volumes); *Big Toys*, pr. 1977; *Signal Driver*, pr. 1982; *Netherwood*, pr., pb. 1983; *Shepherd on the Rocks*, pr. 1987.

POETRY: *The Ploughman, and Other Poems*, 1935.

SCREENPLAY: *The Night of the Prowler*, 1976.

NONFICTION: *Flaws in the Glass: A Self-Portrait*, 1981; *Patrick White Speaks*, 1989; *Letters*, 1996 (David Marr, editor).

BIBLIOGRAPHY

Bliss, Carolyn. *Patrick White's Fiction: The Paradox of Fortunate Failure*. New York: St. Martin's Press, 1986. Offers an excellent introduction to White's overall thematic concerns. Argues that all of White's writing stems from a paradox—that is, the failures so often experienced by the characters can in fact lead to their successful redemption.

Collier, Gordon. *The Rocks and Sticks of Words: Style, Discourse, and Narrative Structure in the Fiction of Patrick White*. Atlanta: Rodopi, 1992. Provides detailed analysis of the themes and techniques in White's fiction, including doublings, narration and character, sentence structure, and indexical detail.

During, Simon. *Patrick White*. New York: Oxford University Press, 1996. Examines White's place in Australian history and culture, arguing that his work reflects the end of the country's colonial relationship with Great Britain. Also analyzes the connection between White's homosexuality and his writing.

Edgecombe, Rodney Stenning. *Vision and Style in Patrick White: A Study of Five Novels.* Tuscaloosa: University of Alabama Press, 1989. Addresses five novels including *The Eye of the Storm*, which Edgecombe considers to be White's greatest. Links the books by exploring the metaphysical thoughts they share and examines White's distinctive style, which affirms his novels' thematic emphasis on alienation, isolation, and the subsequent search for a vision to free the individual from spiritual imprisonment.

Hewill, Helen Verity. *Patrick White: Painter Manqué—Paintings, Painters, and Their Influence on His Writing.* Carlton, Vic.: Miegunyah Press, 2002. Describes how painting was a source of inspiration for White, addressing specifically the influence of twentieth century Australian art and European modernist and Romantic art on his work.

Marr, David. *Patrick White: A Life.* New York: Alfred A. Knopf, 1992. Monumental biography was written with White's cooperation. The dying White found the manuscript painful reading, but he did not ask the author to change a word. Includes detailed notes, bibliography, and helpful appendixes.

Tabron, Judith L. *Postcolonial Literature from Three Continents: Tutuola, H.D., Ellison, and White.* New York: Peter Lang, 2003. Tabron provides her opinions on how to read postcolonial literature, then demonstrates her views by analyzing works by four authors, including a chapter devoted to a postcolonial interpretation of *Voss*.

Weigel, John A. *Patrick White.* Boston: Twayne, 1983. Introduces White and his work by tracing his life and discussing each of his novels and his plays. General work provides a good introduction for the beginning reader of White's fiction. Includes bibliography and chronology.

Williams, Mark. *Patrick White.* New York: St. Martin's Press, 1993. Presents detailed analyses of all of White's novels as well as discussion centered on the themes and contexts of his works. Includes bibliography and index.

Wolfe, Peter. *Laden Choirs: The Fiction of Patrick White.* Lexington: University Press of Kentucky, 1983. While not taking any particular thematic stand, this book offers a substantial analysis of each of White's novels. Focuses in part on White's style, demonstrating how it affects narrative tension, philosophical structure, and the development of character.

_____, ed. *Critical Essays on Patrick White.* Boston: G. K. Hall, 1990. Wide-ranging collection of essays edited by one of White's most astute critics. Includes a section of autobiographical essays by White and a helpful bibliography.

JEANETTE WINTERSON

Born: Manchester, England; August 27, 1959

OTHER LITERARY FORMS

Jeanette Winterson has dramatized several of her own books, most notably *Oranges Are Not the Only Fruit* (1990) for British television. She has written original radio drama and worked on a documentary, *Great Moments in Aviation* (1994), also for British television. She has written short stories, essays, and columns for *The Guardian* and *The Times*. One of her earlier books was a comic book, and she has published several works of children's fiction, including *The King of Capri* (2003) and *Tanglewreck* (2006).

ACHIEVEMENTS

Jeanette Winterson has been in the public eye from the time her first novel won the Whitbread Prize. She was named by *Granta* magazine one of the twenty best young British writers. Other prizes include the Prix d'Argent at the Cannes Film Festival, the Prix Italia, and the BAFTA Best Drama Award for her television adaptation of *Oranges Are Not the Only Fruit*. She won the John Llewellyn Rhys Memorial Prize for *The Passion* and the E. M. Forster Award from the American Academy of Arts and Letters for *Sexing the Cherry*. In 2006, she was awarded the Order of the British Empire (OBE) for services to literature. Her books have been translated into more than one dozen languages.

BIOGRAPHY

Jeanette Winterson was born in 1959 in Manchester, in the northwest of England, and adopted by a childless Pentecostal couple from Accrington, a mill town just outside Manchester. She was raised under strict religious principles and shaped for a career as a missionary. By the age of eight, she was preaching at evangelist tent meetings held by the family's small chapel, and was making converts. Her reading material at home was limited to the Bible and Sir Thomas Malory's *Le Morte d'Arthur* (1485), a strange combination from which she developed a strong feeling for literary style.

At the age of fifteen, Winterson had a lesbian relationship with one of her converts that was strongly denounced by the church. At the age of sixteen, she decided to leave home and took a number of part-time jobs to pay for the academic high school where she was enrolled. When she was eighteen years old, she enrolled at St. Catherine's College, Oxford University, to major in English. She worked for one year at a mental hospital to pay tuition.

After graduation in 1981, Winterson worked in various theaters and began writing what would become her first novel, *Oranges Are Not the Only Fruit*. She finished the novel at the young age of twenty-three years. After it was published in 1985, she began working as an assistant editor for Pandora Press (her early publisher). She began a romantic relationship with Pat Kavanagh, her literary agent. In 1987, Winterson published her second novel, *The Passion*. Its successful reception by readers and critics inspired her to become a full-time writer. The next year she entered a long-term relationship with Peggy Reynolds, an academic and a radio broadcaster. The following year, Winterson published *Sexing the Cherry*.

In 1990, Winterson adapted *Oranges Are Not the Only Fruit* for television in a highly acclaimed dramatization. Her work was embraced in the American market with *Written on the Body* in 1993, ensuring a worldwide readership. Honors and prizes followed, and she became a regular columnist, essayist, writer of children's fiction, and broadcaster. She also bought a delicatessen in central London and a house in Gloucestershire.

ANALYSIS

Jeanette Winterson's novels are at the cusp of modernism, postmodernism, and Magical Realism. Her sheer verbal skills, so evident in her fiction, led to the novels' initial popularity. The novels also were popular because they filled the desire in the mid-1980's for a new lesbian narrative subgenre. In some ways, Winterson steered the postfeminist novel into uncharted territories, especially in terms of narrative. She made gender, along with plot, history, and even narrator, sources of uncertainty. The one certainty in her novels is the story of the truth of love. Other consistent themes include myth and the fairy tale.

Oranges Are Not the Only Fruit, an immediate popular success, is an autobiographical story of lesbian sexuality. The heroine, simply called Jeanette (and later Jess), relates her experiences with a narrow-minded religious sect. With this novel, Winterson joined a long line of writers who were liberated from narrow religious upbringings. (D. H. Lawrence is perhaps the most obvious and most acknowledged of these writers.)

Winterson inherited far more from her religious upbringing than she rejected. She admitted that her readings as a child, narrow and limited as they were, led to her love of words and her sense of style. She became an evangelist, not for religion but for the books themselves, much like the "religion of literature" that the poet Matthew Arnold sought to construct out of the ruins of his childhood faith. Winterson has said that literature, and specifically postmodernist literature, has to redefine the boundaries of truth in terms of love and do so beyond the norms of common sense. As in Lawrence, that love has to be defined in terms of sexuality and passion.

Winterson's next two novels, *The Passion* and *Sexing the Cherry*, play with history, with *The Passion* set in the Napoleonic era. Her fourth novel, *Written on the Body*, is a more somber exploration of what became her typical plot structure, the love triangle of a married couple and a single woman, usually lesbian. Love is challenged by disease, as the heroine is diagnosed with cancer. Love and disease break down boundaries, demanding new ones be constructed. The novel has no plot line and the narrator is not clearly gendered. *Art and Lies* and *Gut Symmetries* are similarly constructed.

After publishing the novels *The Power Book* and *Lighthousekeeping*, Winterson turned to children's science fiction. By invitation of a small Scottish press, she turned to pure myth in the novel *Weight*, which is a retelling of the story of Atlas and Hercules. A growing concern with ecological issues led to the novel *The Stone Gods*, set partly in space in the science fiction format and partly on Easter Island, which suffered desertification at the hands of humans.

SEXING THE CHERRY

Sexing the Cherry is an experiment in postmodern fiction, interweaving strands of history, myth, fairy tale, and Magical Realism. The main plot concerns an orphan named Jordan and his adoptive mother, a large Rabelaisian earth-mother type of woman who lives by the river Thames in London. The time is the seventeenth century, and London is in the throes of civil war. Winterson shows herself with this novel to be deeply reactionary in her politics, siding with King Charles against the Puritans. The tale's search, as it develops, is both for new fruit for Jordan and for love and identity, which includes gender identity, for his mother. A banana comes to symbolize the phallus, and Jordan's mother literally bites off a penis as one would bite off part of a banana. The London portrayed is gross, sordid, and decaying, yet the mythic elements, the search for Fortunata the dancer in particular, prioritize the spiritual. The novel is a bold experiment, and it is left to readers to piece together the fragments.

THE POWER BOOK

Winterson considers *The Power Book* the last of a seven-novel cycle of long fiction. The work is another conscious effort to rewrite the English novel on postmodern terms, this time using the metaphor of the computer and, as one of its loci, cyberspace. In *The Power Book*, word processors are shown to erase what one has written and rewrite what one has erased. Networks are shown to help one find parallel information to the story one is working on, but the information comes in fragments. Nothing is whole or finished.

This process of writing becomes a metaphor for individual lives. Winterson's life is consciously "queer," a term she prefers to lesbian. Queer suggests strange, not straightforward, and it also suggests the ambiguity of the phallus. The novel's opening motif is the tulip, which is used as a phallus for the female body to become male. The consciousness of the presence or absence of the phallus in terms of connection and identity runs throughout the book. The novel's subtexts include the story of gender change and ambiguity in Virginia Woolf's *Orlando: A Biography* (1928). The story's themes are the lifelong search for the grand passion, whether for love or tulips, and how humans keep reinventing themselves to find that grand passion; in finding it, one finds one's true identity.

The main plot, such as it is, centers on two lesbian lovers (one of them married) as they meet in Paris and then continue to Capri. In the second half of the book, Winterson introduces autobiographical fragments from *Oranges Are Not the Only Fruit*. A mother tells her adopted orphan daughter that treasure exists out there in the world, if only one searches for it and even if one has to begin that search in muck and filth. This determination to find the treasure through layers of time and meaning, symbolized by the Thames and London archaeology (as in *Sexing the Cherry*), leads to the realization that the treasure lies within.

LIGHTHOUSEKEEPING

By Winterson's own admission, *Lighthousekeeping* uses the remnants of her autobiography that are not resolved in *Oranges Are Not the Only Fruit*. Silver, the narrator of *Lighthousekeeping*, is an illegitimate orphan girl who finds a home in the Cape Wrath lighthouse in the far north of Scotland, where several different seas meet, setting up dangerous currents. The lighthouse keeper, the blind man Pew, teaches her to tell stories, and local history is constructed as narrative. The novel interweaves several stories toward a personal resolution for Silver as she seeks her identity.

The main story weaves around Babel Dark, a Victorian clergyman who was a minister in the local village of Salts and who knew Charles Darwin and the writer Robert Louis Stevenson. Dark lives a double life and is portrayed as the inspiration for Stevenson's classic novel *The Strange Case of Dr. Jekyll and Mr. Hyde* (1886), which forms one of the novel's subtexts. Dark's own life reverses the Jekyll and Hyde scenario, in that the respectable minister suppresses the former fashionable son of a Bristol merchant who had a passionate affair with Molly, a shop assistant. Dark has escaped the affair by retreating to the north of Scotland and living almost a dead man's life, suppressing all emotion. However, he kept two diaries, one respectable and the other wild and passionate, revealing his inner turmoil. Molly reappears twice to offer Dark a second chance, but he refuses, compromising by going to live with her in Bristol for two months under the alias Lux (or light). In the end, he commits suicide. One of Pew's ancestors, also a lighthouse keeper, recounts Dark's confession.

Dark represents some of the emotional suppression of Winterson's own upbringing. In the other main story, Silver has to find her own identity, especially when the lighthouse is automated and Pew and she are out of a job. She goes to Bristol to seek out some of Dark's roots, then undergoes a number of encounters, some of which seem quite autobiographical. She takes a trip to Capri, where she steals a parrot because the parrot can say "Silver," representing the one thing that knows her name and, therefore, her. Eventually, she has a lover and then resolves to return to the lighthouse, say farewell, and realize the strength of love and the choice for passion which must be made to continue living.

David Barratt

OTHER MAJOR WORKS

SHORT FICTION: *The World and Other Places*, 1998.

PLAY: *The Power Book*, pr. 2002 (based on her novel).

TELEPLAYS: *Oranges Are Not the Only Fruit*, 1990 (based on her novel); *Great Moments in Aviation* (1994).

RADIO PLAYS: *Static*, 1988; *Text Message*, 2001.

NONFICTION: *Art Objects: Essays on Ecstasy and Effrontery*, 1995.

CHILDREN'S LITERATURE: *The King of Capri*, 2003; *Tanglewreck*, 2006.

EDITED TEXT: *Passion Fruit: Romantic Fiction with a Twist*, 1986.

BIBLIOGRAPHY

Andermahr, Sonya. *Jeanette Winterson*. New York: Palgrave Macmillan, 2008. Late biography of Winterson by a scholar of her work. Places her fiction in historical, critical, and theoretical context and analyzes her experimentation with technique and form.

_____, ed. *Jeanette Winterson: A Contemporary Critical Guide*. Harrisburg, Pa.: Continuum International, 2007. Collection of scholarly essays covering the key themes and styles in Winterson's fiction.

Lopez, Gemma. *Seductions in Narrative: Subjectivity and Desire in the Works of Angela Carter and Jeanette Winterson*. Youngstown, N.Y.: Cambria Press, 2007. Scholarly treatise examining through a poststructuralist lens the themes of desire and self-searching in the novels of Winterson and Angela Carter.

Makinen, Merja. *The Novels of Jeanette Winterson*. New York: Palgrave Macmillan, 2005. Traces the reception to Winterson's novels and places them in the context of modern literary debate. Part of the Readers' Guide to Essential Criticism series.

Onega, Susana. *Jeanette Winterson*. New York: Manchester University Press, 2006. Examines the forms, themes, and ideologies of Winterson's novels within the context of the modern British novel. The first full-length study of Winterson's complete oeuvre.

Pressler, Christopher. *So Far So Linear: Responses to the Work of Jeanette Winterson*. Nottingham, England: Paupers' Press, 1997. Brief but comprehensive survey of modern critical responses and analyses of Winterson's works through 1996.

Reynolds, Margaret, and Jonathan Noakes. *Jeanette Winterson: The Essential Guide*. New York: Vintage Press, 2003. Series of interviews with Winterson in which she discusses four of her most popular novels. Includes a biography, questions for discussion, suggestions for further reading, extracts from reviews, a bibliography, and a glossary of literary terms.

BIBLIOGRAPHY

Every effort has been made to include studies published in 2000 and later. Most items in this bibliography contain a listing of secondary sources, making it easier to identify other critical commentary on novelists, movements, and themes.

THEORETICAL, THEMATIC, AND HISTORICAL STUDIES

Altman, Janet Gurkin. *Epistolarity: Approaches to a Form.* Columbus: Ohio State University Press, 1982. Examines the epistolary novel, explaining how novelists use the letter form to develop characterization, further their plots, and develop meaning.

Beaumont, Matthew, ed. *Adventures in Realism.* Malden, Mass.: Blackwell, 2007. Fifteen essays explore facets of realism, which was critical to the development of the novel. Provides a theoretical framework for understanding how novelists attempt to represent the real and the common in fiction.

Brink, André. *The Novel: Language and Narrative from Cervantes to Calvino.* New York: New York University Press, 1998. Uses contemporary theories of semiotics and narratology to establish a continuum between early novelists and those of the postmodern era in their conscious use of language to achieve certain effects. Ranges across national boundaries to illustrate the theory of the development of the novel since the seventeenth century.

Brownstein, Rachel. *Becoming a Heroine: Reading About Women in Novels.* New York: Viking Press, 1982. Feminist survey of novels from the eighteenth century through the latter half of the twentieth century. Examines how "becoming a heroine" defines for women a sense of value in their lives. Considers novels by both men and women, and discusses the importance of the traditional marriage plot.

Bruzelius, Margaret. *Romancing the Novel: Adventure from Scott to Sebald.* Lewisburg, Pa.: Bucknell University Press, 2007. Examines the development of the adventure novel, linking it with the medieval romance tradition and exploring readers' continuing fascination with the genre.

Cavallaro, Dani. *The Gothic Vision: Three Centuries of Horror, Terror, and Fear.* New York: Continuum, 2005. Study of the gothic novel from its earliest manifestations in the eighteenth century to the early twenty-first century. Through the lenses of contemporary cultural theories, examines readers' fascination with novels that invoke horror, terror, and fright.

Doody, Margaret Anne. *The True Story of the Novel.* New Brunswick, N.J.: Rutgers University Press, 1996. Traces the roots of the novel, traditionally thought to have been developed in the seventeenth century, to classical Greek and Latin texts that exhibit characteristics of modern fiction.

Hale, Dorothy J., ed. *The Novel: An Anthology of Criticism and Theory, 1900-2000.* Malden, Mass.: Blackwell, 2006. Collection of essays by theorists and novelists. Includes commentary on the novel form from the perspective of formalism, structuralism, poststructuralism, Marxism, and reader response theory. Essays also address the novel through the lenses of sociology, gender studies, and feminist theory.

_____. *Social Formalism: The Novel in Theory from Henry James to the Present*. Stanford, Calif.: Stanford University Press, 1998. Emphasizes the novel's special ability to define a social world for readers. Relies heavily on the works of contemporary literary and cultural theorists. Provides a summary of twentieth century efforts to identify a theory of fiction that encompasses novels of many kinds.

Hart, Stephen M., and Wen-chin Ouyang, eds. *A Companion to Magical Realism*. London: Tamesis, 2005. Essays outlining the development of Magical Realism, tracing its roots from Europe through Latin America to other regions of the world. Explores the political dimensions of the genre.

Hoffman, Michael J., and Patrick D. Murphy, eds. *Essentials of the Theory of Fiction*. 2d ed. Durham, N.C.: Duke University Press, 1996. Collection of essays by influential critics from the late nineteenth century through the twentieth century. Focuses on the essential elements of fiction and the novel's relationship to the world it depicts.

Lodge, David. *The Art of Fiction: Illustrated from Classic and Modern Texts*. New York: Viking Press, 1993. Short commentaries on the technical aspects of fiction. Examples from important and minor novelists illustrate literary principles and techniques such as point of view, suspense, character introduction, irony, motivation, and ending.

Lynch, Deirdre, and William B. Walker, eds. *Cultural Institutions of the Novel*. Durham, N.C.: Duke University Press, 1996. Fifteen essays examine aspects of long fiction produced around the world. Encourages a redefinition of the genre and argues for inclusion of texts not historically considered novels.

Moretti, Franco, ed. *The Novel*. 2 vols. Princeton, N.J.: Princeton University Press, 2006. Compendium exploring the novel from multiple perspectives, including as an anthropological, historical, and sociological document; a function of the national tradition from which it emerges; and a work of art subject to examination using various critical approaches.

Priestman, Martin, ed. *The Cambridge Companion to Crime Fiction*. New York: Cambridge University Press, 2003. Essays examine the nature and development of the genre, explore works by writers (including women and ethnic minorities) from several countries, and establish links between crime fiction and other literary genres. Includes a chronology.

Scaggs, John. *Crime Fiction*. New York: Routledge, 2005. Provides a history of crime fiction, explores key subgenres, and identifies recurring themes that suggest the wider social and historical context in which these works are written. Suggests critical approaches that open crime fiction to serious study.

Shiach, Morag, ed. *The Cambridge Companion to the Modernist Novel*. New York: Cambridge University Press, 2007. Essays explaining the concept of modernism and its influence on the novel. Detailed examination of works by writers from various countries, all influenced by the modernist movement. Includes a detailed chronology.

Vice, Sue. *Holocaust Fiction*. New York: Routledge, 2000. Examines controversies generated by novels about the Holocaust. Focuses on eight important works, but also offers observations on the polemics surrounding publication of books on this topic.

Zunshine, Lisa. *Why We Read Fiction: Theory of Mind and the Novel*. Columbus: Ohio State University Press, 2006. Applies theories of cognitive psychology to novel reading, explaining how experience and human nature lead readers to constrain their interpretations of a given text. Provides numerous examples from well-known novels to illustrate how and why readers find pleasure in fiction.

Laurence W. Mazzeno

GLOSSARY OF LITERARY TERMS

absurdism: A philosophical attitude, pervading much of modern drama and fiction, that underlines the isolation and alienation that humans experience, having been thrown into what absurdists see as a godless universe devoid of religious, spiritual, or metaphysical meaning. Conspicuous in its lack of logic, consistency, coherence, intelligibility, and realism, the literature of the absurd depicts the anguish, forlornness, and despair inherent in the human condition. Counter to the rationalist assumptions of traditional humanism, absurdism denies the existence of universal truth or value.

allegory: A literary mode in which a second level of meaning, wherein characters, events, and settings represent abstractions, is encoded within the surface narrative. The allegorical mode may dominate an entire work, in which case the encoded message is the work's primary reason for being, or it may be an element in a work otherwise interesting and meaningful for its surface story alone. Elements of allegory may be found in Jonathan Swift's *Gulliver's Travels* (1726) and Thomas Mann's *Der Zauberberg* (1924; *The Magic Mountain*, 1927).

anatomy: Literally the term means the "cutting up" or "dissection" of a subject into its constituent parts for closer examination. Northrop Frye, in his *Anatomy of Criticism* (1957), uses the term to refer to a narrative that deals with mental attitudes rather than people. As opposed to the novel, the anatomy features stylized figures who are mouthpieces for the ideas they represent.

antagonist: The character in fiction who stands as a rival or opponent to the *protagonist*.

antihero: Defined by Seán O'Faoláin as a fictional figure who, deprived of social sanctions and definitions, is always trying to define himself and to establish his own codes. Ahab may be seen as the antihero of Herman Melville's *Moby Dick* (1851).

archetype: The term "archetype" entered literary criticism from the psychology of Carl Jung, who defined archetypes as "primordial images" from the "collective unconscious" of humankind. Jung believed that works of art derive much of their power from the unconscious appeal of these images to ancestral memories. In his extremely influential *Anatomy of Criticism* (1957), Northrop Frye gave another sense of the term wide currency, defining the archetype as "a symbol, usually an image, which recurs often enough in literature to be recognizable as an element of one's literary experience as a whole."

atmosphere: The general mood or tone of a work; atmosphere is often associated with setting but can also be established by action or dialogue. A classic example of atmosphere is the primitive, fatalistic tone created in the opening description of Egdon Heath in Thomas Hardy's *The Return of the Native* (1878).

bildungsroman: Sometimes called the "novel of education," the bildungsroman focuses on the growth of a young *protagonist* who is learning about the world and finding his or her place in life; typical examples are James Joyce's *A Portrait of the Artist as a*

Young Man (1914-1915, serial; 1916, book) and Thomas Wolfe's *Look Homeward, Angel* (1929).

biographical criticism: Criticism that attempts to determine how the events and experiences of an author's life influence his or her work.

bourgeois novel: A novel in which the values, preoccupations, and accoutrements of middle-class or bourgeois life are given particular prominence. The heyday of the bourgeois novel was the nineteenth century, when novelists as varied as Jane Austen, Honoré de Balzac, and Anthony Trollope both criticized and unreflectingly transmitted the assumptions of the rising middle class.

canon: An authorized or accepted list of books. In modern parlance, the literary canon comprehends the privileged texts, classics, or great books that are thought to belong permanently on university reading lists. Recent theory—especially feminist, Marxist, and poststructuralist—critically examines the process of canon formation and questions the hegemony of white male writers. Such theory sees canon formation as the ideological act of a dominant institution and seeks to undermine the notion of canonicity itself, thereby preventing the exclusion of works by women, minorities, and oppressed peoples.

character: Characters in fiction can be presented as if they were real people or as stylized functions of the plot. Usually characters are a combination of both factors.

classicism: A literary stance or value system consciously based on the example of classical Greek and Roman literature. While the term is applied to an enormous diversity of artists in many different periods and in many different national literatures, "classicism" generally denotes a cluster of values including formal discipline, restrained expression, reverence for tradition, and an objective rather than a subjective orientation. As a literary tendency, classicism is often opposed to *Romanticism*, although many writers combine classical and romantic elements.

climax/crisis: The term "climax" refers to the moment of the reader's highest emotional response, whereas "crisis" refers to a structural element of plot, a turning point at which a resolution must take place.

complication: The point in a novel when the *conflict* is developed or when the already existing conflict is further intensified.

conflict: The struggle that develops as a result of the opposition between the *protagonist* and another person, the natural world, society, or some force within the self.

contextualist criticism: A further extension of *formalist criticism*, which assumes that the language of art is constitutive. Rather than referring to preexistent values, the artwork creates values only inchoately realized before. The most important advocates of this position are Eliseo Vivas (*The Artistic Transaction*, 1963) and Murray Krieger (*The Play and Place of Criticism*, 1967).

conventions: All those devices of stylization, compression, and selection that constitute the necessary differences between art and life. According to the Russian Formalists, these conventions constitute the "literariness" of literature and are the only proper concern of the literary critic.

deconstruction: An extremely influential contemporary school of criticism based on the works of the French philosopher Jacques Derrida. Deconstruction treats literary works as unconscious reflections of the reigning myths of Western culture. The primary myth is that there is a meaningful world that language signifies or represents. The deconstructionist critic is most often concerned with showing how a literary text tacitly subverts the very assumptions or myths on which it ostensibly rests.

defamiliarization: Coined by Viktor Shklovsky in 1917, this term denotes a basic principle of Russian Formalism. Poetic language (by which the Formalists meant artful language, in prose as well as in poetry) defamiliarizes or "makes strange" familiar experiences. The technique of art, says Shklovsky, is to "make objects unfamiliar, to make forms difficult, to increase the difficulty and length of perception. . . . Art is a way of experiencing the artfulness of an object; the object is not important."

detective story: The so-called classic detective story (or mystery) is a highly formalized and logically structured mode of fiction in which the focus is on a crime solved by a detective through interpretation of evidence and ratiocination; the most famous detective in this mode is Arthur Conan Doyle's Sherlock Holmes. Many modern practitioners of the genre, however, such as Dashiell Hammett, Raymond Chandler, and Ross Macdonald, have de-emphasized the puzzlelike qualities of the detective story, stressing instead characterization, theme, and other elements of mainstream fiction.

determinism: The belief that an individual's actions are essentially determined by biological and environmental factors, with free will playing a negligible role. (See *naturalism.*)

dialogue: The similitude of conversation in fiction, dialogue serves to characterize, to further the *plot*, to establish *conflict*, and to express thematic ideas.

displacement: Popularized in criticism by Northrop Frye, this term refers to the author's attempt to make his or her story psychologically motivated and realistic, even as the latent structure of the mythical motivation moves relentlessly forward.

dominant: A term coined by Roman Jakobson to refer to that which "rules, determines, and transforms the remaining components in the work of a single artist, in a poetic canon, or in the work of an epoch." The shifting of the dominant in a *genre* accounts for the creation of new generic forms and new poetic epochs. For example, the rise of *realism* in the mid-nineteenth century indicates realistic conventions becoming dominant and *romance* or fantasy conventions becoming secondary.

doppelgänger: A double or counterpart of a person, sometimes endowed with ghostly qualities. A fictional character's doppelgänger often reflects a suppressed side of his or her personality. One of the classic examples of the doppelgänger motif is found in

Fyodor Dostoevski's novella *Dvoynik* (1846; *The Double*, 1917); Isaac Bashevis Singer and Jorge Luis Borges, among others, offer striking modern treatments of the doppelgänger.

epic: Although this term usually refers to a long narrative poem that presents the exploits of a central figure of high position, the term is also used to designate a long novel that has the style or structure usually associated with an epic. In this sense, for example, Herman Melville's *Moby Dick* (1851) and James Joyce's *Ulysses* (1922) may be called epics.

episodic narrative: A work that is held together primarily by a loose connection of self-sufficient episodes. *Picaresque novels* often have episodic structure.

epistolary novel: A novel made up of letters by one or more fictional characters. Samuel Richardson's *Pamela: Or, Virtue Rewarded* (1740-1741) is a well-known eighteenth century example. In the nineteenth century, Bram Stoker's *Dracula* (1897) is largely epistolary. The technique allows for several different points of view to be presented.

euphuism: A style of writing characterized by ornate language that is highly contrived, alliterative, and repetitious. Euphuism was developed by John Lyly in his *Euphues, the Anatomy of Wit* (1578) and was emulated frequently by writers of the Elizabethan Age.

existentialism: A philosophical, religious, and literary term, emerging from World War II, for a group of attitudes surrounding the pivotal notion that existence precedes essence. According to Jean-Paul Sartre, "Man is nothing else but what he makes himself." Forlornness arises from the death of God and the concomitant death of universal values, of any source of ultimate or a priori standards. Despair arises from the fact that an individual can reckon only with what depends on his or her will, and the sphere of that will is severely limited; the number of things on which he or she can have an impact is pathetically small. Existentialist literature is antideterministic in the extreme and rejects the idea that heredity and environment shape and determine human motivation and behavior.

exposition: The part or parts of a fiction that provide necessary background information. Exposition not only provides the time and place of the action but also introduces readers to the fictive world of the story, acquainting them with the ground rules of the work.

fantastic: In his study *The Fantastic* (1970), Tzvetan Todorov defines the fantastic as a *genre* that lies between the "uncanny" and the "marvelous." All three genres embody the familiar world but present an event that cannot be explained by the laws of the familiar world. Todorov says that the fantastic occupies a twilight zone between the uncanny (when the reader knows that the peculiar event is merely the result of an illusion) and the marvelous (when the reader understands that the event is supposed to take place in a realm controlled by laws unknown to humankind). The fantastic is thus essentially unsettling, provocative, even subversive.

feminist criticism: A criticism advocating equal rights for women in political, economic, social, psychological, personal, and aesthetic senses. On the thematic level, the feminist reader should identify with female characters and their concerns. The object is to provide a critique of phallocentric assumptions and an analysis of patriarchal ideologies inscribed in a literature that is male-centered and male-dominated. On the ideological level, feminist critics see gender, as well as the stereotypes that go along with it, as a cultural construct. They strive to define a particularly feminine content and to extend the *canon* so that it might include works by lesbians, feminists, and women writers in general.

flashback: A scene in a fiction that depicts an earlier event; it may be presented as a reminiscence by a character in the story or may simply be inserted into the narrative.

foreshadowing: A device to create suspense or dramatic irony in fiction by indicating through suggestion what will take place in the future.

formalist criticism: Two particularly influential formalist schools of criticism arose in the twentieth century: the Russian Formalists and the American New Critics. The Russian Formalists were concerned with the conventional devices used in literature to defamiliarize that which habit has made familiar. The New Critics believed that literary criticism is a description and evaluation of its object and that the primary concern of the critic is with the work's unity. Both schools of criticism, at their most extreme, treated literary works as artifacts or constructs divorced from their biographical and social contexts.

genre: In its most general sense, this term refers to a group of literary works defined by a common form, style, or purpose. In practice, the term is used in a wide variety of overlapping and, to a degree, contradictory senses. Tragedy and comedy are thus described as distinct genres; the novel (a form that includes both tragic and comic works) is a genre; and various subspecies of the novel, such as the *gothic* and the *picaresque*, are themselves frequently treated as distinct genres. Finally, the term "genre fiction" refers to forms of popular fiction in which the writer is bound by more or less rigid conventions. Indeed, all these diverse usages have in common an emphasis on the manner in which individual literary works are shaped by particular expectations and conventions; this is the subject of genre criticism.

genre fiction: Categories of popular fiction in which the writers are bound by more or less rigid conventions, such as in the *detective story*, the *romance*, and the *Western*. Although the term can be used in a neutral sense, it is often used dismissively.

gothic novel: A form of fiction developed in the eighteenth century that focuses on horror and the supernatural. In his preface to *The Castle of Otranto* (1765), the first gothic novel in English, Horace Walpole claimed that he was trying to combine two kinds of fiction, with events and story typical of the medieval romance and character delineation typical of the realistic novel. Other examples of the form are Matthew Gregory

Lewis's *The Monk: A Romance* (1796; also known as *Ambrosio: Or, The Monk*) and Mary Wollstonecraft Shelley's *Frankenstein: Or, The Modern Prometheus* (1818).

grotesque: According to Wolfgang Kayser (*The Grotesque in Art and Literature*, 1963), the grotesque is an embodiment in literature of the estranged world. Characterized by a breakup of the everyday world by mysterious forces, the form differs from fantasy in that the reader is not sure whether to react with humor or with horror and in that the exaggeration manifested exists in the familiar world rather than in a purely imaginative world.

Hebraic/Homeric styles: Terms coined by Erich Auerbach in *Mimesis: The Representation of Reality in Western Literature* (1953) to designate two basic fictional styles. The Hebraic style focuses only on the decisive points of narrative and leaves all else obscure, mysterious, and "fraught with background"; the Homeric style places the narrative in a definite time and place and externalizes everything in a perpetual foreground.

historical criticism: In contrast to *formalist criticism*, which treats literary works to a great extent as self-contained artifacts, historical criticism emphasizes the historical context of literature; the two approaches, however, need not be mutually exclusive. Ernst Robert Curtius's *European Literature and the Latin Middle Ages* (1940) is a prominent example of historical criticism.

historical novel: A novel that depicts past historical events, usually public in nature, and features real as well as fictional people. Sir Walter Scott's Waverley novels established the basic type, but the relationship between fiction and history in the form varies greatly depending on the practitioner.

implied author: According to Wayne Booth (*The Rhetoric of Fiction*, 1961), the novel often creates a kind of second self who tells the story—a self who is wiser, more sensitive, and more perceptive than any real person could be.

interior monologue: Defined by Édouard Dujardin as the speech of a character designed to introduce the reader directly to the character's internal life, the form differs from other kinds of monologue in that it attempts to reproduce thought before any logical organization is imposed on it. See, for example, Molly Bloom's long interior monologue at the conclusion of James Joyce's *Ulysses* (1922).

irrealism: A term often used to refer to modern or postmodern fiction that is presented self-consciously as a fiction or a fabulation rather than a mimesis of external reality. The best-known practitioners of irrealism are John Barth, Robert Coover, and Donald Barthelme.

local colorists: A loose movement of late nineteenth century American writers whose fiction emphasizes the distinctive folkways, landscapes, and dialects of various regions. Important local colorists include Bret Harte, Mark Twain, George Washington Cable, Kate Chopin, and Sarah Orne Jewett. (See *regional novel*.)

Marxist criticism: Based on the nineteenth century writings of Karl Marx and Friedrich Engels, Marxist criticism views literature as a product of ideological forces determined by the dominant class. However, many Marxists believe that literature operates according to its own autonomous standards of production and reception: It is both a product of ideology and able to determine ideology. As such, literature may overcome the dominant paradigms of its age and play a revolutionary role in society.

metafiction: This term refers to fiction that manifests a reflexive tendency, such as Vladimir Nabokov's *Pale Fire* (1962) and John Fowles's *The French Lieutenant's Woman* (1969). The emphasis is on the loosening of the work's illusion of reality to expose the reality of its illusion. Other terms used to refer to this type of fiction include "irrealism," "postmodernist fiction," "antifiction," and "surfiction."

modernism: An international movement in the arts that began in the early years of the twentieth century. Although the term is used to describe artists of widely varying persuasions, modernism in general was characterized by its international idiom, by its interest in cultures distant in space or time, by its emphasis on formal experimentation, and by its sense of dislocation and radical change.

motif: A conventional incident or situation in a fiction that may serve as the basis for the structure of the narrative itself. The Russian Formalist critic Boris Tomashevsky uses the term to refer to the smallest particle of thematic material in a work.

motivation: Although this term is usually used in reference to the convention of justifying the action of a character from his or her psychological makeup, the Russian Formalists use the term to refer to the network of devices that justify the introduction of individual *motifs* or groups of motifs in a work. For example, "compositional motivation" refers to the principle that every single property in a work contributes to its overall effect; "realistic motivation" refers to the realistic devices used to make a work plausible and lifelike.

multiculturalism: The tendency to recognize the perspectives of those traditionally excluded from the canon of Western art and literature. In order to promote multiculturalism, publishers and educators have revised textbooks and school curricula to incorporate material by and about women, members of minority groups, persons from non-Western cultures, and homosexuals.

myth: Anonymous traditional stories dealing with basic human concepts and antinomies. According to Claude Lévi-Strauss, myth is that part of language where the "formula *tradutore, tradittore* reaches its lowest truth value. . . . Its substance does not lie in its style, its original music, or its syntax, but in the story which it tells."

myth criticism: Northrop Frye says that in myth "we see the structural principles of literature isolated." Myth criticism is concerned with these basic principles of literature; it is not to be confused with mythological criticism, which is primarily concerned with finding mythological parallels in the surface action of the *narrative*.

narrative: Robert Scholes and Robert Kellogg, in *The Nature of Narrative* (1966), say that by "narrative" they mean literary works that include both a story and a storyteller. The term "narrative" usually implies a contrast to "enacted" fiction such as drama.

narratology: The study of the form and functioning of *narratives*; it attempts to examine what all narratives have in common and what makes individual narratives different from one another.

narrator: The *character* who recounts the *narrative*, or story. Wayne Booth describes various dramatized narrators in *The Rhetoric of Fiction* (1961): unacknowledged centers of consciousness, observers, narrator-agents, and self-conscious narrators. Booth suggests that the important elements to consider in narration are the relationships among the narrator, the author, the characters, and the reader.

naturalism: As developed by Émile Zola in the late nineteenth century, naturalism is the application of the principles of scientific *determinism* to fiction. Although it usually refers more to the choice of subject matter than to technical conventions, those conventions associated with the movement center on the author's attempt to be precise and scientifically objective in description and detail, regardless of whether the events described are sordid or shocking.

New Criticism: See *formalist criticism.*

novel: Perhaps the most difficult of all fictional forms to define because of its multiplicity of modes. Edouard, in André Gide's *Les Faux-monnayeurs* (1925; *The Counterfeiters*, 1927), says the novel is the freest and most lawless of all *genres*; he wonders if fear of that liberty is the reason the novel has so timidly clung to reality. Most critics seem to agree that the novel's primary area of concern is the social world. Ian Watt (*The Rise of the Novel*, 2001) says that the novel can be distinguished from other fictional forms by the attention it pays to individual characterization and detailed presentation of the environment. Moreover, says Watt, the novel, more than any other fictional form, is interested in the "development of its characters in the course of time."

novel of manners: The classic examples of this form might be the novels of Jane Austen, wherein the customs and conventions of a social group of a particular time and place are realistically, and often satirically, portrayed.

novella, novelle, nouvelle, novelette, novela: Although these terms often refer to the short European tale, especially the Renaissance form employed by Giovanni Boccaccio, the terms often refer to that form of fiction that is said to be longer than a short story and shorter than a novel. "Novelette" is the term usually preferred by the British, whereas "novella" is the term usually used to refer to American works in this *genre*. Henry James claimed that the main merit of the form is the "effort to do the complicated thing with a strong brevity and lucidity."

phenomenological criticism: Although best known as a European school of criticism practiced by Georges Poulet and others, this so-called criticism of consciousness is also propounded in the United States by such critics as J. Hillis Miller. The focus is less on individual works and *genres* than it is on literature as an act; the work is not seen as an object but rather as part of a strand of latent impulses in the work of a single author or an epoch.

picaresque novel: A form of fiction that centers on a central rogue figure, or picaro, who usually tells his or her own story. The plot structure is normally *episodic*, and the episodes usually focus on how the picaro lives by his or her wits. Classic examples of the mode are Henry Fielding's *The History of Tom Jones, a Foundling* (1749; commonly known as *Tom Jones*) and Mark Twain's *Adventures of Huckleberry Finn* (1884).

plot/story: "Story" refers to the full *narrative* of *character* and action, whereas "plot" generally refers to action with little reference to character. A more precise and helpful distinction is made by the Russian Formalists, who suggest that "plot" refers to the events of a narrative as they have been artfully arranged in the literary work, subject to chronological displacement, ellipses, and other devices, while "story" refers to the sum of the same events arranged in simple, causal-chronological order. Thus story is the raw material for plot. By comparing the two in a given work, the reader is encouraged to see the narrative as an artifact.

point of view: The means by which the story is presented to the reader, or, as Percy Lubbock says in *The Craft of Fiction* (1921), "the relation in which the narrator stands to the story"—a relation that Lubbock claims governs the craft of fiction. Some of the questions the critical reader should ask concerning point of view are the following: Who talks to the reader? From what position does the narrator tell the story? At what distance does he or she place the reader from the story? What kind of person is he or she? How fully is he or she characterized? How reliable is he or she? For further discussion, see Wayne Booth, *The Rhetoric of Fiction* (1961).

postcolonialism: Postcolonial literature emerged in the mid-twentieth century when colonies in Asia, Africa, and the Caribbean began gaining their independence from the European nations that had long controlled them. Postcolonial authors, such as Salman Rushdie and V. S. Naipaul, tend to focus on both the freedom and the conflict inherent in living in a postcolonial state.

postmodernism: A ubiquitous but elusive term in contemporary criticism, "postmodernism" is loosely applied to the various artistic movements that followed the era of so-called high modernism, represented by such giants as James Joyce and Pablo Picasso. In critical discussions of contemporary fiction, the term "postmodernism" is frequently applied to the works of writers such as Thomas Pynchon, John Barth, and Donald Barthelme, who exhibit a self-conscious awareness of their modernist predecessors as well as a reflexive treatment of fictional form.

protagonist: The central *character* in a fiction, the character whose fortunes most concern the reader.

psychological criticism: While much modern literary criticism reflects to some degree the impacts of Sigmund Freud, Carl Jung, Jacques Lacan, and other psychological theorists, the term "psychological criticism" suggests a strong emphasis on a causal relation between the writer's psychological state, variously interpreted, and his or her works. A notable example of psychological criticism is Norman Fruman's *Coleridge, the Damaged Archangel* (1971).

psychological novel: A form of fiction in which *character*, especially the inner lives of characters, is the primary focus. This form, which has been of primary importance at least since Henry James, characterizes much of the work of James Joyce, Virginia Woolf, and William Faulkner. For a detailed discussion, see *The Modern Psychological Novel* (1955) by Leon Edel.

realism: A literary technique in which the primary convention is to render an illusion of fidelity to external reality. Realism is often identified as the primary method of the novel form: It focuses on surface details, maintains a fidelity to the everyday experiences of middle-class society, and strives for a one-to-one relationship between the fiction and the action imitated. The realist movement in the late nineteenth century coincides with the full development of the novel form.

reception aesthetics: The best-known American practitioner of reception aesthetics is Stanley Fish. For the reception critic, meaning is an event or process; rather than being embedded in the work, it is created through particular acts of reading. The best-known European practitioner of this criticism, Wolfgang Iser, argues that indeterminacy is the basic characteristic of literary texts; the reader must "normalize" the text either by projecting his or her standards into it or by revising his or her standards to "fit" the text.

regional novel: Any novel in which the character of a given geographical region plays a decisive role. Although regional differences persist across the United States, a considerable leveling in speech and customs has taken place, so that the sharp regional distinctions evident in nineteenth century American fiction have all but disappeared. Only in the South has a strong regional tradition persisted to the present. (See *local colorists*.)

rhetorical criticism: The rhetorical critic is concerned with the literary work as a means of communicating ideas and the means by which the work affects or controls the reader. Such criticism seems best suited to didactic works such as satire.

roman à clef: A fiction wherein actual people, often celebrities of some sort, are thinly disguised.

romance: The romance usually differs from the novel form in that the focus is on symbolic events and representational characters rather than on "as-if-real" characters and events. Richard Chase says that in the romance, character is depicted as highly stylized, a function of the plot rather than as someone complexly related to society. The romancer is more likely to be concerned with dreamworlds than with the familiar world, believing that reality cannot be grasped by the traditional novel.

Romanticism: A widespread cultural movement in the late eighteenth and early nine-teenth centuries, the influence of which is still felt. As a general literary tendency, Ro-manticism is frequently contrasted with *classicism.* Although many varieties of Ro-manticism are indigenous to various national literatures, the term generally suggests an assertion of the preeminence of the imagination. Other values associated with vari-ous schools of Romanticism include primitivism, an interest in folklore, a reverence for nature, and a fascination with the demoniac and the macabre.

scene: The central element of *narration;* specific actions are narrated or depicted that make the reader feel he or she is participating directly in the action.

science fiction: Fiction in which certain givens (physical laws, psychological principles, social conditions—any one or all of these) form the basis of an imaginative projection into the future or, less commonly, an extrapolation in the present or even into the past.

semiotics: The science of signs and sign systems in communication. According to Roman Jakobson, semiotics deals with the principles that underlie the structure of signs, their use in language of all kinds, and the specific nature of various sign systems.

sentimental novel: A form of fiction popular in the eighteenth century in which emotion-alism and optimism are the primary characteristics. The best-known examples are Samuel Richardson's *Pamela: Or, Virtue Rewarded* (1740-1741) and Oliver Gold-smith's *The Vicar of Wakefield* (1766).

setting: The circumstances and environment, both temporal and spatial, of a *narrative.*

spatial form: An author's attempt to make the reader apprehend a work spatially in a mo-ment of time rather than sequentially. To achieve this effect, the author breaks up the *narrative* into interspersed fragments. Beginning with James Joyce, Marcel Proust, and Djuna Barnes, the movement toward spatial form is concomitant with the *modern-ist* effort to supplant historical time in fiction with mythic time. For the seminal discus-sion of this technique, see Joseph Frank, *The Widening Gyre* (1963).

stream of consciousness: The depiction of the thought processes of a *character,* insofar as this is possible, without any mediating structures. The metaphor of consciousness as a "stream" suggests a rush of thoughts and images governed by free association rather than by strictly rational development. The term "stream of consciousness" is often used loosely as a synonym for *interior monologue.* The most celebrated example of stream of consciousness in fiction is the monologue of Molly Bloom in James Joyce's *Ulysses* (1922); other notable practitioners of the stream-of-consciousness technique include Dorothy Richardson, Virginia Woolf, and William Faulkner.

structuralism: As a movement of thought, structuralism is based on the idea of intrinsic, self-sufficient structures that do not require reference to external elements. A structure is a system of transformations that involves the interplay of laws inherent in the system itself. The study of language is the primary model for contemporary structuralism. The structuralist literary critic attempts to define structural principles that operate intertextually throughout the whole of literature as well as principles that operate in *genres* and in individual works. One of the most accessible surveys of structuralism and literature available is Jonathan Culler's *Structuralist Poetics* (1975).

summary: Those parts of a fiction that do not need to be detailed. In *Tom Jones* (1749), Henry Fielding says, "If whole years should pass without producing anything worthy of . . . notice . . . we shall hasten on to matters of consequence."

thematics: According to Northrop Frye, when a work of fiction is written or interpreted thematically, it becomes an illustrative fable. Murray Krieger defines thematics as "the study of the experiential tensions which, dramatically entangled in the literary work, become an existential reflection of that work's aesthetic complexity."

tone: The dominant mood of a work of fiction. (See *atmosphere*.)

unreliable narrator: A narrator whose account of the events of the story cannot be trusted, obliging readers to reconstruct—if possible—the true state of affairs themselves. Once an innovative technique, the use of the unreliable narrator has become commonplace among contemporary writers who wish to suggest the impossibility of a truly "reliable" account of any event. Notable examples of the unreliable narrator can be found in Ford Madox Ford's *The Good Soldier* (1915) and Vladimir Nabokov's *Lolita* (1955).

Victorian novel: Although the Victorian period extended from 1837 to 1901, the term "Victorian novel" does not include the later decades of Queen Victoria's reign. The term loosely refers to the sprawling works of novelists such as Charles Dickens and William Makepeace Thackeray—works that frequently appeared first in serial form and are characterized by a broad social canvas.

vraisemblance/verisimilitude: Tzvetan Todorov defines vraisemblance as "the mask which conceals the text's own laws, but which we are supposed to take for a relation to reality." Verisimilitude refers to a work's attempts to make the reader believe that it conforms to reality rather than to its own laws.

Western novel: Like all varieties of *genre fiction*, the Western novel—generally known simply as the Western—is defined by a relatively predictable combination of *conventions*, *motifs*, and recurring themes. These predictable elements, familiar from many Western films and television series, differentiate the Western from *historical novels* and idiosyncratic works such as Thomas Berger's *Little Big Man* (1964) that are also set in the Old West. Conversely, some novels set in the contemporary West are regarded as Westerns because they deal with modern cowboys and with the land itself in the manner characteristic of the *genre*.

Charles E. May

GUIDE TO ONLINE RESOURCES

WEB SITES
The following sites were visited by the editors of Salem Press in 2009. Because URLs frequently change, the accuracy of these addresses cannot be guaranteed; however, longstanding sites, such as those of colleges and universities, national organizations, and government agencies, generally maintain links when sites are moved or updated.

American Literature on the Web
http://www.nagasaki-gaigo.ac.jp/ishikawa/amlit

Among this site's features are several pages providing links to Web sites about specific genres and literary movements, southern and southwestern American literature, minority literature, literary theory, and women writers, as well as an extensive index of links to electronic text collections and archives. Users also can access information for five specific time periods: 1620-1820, 1820-1865, 1865-1914, 1914-1945, and since 1945. A range of information is available for each period, including alphabetical lists of authors that link to more specific information about each writer, time lines of historical and literary events, and links to related additional Web sites.

Books and Writers
http://www.kirjasto.sci.fi/indeksi.htm

This broad, comprehensive, and easy-to-use resource provides access to information about hundreds of authors throughout the world, extending from 70 B.C.E to the twenty-first century. Links take users from an alphabetical list of authors to pages featuring biographical material, lists of works, and recommendations for further reading about individual authors; each writer's page also includes links to related pages on the site. Although brief, the biographical essays provide solid overviews of the authors' careers, their contributions to literature, and their literary influences.

The Canadian Literature Archive
http://www.umanitoba.ca/canlit

Created and maintained by the English Department at the University of Manitoba, this site is a comprehensive collection of materials for and about Canadian writers. It includes an alphabetical listing of authors with links to additional Web-based information. Users also can retrieve electronic texts, announcements of literary events, and videocasts of author interviews and readings.

A Celebration of Women Writers

http://digital.library.upenn.edu/women

This site presents an extensive compendium of information about the contributions of women writers throughout history. The "Local Editions by Authors" and "Local Editions by Category" pages include access to electronic texts of the works of numerous writers, including Louisa May Alcott, Djuna Barnes, Grazia Deledda, Edith Wharton, and Virginia Woolf. Users can also access biographical and bibliographical information by browsing lists arranged by writers' names, countries of origin, ethnicities, and the centuries in which they lived.

Contemporary Writers

http://www.contemporarywriters.com/authors

Created by the British Council, this site offers "up-to-date profiles of some of the U.K. and Commonwealth's most important living writers (plus writers from the Republic of Ireland that we've worked with)." The available information includes biographies, bibliographies, critical reviews, news about literary prizes, and photographs. Users can search the site by author, genre, nationality, gender, publisher, book title, date of publication, and prize name and date.

Internet Public Library: Native American Authors

http://www.ipl.org/div/natam

Internet Public Library, a Web-based collection of materials, includes this index to resources about writers of Native American heritage. An alphabetical list of authors enables users to link to biographies, lists of works, electronic texts, tribal Web sites, and other online resources. The majority of the writers covered are contemporary Indian authors, but some historical authors also are featured. Users also can retrieve information by browsing lists of titles and tribes. In addition, the site contains a bibliography of print and online materials about Native American literature.

LiteraryHistory.com

http://www.literaryhistory.com

This site is an excellent source of academic, scholarly, and critical literature about eighteenth, nineteenth, and twentieth century American and English writers. It provides numerous pages about specific eras and genres, including individual pages for eighteenth, nineteenth, and twentieth century literature and for African American and postcolonial literature. These pages contain alphabetical lists of authors that link to articles, reviews, overviews, excerpts of works, teaching guides, podcast interviews, and other materials. The eighteenth century literature page also provides access to information about the eighteenth century novel.

Literary Resources on the Net

http://andromeda.rutgers.edu/~jlynch/Lit

Jack Lynch of Rutgers University maintains this extensive collection of links to Internet sites that are useful to academics, including numerous Web sites about American and English literature. This collection is a good place to begin online research about the novel, as it links to hundreds of other sites with broad ranges of literary topics. The site is organized chronically, with separate pages for information about the Middle Ages, the Renaissance, the eighteenth century, the Romantic and Victorian eras, and twentieth century British and Irish literature. It also has separate pages providing links to Web sites about American literature and to women's literature and feminism.

LitWeb

http://litweb.net

LitWeb provides biographies of more than five hundred world authors throughout history that can be accessed through an alphabetical listing. The pages about each writer contain a list of his or her works, suggestions for further reading, and illustrations. The site also offers information about past and present winners of major literary prizes.

The Modern Word: Authors of the Libyrinth

http://www.themodernword.com/authors.html

The Modern Word site, although somewhat haphazard in its organization, provides a great deal of critical information about writers. The "Authors of the Libyrinth" page is very useful, linking author names to essays about them and other resources. The section of the page headed "The Scriptorium" presents "an index of pages featuring writers who have pushed the edges of their medium, combining literary talent with a sense of experimentation to produce some remarkable works of modern literature." The site also includes sections devoted to Samuel Beckett, Umberto Eco, Gabriel García Márquez, James Joyce, Franz Kafka, and Thomas Pynchon.

Novels

http://www.nvcc.edu/home/ataormina/novels/default.htm

This overview of American and English novels was prepared by Agatha Taormina, a professor at Northern Virginia Community College. It contains three sections: "History" provides a definition of the novel genre, a discussion of its origins in eighteenth century England, and separate pages with information about genres and authors of nineteenth century, twentieth century, and postmodern novels. "Approaches" suggests how to read a novel critically for greater appreciation, and "Resources" provides a list of books about the novel.

Outline of American Literature

http://www.america.gov/publications/books/outline-of-american-literature.html

This page of the America.gov site provides access to an electronic version of the ten-chapter volume *Outline of American Literature*, a historical overview of prose and poetry from colonial times to the present published by the U.S. Department of State. The work's author is Kathryn VanSpanckeren, professor of English at the University of Tampa. The site offers links to abbreviated versions of each chapter as well as access to the entire publication in PDF format.

Voice of the Shuttle

http://vos.ucsb.edu

One of the most complete and authoritative places for online information about literature, Voice of the Shuttle is maintained by professors and students in the English Department at the University of California, Santa Barbara. The site provides thousands of links to electronic books, academic journals, association Web sites, sites created by university professors, and many, many other resources about the humanities. Its "Literature in English" page provides links to separate pages about the literature of the Anglo-Saxon era, the Middle Ages, the Renaissance and seventeenth century, the Restoration and eighteenth century, the Romantic age, the Victorian age, and modern and contemporary periods in Britain and the United States, as well as a page focused on minority literature. Another page on the site, "Literatures Other than English," offers a gateway to information about the literature of numerous countries and world regions.

ELECTRONIC DATABASES

Electronic databases usually do not have their own URLs. Instead, public, college, and university libraries subscribe to these databases, provide links to them on their Web sites, and make them available to library card holders or other specified patrons. Readers can visit library Web sites or ask reference librarians to check on availability.

Canadian Literary Centre

Produced by EBSCO, the Canadian Literary Centre database contains full-text content from ECW Press, a Toronto-based publisher, including the titles in the publisher's Canadian fiction studies, Canadian biography, and Canadian writers and their works series, *ECW's Biographical Guide to Canadian Novelists*, and *George Woodcock's Introduction to Canadian Fiction*. Author biographies, essays and literary criticism, and book reviews are among the database's offerings.

Literary Reference Center

EBSCO's Literary Reference Center (LRC) is a comprehensive full-text database designed primarily to help high school and undergraduate students in English and the humanities with homework and research assignments about literature. The database contains massive amounts of information from reference works, books, literary journals, and other materials, including more than 31,000 plot summaries, synopses, and overviews of literary works; almost 100,000 essays and articles of literary criticism; about 140,000 author biographies; more than 605,000 book reviews; and more than 5,200 author interviews. It also contains the entire contents of Salem Press's MagillOnLiterature Plus. Users can retrieve information by browsing a list of authors' names or titles of literary works; they can also use an advanced search engine to access information by numerous categories, including author name, gender, cultural identity, national identity, and the years in which he or she lived, or by literary title, character, locale, genre, and publication date. The Literary Reference Center also features a literary-historical time line, an encyclopedia of literature, and a glossary of literary terms.

MagillOnLiterature Plus

MagillOnLiterature Plus is a comprehensive, integrated literature database produced by Salem Press and available on the EBSCO*host* platform. The database contains the full text of essays in Salem's many literature-related reference works, including *Masterplots*, *Cyclopedia of World Authors*, *Cyclopedia of Literary Characters*, *Cyclopedia of Literary Places*, *Critical Survey of Long Fiction*, *Critical Survey of Short Fiction*, *World Philosophers and Their Works*, *Magill's Literary Annual*, and *Magill's Book Reviews*. Among its contents are articles on more than 35,000 literary works and more than 8,500 writers, poets, dramatists, essays, and philosophers, more than 1,000 images, and a glossary of more than 1,300 literary terms. The biographical essays include lists of authors' works and secondary bibliographies, and almost four hundred overview essays offer information about literary genres, time periods, and national literatures.

NoveList

NoveList is a readers' advisory service produced by EBSCO. The database provides access to 155,000 titles of both adult and juvenile fiction as well information about literary awards, book discussion guides, feature articles about a range of literary genres, and "recommended reads." Users can search by author name, book title, or series title or can describe the plot to retrieve the name of a book, information about the author, and book reviews; another search engine enables users to find titles similar to books they have enjoyed reading.

Rebecca Kuzins

GEOGRAPHICAL INDEX

SUBJECT INDEX